S0-BEZ-281

OXFORD WORLD'S CLASSICS

THE OXFORD SHAKESPEARE

General Editor · Stanley Wells

The Oxford Shakespeare offers new and authoritative editions of Shakespeare's plays in which the early printings have been scrupulously re-examined and interpreted. An introductory essay provides all relevant background information together with an appraisal of critical views and of the play's effects in performance. The detailed commentaries pay particular attention to language and staging. Reprints of sources, music for songs, genealogical tables, maps, etc. are included where necessary; many of the volumes are illustrated, and all contain an index.

RENÉ WEIS is Professor of English Literature at University College London, where he has taught since 1980. He has twice been a Visiting Professor at Dartmouth College, NH, and his publications include *Criminal Justice: The True Story of Edith Thompson* (Hamish Hamilton, 1988) and *King Lear: A Parallel Text Edition* (Longman, 1993). He has written extensively on Shakespeare and is the editor of *Henry IV, Part 2* in the Oxford Shakespeare and *The Duchess of Malfi and Other Plays* in Oxford World's Classics.

THE OXFORD SHAKESPEARE

Currently available in paperback

All's Well that Ends Well
Anthony and Cleopatra
As You Like It
The Comedy of Errors
The Complete Sonnets
  and Poems
Coriolanus
Cymbeline
Hamlet
Henry V
Henry IV, Part 1
Henry IV, Part 2
Henry VI, Part Two
Henry VI, Part Three
Julius Caesar
King Henry VIII
King John

King Lear
Love's Labour's Lost
Macbeth
Measure for Measure
The Merchant of Venice
The Merry Wives of Windsor
A Midsummer Night's Dream
Much Ado About Nothing
Richard III
Romeo and Juliet
The Taming of the Shrew
The Tempest
Titus Andronicus
Troilus and Cressida
Twelfth Night
The Two Noble Kinsmen
The Winter's Tale

The rest of the plays are forthcoming

OXFORD WORLD'S CLASSICS

WILLIAM SHAKESPEARE

Henry IV, Part 2

Edited by
RENÉ WEIS

OXFORD
UNIVERSITY PRESS

To Jean in Deepest gratitude

OXFORD
UNIVERSITY PRESS

Great Clarendon Street, Oxford OX2 6DP

Oxford University Press is a department of the University of Oxford.
It furthers the University's objective of excellence in research, scholarship,
and education by publishing worldwide in

Oxford New York
Auckland Cape Town Dar es Salaam Hong Kong Karachi Kuala Lumpur
Madrid Melbourne Mexico City Nairobi New Delhi Shanghai
Taipei Toronto

With offices in
Argentina Austria Brazil Chile Czech Republic France Greece
Guatemala Hungary Italy Japan South Korea Poland Portugal
Singapore Switzerland Thailand Turkey Ukraine Vietnam

Oxford is a registered trade mark of Oxford University Press
in the UK and in certain other countries

Published in the United States
by Oxford University Press Inc., New York

© René Weis 1997

First published by the Clarendon Press 1997
First published as an Oxford World's Classics paperback 1998

All rights reserved. No part of this publication may be reproduced,
stored in a retrieval system, or transmitted, in any form or by any means,
without the prior permission in writing of Oxford University Press,
or as expressly permitted by law, or under terms agreed with the appropriate
reprographics rights organization. Enquiries concerning reproduction
outside the scope of the above should be sent to the Rights Department,
Oxford University Press, at the address above

You must not circulate this book in any other binding or cover
and you must impose this same condition on any acquirer

British Library Cataloguing in Publication Data

Data available

Library of Congress Cataloging in Publication Data

Data available

ISBN-13: 978-0-19-283143-9
ISBN-10: 0-19-283143-7

4

Printed in Great Britain by
Clays Ltd, St Ives plc

ACKNOWLEDGEMENTS

It is a pleasure to record my indebtedness to the many who have assisted me in the preparation of this edition.

My first debt is to my distinguished predecessors in the field. The modern editor of *Henry IV Part 2* is fortunate to follow in the footsteps of A. R. Humphreys, and to be able to draw on the pioneering work of Matthias A. Shaaber, whose Variorum edition remains as valuable now as it was over fifty years ago. The labours of subsequent editors and scholars have further lightened the burden of editing the text of the play, and of attempting to elucidate some of its cruces.

A number of friends and scholars generously responded to my requests for guidance.

George Walton Williams closely read the General Introduction and commented on it with characteristic verve and acumen. My friend and colleague Henry Woudhuysen again scrutinized my material. It is a pleasure to thank both of them for allowing me to benefit from their learning and bibliographical expertise. The General Editor of the Oxford Shakespeare, Stanley Wells, was efficient, incisive, and constructive in his comments on the typescript.

I wish to record here my debt to David Bevington whose scrupulous edition of *Henry IV Part 1* in the Oxford series set a high standard which, if I could not hope to match, I could at least aim for.

I am grateful to John Jowett for taking time to read, and offer helpful suggestions on, the textual section of my Introduction. Peter Swaab also commented on the Introduction at length, and caused me to rethink some of my views on Falstaff and the role of anarchy in Bolingbroke's world of power-politics and civil strife. Philip Horne convinced me that *Chimes at Midnight* is a visionary rendering of the glory that was Falstaff. Penny Hicks kindly assisted me with the search for post-Restoration and eighteenth-century productions of *Henry IV*; and my friend Keith Walker generously plied me with books and frequently entertained me with jokes. I am grateful to David Kastan for allowing me a preview of his valuable essay on Oldcastle and Falstaff. I am, of course, alone responsible for any remaining errors.

John Sutherland granted me sabbatical leave during which to complete this edition. I am grateful to him for his generous support over many years, and to my department for financial assistance with the illustrations. Rosemary Ashton, David Daniell, Dan Jacobson, and Karl Miller have at various times shared with me their enthusiasm for the *Henry IV* plays, and Sarah Wintle reminded me that Shakespeare 'invented' Gloucestershire in *Henry IV Part 2*. I owe them all a debt of gratitude.

Kathy Metzenthin provided me with much electronic equipment and guidance for which I am grateful. I was frequently assisted in the course of my work by the ISD department at UCL, particularly Nafisa Taylor.

I am thankful for their help to the staff of the British Library, the University of London Library at Senate House, the Shakespeare Centre in Stratford-upon-Avon, the Theatre Museum in Covent Garden, the County Library Department of Hampshire County Council, and the Gloucestershire Record Office, particularly Mrs K. Haslem. Guilland Sutherland, and Thomas Lange of the Huntington Library, came to my rescue over two of the illustrations. I owe special thanks to John Allen and John Spiers of the University College London Library. Their help and relentless good humour are inspirational.

I am grateful to Frances Whistler at Oxford University Press for seeing the typescript through its final stages, and particularly to Christine Buckley for doing such an exemplary job as copy-editor.

I have learnt much from the students of the UCL Shakespeare course, and I must thank them for their enthusiasm and bracing scepticism.

Thinking of Maryse never failed to remind me that there is a world elsewhere. My greatest debt of all is acknowledged in the dedication.

RENÉ WEIS
University College London, 1997

CONTENTS

List of Illustrations   viii

Introduction   I
  The Play   I
    The Date   8
    The Sources   16
    What's in a name?   27
    Falstaff versus Oldcastle   31
    Falstaff   40
    Whose 'commandment'?   44
    Father and Son: Act 4, Scene 3   48
    Language and Comic Structures   50
  The Play in Performance   58
  The Texts of 2 Henry IV   78
    The Control-Text   78
    Act 3, Scene 1: QA, QB, F   79
    The F-only Passages   84
    Quarto 1600   90
    The Copy for Folio   91

Editorial Procedures   101
  Abbreviations and References   103

THE HISTORY OF KING HENRY THE FOURTH,
PART 2   113

Index   275

LIST OF ILLUSTRATIONS

1. John Neville as Pistol and Gwen Cherrell as Doll Tearsheet
   in the 1955 Old Vic production of *2 Henry IV*   2
   (By courtesy of the Trustees of the Victoria and Albert Museum)

2. Emrys James as Bolingbroke and Alan Howard as Hal in
   the 1975 RSC production at Stratford-upon-Avon   5
   (By permission of the Shakespeare Centre Library)

3. The martyrdom of Sir John Oldcastle, from Foxe's *Book
   of Martyrs* (1563)   5
   (By permission of the British Library)

4. The title-page of the 1600 Quarto (QB)   8
   (By permission of the Huntington Library)

5. The Coronation of Henry V, a sculpture in Westminster Abbey   25
   (By courtesy of the Dean and Chapter of Westminster)

6. Richard Burton as Hal, Heather Stannard as Doll Tearsheet,
   Alan Badel as Poins, and Anthony Quayle as Falstaff in
   the 1951 production at Stratford-upon-Avon   28
   (By permission of the Angus McBean Estate)

7. Irene Palmer (Lady Percy), Cecil Trouncer (Northumberland),
   and Phyllis Hatch (Lady Northumberland) in the 1935 Old
   Vic production   51
   (By courtesy of the Trustees of the Victoria and Albert Museum)

8. James Grout as Silence, Paul Eddington as Shallow, and
   director John Caird in the 1995 BBC production   76
   (By permission of James Grout, the Estate of Paul Eddington, and
   the BBC)

9. Sig. g3 recto of the 1623 Folio   94
   (By permission of W. W. Norton)

10. The last page of the 1623 Folio *2 Henry IV*   94
    (By permission of W. W. Norton)

INTRODUCTION

The Play

IT is never easy to come second. For Shakespeare to have written a play called '*The Second Part of Henry the Fourth*', in both quarto and Folio, seems therefore to be a particularly confident stroke, because the new (albeit 'second') play is clearly expected to repeat the success of the one whose title it echoes, '*The First Part of Henry the Fourth*'. It also appears to assume that its audiences know *Part 1*. Whereas *Richard II* or *1 Henry IV*, the first two members of the second tetralogy, or *Henry V*, the play which completes the cycle, all enjoy a considerable degree of autonomy, *Part 2* of *Henry IV* is connected to *Part 1* in a seamless join. 'Rumour', the Induction, enters at a dramatic point located before the dramatic action of *Part 1* has fully finished (see below, p. 9). In terms of plot and imaginative chronology, Shakespeare's completing his dramatization of Bolingbroke's reign in *2 Henry IV* revisits the end of *Part 1*. The sequel starts *in medias res*, in the immediate aftermath of the climactic action which concludes *1 Henry IV*, the Battle of Shrewsbury.

The apparent disadvantage of an umbilical dependence on the plot of another member of the tetralogy may be thought to be compounded by the absence from the sequel of the heroic, and at times youthfully idealistic, strains of the high plot of *Part 1*. There is no Hotspur any longer to challenge Hal for the succession (as well as the loyalty of the audience), and our only view of the indomitable Kate Percy is as Hotspur's grieving widow, in a scene which is often cut in performance. Moreover, in *Part 2* the Prince of Wales disdainfully transcends his madcap Eastcheap adventures which account for much of the attraction of *Part 1*. His brief appearance at the Boar's Head tavern in *Part 2* is almost grudging. If the three *Henry* plays of the second tetralogy are viewed primarily as stations of the prodigal's progress towards the crown, then *2 Henry IV* is the most isolated and transitional of them, a mere prelude to the epic of *Henry V*. At worst it could be seen to be marking time until the coronation in its fifth Act, which empowers Henry to launch into his French campaign. The obsession with sickness in *2 Henry IV* (see Wells, 1994, p. 147, and below, p. 47) creates a sense of weariness, and its incessant retrospection may give the impression that the play is too timid to cut loose from its elder brother.

That Shakespeare was alert in *Part 2* to problems with novelty and transitoriness is clear from the emphasis in the quarto title-page on the continued presence in the second part of Falstaff (he had clearly been a resounding triumph in performances of *Part 1*, and could be trusted to deliver again), and the introduction of a flamboyant new character, the trendily 'intertextual' Pistol, Falstaff's ensign. There are other newcomers, notably Doll Tearsheet, Falstaff's occasional concubine, the country justices Shallow and Silence, and the poor recruits who refuse to slip into the cartoon

Figure 1. John Neville as Pistol and Gwen Cherrell as Doll Tearsheet in the 1955 production (directed by Douglas Seale) of *2 Henry IV* at the Old Vic.

roles that their betters propose for them (see below, p. 45); and finally there is the austere figure of the Lord Chief Justice.

Part 2 revisits *1 Henry IV* in ways which are far from mechanical. Rather, it uses the many superficial similarities and continuities between the two plays to generate an imaginative conception which significantly differs from its predecessor and thereby in turn, almost incidentally, affords fascinating insights into Shakespeare's dramatic construction, as for instance in the case of the first scene of Act 3 (see below, p. 82 n.). As Hal moves closer to the crown Shakespeare seems keen to ensure that the Prince's hands should be free from the taint of usurpation. Conflicting teleologies and their ideological baggage are less prominent here than in either *Richard II* or *1 Henry IV*. The approach Shakespeare adopts in this play is domestically angled, whether at the national levels of London and Gloucestershire, or in the intimacy of the Jerusalem Chamber in Westminster.

In *Part 2* the wider politics of the realm are marginalized to a degree that is unthinkable in the earlier play-world which included Hal and Hotspur as well as the King, Northumberland, and Glyndŵr. The political factions in *1 Henry IV* consisted of powerful antagonistic warlords, whereas in the imagined world of *2 Henry IV* the historical confrontations of the first play are largely resolved or temporarily suspended. Rather more sanguinely than is licensed by the chronicles he used, Shakespeare creates a necessary space from political conflicts in the play-world of *Part 2*. The half-hearted Scrope rising (as portrayed in *Part 2*) is merely a bloodstained footnote in the history of the realm. Its successful resolution does not even involve the Prince of Wales. The rebellion, the only significant martial and political event in the play, is squashed by a cynically equivocating royal deputy. The engagement at Gaultres could hardly be further from the manly duel of Hal and Hotspur at Shrewsbury, which ends with Hal speaking his chivalrous opponent's epitaph.

In *Part 2* the royal family's tug-of-war is no longer parodied and counterbalanced by Hal paying filial mock-homage to Falstaff. The symbolic politics of the crown are split off from the mayhem that floats in the wake of a larger-than-life Falstaff. It is as if Shakespeare had decided to separate out the two intermingled strands of *Part 1* by rewriting them in *Part 2* as a Falstaff comedy which runs in tandem, but no longer intersects, with a poignant royal father–son tragicomedy.

In the long third scene of Act 4 Shakespeare develops the father–son relationship launched in *1 Henry IV*. The issue may have been particularly close to Shakespeare's heart at this time, because his son Hamnet died in August 1596 (at the age of eleven and a half), when Shakespeare was (probably) well into writing *2 Henry IV*. It is possible that the revisiting in *Part 2* of the father–son scene from *1 Henry IV* 3.2 reflects an urgent desire in Shakespeare to rene-gotiate the rhetoric and feelings of that earlier scene, this time in terms of a permanent parting. But it is also true that the royal family divisions of *1 Henry IV* were left unresolved, and the second *Henry* play was probably planned as a separate work from the start.[1] Another father–son scene was inevitable, because without such a scene *Part 2* could hardly stand on its own. *Part 2* may be a sequel, but it also needs to be self-contained to some degree; and there can be no Henry V without some symbolic gesture of handing-over by Henry IV. Bolingbroke's soliloquy in 3.1 and his tête-à-tête, on the verge of death, with Hal in 4.3 attempt to legitimate the crown before it is passed on by the usurper to the Prince of Wales.[2]

[1] Jenkins has argued that the sheer bulk of his material overtook Shakespeare's design halfway through *Part 1*, and that it was this congestion which decided him to use Shrewsbury as the climax of the first play, in the knowledge (by then) that a second play would allow him to complete the story. Jenkins's hypothesis about the single play which unintentionally became two separate works is scrupulously analysed, and then rejected, by Humphreys (pp. xxv–xxviii) who concludes 'that Shakespeare seemingly intended two plays from the outset, or very near it'. Mel-chiori (p. 15) suggests that Shakespeare's '*Henry IV* was not only conceived but also written and performed in 1596 as a one-play remake of the first part of *Famous Victories*', and that it was this Shakespearian *Ur-Henry*, an earlier non-extant version of a text from which extant texts independently derive, featuring Sir John Oldcastle, Sir John Russell, Harvey, and Poins, which attracted the ire of the Lord Chamberlain.

[2] Jonathan Crewe argues that *Part 2* 'reveals a deepening Shakespearean pre-occupation with mechanisms of "legitimate" change and succession' which ex-tends beyond the historical narrative of the *Henry* plays into the act of textual composition itself ('Reforming Prince Hal: The Sovereign Inheritor in *2 Henry IV*', *Renaissance Drama*, NS 21 (1990), 225–42; p. 226). That the play self-reflexively explores similar issues on different levels is also stressed by David M. Bergeron in 'Shakespeare Makes History: *2 Henry IV*' (*SEL* 31 (1991), 231–45). He points out that *Part 2* stands out among the plays of the second tetralogy by virtue of an acute literary self-awareness, and sees it as simultaneously tackling three layers of 'his-tory': the 'ahistory' of Falstaff, the '*national*' history of politics, and the '*literary*' history of texts echoing one another.

Figure 2. Emrys James as Bolingbroke and Alan Howard as Hal in the 1975 RSC production (directed by Terry Hands) at the Royal Shakespeare Theatre, Stratford-upon-Avon.

Figure 3. The martyrdom of Sir John Oldcastle, from Foxe's *Book of Martyrs* (1563).

The description of the cruell Martyrdome of
fyr Iohn Oldecaftle Lord Cobham.

As touching the pretenced treafon of this Lord Cob   martyrdome. And thus much for the death and execut

The sequel sternly emphasizes that the crown cannot descend to Hal without a full avowal of guilt by the man who first illicitly snatched it from Richard II. Whereas in the earlier encounter of father and son (*1 Henry IV* 3.2.1–161) the King explained to Hal his strategies to secure the crown with reference both to specific incidents from the past and the requirements of the political situation of the present, here the King's deathbed candour is total and unpremeditated. Like Hamlet's father (Hal shares more than just the first letters of his name with Hamlet), Bolingbroke momentarily returns from the outer edges of existence for one final briefing of the future king. Free from 'the spiritual wickednesses, which are in the hie places', and armed instead with the truth like St Paul's good Christian (Ephesians 6: 12–7), Hal is launched into *Henry V*.

Before reaching that point, however, Henry V has to reject Falstaff. The political containment of Falstaff is symbolized at both the start and the end of the play by his nemesis, the figure of the Lord Chief Justice, and his excesses are confined to the twilight world of London whores, drunkards, and conmen, and the stringing along of foolish and aged country justices. The waning of his political influence is, however, offset by an imaginative expansion of the character. For Falstaff the contraction in *Part 2* of the world of history does not necessarily signal an impoverishment. Rather, it unshackles and releases the energy that is Falstaff.[1] If the Prince of *Part 1* is in the sequel freed from the shadow of Falstaff, the same can be said *mutatis mutandis* about Falstaff. The separation of Falstaff from the politically oppressive presence of the Prince emancipates the character (in *Part 1* we never really forget that Hal's days in Eastcheap are a controlled and even manipulative Saturnalian indulgence: see below, p. 41). He who claims to be a monarch of wit in his first lines in the play (1.2.6–14) is given a chance fully to prove his claim to that throne in the great comic scenes in London and the country. More so than

[1] In *The End Crowns All: Closure and Contradiction in Shakespeare's History* (1991), Barbara Hodgdon similarly notes that as well as reworking the 'oppositional economy' of *Part 1*, *Part 2* 'also consumes and subsumes its historical subject matter by positioning Falstaff, not Henry IV or Hal, as the play's central figure. As much as, if not more than, the royal succession, it is his dramatic succession that is at issue...' (p. 167). The fullest, and most suasive, argument to the effect that in *Part 2* 'Falstaff's status is lowered by his isolation' and by the prominence granted to Pistol, Doll, Quickly, and Shallow is advanced by Vickers (pp. 118–41).

Part 1, 2 Henry IV is dominated by a Falstaff prose comedy of sex and money, whose function may well ultimately be to subvert royal power by ensuring that the 'historical world never takes on the illusion of full presence'.[1] If so, it is acutely ironic that it should be Falstaff's first, and intentional, incarnation as the emphatically historical Sir John Oldcastle that nearly brought about the demise of both the *Henry IV* plays.

That Falstaff was originally called Oldcastle, the name of a famous Protestant martyr, is universally recognized. To the over-whelming majority of audiences, however, the Falstaff–Oldcastle debate is in the strictest sense a scholastic one. Since the first printing of the play in 1600 the famous reprobate has been known, and often been loved, by the name of 'Falstaff'. The fact, however, that Falstaff was at some earlier point called Oldcastle becomes acutely important when the wider political and religious implications (the two are not easily distinguishable in this period) of the name Oldcastle are realized. The bulk of recent scholarship on the play has homed in on the controversial Falstaff–Oldcastle issue, and any modern edition is bound to reflect this.

There is little doubt that the dispute over Falstaff and Oldcastle goes to the heart of the *Henry IV* plays. But it has tended to focus on *1 Henry IV* almost to the exclusion (again) of *2 Henry IV*. At most *Part 2* has been mined for the occasional nugget such as the speech-prefix '*Old.*' that it could provide for one side rather than another in this debate. This edition will instead aim to establish that the impetus for the change from Oldcastle to Falstaff in both *Henry IV* plays came initially in response not to *Part 1*, as is commonly argued, but to *Part 2*.

All roads in *2 Henry IV*, including its textual and bibliographical history, sooner or later lead to Falstaff and Oldcastle. The wider ramifications of the Falstaff–Oldcastle controversy also help to date *2 Henry IV* by providing important information which may be corroborated by *Merry Wives*, with which *2 Henry IV* shares several characters and which, through its nomenclature, may touch on germane issues.

[1] Phyllis Rackin, *Stages of History: Shakespeare's English Chronicles* (1990), p. 139. Rackin notes further that 'The double plot [Falstaffian comedy *versus* national politics] in the Henry IV plays . . . can be seen as a kind of allegory of mediation, representing in dramatic structure the split between the historical past that is represented and the theatrical mediation required to make it present.'

The Date. The Stationers' Register records that on 23 August 1600 Andrew Wise and William Aspley

Entred for their copies vnder the handes of the wardens. Twoo bookes. the one called: Muche a doo about nothinge. Thother the second p[ar]te of the History of Kinge Henry the iiij[th] w[th] the humo[rs] of S[r] Iohn Fallstaff: Wrytten by m[r] Shakespere. xij[d]

The title-page of the quarto, which was published not long afterwards, and which remained the only printed version of the play until the 1623 Folio, expands on this by advertising its further contents, the coronation of Henry V and the introduction of a new character, Pistol (see Fig. 4). If 23 August 1600 provides the final date, *1 Henry IV* provides the earliest, in 1596; and if the exact date

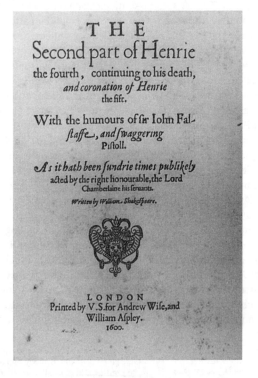

Figure 4. The title-page of the 1600 Quarto (QB, Huntington 69318, B & P 343).

of *1 Henry IV* is itself thought to be too elusive to support a date for
Part 2, then certainly the accession of the fratricidal Muhammad
III to the Turkish Sultanate in January 1596 does, because it is
alluded to at *2 Henry IV* 5.2.47–8.

Shakespeare had probably finished *1 Henry IV* by the spring of
1596,[1] within some six months of completing *Richard II*, and the
play would have been licensed by the Office of the Revels under
Henry Carey, first Lord Hunsdon, the Queen's first cousin, who
had been the patron of the Lord Chamberlain's Men since they rose
from the ashes of Strange's Men in the summer of 1594. At that
point the character we know as Falstaff was called Oldcastle, based
on an ancestor of Sir William Brooke, Lord Cobham. It is Cobham
who, as Lord Chamberlain from 8 August 1596 to 5 March 1597,
appears to have forced Shakespeare to change Oldcastle to Falstaff
in what has become the most celebrated act of Elizabethan censorship. There are good reasons for believing that *1 Henry IV* played in
London at first, and then, after the closure of the London theatres
on 22 July 1596, toured in the provinces where, during the
interdict, the company probably performed at Rye (August), and
at Dover and Bristol (September).[2] The dramatic action of *Part 2*
picks up directly where *Part 1* leaves off, in such a manner as to
suggest that Shakespeare embarked on the 'sequel' almost at once.
In fact, the opening scene of *2 Henry IV*, with the Earl of Northumberland waiting for news of Shrewsbury, takes the audience
back to just *before* the end of *1 Henry IV*, to 5.4, set on the battlefield at Shrewsbury, rather than 5.5 which marks the triumph of
the royalist party. It is as if the audience were expected to be freshly
familiar with *1 Henry IV*.

Against this suggestion for an early date of *2 Henry IV* Francis
Meres's *Palladis Tamia*, which was entered in the Stationers' Register on 7 September 1598, is sometimes adduced. Meres cites
'*Henry the 4*' among works demonstrating Shakespeare's excellence for tragedy. Meres's failure to distinguish between *Part 1* and
Part 2 does not by itself provide strong evidence for believing that
he therefore knew only *Part 1*. Even if he did know only the first

---

[1] Cf. Humphreys (1960, p. xiii); Honigmann (pp. 122–3); Taylor (1987, pp. 347–52).

[2] See Chambers, 1923 (ii. 196). That *1 Henry IV* was almost certainly performed with Oldcastle in the public theatres before the 1596–7 Christmas season and occasionally, and privately, *after* 1597, is argued by Taylor (1985, p. 90).

play, that would not be itself any kind of proof of the non-existence by then of *Part 2*, because he would know of it only if it had been acted at a public theatre, or else if it had been published.[1] It is also possible that Meres thought of the two *Henry IV* plays as a single dramatization of the reign of Henry IV, and called it a 'tragedy' because he had been impressed above all by the death of Henry IV in Act 4 of *Part 2*. The view that Meres failed to see the two plays as separate works may, however, be thought to acquire some authority from the Stationers' Register for 25 February 1598, which records the entry for publication of *Part 1* as

a booke intituled The historye of Henry the iiijth wth his battaile at Shrewsburye against Henry Hottspurre of the Northe wth the conceipted mirthe of Sr Iohn Falstoff.

The additional fact that the title-page of the second 1598 Q (commonly known as Q1) also describes the play as simply 'THE | HISTORY OF | HENRIE THE | FOVRTH' may be thought to be similarly surprising if *Part 2* was already in existence.[2] But then the third edition of a *1 Henry IV* quarto, 'Newly corrected', in 1599, and others thereafter (by which time *2 Henry IV* was indisputably in existence) similarly fail to call themselves the 'first part'.[3] The Folio of 1623, on the other hand, properly calls the two plays 'The First Part' and 'The Second Part'.

The evidence against an early date is therefore based on an ambiguous report by Meres and the unreliable witness of the title-pages of *1 Henry IV* quartos. The latest date for *2 Henry IV* can be brought forward with reasonable confidence from 1600 with reference to the date of *Merry Wives*, which is now generally (though not universally) accepted to have been performed at the Garter Feast on St George's Day, 23 April 1597, a month before the formal installation of the Knights of the Garter at Windsor.[4] In 1597 this included the elevation of George Carey, second Lord Hunsdon, who (after the brief Cobham interregnum) succeeded his

---

[1] Meres misses out *Shrew* and also *Merry Wives*, the latter probably because it had as yet been performed only at Court.

[2] There were two quartos that year, but only a fragment of the first quarto (commonly denoted Q0, but called Q1 by *Textual Companion*) survives.

[3] Q3 (1604), Q4 (1608), Q5 (1613), Q6 (1622): none of them calls *1 Henry IV* anything other than 'The History of Henry The Fourth'.

[4] Cf. Hotson (pp. 111–22), and Oliver (pp. xlv–xlvi).

father in the office of Lord Chamberlain on 17 April 1597, and inherited also the patronage of Shakespeare's company.

Like *1 Henry IV* and *2 Henry IV*, *Merry Wives* is a Falstaff play. That *Merry Wives* and *2 Henry IV* may be closely connected is suggested by the presence of new characters shared between them, notably Shallow and Pistol, and particularly by the occurrence of words and phrases unique to them both, including Shallow's 'By cock and pie' and 'pippin', and the Page's 'Ephesians' (respectively, 5.1.1, 5.3.2, 2.2.142; *Merry Wives* 1.1.283, 1.2.12, 4.5.16).[1] But which of the two plays comes first? If *Merry Wives* was indeed commissioned by Hunsdon as a thanksgiving offering to the Queen (for his appointment to the Revels and elevation to the Garter), then *Merry Wives* must have been composed in a matter of weeks, to be ready for the Garter Feast itself in April, or, at the latest, for the installation in May 1597.

Tantalizingly *Merry Wives* also seems to be embroiled in the Cobham–Brooke business, since the needlessly jealous and ridiculous Ford's assumed name in disguise is 'Brooke'. 'Brooke', which is the correct form and the one reproduced in Q, is nevertheless changed in Folio to 'Broome'.[2] Does this suggest that Shakespeare, who was forced to change Oldcastle to Falstaff, was satirizing his tormentor in *Merry Wives*? If he did, then we would be on surer ground in maintaining that *Merry Wives* comes sometime soon after Cobham's death, which would leave the period from 6 March to 23 April or May 1597 for the writing of the comedy. The fact that in *Merry Wives* Pistol, who was accorded the accolade of title-page mention in the 1600 quarto of *2 Henry IV*, is almost casually introduced ('your cony-catching rascals, Bardolph, Nim, and Pistol'), and the further fact that the play starts with Justice Shallow (who is also introduced for the first time in *2 Henry IV*), implies a continuation with *Part 2* of the Lancastrian history cycle. Moreover Shallow is older in *Merry Wives* (see below, pp. 43–4), and although his more advanced age may not matter in a de-historicized context which places the same characters in two different centuries (in 1413 and 1597), Shakespeare may have wished his cast to be older, simply because the play they are in now is a later play.

[1] Oliver (p. lv).

[2] The line commonly cited in support of 'Brooke' is 'Such Brookes are welcome to me, that o'erflows such liquor' (*Merry Wives* 2.2.146–7).

While the character of Shallow in *Merry Wives* clearly connects with the character in *2 Henry IV*, the puzzling location of Shallow's residence in Gloucestershire in the later stages of *2 Henry IV* has been attributed to the Gloucestershire reference in *Merry Wives* 1.1.3–5.[1] That Falstaff should need to pass through Gloucestershire on his way to York and Gaultres is geographically perplexing, as is Shallow's question to Silence about the price of cattle at Stamford Fair in Lincolnshire (3.2.36). It is only when Falstaff requests permission of Prince John 'to go through Gloucestershire' (4.2.78–9) on his way to London that the location is actually given. Up to that point the evidence afforded by the play has put Shallow somewhere in Lincolnshire. The solution proposed by H. J. Oliver, that Shakespeare temporarily interrupted work on *2 Henry IV* to write *Merry Wives* to order, elegantly addresses a number of questions raised by the apparent change of mind over the location of Shallow's estate. It assumes that by the time *Merry Wives* was commissioned, perhaps immediately after Cobham's death, Shakespeare had got as far as at least *2 Henry IV* 3.2.36, and possibly beyond, but not to the point of Falstaff's decision to fleece Shallow in Gloucestershire on his way down to London from Gaultres.[2] By the time he returned to *2 Henry IV* in the late spring or summer of 1597, he had allegedly written himself into a Gloucestershire corner through the first lines of *Merry Wives*.

While this hypothesis offers a plausible explanation of the problem with Shallow's location, it does not necessarily exclude others. The Gloucestershire location is so precisely specified by the two litigants before Davy and Shallow (see 5.1.32–3) as to make one wonder about other reasons that Shakespeare may have had for apparently relinquishing an original idea about Lincolnshire in favour of Gloucestershire. Is it really likely that, as he sat down to start, in some haste, on *Merry Wives*, Shakespeare forgot about a northern Shallow whom he had just left behind in the pages of *2 Henry IV*?

There is another reason for scepticism. The Oliver scenario would suggest that between finishing *1 Henry IV* (the spring of 1596) and embarking on *Merry Wives* sometime in March 1597, Shakespeare wrote a mere three acts. His writing pattern over twenty years, and some forty plays, argues otherwise, as indeed

[1] Oliver (p. lv).   [2] Humphreys (pp. 235–6); Oliver (pp. lv–lvi).

does the remarkable speed of the composition of *Merry Wives*. Although Shakespeare must have known periods of greater and lesser productivity—and his son died in 1596—he may well have had an unusual amount of time on his hands, because of the summer closure of the theatres. Commenting on these and related issues in the introduction to the Oxford *1 Henry IV*, David Bevington (1987, p. 9) notes that Shakespeare

must have written, or at least begun, *2 Henry IV* by then [early 1597] as well, for *Merry Wives* makes use of comic types introduced into *Part 2*. Such a comparatively early date for the composition of *2 Henry IV* would also explain the Oldcastle echoes, which must date from before the outcry.

This position can be cautiously developed further. Since *2 Henry IV* contains Oldcastle 'echoes' as well as a quarto (and therefore manuscript-derived) stage direction which includes a 'sir Iohn Russel' (see below, p. 29), it can be legitimately argued that the play may have been finished before 26 December 1596, when the Lord Chamberlain's Men started their performances at Court under the watchful eye of Cobham. It is very difficult to believe that Oldcastle 'echoes' (in the speech-prefix at 1.2.117, and hypothesized allusions to the name as in 'Do you set down your name in the scroll of youth, that are written down old with all the characters of age?', 1.2.173–5) would have crept into the text of the play after Cobham's objections were raised. In other words, there is evidence which strongly suggests that shortly after *1 Henry IV* (with Oldcastle) Shakespeare embarked on the sequel, and wrote and completed it during the second half of 1596.

But because of the evidence provided by Richard James (see below, p. 36), the entries in the Stationers' Register, the *1 Henry IV* quarto title-pages, and *Palladis Tamia*, it may that *2 Henry IV* had not yet been acted when the axe came down on 'Oldcastle'. There may have been enough of a question mark hanging over the manuscript of *2 Henry IV* from the fallout of the Cobham intervention for the company not to announce *Part 2* in February 1598; or perhaps the manuscript was being scrutinized for publication, and the signs were that permission to print it, along with the quarto of *1 Henry IV*, was not to be readily forthcoming, and might not be granted at all. The precipitate publication in quick succession of two quartos of *1 Henry IV* prominently displaying the name of Falstaff (as if to reassure the authorities) may suggest that the issue had not been laid to rest entirely even after Cobham's death.[1] Certainly the printing history of *2 Henry IV*, the many differences between its quarto and Folio texts, and therefore between foul papers and another manuscript which probably collates a prompt-book and the first quarto (see below, pp. 78 ff.), reveal a publication history which is more complex and puzzling than that of *1 Henry IV*.

The differences between the Q and F Epilogues may provide a further clue to the date of the play. The arrangement in this edition, which follows quarto as control-text, may be taken to suggest that the last line of the first paragraph of the Epilogue, with its prayer for the Queen, originally concluded *2 Henry IV*. The two paragraphs which follow in both Q and F combine a traditional '*captatio beneuolentiae*' (the rhetorical enlisting of the audience's good will and empathy) which is tendered, it would appear, by an actor adept at dancing,[2] with an apology for the Oldcastle–Falstaff confusion, and may have been added at a later stage. Although this has been interpreted as corroborative proof of the fact that Oldcastle was no longer called that in *2 Henry IV*, the obvious question remains why the 'apology' was not proffered at the end of *1 Henry IV*.[3]

Perhaps the most plausible line of argument would be to suggest that the two concluding paragraphs of the Epilogue were added sometime between the completion of the play in late 1596 and before the death of Cobham in March 1597, in other words as soon as was practical after the play first ran into difficulties. That would go some way towards explaining why both Q and F have all the

---

[1] See Williams (p. 179) who argues that the quartos of both the *Henry IV* plays were printed to reassure 'Oldcastle's angry posterity'; similarly Kastan notes that the 1598 printing of the quarto of *1 Henry IV* 'was perhaps demanded as proof of Shakespeare's willingness to respond to the concerns of the authorities' (forthcoming).

[2] Pope first noted that the actor was probably a dancer. The Epilogue's two references to his legs (ll. 18 and 31) and his desire to 'dance out' of the audience's 'debt' might indeed suggest this, although they could also simply denote the fact that he is standing up and is eager to be released by the audience's plaudits. Davison (p. 285) is sceptical about the idea of a dancing Epilogue, but points out that the Lord Chamberlain's Men's clown, Will Kemp, was a famous dancer and that he might well have spoken the Epilogue.

[3] Taylor (1987, p. 343) asserts that 'The Epilogue, rather than confirming that Oldcastle originally appeared in *Part Two*, suggests instead that Shakespeare had disclaimed that identification by the time he finished his first complete draft'.

material, even though F shifts the genuflecting prayer for the Queen from the end of the first to the end of the third paragraph.

The scenario (see particularly 'The Texts of 2 *Henry IV* ', below, pp. 78–99) would be something like this: after finishing the play in time for Christmas 1596, to partner 1 *Henry IV* (with Oldcastle), Shakespeare was forced into a change of nomenclature in *both* the *Henry IV* plays after submitting the prompt-book of *Part 2* for licensing.[1] If the second and third paragraphs of the Epilogue had been written some time later, just before *Henry V* or for the 1600 publication of quarto, they would not have appeared in Folio. The text in Folio (with its prompt-book pedigree) would in that case exhibit only the first paragraph of the Epilogue, since the prompt-book would have been copied from foul papers immediately after the play was finished, precisely with a view to securing a licence for performance; and in this case both foul papers and prompt-book reflect the revised material in the Epilogue. The last two paragraphs were probably written in response to the Cobham intervention, and copied simultaneously into the prompt-book and the foul papers. But in foul papers they were simply added, whereas in the prompt-book the prayer to the Queen was tactically shifted to the end of the Epilogue, perhaps further to protest the loyalty to established power of this sometime wayward author.[2]

The fact that the final paragraph of the Epilogue anticipates *Henry V* need not indicate that it was therefore written in close temporal proximity to *Henry V*. All that the final paragraph demonstrates is that Shakespeare clearly intended to conclude the Lancastrian tetralogy. His failure to deliver on his promise to

[1] In other words, it is the appearance of Oldcastle in *2 Henry IV* which precipitated the intervention by Cobham in both plays, because *Part 2* was submitted for licensing during his tenure of the office of Lord Chamberlain (*Part 1* had already been licensed and had played for probably over half a year before its Oldcastle was changed to Falstaff).

[2] It may be due to the late insertion of parts of the Epilogue into foul papers that the space between the first and second quarto paragraphs is wider than that separating the second and third. It is interesting to note also that only in quarto does Shakespeare preserve what appears to be an over-arching echo of Hal's parting words to Falstaff. Hal's last two words to Falstaff before the coronation are 'good night' (2.4.361), and those are also the last words in the quarto version of the play when the Epilogue, which may have been written for Falstaff (i.e. Kemp, who was an accomplished dancer), says 'I will bid you good night'. Is it fanciful to suspect a closing pun on 'knight'?: see Epilogue 16 n.

feature 'Sir John in it' might argue in the opposite direction: that these lines were written well before work on *Henry V* seriously got under way. The additional material in the Epilogue allowed Shakespeare simultaneously to advertise the new play, and once and for all to settle the contentious matter of Oldcastle. But notwithstanding Shakespeare's concessions to the authorities, the transition from script to printed text would turn out to be far from smooth; other interests and other censors were waiting to enter the fray with *2 Henry IV*.

The Sources. By writing *2 Henry IV* hard on the heels of *1 Henry IV*, and not long after *Richard II*, Shakespeare returned to familiar historical territory. His main sources for *2 Henry IV* were, again, Raphael Holinshed's *The Third Volume of Chronicles* (1587, second edn.), and the rambling anonymous chronicle play *The Famous Victories of Henry the Fifth*. This was entered in the Stationers' Register on 14 May 1594, but its first known edition dates from 1598, later than the writing of the two *Henry IV* plays. Shakespeare again used, or recalled to effect, Samuel Daniel's *The First Fowre Bookes of the Civile Wars* (1595), Edward Hall's *The Union of the Two Noble and Illustre Famelies of Lancastre and Yorke* (1548) from which he had worked earlier during the first cycle of history plays, John Stow's *The Chronicles of England* (1580), Sir Thomas Elyot's *The Governour* and, perhaps, *A Myrroure for Magistrates* (1559). There was also a *Henry IV/Henry V* play in existence before 1588, when Richard Tarlton died. He had appeared in a play at the Bull in Bishopsgate during which 'the judge was to take a box on the eare' (Bullough, p. 289), a reference to the infamous (and probably apocryphal) incident of Hal's striking the Lord Chief Justice and therefore being committed to prison.

Of these texts the first two, Holinshed's *Chronicles* (to which Stow, Fleming, and Harrison contributed after Holinshed's death in 1580) and *The Famous Victories*, are the most important. Holinshed above all provided Shakespeare with a rich source of information in no fewer than thirteen plays, and he 'must have owned his own copy'.[1] At times, as in the Archbishop of Canterbury's Salic Law speech in *Henry V*, Shakespeare followed Holin-

---

[1] Gurr (p. 231).

shed's text almost to the letter, as faithfully there as he did Plutarch in the Roman plays.[1]

The sources listed so far in relation to *2 Henry IV* bear almost exclusively on the 'high' political plot of the play, which in point of fact runs to 10,289 words in Q (F = 11,647) compared to 12,576 Q words (F = 12,413) of the sub-plot presided over by Falstaff.[2] For a substantial part of the play therefore Shakespeare was at liberty with regard to his material. This is not to deny the importance of a number of other materials that he used for the 'non-historical' parts of the plot, some of which are openly alluded to and even quoted. These include John Eliot's *Ortho-epia Gallica* (1593), two plays by George Peele (one of them lost, the other being *The Battle of Alcazar*, 1594), and Marlowe's *Tamburlaine* (1587)—all particularly relevant to the new and prominently advertised character of Pistol—and the Bible is repeatedly drawn on by Falstaff and also the conspirators.

It is the uses of Holinshed in *2 Henry IV* that need to be addressed above all. Clearly the writing of a history play, whether English or Roman, puts special constraints on the author. His room for manoeuvre is circumscribed by the established facts of the real world, as they are set out in the sources. No amount of creativity can undo the deposition of Richard II by Henry Bolingbroke in a play about those events, or allow the Archbishop of York, Richard Scrope, to see through the ruse at Gaultres or to triumph over his enemies. But if the essential facts cannot be changed, they can, and need to be, restructured in the dramatic exposition. It is not Shakespeare's purpose to offer a chronicled narrative of the last nine years and eight months of the reign of Henry IV which are covered by the play, from the aftermath of the Battle of Shrewsbury (21 July 1403) to Henry's death in Westminster on 20 March 1413. There would not be the space for him to do so, even if he wished.

---

[1] In *The Sources of Shakespeare's Plays* (1977) Kenneth Muir writes that 'Shakespeare is at his worst when he is slavishly following Holinshed's narrative . . . The feebleness of this speech [on the Salic law] suggests that Shakespeare's imagination was not engaged . . .' (pp. 107–9).

[2] These figures are approximate because Hal in particular straddles the division between 'high' and 'low' plots, but they are nevertheless indicative of the play's general balance between, or even tilt towards, a Falstaffian rather than a Lancastrian world; on respective word counts, see below, p. 42.

Shakespeare's powers of pertinent selectivity are such that not only is an audience of *2 Henry IV* unaware of, or undisturbed by, 'gaps' in the narrative, the play can even afford the luxury of repeatedly, and at some length, referring back to its own past history, and particularly to the forced abdication of Richard II. That this is a leitmotif in the play's politics is acknowledged by the dying Bolingbroke: 'For all my reign hath been but as a scene | Acting that argument' (*2 Henry IV* 4.3.327–8). It occurs throughout the *Henry IV* and *Henry V* plays, and comes to rest only when Henry V, in a gesture of extenuation, removes Richard's body from King's Langley to the Chapel in Westminster Abbey, built by Richard himself for the express purpose of his burial (*Henry V* 4.1.286–302). Holinshed makes it clear that the usurpation lies at the root of the turbulence of the reign of Henry IV:

And to speake a truth, no marvell it was, if manie envied the prosperous state of king Henrie, sith it was evident inough to the world, that he had with wrong usurped the crowne, and not onelie violentlie deposed king Richard, but also cruellie procured his death; for the which undoubtedlie, both he and his posteritie tasted such troubles, as put them still in danger of their states, till their direct succeeding line was quite rooted out by the contrarie faction, as in Henrie the sixt and Edward the fourth it may appeare. (Bullough, p. 188)

Others kept an open or sceptical mind about the death at Pomfret of Richard II. But Holinshed, who elsewhere is scrupulously reticent to the point of deferring to his readers' judgement and discretion,[1] is in no doubt here that Henry IV ordered the murder of his deposed predecessor. Although less explicitly, Shakespeare followed Holinshed's lead here.

Elsewhere his repeating Holinshed's errors suggests that he did not always check his history beyond the chronicles' accounts, or was prepared to follow their licence. This can be seen in the perhaps understandable confusion (which Daniel also perpetrates in *Civil Wars* followed by Shakespeare) between Sir Edmund Mor-

[1] As, for example, in relating (while not necessarily crediting) the story of Henry IV's dying words about the Jerusalem Chamber (4.3.365–70: cf. Bullough, p. 278), where again one senses his hostility to Henry IV. In her chapter 'Censorship', Patterson (pp. 234–63) repeatedly refers to Holinshed's characteristic 'protocols' of 'multivocality and verbatim reporting' which left its mark even on the controversial (and subsequently censured) Elizabethan section (notably the Babington conspiracy) written by Abraham Fleming (see below, p. 33).

timer, the brother-in-law of Hotspur, who marries the daughter of Glyndŵr, and Edmund Mortimer, fifth Earl of March, grandson of 'the lady Philip, daughter of Lionel Duke of Clarence, the third son of King Edward the third' (Bullough, p. 184), and recognized as heir designate by Richard II.[1]

On the other hand, where Holinshed follows Hall in wrongly calling Elizabeth Mortimer 'Elianor', Shakespeare calls her Kate, perhaps exploiting the chroniclers' confusion to artistic ends. He is eager to emphasize the structural parallel between Hotspur and Hal (Henry V also marries a Kate), which further necessitates an imaginative recasting of Hotspur as Hal's contemporary in age: Hal was born in 1387, whereas Hotspur, his almost changeling in the play (*1 Henry IV* 1.1.85–9), was born in 1364 (three years before Bolingbroke), and was therefore Hal's senior by twenty-three years. A similar licence with age arises in *2 Henry IV*, where Hotspur's father Northumberland and Henry IV appear to be equally aged and ailing, even though Northumberland, who was born in 1341, was Bolingbroke's senior by twenty-six years, a generation. Shakespeare's attitude to Holinshed in both the *Henry IV* plays is essentially flexible and pragmatic, unlike that in *Richard II* in which he followed the politico-historical plot closely. The fact that in both *Henry IV* plays the action weaves in and out of politics and comedy, so that the focus of the audience is not sustainedly on the King's battle with disenchanted nobles and prelates, requires an unusually high degree of telescoping and compression.

The play starts in 1403 in the immediate aftermath of Shrewsbury, so 'immediate' in fact that confirmed news of its outcome has not yet reached Warkworth Castle, where the first scene is set. The action is clearly meant to be continuous with *1 Henry IV*, and Rumour reminds us exactly of where we are and where not, by first telling us the true version of events and then, in confidence, its intention to deceive and raise false expectations. The political plot moves straight from Warkworth to the Scrope conspiracy (1.3) which Morton (who is wholly Shakespeare's invention) urges

---

[1] At *1 Henry IV* 1.3.140 Hotspur calls Mortimer 'my wife's brother' (see also *1 Henry IV* 2.4.79) when he is in fact her nephew, which Shakespeare seems to know since later, at 3.1.192, the same Mortimer refers to Kate Percy as 'my aunt Percy'. For a full exposition, see Bevington (1987, pp. 287–8).

Northumberland to join because, unlike Hotspur, the Archbishop has it in his power to turn 'insurrection to religion'. But in Holinshed Northumberland submits at least temporarily to the King (Bullough, p. 269) after Shrewsbury.

Shakespeare ignores the plundering by Glyndŵr in the English marches in 1404, and concentrates instead, as does Holinshed, on the Scrope uprising. Compared to this, Glyndŵr and Northumberland are shifted about in the play to fit in with dramatic expediency. Glyndŵr's death is reported to Henry IV by Warwick in 3.1.102. Since 3.1 specifically refers back to 1399 as 'eight years since' and is therefore set in 1407, it appears that Shakespeare has brought forward Glyndŵr's death by two years from Holinshed's claiming, wrongly, that Glyndŵr died 'in this tenth yeare of king Henrie his reigne' (Bullough, p. 276).[1]

Similarly, the defeat of Northumberland and Bardolph at Bramham Moor (1408) is announced by Harcourt to the ailing King in 4.3, twelve lines after Westmorland's breaking the news of the defeat of Mowbray, Scrope, and Hastings at Gaultres. Imaginative chronology is at odds here with both reality and source: in 3.1 the scene was set in 1407, but in 4.3 the outcomes of the battles of Gaultres (1405) and Bramham Moor (1408) are reported as simultaneous events in a scene which appears to be set in 1413, shortly before the death of Henry IV. A logical (as opposed to 'poetic') sequence would demand at least one other scene (about Bramham Moor) after 4.2, but that would be to misunderstand the drift of the play. By 4.3 Shakespeare is eager to wind up the dying King's involvement in politics in anticipation of the encounter between father and son, Henry IV and the future Henry V. If Northumberland's final and fatal rebellion is therefore given short, or even almost perfunctory, shrift, then that is no different from the compressing of the last fairly peaceful years of Bolingbroke's reign into the agonized final moments that follow the apoplexy suffered by the King on hearing the news in 4.3.102 ('And wherefore should these good news make me sick?').

Shakespeare makes no mention here either of Hal's prominent role on the King's Council during 1411–12, when his uncle

---

[1] That is, in 1409; in fact Glyndŵr probably died in *c.*1415–16: see R. R. Davies, *The Revolt of Owain Glyn Dŵr* (Oxford, 1995), pp. 326–7.

Henry Beaufort, Bishop of Winchester, suggested that the ailing Henry IV might abdicate in Hal's favour.[1] In the ensuing rift with the King, Hal and his followers were dismissed from the Council, and he was replaced by the second of his three brothers, Thomas of Clarence. It may be this rift—which was healed before Henry IV died—which makes Shakespeare's Henry IV single out Clarence in 4.3.20 ff., and urge him to stay close to his brother, the future king.

Moreover, in *The Chronicles of England* (1580) and *The Annales of England* (1592), Stow makes the dying King voice his concern about Clarence and Hal becoming bitter rivals after his death and thus bringing the realm 'to destruction and misery'. It may be Shakespeare's reading of this in Stow, as well as the massacre by the newly installed Sultan of his brothers in 1596, which makes Henry V urge his brothers not to mingle their sorrow with fear (see below, 5.2.48 n.). The royal family as a family is accorded greater prominence by Shakespeare in both plays than it is in his sources. Just as Hal, who was only sixteen at Shrewsbury, is made to fight an apocryphal duel with Hotspur, so it is Prince John of Lancaster who tricks Scrope and the conspirators at Gaultres (and not Westmorland as in Holinshed).

The final reconciliation between Hal and Henry, with its long passages of intense solemnity and Hal's premature snatching (like his father) of the crown, is inspired by a few, albeit striking, sentences and exchanges in Holinshed, and more specifically in *Civil Wars* and *Famous Victories* (see below, pp. 25–6). Shakespeare recalls, but does not show, the incident of Hal's striking the Lord Chief Justice of the day, Sir William Gascoigne, reported by Holinshed, Hall, *Famous Victories* and, in a modified form, by Sir Thomas Elyot. Shakespeare, however, departs from history and his authorities by making the Lord Chief Justice's steadfast and principled response the reason not only for his keeping on, but for Henry V's adopting this 'Lord of Rule' as a surrogate 'father to my youth', just before he discards

---

[1] At *1 Henry IV* 3.2.32 Hal is told 'Thy place in Council thou hast rudely lost'. Bevington (1987, p. 223) and Humphreys (p. 102) rightly read this as a reference to the striking of the Lord Chief Justice rather than to the later political struggle for supremacy at Court. Also, 3.2 is set before the Battle of Shrewsbury, i.e. before 1403.

Falstaff.[1] Shakespeare sharpened the relationship that he found in *Famous Victories*, where the Lord Chief Justice is appointed by Henry 'to be my Protector over my Realme' (Bullough, p. 325).

Another important departure from his sources in the direction of family domesticities is the depiction of Northumberland as a married man who is persuaded not to join the archiepiscopal party by his wife and widowed daughter-in-law. The play, though not Holinshed, makes it clear that Northumberland wilfully failed his son and brother at Shrewsbury, and at Kate Percy's pleading so he will the Archbishop. Shakespeare may well have known that Richard Scrope, a cousin of the William Scrope whom Bolingbroke executed as one of 'the caterpillars of the commonwealth', was linked to the Percies through his brother's marriage to the widow of Hotspur's brother, so that his flight to Scotland becomes a second betrayal of family links. The unsympathetic portrayal of Northumberland from *Richard II* to *2 Henry IV* owes something to Holinshed, who portrays him as a schemer who marched a large army 'either to aid his sonne and brother (as was thought) or at the least towards the king, to procure a peace' (Bullough, p. 269), and as a perennial conspirator in the home nest (Bullough, p. 270; see also 3.1.57–70).

Shakespeare had drawn on Daniel's *Civil Wars*, 3.111 in *1 Henry IV* 5.4, when at Shrewsbury Hal rescued his father from Douglas. From an apostrophe to Hotspur there ('Such wracke of others bloud thou didst behold | O furious *Hotspur*, ere thou lost thine owne!') Daniel moves at once to the sleepless guilt-ridden King's sickening. Within four stanzas of his account of Shrewsbury, in lines which correspond to 3.1 in *2 Henry IV*, Daniel has the King lying on his deathbed, as if the battle and the apoplexy ten years later were immediately and causally linked (see below, p. 47). If Shakespeare compresses five historical and Holinshedian years into a seeming few frantic weeks between 1.1 and 4.3, Daniel renders double the time in a blank transition between two stanzas, 114 and 115. The contemplation of his crown which is set 'in his sight' triggers a soliloquy by the King during which his soul temporarily separates from his body and leaves it for dead, in the

---

[1] In fact, Gascoigne died on 17 December 1413 (some nine months after Henry IV, and after serving as Lord Chief Justice since 15 November 1401), and was succeeded under the new regime by Sir William Hankford.

course of an abstract search for repentance, expiation, and hope of mercy. While the King considers that the only redress is the surrendering of the crown back to its original owner, Richard II,[1] Hal takes it away. When Henry IV awakes, he urges Hal (presumably as instructed by his soul), to part with the tainted crown. But Hal refuses, because 'Time will appease them well that now complaine, | And ratefie our interest in the end' (*CW*, 3.125; Bullough, p. 284). Whereas in *2 Henry IV* the dying King bequeathes the crown to Hal in the hope that the smooth succession of the father by the son, the King by the Prince of Wales, will mitigate the criminality of the deposition of 1399 in the minds of the nobles and the people, in *Civil Wars* the Prince of Wales is ruthlessly ambitious. He declines to heed his father's advice with 'Nay father, since your fortune did attaine | So hye a stand: I mean not to descend' (*CW*, 3.125; Bullough, p. 284). Shakespeare closely follows the train of thought in *Civil Wars*, 3.127 in *2 Henry IV* 4.3.339–45, when Henry IV reveals to his son his purpose of a crusade to the 'Holy Land' ('this sacred warre I tooke in hand'), because it is political wisdom 'to busy giddy minds | With foreign quarrels' (*CW*, 3.127: 'But some great actions entertaine thou still | To hold their mindes who else will practise ill'; Bullough, p. 285).

Famous Victories bears on both the 'high' and 'comedic' or 'low' plots of the *Henry IV* plays. As printed in 1598, this twenty-scene picaresque work stretches over 1,552 lines from the robbing of the Receivers (the model for the Gad's Hill robbery in *1 Henry IV*, Act 2) to the coronation of Henry V and his subsequent conquest of France, and it ends by announcing the wedding date of Henry to Katherine of France. Although in its extant version it is a single play,[2] it divides into roughly two equal parts as far as Shakespeare's uses of it are concerned. The first ten scenes loosely correspond to *1 Henry IV* (Scenes I to VI) and *2 Henry IV* (VII to Scene IX.756), while Scenes IX.757 to XX relate the build-up to,

---

[1] Or it could mean surrendering the crown to Edmund Mortimer, chosen by Richard as his heir (see Humphreys, p. xxxiv). But Bolingbroke is hallucinating at this point (his soul is said to be 'sad' and 'confused') and not likely to be thinking in clear dynastic terms.

[2] It may be a run-together, truncated version of two separate plays, or perhaps even a memorially reconstructed one from the period 1592–4, when the theatres in London were closed: see Humphreys, p. xxxii.

and execution of, the French campaign dramatized by Shakespeare in *Henry V*. At the same time the tense encounter between the not-yet-crowned Henry V and the Lord Chief Justice who committed him to prison occurs here *after* the King has been insulted by the Dauphin's tennis balls, and decided to make for Southampton (*Henry V* 1.2.299–310; *Famous Victories* IX.868–75).[1] Similarly the press-ganging of the reluctant John Cobler (i.e. cobbler, or shoemaker) in front of his wife by a captain may have influenced 2 *Henry IV* 3.2, as is signalled particularly by the degree of overlap between the respective domestic circumstances (Mouldy's mother and John Cobler's wife), trade (Feeble is a tailor), and sickness (Bullcalf also claims to be 'diseased'). But the tender parting of John Cobler and his wife, and her sudden concern for her husband to whom she may previously have behaved like a shrew, also bring to mind the sudden burst of sentiment and affection in Mistress Quickly and, unexpectedly, Doll Tearsheet, as Falstaff in turn departs to the wars.

In 2 *Henry IV* Shakespeare worked from some raw materials that occur in *Famous Victories*, particularly between Scenes VII and IX.756. But he also drew on the 1 *Henry IV* parts of *Famous Victories*. The recollection of Hal's assault on the dignity of the person and office of the Lord Chief Justice is spelt out in Scene IV where the 'box [o]' the ear' is dramatized. The Lord Chief Justice looms larger in Scenes V and VI than in any other source for the play. In Scene V Dericke and John Cobler re-enact the scene of Hal's striking the judge, and in the following scene Hal, who is called 'the young Prince', but is throughout denoted by the speech-prefix *Hen.*5, promises Ned (who corresponds to the 'Ned', 'Edward', 'Yedward' Poins of the *Henry IV* plays as the closest of the prince's scapegrace boon companions) the office of Lord Chief Justice, thereby anticipating the unique prominence Shakespeare accords the judge in 2 *Henry IV*.

Although at the coronation Henry V (who also banishes his 'misrulie mates' in Holinshed: Bullough, p. 280) firmly rejects Ned who publicly reminds him of his promise (*FV* IX; Bullough, pp. 320–1), nothing in the earlier scenes suggests that this Hal

---

[1] On this occasion Shakespeare demonstrably remembered *Famous Victories* in *Henry V*, when he echoed *Famous Victories*' 'tunne' which originates in Hall (Holinshed writes of a 'barrell' of tennis balls: cf. Gurr, p. 16).

Figure 5. The Coronation of Henry V, a sculpture in stone in the Henry V Chantry in Westminster Abbey.

knows them all and indulges the unyoked idleness of their humour only to offset his own imperial glory the more effectively later. Rather the Prince of *Famous Victories* is a ruthless and reckless character most of whose unsavoury traits Shakespeare transfers to Hal's companions and Falstaff. Although *Famous Victories* does have its Sir John Oldcastle, also known as 'Jockey', he is a minor figure and in no way, physical or other, recognizable as the ancestor of Shakespeare's gargantuan rogue. More intriguing perhaps is the fact that he features here among Hal's rowdy companions under the name of Oldcastle, in a text printed within a year of the Falstaff–Oldcastle fiasco.

The most noteworthy similarity is between *2 Henry IV* 4.3.131–370 and *Famous Victories* Scene VIII, an earlier version of which may also have left its mark on *Civil Wars*, 3.121, as the Prince's two references to the 'melancholy soul' of his father's body and the surrounding context may suggest (*FV* 620–1; 651–3). The use of music in *Famous Victories* and by Shakespeare at the King's request (*FV* 616; *2 Henry IV* 4.3.135), the Prince's begging forgiveness of his dying father (ll. 268–306), and the King's virtual admission in both texts of foul play in the achieving of the crown, demonstrate a close influence.[1] Such evidence may also suggest that the version (or even copy) of the play that Shakespeare knew was, in this scene at least, essentially the same as the 1598 version. This may have been an edition which appeared shortly after its entry in the Stationers' Register (Chambers, 1930, i. 384), or an earlier version of it. Its title-page states that it was played by 'the Queenes Maiesties Players', a company which flourished in the 1580s, and whose clown was Tarlton (see Bevington, 1987, pp. 17–19) so that the scene described in *Tarlton's Jests* (printed in 1638; Bullough, p. 289), which comes from 'a play of Henry the fift, wherein the judge was to take a box on the eare', could be Scene IV of *Famous Victories*. His use of *Famous Victories* illustrates that even when Shakespeare draws on a source for parts of the low-life plot, it supplies inspiration also for the high plot, both its politics and its affective relationships, as in the deathbed scene. Shakespeare clearly supplemented his reading of Holinshed by a number of other accounts, including poetic and dramatic ones, primarily with a view to consolidating his knowledge of the history of the period.[2]

That Hal had enjoyed a wild, even riotous youth, was widely known in Elizabethan England, and is alluded to by Shakespeare in *Richard II* 5.3.1–22, already with half an eye on *1 Henry IV* and the tetralogy as a whole. That the stories may be more than anecdotal truth is suggested by the fact that they originate with contempor-

---

[1] A brief checklist of the main similarities between *2 Henry IV* 4.3.131–370 and *Famous Victories* (Bullough, pp. 315–19) is as follows:
175–8: *FV* VIII 678–81; 236: *FV* VI 540–74; 268–9: *FV* VIII 625–8, 655; 279: *FV* VIII 655; 279–81: *FV* VIII 652–3; 311–16: *FV* VIII 666, 674–5; 350–4: *FV* VIII 676–81 (cf. 175–8).

[2] At times he followed the detail of his sources to such an extent that we can confidently conclude that he used the 1587 (rather than the 1577) edition of Holinshed (which lacks the phrase 'pickthanks' which Shakespeare uses at *1 Henry IV* 3.2.25), or that the Archbishop's word 'schedule' derives from Stow's *Chronicles* or *Annales* rather than from Holinshed, even as he tirelessly restructured the information they offered.

aries of King Henry himself, notably the fourth Earl of Ormonde who was knighted at Agincourt (October 1415) by Henry. The main written conduits for the madcap Hal stories are by Hal's contemporary Thomas of Walsingham in his *Historia Anglicana* (1418), by Tito Livio's *Vita Henrici* (c.1437),[1] and by Caxton's version of the Brut Chronicle (1482). Robert Fabyan's *Chronicle* (1516) states that on his coronation Henry V 'became a newe man' and in order not to slide back into bad ways he banished his companions from his presence: 'charged them upon paine of their lives, that none of them were so hardy as to come within X. mile of suche place as he were lodged in' (Bullough, p. 354). Fabyan is the first to record this detail, while Sir Thomas Elyot's *The Governour* (1531) first mentions Hal's threatening (though not perpetrating) violence against the Lord Chief Justice.[2] In *The Union of the Two Noble and Illustre Famelies of Lancastre and Yorke* (1548), however, Hall writes that Hal 'strake the Chiefe Justice with his fiste on the face' (Bullough, p. 286), which Holinshed closely echoes in his account. Shakespeare's approach to his material is, as his use of multiple sources demonstrates, eclectic in the extreme. Even 'historical' matter is not allowed entirely to override the needs of dramatic and imaginative structure, as the unhistorical prominence in *2 Henry IV* of various low-life characters shows further and specifically.

What's in a name? In view of this, and in view particularly of the independence of the low plot, which merely gestures towards received history through the use of anecdotes, the question must

[1] This was translated into English, and augmented, in a 1513 manuscript, by details from the *Chroniques* by Enguerrand de Monstrelet and information from the Earl of Ormonde. This version for the first time relates the incident of Hal's ambushing his receivers as well as the business of the crown and pillow (*2 Henry IV* 4.3). Because the pedigree of this version stretches back into the early fifteenth century and to a contemporary of Henry V (only five years his junior), it has some authority.

[2] Sir Thomas Elyot, *The Governor* (Book II, chapter vi: Bullough, pp. 288–9) in a passage which Shakespeare echoes at *2 Henry IV* 5.2.67–100. According to Elyot the Prince of Wales only threatened the Lord Chief Justice ('[Hal] being set all in a fury, all chafed, and in a terrible maner, came up to the place of judgement'), because one of his servants (not specifically Bardolph, as Shakespeare suggests in *2 Henry IV* 1.2.52–3) 'was arrayned at the kynges benche'. In the anonymous *The Famous Victories of Henry the Fifth* which was performed before *2 Henry IV* Hal strikes the judge: 'He giveth him a boxe on the eare' (Bullough, p. 309); cf. also *1 Henry IV* 3.2.32–3 for a further possible allusion to this.

Figure 6. Richard Burton as Hal, Heather Stannard as Doll Tearsheet, Alan Badel as Poins, and Anthony Quayle as Falstaff in the 1951 production (directed by Michael Redgrave) at the Shakespeare Memorial Theatre in Stratford-upon-Avon.

be asked why the comic characters' names are nevertheless historical. Shakespeare substitutes the historical Oldcastle with a transliterated version of the name of another historical figure, Sir John Fastolf (1378–1459), an exact contemporary of Oldcastle (c. 1378–1417), even though the character's visual and other aspects (see below, p. 39) differ from historical reality.[1] Fastolf had fought under Henry V in France, and had already appeared on the

---

[1] The birth dates for Oldcastle and Fastolf are from *DNB*. That Falstaff is a transliterated version of Fastolf is not universally accepted. In 'Second Thoughts on Falstaff's Name' (*SQ* 30 (1979), 82–4), George Walton Williams argues that Fastolf and Falstaff are distinct: 'It seems unlikely . . . that Shakespeare would think it appropriate to replace the name of one historical personage with the name of another historical personage'. He finds support for a clear distinction between 'Fastolf' and 'Falstaff' in the fact that the speech-prefixes of the single surviving sheet C (sig. 4) of Qo (1598) of *1 Henry IV* are '*Fast.*', and concludes that Shakespeare may have 'wanted the sound of the new name to be suggestive of falling and falsity'. That Falstaff could be suggestive of 'false staff' was noted by Ax (pp. 101 ff.), who additionally noted that the name 'contains as it were the word "fat" twice, firstly if we begin reading as usually, omitting the l & s, and especially reading the last syllable backwards'.

stage a few years earlier in Shakespeare's *1 Henry VI*.[1] Moreover, the Prince's satellite in *Famous Victories*, Ned, who does not there have a surname (in the *Henry IV* plays the character splits into both Falstaff and Ned Poins) may contain more than a glancing allusion to the Poins/Points/Poyntz family. By calling him 'Poins', Shakespeare turns him into a character whose family name was certainly known and respected at the time of writing: Elizabeth's Vice-Chamberlain, Sir Thomas Heneage, had been married to Anne Points (her family quartered the arms of Bardolph) and he was therefore related to the same Brookes who were briefly to hold the office of Lord Chamberlain.[2] If the Ned Poins of *1 Henry IV* is indeed a scion of the ancient family of Sir Francis Poyntz of Gloucestershire (Shaaber, p. 3), then there would be further grounds for arguing that the two *Henry* plays were from the start conceived as a two-part drama, because though Gloucestershire does not feature in *1 Henry IV*, it does emphatically in the sequel.

The names Russell and Harvey both occur in *1 Henry IV*, but neither Harvey nor Russell is mentioned in *Famous Victories*. Harvey and Russell were contemporary names associated with prominent Elizabethan families, the Southamptons (Harvey was the stepfather of Shakespeare's patron Henry Wriothesley) and the Earls of Bedford. In the stage direction at *2 Henry IV* 2.2.0.1 Shakespeare furthermore seems to have changed the name of '*sir Iohn Russel*' (in quarto) to Bardolph (Folio's reading). Following that lead, for QF '*Rossill*' and '*Haruey*' (*1 Henry IV* 1.2.160) most editors since Theobald[3] print 'Bardolph' and 'Peto' respectively (Humphreys, p. xv).[4] The change in nomenclature downgraded the characters on the social scale. Peto may (just possibly) allude to the priest, and later cardinal, William Peto, who opposed Henry VIII's desire to divorce Katherine of Aragon (Bullough, p. 176),

[1] In Folio, the only authority for the text of *1 Henry VI*, he is called '*Falstaffe*'.

[2] See Sharpe (p. 95), who also thinks that there might be possible links between Heneage and Shakespeare's portrayal of Pistol in *2 Henry IV*. See also p. 31 below, and McKeen (p. 137).

[3] The exception is the Oxford *Complete Works*.

[4] *1 Henry IV* quartos print speech-prefix '*Ross.*' at 2.5.175, 177, 181 where F reads '*Gads.*'. Chambers (1923, ii. 200) writes that 'Two other minor actors in the company about 1597 were probably Harvey and Rossill, whose names appear to have got into the text of *1 Henry IV* in place of those of Bardolph and Peto, whom they represented.' If this is the case, then the situation would be analogous to the appearance of Sincklo in the quarto of *Part 2* and the suspected presence of Kemp in a speech-prefix in 2.4.

but his role in *Part 2*, where he speaks a mere forty words, is so small as to be almost insignificant. The point is that even in the case of a tiny part such as Peto's the new name may be historical, as indeed is Bardolph's, since a Johan Bardolf served under Fastolf at Honfleur in France in 1428 (by which time Henry V had been dead for six years). But the choice of Bardolph, coincidentally also a Stratford name at the time, has the consequence for *2 Henry IV* of featuring two Bardolphs: the 'irregular humourist' already much in evidence as a splendid caricature in *1 Henry IV*, and the historical Baron Thomas Bardolph, who was Northumberland's ally and who died of wounds shortly after the Battle of Bramham Moor (19 February 1408).

Should this suggest that Shakespeare had not yet started work on *2 Henry IV* when he changed the names in *1 Henry IV*, particularly since it is 'Lord Bardolph' who speaks the very first line in the play after Rumour: 'Who keeps the gate here, ho?' (1.1.1)?[1] It would do so only if we started from the premise that Shakespeare wanted to avoid duplication. But such duplication need not cause confusion. Indeed, the third line of the play proper (after Rumour) identifies the speaker as 'Lord Bardolph'. In any case the red-nosed appearance of Bardolph whom Falstaff can never look at 'but I think upon hell-fire and Dives that lived in purple' (*1 Henry IV* 3.3.30–1), his casting as 'the Knight of the Burning Lamp' (*1 Henry IV* 3.3.25–6), rules out visual confusion.[2]

Furthermore, both the *Henry* plays structure their actions through a series of foils and antitheses at the levels of scene, genre, and character, as in Hal–Hotspur, Falstaff–Henry IV, and Falstaff/Henry IV–Lord Chief Justice (see below, pp. 44–5). It may be therefore that the change to Bardolph in *1 Henry IV* was *inspired* by the serendipitous presence of Lord Bardolph in the historical material pertinent to *2 Henry IV*, in which case one would be forced to conclude that the changes were implemented almost certainly *after* the completion, or at least the start, of the second play. In the context of the play's opposing a crumbling main plot in its final throes to an equally collapsing low plot, the two Bardolphs

---

[1] Cf. similarly Shaaber (p. 3), Davison (p. 6).

[2] There is the further oddity in *1 Henry IV* of the homophones 'Gadshill' and 'Gad's Hill' denoting a character and a place respectively; and there are of course two 'Jaques' names in *As You Like It* (as well as two Olivers).

(in the quarto of *2 Henry IV* their parts are of not dissimilar length: Lord Bardolph 391 words; Bardolph 307) pose similar threats to the welfare of the kingdom, through high treason and corruption of the heir to the throne respectively. Certainly, *if* the changes in nomenclature occurred after work on *2 Henry IV* had started, then the conclusion must be that Shakespeare willed *2 Henry IV* to have two Bardolphs, turning the necessity of renaming into a virtue whose merits as yet require further investigation. Did Shakespeare know that Bardolph was also the family name of Sir Reginald Cobham's wife, of the same Cobham/Brooke/Oldcastle family which caused the players so much grief?

Falstaff versus Oldcastle. That Falstaff started his theatrical existence in *1 Henry IV*, and very probably in *2 Henry IV*, as Oldcastle is almost certain, and there is the strongest likelihood that Shakespeare was compelled to change the name of his great comic character on the insistence of Sir William Brooke, the seventh Lord Cobham and briefly Lord Chamberlain, and his son Sir Henry Brooke, eighth Lord Cobham.[1] The Brookes were descended from Lady Joan Cobham (b. 1387), a widowed Kentish heiress whom Sir John Oldcastle married in 1409. The sixty-nine-year-old Brooke's seven-month tenure was sandwiched between the eleven years of the first Lord Hunsdon and his son George Carey, second Lord Hunsdon, who inherited his father's patronage of Shakespeare's company; and by the time the First Folio was printing the Cobhams were in disgrace. Henry Brooke was arrested and convicted of treason in November 1603 and died in the Tower sixteen years later (1619), still a prisoner. The family title was not filled again until 1645.

If the long arm of the Brookes indeed managed to erase the name of their illustrious ancestor from the printed versions of Shakespeare's play in the immediate aftermath of writing, one must wonder why the four post-1603 quartos of *1 Henry IV* (Q3, Q4, Q5, Q6), and of course the 1623 Folio of both the *Henry IV* plays did not restore the name of Oldcastle. It was after all, according to Heminge and Condell in their address 'To the great Variety of

---

[1] Kastan calls them the tenth and eleventh holders of the title, after *The Complete Peerage of England, Scotland, and Ireland* (G. E. Cockayne, rev. Vicary Gibbs, 1913), 341–51, and McKeen (pp. 700–2).

Readers', one of the professed aims of the volume to print the texts the way Shakespeare 'conceived them', and not as in some of the earlier imperfect states in the quartos.[1] Similarly surprising is the change to 'Broome' in Folio of the punning use of the name Brooke in 1602 quarto of *Merry Wives* (see above, p. 11), at a time when there could be no obvious reason connected to the Cobhams for such reticence.[2]

The Brookes may not have been antagonistic to the theatre per se. The questionable assumption that they were has arisen in the wake of the *Henry IV* controversy, and the complaint (in a letter to William Cotton) by Thomas Nashe, within a month of Cobham's tenure of office, that under the former Lord Chamberlain the players had been safe from the persecutions of the Lord Mayor and his aldermen, but that their state 'is now so vncertayne they cannot build vpon it'.[3] Brooke's verifiable behaviour argues otherwise. Thus in November 1596 he pointedly refused to sign a petition against the opening of a new playhouse by James Burbage next door to him in Blackfriars, even though the purpose of the petition mentions the vicinity of the new venue to the Lord Chamberlain's residence (Chambers, 1923, iv. 319–20). Far from being a Puritan zealot, Brooke may have been a forbearing patron of the arts.[4]

[1] Although, as Stanley Wells reminds me, the Folio regularly treats foul-paper texts with more or less close conformity with the plays as acted rather than as 'conceived', as for instance *Hamlet* and *Lear*.

[2] Unless one assumes that the change to 'Broome' alludes to what may have been a real-life Broome–Mrs Broome–Cobham sexual triangle, as Honigmann (pp. 128–9) has argued, in which case the burden of insult would shift from the Brooke family more specifically to William Brooke's immediate private and domestic circumstances. That the widowed Cobham had earlier (1592) been spectacularly and famously rebuffed in a marriage suit to Lady Montague may have fuelled Shakespeare's imagining of Falstaff in *Merry Wives*, *if* he was hostile, and dared to express it, to the Brookes.

[3] Chambers (1923, iv. 319). It was the same Nashe's collaboration with Jonson on *The Isle of Dogs* which caused the closure of the theatres from July to October 1597. Presumably their play had been duly licensed for performance under the second Hunsdon dispensation, but this did not, it appears, protect the players from the censure which followed.

[4] See McKeen (pp. 648–50). The suspicion about Brooke's Puritan leanings derives partly from William Harrison's conclusion of 'The Epistle Dedicatorie' of Holinshed's *Chronicles*, second edn. (1587), to which he contributed. Harrison ('a shallow and foolish man who wrote a dull book'—Booth, p. 28) became chaplain to William Brooke, who appointed him vicar of Radwinter in Essex. In his epistle he wishes Cobham well, 'and the rest of your reformed familie, vnto whom I wish farder increase of his holie spirit, vnderstanding of his word, augumentation of

His initial period of office coincides with the closure of the London theatres by the Privy Council (22 July 1596), in the wake of fears about the plague (Chambers, 1923, iv. 319). All the signs are that by then 1 *Henry IV* was playing with Oldcastle as the fat knight. Its licence for performance would have been issued by the experienced and long-serving Master of the Revels from 1579 to 1609, Edmund Tilney, under Hunsdon as Lord Chamberlain.[1] That Shakespeare would have been unaware of the connection between Cobham/Brooke and Oldcastle is inconceivable. The connection is made explicitly in the Elizabethan section of Holinshed, where the long 'Treatise of the Lord Cobhams . . .' contains extended, and even mystical, references to Oldcastle. The Cobham section, like the Babington material, is among the five sections in the 1587 edition that the Privy Council ordered to be removed, as a consequence of which they survive only in a few examples of the extant copies. It is not at all clear why the innocuous-seeming Cobham section was cut to the point of being described as 'the most extensive interference on the part of the government [of the time] in a literary work'.[2] Even if Shakespeare's Holinshed lacked these censored pages (they demonstrate that the Cobham family and their history were part of the nation's common heritage), it is very probable that when Shakespeare wrote Oldcastle he meant to write Oldcastle, in the full knowledge of the character's history as recorded in Foxe's huge section in *Acts and Monuments*, 'The Trouble and Persecution of the most valiant and worthy Martyr of Christ, Sir John Oldcastle, Knight, Lord

honor, and continuance of zeale to follow his commandements'. But McKeen (p. 238) does not view this as a gesture towards Puritanism, notwithstanding the loaded resonance in the period of phrases like 'reformed' and 'zeale'; cf. similarly Clare (p. 77) who notes that there is no 'concrete' evidence to suggest that Cobham was hostile to the theatre.

[1] Tilney might have been reluctant to issue a licence under the new Lord Chamberlain who, as a member of the Privy Council in 1587, had already shown his sensitivity to issues affecting his family by being a direct party to the censoring of Holinshed. At the same time it is worth stressing that the shrewd Tilney does not seem earlier to have baulked at the idea of Oldcastle as portrayed in 1 *Henry IV*. There is some evidence from a chance remark in Tilney's correspondence which suggests that the Master of the Revels and Brooke as Lord Chamberlain clashed over a matter relating to the Court performances of the 1596–7 Christmas season, possibly Oldcastle: see Fehrenbach (p. 96).

[2] Donno (pp. 229–48).

Cobham'.[1] What he could not have anticipated was that within a few months a nearly septuagenarian descendant (albeit collateral) of the same family should be empowered to vet plays.

If *1 Henry IV* played in the provinces in the spring and late autumn of 1596, we can be reasonably sure that it did so with Oldcastle as its star role. It may occasionally have continued to do so even after the Oldcastle embargo, for in 1600 the then new Lord Chamberlain entertained a foreign dignitary with a private performance of a play called 'Sir John Oldcastle', which was almost certainly Shakespeare's *1 Henry IV* rather than the collaborative Admiral's Men's 'Oldcastle' play (see below, p. 35); and as late as *c.*1610–11 Nathan Field alluded to Falstaff's lines on honour (*1 Henry IV* 5.1.127–40) by attributing them to 'the fat knight hight Oldcastle' (Bevington, 1987, p. 7).[2]

In 1596 the then latest play, and its sequel, by the foremost dramatist in the land, were bound to be considered by the Lord Chamberlain's office for the Christmas Court performances of the 1596–7 season. It must have been sometime during this period, from 26 December to 8 February (Shakespeare's company played at Court on 26 and 27 December, 1 and 6 January, 6 and 8 February) that the change of name, and it appears of name only, was requested and implemented. But the damage was done. Just over a year after the implementation of the change, the Earl of Essex could write to Sir Robert Cecil suggesting that he might

[1] Shakespeare was fully conversant with Foxe's vast and influential *Acts and Monuments* which he used elsewhere, as in *All is True* 5.1.136–58. No fewer than six editions of Foxe's book were published during Shakespeare's life, and one of them appeared in 1596, the year of the *Henry IV* plays. The Oldcastle sections of Foxe's book are to be found in *The Acts and Monuments of John Foxe*, 8 vols. (New York, 1965), iii. 321–401; 541–2; see also the woodcut on p. 5 showing the martyrdom of Oldcastle and reproduced from the 1563 edition of Foxe. Booth (p. 66) argues that Foxe's *Acts and Monuments* influenced the 1587 edition of Holinshed's *Chronicles*, through the 'Continuation' by Abraham Fleming, to such an extent that the revised *Chronicles* become, like Foxe's, a book that makes 'history illustrate the active Protestantism of God'; on Foxe and the place of Oldcastle in English Protestant martyrology, see further John R. Knott, *Discourses of Martyrdom in English Literature, 1563–1694* (1993).

[2] Paraphrasing the same lines in *An Antidote Against Purgatory* (1634), the Catholic polemicist Jane Owen attributes them to '*Syr Iohn Oldcastle* being exprobated of his Cowardlynes ...' In 'A Catholic Oldcastle' (*N & Q* NS 40 (1993), 185–6) R. W. F. Martin concludes from this that Owen knew Falstaff as Oldcastle 'perhaps from past stage performances', and notes that the surprising use in the period of a Protestant martyr by a Catholic writer may reflect an incipient rapprochement between the two sides of the sectarian divide.

inform Sir Alex Ratcliffe that 'his sister is married to Sir John Falstaff'. The Sir John Falstaff referred to here is Sir Henry Brooke, the Lord Chamberlain's son, and coincidentally Sir Robert Cecil's brother-in-law, because Cecil had married Elizabeth Cobham, who died in childbirth on 24 January 1597, to be followed not long after by her grieving father. The only way Brooke and Falstaff could be linked was of course through the common knowledge, at least in political circles, of Falstaff's origin in the Brookes' ancestry; and Essex may well be wishing to needle Cecil here, because the Essex faction, which included Shakespeare's patron Southampton, was at odds with the Cobhams and would therefore have been delighted by their discomfiture over Oldcastle.[1]

Political loyalties as much as a sense of injured dignity may have joined forces to commission the pro-Puritan *1 Sir John Oldcastle* (by Michael Drayton, Richard Hathaway, Antony Munday, and Robert Wilson) which was produced by the Lord Admiral's Men in October 1599.[2] Its intention was, in the words of the Prologue, to set the record straight and to present Oldcastle as 'no pampered glutton ... Nor agèd counsellor to youthful sin'. Instead, the Oldcastle of the play is a courageous philanthropist who feeds the poor who, pointedly in view of Falstaff's shameful recruiting practices in the *Henry IV* plays, are demobbed and errant soldier–beggars. As Honigmann (p. 124) notes, the play's genesis may not be unconnected to the fact that the widowed Countess of Kildare, the daughter of the Lord Admiral, was in January 1599 rumoured to be thinking of marrying Sir Henry Brooke, the new Lord Cobham.

The Oldcastle–Falstaff débâcle may have gone to the heart of the power struggles at the Court and the cliques that managed them, without Shakespeare's intending it to do so, but the evidence is not conclusive. It is far from likely, let alone certain, that Shakespeare intended to write politically barbed and controversial plays in the *Henry IV* plays, as Gary Taylor (1985, 1987) has argued. Nor is it necessary to conclude that the substitution of Falstaff (and Taylor is adamant that the change is to the nomenclature alone) sanitizes, generalizes, and even emasculates the play. But Taylor's polemical argument primarily addresses the Oldcastle–Falstaff issue in *1*

---

[1] The picture may, however, be less clear-cut as Honigmann (pp. 120–2) notes, since in the 1590s the Cobhams and Southampton were at times on friendly, and even mutually supportive, terms.

[2] ed. Corbin.

Henry IV, while it is this edition's contention that the character was 'conceived' (the word used by the Folio syndicate: see above, p. 32) originally as Oldcastle in *Part 2* as well. The lone '*Old.*' speech-prefix (1.2.117), where there should be a 'Falstaff' or a 'Sir John', indeed provides strong evidence in support of the continuation of Oldcastle in the second part, and not, as some hold, a foul-paper fossil which originated in absent-mindedness during the writing of the sequel.

One of the most important witnesses in the Falstaff–Oldcastle debate here is Sir Robert Cotton's librarian, Richard James. When James was asked to account for the discrepancies between the historical Fastolf and Shakespeare's two different Falstaffs in the *Henry IV* plays and *1 Henry VI*, he explained

that in Shakespeare's first show of Harry the fifth, the person with which he undertook to play a buffoon was not Falstaff, but Sir John Oldcastle . . . who gave witness unto the truth of our reformation with a constant and resolute martyrdom, unto which he was pursued by the priests, bishops, monks, and friars of those days.

Richard James, though he wrote some thirty-seven years after the first performances to which he refers, is the most explicit contemporary source for our knowing that offence was 'worthily taken by personages descended from . . . [Oldcastle's] title'. He has been interpreted as clearly stating that it was *1 Henry IV* ('first show of Harry the fifth') in which the character was called Oldcastle. But this passage does not necessarily support that interpretation. By 'first show' he could have meant (*pace* Taylor) either that (*a*) *1 Henry IV* was performed with Oldcastle in it (that proposition does not exclude Oldcastle from *2 Henry IV*), or (*b*) the *Henry IV* plays (as opposed to *Henry V*) were performed at first with Oldcastle rather than Falstaff.

To underpin his views on Oldcastle and the *Henry IV* plays, Taylor offers a metrical analysis of the occurrences of Falstaff and Oldcastle in the two plays. Because the six occurrences in verse of 'Falstaff' in *2 Henry IV* (like the ones in *Merry Wives* and *Henry V*) are metrical each time and the one occurrence in *1 Henry IV* is not,[1] Taylor concludes that by the time Shakespeare wrote *2*

[1] In fact the first 'Falstaff' in verse in *2 Henry IV* occurs in a hendecasyllabic line (2.4.355), as does the fourth (4.2.81), where the syllabic count may yield twelve syllables with Oldcastle and eleven with Falstaff. Regarding *1 Henry IV* 2.3.16,

Henry IV (within less than a year), he had fully reconceptualized Oldcastle as Falstaff, and not just, as in *1 Henry IV*, renamed him.[1] Taylor consequently plays down the significance for *2 Henry IV* of the speech-prefix *Old.*, or the Epilogue's famous disclaimer that 'Falstaff shall die of a sweat ... Oldcastle died martyr, and this is not the man'. Although the sweat here most immediately denotes the 'sweating-sickness' (i.e. the plague or venereal disease, neither of which in the end kills Falstaff in *Henry V*), it may also allude to the manner of Oldcastle's death in St Giles' Field on Christmas Day 1417, when he was burnt as a heretic hanging in chains.[2] If so, it would indicate that Oldcastle lurks just beneath the surface of Falstaff, that Shakespeare wished to remind his audience of the true submerged identity of the riotous companion of Henry V. It is certainly intriguing that Shakespeare had already used the word 'sweat' earlier in *1 Henry IV*, in a way which anticipates the Oldcastle reference of the Epilogue. After robbing the robbers at Gad's Hill, Hal turns to Poins with 'Away, good Ned. Oldcastle [Falstaff] sweats to death, | And lards the lean earth as he walks along' (*1 Henry IV* 2.3.16–17). It is line 16 which, metrically, would be a perfect pentameter if instead of 'Falstaff' the trisyllabic 'Oldcastle' were used, as the Oxford Shakespeare does; and it might arguably confer a piquancy (perhaps even poignancy) on the comic idiom of sweating and lard that audiences of a Protestant nation reared on Foxe's *Acts and Monuments* could perhaps be trusted to recognize.

But the metrical argument about Oldcastle and Falstaff here is not entirely convincing, because the syllabic count (if it is indeed a matter of a missing syllable) of the line (nine with Falstaff, ten with Oldcastle) matters less than the timed stresses (five in each case)— in the Arden text (with Falstaff) Humphreys very effectively uses a

---

Pendleton (p. 62) notes that 'the supposed necessity that the line in question be regularly decasyllabic must be upheld in face of the fact that within the same seven-line speech, two other lines (105 [13], 106 [14]) have an extra syllable'.

[1] Taylor (1987) argues rather tenuously that the Lord Chief Justice's question after Falstaff's identity in *2 Henry IV* 1.2 serves to remind us that this is a different man, newly named.

[2] The comparison of Falstaff to 'that roasted Manningtree ox with the pudding in his belly' (*1 Henry IV* 2.5.457), particularly when taken in conjunction with Foxe's picture of Oldcastle's death, could irreverently be interpreted as a grotesque barbecuing reference: cf. also Hal's addressing Falstaff as 'my sweet beef' (*Part 1* 3.3.178).

pause to compensate for the missing syllable. The point is further weakened by the fact that *all* quartos and Folio print this passage as prose. It is not until Pope's 1725 edition of Shakespeare that the passage is first set out as verse. Nevertheless, it is hard to avoid the suspicion that 'sweating' is a phrase submergedly connected to the manner of Oldcastle's death. All four uses of 'sweat' in *2 Henry IV* refer to Falstaff (1.2.204; 4.2.12 (twice); Epilogue 29), as does the single occurrence of 'sweatest' (*2 Henry IV* 2.4.214: Doll on Falstaff) and 'sweating' (5.5.23). In this respect the phrase performs a function similar to 'my old lad of the castle' (*1 Henry IV* 1.2.41–2) which is a cant term for a roisterer; or it denotes somebody who frequents 'The Castle', a brothel in Southwark (as Falstaff might well have done), but it unmistakably also alludes to Oldcastle, and this may well be the primary reason for its presence in the text. Shakespeare's use of 'sweat' may be echoed in the Epilogue to signal that he has still not entirely let go of his character Oldcastle.

Since Shakespeare intended to call the character Oldcastle, and did so before the Cobhams held the office of Lord Chamberlain, what could he have hoped to achieve thereby? Lampooning real-life characters in an Aristophanic mode is not a readily recognizable trait of Shakespeare's art and craft. When he does mention a real-life person like the Earl of Essex (or Mountjoy?) in *Henry V*, it is to praise him, opportunistically almost, at just the time when he seemed poised to deck himself in glory. That the opposite happened is a tragic irony of the kind that Shakespeare might have appreciated. Perhaps Innogen's giving her master's name as 'Richard du Champ' (*Cymbeline* 4.2.379), which is generally taken to allude to Shakespeare's Stratford friend (as he probably was), Richard Field, the printer of both Shakespeare's *Venus and Adonis* and *Lucrece*, would be a more mundane example of a cheekily affectionate, and certainly apolitical, allusion to an acquaintance.

While critics continue to disagree about the Oldcastle–Falstaff business, common sense as well as Shakespeare's practice elsewhere suggests that he would not have set out deliberately to provoke the Lord Chamberlain, even if by doing so he were to please Essex and his powerful friends.[1] Although the character in Shakespeare's play is named after a real person of very consider-

[1] But Honigmann stresses the enmity between Essex and the Cobhams and, noting Shakespeare's support for the former, argues that the *Henry IV* plays were written with an eye to the rivalry, and therefore before Cobham became Lord

able national fame, he is in the final analysis above all a fictional being, who differs from the real character in every recognizable detail. Shakespeare's Falstaff is nearly sixty in *1 Henry IV* (he is older in *Part 2*: see below, p. 43), huge in girth (to contrast with Hal's leanness), and a notorious coward, both at Gad's Hill and in battle, whether fighting and deceiving Douglas at Shrewsbury, or abusing Hotspur's dead body, or in his comic, and unexpectedly victorious, encounter with Coleville of the Dale at Gaultres in *2 Henry IV*; and he is famously rejected at the coronation. Oldcastle, on the other hand, was Hal's senior by a mere nine years, had a reputation for courage (Holinshed calls him 'a valiant capteine'), is nowhere said to be fat, and died at the age of thirty-nine after being friends with Henry as both Prince of Wales and for a while as King Henry V.[1]

If one accepts that the only substantial change to the texts of the *Henry IV* plays ensuing from the Oldcastle–Falstaff débâcle was the name, one must also grant that the differences between the real Oldcastle and his fictional counterpart were from the start of such a magnitude that the mere change of nomenclature sufficed to render him unrecognizable, and therefore hardly likely to have been conceived in the first place as a polemical, sectarian figure.[2] It is at least possible that, following the 'Jockey' from *Famous Victories*, Shakespeare may have been intending to offer a more conciliatory and irenic view of the reigns of Henry IV and Henry V than reality afforded, by stripping his imaginative vision of them of the horror of the historical religious sectarianism. The question is now whether the two Falstaffs, the Falstaff/Oldcastle of *1 Henry IV* and the Falstaff/Oldcastle of *2 Henry IV*, are indeed differently 'conceived' creatures. It is hard to see that anything is gained in a modern edition from calling the character Oldcastle, because to

Chamberlain. At the same time Honigmann concedes that 'In *Henry IV* Shakespeare's treatment of Oldcastle seems to me more amusing than malicious' (p. 128).

[1] Shakespeare's change of Oldcastle to Falstaff may have been inspired by the (unhistorical) rejection for cowardice of Fastolf at the coronation of Henry VI in France (*The First Part of Henry the Sixth* 4.1.9–17). The fact is that Fastolf withdrew from the battle at Patay, and was subsequently summoned to a court martial for conduct unbecoming if not cowardice. He was cleared.

[2] In 'Saints Alive!' (*SQ* 46, (1995), 47–75), Kristen Poole argues against reinstating Oldcastle, and instead, reading the plays against the background of the Marprelate controversy, suggests that in 'many ways Falstaff epitomizes the image of the grotesque puritan'.

modern audiences the characters of Oldcastle and Falstaff are historically equally abstract, whereas Falstaff has become powerfully real through being a fiction. If the Folio syndicate decided not to reinstate the name because it was best to let sleeping dogs lie, the modern editor need not be so intimidated. But the decision to restore Oldcastle is bound to focus any audience's attention on the change itself and its legitimacy, at the expense of the imaginative part played by the character.[1]

Falstaff. It has become a critical commonplace to state that the Falstaff of *2 Henry IV* is a mere shadow of the flamboyant, even outrageous, companion of the Prince of Wales in *Part 1*. When he claims to be full of wit himself, as well as the cause of wit in other men, we recall the quipping Falstaff of *1 Henry IV*, whose '*humorous conceits*' were advertised on the title-page of the quarto of that play. Certainly the relationship between the Prince and the 'Lord of Misrule' is closer and more privileged in *Part 1* than in *Part 2*. Whereas in the second play Falstaff shares just two scenes with Hal/Henry V, 2.4 (the tavern scene) and 5.5 (the rejection), in *1 Henry IV* there are no fewer than nine scenes (1.2; 2.2; 2.3; 2.5; 3.3; 4.2; 5.1; 5.3; 5.4) during which Hal and Falstaff interact on the stage. But the imaginative greatness of Falstaff does not depend primarily on the reflected glory from the heir to the throne, even though his political standing may well do.

The fact that he is famously unwell at the start of *2 Henry IV*, to the point of needing to have his 'water' examined by the doctor (and the report is not good), is comically appropriate and neatly counterpoints the opening reference to 'drinking of old sack' in *1 Henry IV* 1.2.2–3. The audience is clearly expected to be familiar with Falstaff's earlier exploits, and it may be prepared for the news that his drinking and wenching escapades have penalty tags, in the form perhaps of venereal disease (Falstaff uses the word 'pox' three times,[2] and he knows that he may 'catch' from Doll) or, as here, of gout. Falstaff is not discernibly subdued by failing health, however, in spite of his comments on its effects. His losing the first and second rounds to the Lord Chief Justice is a more menacing sign of things to come. But then the Falstaff of *1 Henry IV* never

---

[1] On the conceptual relevance of 'fiction' (as opposed to documentary fact) in deciding this issue, see Bevington (1987, p. 108).

[2] At 1.2.225, 238 (twice). The only other use of the phrase is Doll's at 2.4.39.

fought a real bout with the powers of the Lancastrian state either.[1]
In spite of Falstaff's seeming sway over Hal, and his undoubted
ability to corrupt, the Prince of Wales is never threatened by
Falstaff's antics. Hal assures us early on in *1 Henry IV* (1.2.192–
214) that he knows them all, and that he plans to use his riotous
companions for his own purposes.

Falstaff was licensed by the Prince of Wales to run riot rather in
the way the devil is let loose to walk the earth for a while. In this
capacity he is allowed to taunt and parody the royal household.
Whatever the deeper and even symbolic implications of his actions
may be, he does not encounter the real world of domestic politics
until after his bogus achievement at Shrewsbury. It is his own false
report (with Hal's tacit collusion) of his victory over Hotspur
which saves him from retribution over Gad's Hill, allows him
(with impunity, he thinks) to flout the authority of the Lord Chief
Justice ('all you that kiss my lady Peace at home'), and even buys
him some temporary credit with John of Lancaster.[2] It is para-
doxically his coward's resourcefulness at Shrewsbury that at Gaultres inspires him successfully to dupe and arrest Coleville of the
Dale. But whenever Falstaff comes face to face with the authority
of the legitimate state (as he does in *2 Henry IV*), his banter and
attempts at tomfoolery fall on barren ground.

If his vistas in *2 Henry IV* have contracted largely to the levels of
Mistress Quickly and Doll Tearsheet (tavern and brothel), and to
the gulling of a foolish and corrupt Justice of the Peace, this is
because in the *1 Henry IV* part of the story he could always hide
behind Hal and so never needed to confront personally any office-
bearers such as the sheriff in *1 Henry IV* 2.5. If the worsting of
Falstaff by the Lord Chief Justice in Act 1 does not in itself diminish
Falstaff, the reason is that he was never in the first place in a league
politically or morally to be thereby reduced. Justice Shallow is
more his measure.

Although Shakespeare is scaling down Falstaff's access to the
Prince of Wales as the play draws towards the coronation, his
treatment of Falstaff's rhetoric has undergone little change. He
still favours an ironically homiletic style (as in his encomium on

---

[1] As Humphreys (p. 23) also notes in his comment on the stage direction to 5.4.

[2] But Kate Percy knows that it was Hal ('Monmouth') who killed her husband,
because Morton relates Hotspur's death at the hands of 'Harry Monmouth' at *2
Henry IV* 1.1.107–11.

the benefits of sack, 4.2.93–120), and peppers it with literary allusiveness as pervasively as in his echoes of Lyly's *Euphues or the Anatomy of Wit* in *1 Henry IV*. While it is tempting to lay his biblical learning (as in his pointed references to Achitophel, Job, the Prodigal Son, and Lucifer) at the door of a parodically Protestant Falstaff (or Oldcastle) citing Scripture, it may be rather that the Morality-play structuring of the relationship between the young lean Hal and the old fat Vice Falstaff is the determining factor here. Conversely it may be the plays' interest in father–son relationships which accounts for the pervasive use of the parable of the Prodigal Son, just as the Dives–Lazarus parable is made to underpin their concern with 'gluttony', a topos which seems to be an almost exclusive preoccupation of the *Henry IV* plays among Shakespeare's dramatic works.[1]

Far from being a reduced figure, the Falstaff of *2 Henry IV* is a massive presence. As he cheerfully announces, 'I do here walk before thee like a sow that hath overwhelmed all her litter but one' (1.2.10–12). The fact that he and the Prince have been separated works to Falstaff's advantage as a dramatic character. Whereas earlier his energy was devoted largely to controlling his parasitic gravitations around Hal and the King, in *2 Henry IV* he is liberated, free to lord it over his world of down-and-outs and to concentrate on the rich pickings in Gloucestershire.

His part in *2 Henry IV* is by far the largest in the play. At 5,477 words (Q; 5,351 F) his is longer than the second and third longest, Henry IV's (Q 2,290; 2,261 F) and Hal's (Q 1,789; 1,752 F), added together. He speaks more lines in this play than in *1 Henry IV*, and he appears in eight scenes to Hal's five and the King's two. If sheer length were a legitimate gauge of the imaginative focus of the play, *2 Henry IV* should be known by the title of *Falstaff*. It was indeed so listed in the Chamber Accounts for the 1612–13 festive season, when a play called 'Sir Iohn Falstaffe', almost certainly *2 Henry IV*, was performed in Whitehall.[2]

[1] The only other works by Shakespeare in which the topos is mentioned as such are *Timon*, *Venus*, and *Sonnets*. Henry V pointedly instructs Falstaff to 'Leave gormandizing' (*2 Henry IV* 5.5.52), and the charge of gluttony was rejected specifically by the authors of *1 Sir John Oldcastle*.

[2] During the same season there was also a play called 'The Hotspur', i.e. *1 Henry IV*. A similarly motivated renaming, for the purpose of instant topical recognition, happened when Orson Welles's film *Chimes at Midnight* (below, p. 69) was originally released in the USA as *Falstaff*.

Not only are we given Falstaff in the present, as we were in *1 Henry IV*, but now his background and past life are explored by Shallow and by Falstaff himself in a series of unforgettable vignettes. We have a glimpse of Falstaff's boyhood: 'Then was Jack Falstaff, now Sir John, a boy, and page to Thomas Mowbray, Duke of Norfolk' (3.2.22–4). Echoing Shaaber (p. 238), Humphreys remarks that

This unexpected sidelight is sometimes said to be historically true of both Fastolf and Oldcastle, but the only source of the idea seems to be the passage itself. It is rather one of the many imaginative retrospective touches which so extend the living reality of the characters. (p. 96)[1]

From the synchronic Falstaff of *1 Henry IV* we have in the sequel moved to a diachronic one. The diachronic construction of Falstaff in *2 Henry IV* distances the character from the realities of English history. If the play was originally completed with Oldcastle as Falstaff, then the fleshing out of the character bears witness further to a conception that is not primarily polemical, let alone sectarian, but wholeheartedly imaginative.

The fact that Falstaff and Shallow were contemporaries as students at Clement's Inn, starting there fifty-five years earlier according to Silence (3.2.203), takes the characters back from the time of Gaultres in 1405 to 1350. Alternatively, we may choose to accept Falstaff's version of his age, 'some fifty, or, by'r Lady, inclining to threescore' (*1 Henry IV* 2.5.427–8), as being in his late fifties or at most sixty (Falstaff may of course be knocking a few years off his age) rather than the seventy upwards that is suggested by Silence's reply to Shallow's reminiscences of Jane Nightwork's domestic circumstances.[2] The period in question is the 1350s or 1360s, the time of the long rule of Edward III (1327–77). When Shakespeare's Falstaff was a young man sowing his wild oats to the

---

[1] In creating his own fictional historical past, Shakespeare has made it remarkably consistent: if the young Falstaff had indeed been page to Mowbray, as in *Richard II* for example, then he would have been in opposition to Bolingbroke, just as he is now.

[2] It is intriguing to note that the upwards revising of Falstaff's age in *2 Henry IV* renders him roughly the same age as Lord Cobham in late 1596. In the Falstaff plays the age issue is perplexing, not least because Shallow in *Merry Wives* is eighty. But in *Merry Wives* there is no attempt to historicize the characters, since they have been obviously transported back to the future, from 1405 into late Elizabethan England.

43

'chimes at midnight' in the company of various Shallows, the historical Oldcastle and Fastolf were not even born. Neither was Bolingbroke, let alone Hal. If Falstaff belongs to the generation which experienced the fifty-year reign of Edward III, which was followed by a smooth transition to the reign of Richard II, his socially anarchic nature might be partly seen as a phenomenon on the lower level complementary to the phenomenon on the royal level. The King admits that he 'stole' the crown; why should Falstaff not follow suit and steal a few purses? In fact, we should expect no other.

Whose 'commandment'? As Shakespeare knew from reading Holinshed, and as he intimates in his four plays dealing with the period from 1398 to 1422, the people of England never fully accepted Bolingbroke's legitimacy. The division in the kingdom of the *Henry IV* plays is on both the North–South and East–West axes: the northern forces of the Percies of Northumberland and the Archbishop of York against the southern authority of the Crown and London; and the world of Eastcheap against the power of Westminster, with Falstaff, as Lord of Misrule and mock-usurper,[1] who believes that the laws of the realm are within his reach, pitted against the Lord Chief Justice and the King. If the horizontal fault line in the country reflects the history of the period, the intersecting vertical one is of Shakespeare's making, and is largely of metaphorical significance. It is an opposition between the worlds of comedy and reality that anticipates the comparable East–West split in *Antony and Cleopatra*. That Falstaff and Cleopatra share variety, ambition, and an addiction to pleasure, while challenging in different ways the austerer, and (self-appointedly) morally superior, worlds of Westminster and Rome has often been noticed.[2] In the *Henry IV* plays it seems that the Bacchanalian element provided by the low plot as it is presented in the plays is almost a required part of the social fabric. That in *2 Henry IV* the two worlds are perceived by the author to run on parallel tracks is signalled by the shared condition of ailing between the King and

---

[1] See C. L. Barber, *Shakespeare's Festive Comedy* (1972), pp. 68–73. In *William Shakespeare* (1986), pp. 15–16, Terry Eagleton describes Falstaff as 'one of Shakespeare's most shameless verbal mystifiers' whose 'reductive materialism and verbal licence—belong to the carnivalesque, the satiric comedy of the people'.

[2] See Bradley (pp. 299–300).

Falstaff; and while Falstaff bounces back, the King is seen only in the process of declining.

It is left to Hal to overcome the threat posed by Falstaff at the coronation, just as at the end of *1 Henry IV* he conquered Hotspur. But if personal glory at Shrewsbury could be readily shared, and even yielded, by Hal to his boon companion, the crown, symbolizing the commonwealth, cannot be shared. Shakespeare prepares us well in the text of *2 Henry IV* for Falstaff's rejection by Hal and his final humiliation at the hands of the Lord Chief Justice, not least in Falstaff's segregation from the future king and a moral degeneration to the point where he is little more than a predator: 'If the young dace be a bait for the old pike, I see no reason in the law of nature but I may snap at him' (3.2.314–16). He mercilessly exploits Mistress Quickly, Doll Tearsheet, and possibly a Mistress Ursula,[1] and he accepts bribes while recruiting under royal warrant for the defence of the realm, thus abusing a position of trust, as well as offending basic moral decency. In the words of Dr Johnson's apostrophe, 'But Falstaff unimitated, unimitable Falstaff, how shall I describe thee? Thou compound of sense and vice; of sense which may be admired but not esteemed, of vice which may be despised, but hardly detested.'[2]

If Falstaff were allowed privileged access to Hal after the coronation, the whole country might suffer the fate of the poignantly individuated recruits of 3.2, the 'pitiful rascals' as Hal called them: 'Tut, tut, good enough to toss, food for powder, food for powder. They'll fill a pit as well as better' (*1 Henry IV* 4.2.65–6).[3] Shakespeare shows us Falstaff not just once but twice in charge, and on each occasion he turns out to be deeply corrupt. This is not to deny that he makes a great deal of sense, whether in questioning the

[1] If she is indeed another woman: she appears in *Falstaff's Wedding* by W. Kenrick published in 1760: see below, p. 63, and see 1.2.234 n.

[2] *Samuel Johnson on Shakespeare*, ed. with an Introduction by H. R. Woudhuysen (1989), p. 205.

[3] Humphreys (p. 101) notes that there was considerable anxiety at the time about corrupt recruiting practices and refers to the 1596 (also the date of the play) Star Chamber trial of Sir John Smythe for inciting mutiny in this connection. Smythe had earlier protested to Lord Burghley about the urgent need to recruit with greater care in order to avoid the unnecessary waste of human life. In *The Names of Comedy* (1990), Anne Barton writes of Falstaff's 'dehumanizing attempt to reduce them [the recruits] to their surnames' (p. 109), and stresses that Falstaff's 'callous and unimaginative cratylism' is counteracted by the amount of 'quotidian detail' that surrounds them.

validity of a code of honour which has just brought about the futile death of a noble soldier and husband like Hotspur, or in his dislike of the abstemious killjoy and Machiavel John of Lancaster, a revulsion that we share at the same time that we gleefully contemplate the effect manuring by sack might have on him. Shakespeare's divided response to Falstaff, who may be his most famous creation after Hamlet, is reflected in the moving account of his death in *Henry V* 2.3.9–25 by Mistress Quickly, who tells us that 'The King has killed his heart' (2.1.84).

To read Falstaff sentimentally, however, is to misunderstand the seriousness of Shakespeare's conception of politics in the plays. However empowering the humorous anarchic vistas conjured up by Falstaff may be, they are not intended to make us renege on our responsibilities. A. C. Bradley's brilliant dictum about Falstaff, that in him Shakespeare 'created so extraordinary a being, and fixed him so firmly on his intellectual throne, that when he sought to dethrone him he could not' (Bradley, p. 259), is not justified by the play. However much one sympathizes with Bradley's notion that the 'main source, then, of our sympathetic delight in Falstaff is his humorous superiority to everything serious, and the freedom of soul enjoyed in it' (Bradley, pp. 268–9), the fact is that Falstaff does not exist solipsistically; nor is he remotely comparable to 'Punch or Reynard the Fox', whom Bradley adduces as other examples of figures who behave atrociously but do not attract moral opprobrium.[1]

The striving in the *Henry IV* plays towards a form of order, peace, and above all legitimacy, is very powerful. Shakespeare's determined mining, and early launching, of the riotous youth theme (see above, pp. 26–7) may itself be inspired by a long-range desire to isolate the Prince from the usurping father. It takes two full-scale reconciliations (*1 Henry IV* 3.2 and *2 Henry IV* 4.3), which mirror each other, for the father to be reassured of his son's love and allegiance. The disruption by Bolingbroke of the established political order, which Tudor historiography liked to dress for public consumption in the rhetorical garb of divine institution (as in the long 1574 homily *Against Disobedience and Wilful*

---

[1] Bradley might have heeded Dr Johnson's response (which he quotes) to Maurice Morgann's 'Essay on the Dramatic Character of Sir John Falstaff' (1777), that now that Morgann 'has proved Falstaff to be no coward, he may prove Iago to be a very good character' (p. 275).

Rebellion), is reflected in the microcosm of his family. In Shakespeare's histories, Bolingbroke inherits the mantle of Richard III rather than that of Richard II, who on his return from Ireland knelt on English earth and embraced it 'As a long-parted mother' does her child (*Richard II* 3.2.5–7). But pitted against the realpolitik of Bolingbroke (which, as Henry IV, he repeatedly expounds to his son), Richard's inept idealism was destined to fail. Although Shakespeare treads the finest tightrope between the two positions in *Richard II*, not least because history is famously written by the victors, in this case the Lancastrians, his sympathies must be thought to lie with the deposed king. What redeems Bolingbroke's reign in the hindsight of the three plays which complete the tetralogy is its becoming the conduit for Hal, and finally Henry V.

The roles of Bolingbroke in both the plays which bear his crowned name are remarkably limited, particularly in *2 Henry IV*. In *1 Henry IV* he shares the play with both Falstaff and the irrepressible Hotspur, whose stinging criticisms of the King, 'this vile politician, Bolingbroke . . . this king of smiles, this Bolingbroke' ring the truer because of Hotspur's own guilelessness, while at the same time the King's only moments of credibility and spiritual intensity occur in his candid, even confessional, meeting with Hal in *1 Henry IV* 3.2. In *2 Henry IV* the situation has deteriorated further to the point that it is the conspirators who open the play. By compressing his dramatic narrative against the authority of the sources, so that Shrewsbury (1403), Gaultres (1405), Bramham Moor (1408), and the death of Henry IV (1413) become closely connected and almost simultaneous events, Shakespeare portrays a harried kingdom in the throes of permanent civil strife and turmoil. The first words spoken in the play by the Prince of Wales are 'Before God, I am exceeding weary' (2.2.1). He confirms Falstaff's claim (1.2.104–5) that the King is very sick, a sickness which in the telescoped time-scheme of Shakespeare's play is connected directly to the illness which causes his death in 4.3, even though historically eight years separate the two scenes (1405 and 1413).[1]

[1] The Lord Chief Justice is also 'rumoured' to be sick, as Falstaff reminds him, and Northumberland is said by Rumour to be 'crafty-sick'. It is as if all the leading characters in the play were either sick, pretending to be so, or tired, as the reign of Bolingbroke draws to a close; the Archbishop notes that the 'commonwealth is sick' (1.3.87), and he complains that 'we are all diseased'.

When we first see the King in 3.1 the rebellion, spearheaded by
the Archbishop of York, is gathering momentum while the ailing
and insomniac monarch surrenders to a moment of contemplation in the manner of Richard II. Bolingbroke is a prototypical
Macbeth figure. The difference is that he is comforted by the
thought that if he defiled his soul it will have been for the benefit
of his own son ultimately. As he tells Hal, 'How I came by the
crown, O God forgive, | And grant it may with thee in true peace
live!' (4.3.348–9).

Father and Son : Act 4, Scene 3. There is no scene quite like 4.3.151–
370 in the second tetralogy for its skill in synchronizing the domestic and political concerns that it explores. It is both intimate
and poignant in the extreme, a father and son becoming reconciled
on the father's deathbed, and yet conceived on a grand scale,
because both participants are acutely aware also that their final
encounter revolves around the crown and will therefore shape the
destiny of a nation. In a reign haunted to the end by the usurpation
which initiated it, it is profoundly ironic, as well as symbolic, that
the heir to the throne crowns himself in an act of political auto-
genesis; and he does so in the presence of the unconscious and
dying King, thus ensuring, in political–theological terms, that he
does not initially receive the crown from the hand of the usurper. It
is above all in his role as father, and not as king, that the dying
Bolingbroke is allowed to communicate with Hal. Hal's taking of
the crown is carefully motivated by Shakespeare through a soliloquy (4.3.152–78) which clearly indicates that Hal does think that
his father is dead, and promises to mourn him (he is weeping),
while at the same time coolly assuming his 'due' from the King, the
'imperial crown'. This member of the royal family certainly knows
how to distinguish effectively between the king's two bodies.

To the extent that the audience has of course been privy to the
soliloquy it becomes a hostage to fortune when Hal is challenged
by his father to explain his reasons for the taking of the crown. His
report (ll. 288–306) differs significantly from the 'true' version of
events. It is the most striking of the several echoic narratives in the
tetralogy, events dramatized in one of the plays which are then
recalled, or distorted, either in the same play or in a later play.[1] Hal

[1] As in the case of Richard's comparison of Northumberland to a 'ladder', which
is quoted by Henry IV in *2 Henry IV* 3.1 from *Richard II* 5.1.55–68.

now remembers his deed as an apostrophic and hostile address to the crown's deleteriously precious metal which eats up its owner like a cancer. The eager assumption of the crown is interpreted to Bolingbroke as the dutiful act of a son avenging his father's death. Hal concludes by disclaiming emphatically any pleasure in the crown's possession and invites divine retribution if pride or 'any rebel or vain spirit of mine | Did with the least affection of a welcome' (301–2) consider its resting on his head. This compares strangely with

> Lo where it sits,
> Which God shall guard; and put the world's whole strength
> Into one giant arm, it shall not force
> This lineal honour from me.

$$(4.3.174-7)$$

Not entirely unlike his father, who proposed a crusade to the Holy Land,[1] Hal enlists God's help almost as a mercenary ('God shall guard') at first, only to evoke God's curse cynically on himself if he ever desired the crown for any reason other than out of a sense of painful duty. His father's reply ('God put it in thy mind to take it hence') again enlists the Deity in an effort to lubricate acceptance of the actions by the House of Bolingbroke, just as he had earlier laid the blame for the usurpation of Richard II at the door of fate, by the simple expedient of the use of the passive:

> Though then, God knows, I had no such intent
> But that necessity so bowed the state
> That I and greatness were compelled to kiss...

$$(3.1.71-3)$$

This is Bolingbroke speaking with his public royal voice (cf. also 'Are these things then necessities? | Then let us meet them like necessities'), intent on misleading even his councillors, as we and Hal know from *1 Henry IV* 3.2.[2] It appears therefore that Hal has

---

[1] It was intended to keep the nobles preoccupied and prevent their thoughts from straying to trouble at home, while coincidentally earning credit with the divine powers.

[2] Mowbray similarly rewrites history and blames abstract necessity for his father's exile under Richard II. The reason is that in his confrontation with the powers of Henry IV he cannot blame Richard II, but pretends to believe that Richard II could do wrong only by necessity overriding: 'The King that loved him, as the state stood then, | Was force perforce compelled to banish him' (*2 Henry IV* 4.1.113–14). In 'Invisible Bullets' (in Bloom, 1987), pp. 146–7, however, Green-

assimilated his father's political shrewdness. He is equipped, it is suggested, to rule in his father's mould, but crucially—and this is the *raison d'être* of the scene—his is a lineal succession to the throne. In preparation for this reign by a king whom Shakespeare admired (whatever his reservations about Henry's use of power might have been), it is important that the issues which threatened its foundations should be confronted and, if possible, exorcized. By listening to his father's confession (because that is what Bolingbroke's speeches are) Hal becomes the trustee and heir of that past history with all its blemishes and promises. Before Hal can assume the crown his father needs to repent in order to cleanse the guilt that clings to the Lancastrian possession of it. Just as we needed to be reassured by the soliloquy in *1 Henry IV* that the Prince of Wales would not be morally swamped by the antics of Falstaff and his dissolute companions, and thus as audience were afforded a radically different perspective from that of the characters in the play (not least to allow us to enjoy the comedy of Falstaff from the moment his political power is known to be neutered), so here the lie of Bolingbroke's reign is fully exposed and rejected. The new king will start with as clean a slate as is possible under the circumstances.

Language and Comic Structures. The intense confrontation between the King and the Prince of Wales, father and son, marks the most significant point in the political plot of the play. Of the five scenes with the rebels, two are similarly sustained by the memory of a public man as primarily son and husband. It is the news of Hotspur's death that galvanizes his father into action and produces dramatic poetry of a high order in 1.1, as it does again in Kate Percy's elegy 'The time was, father...' in 2.3. It is the reactions at the domestic level of the family which dictate the course of world politics, and it may also be subliminal family loyalties which determine the Archbishop of York to take up arms against the King. But once Northumberland and his clan are removed from the frame, the rebellion shrinks to a mere three scenes (1.3; 4.1; 4.2).

blatt suggests that Bolingbroke's hypocrisy is so deep that he may himself believe it, that it is only through our 'privileged access to Falstaff's cynical wisdom' that we, the audience, see through the moral corruption of Bolingbroke's order.

Figure 7. Irene Palmer (Lady Percy), Cecil Trouncer (Northumberland), and Phyllis Hatch (Lady Northumberland) in the 1935 production of *2 Henry IV* (directed by Henry Cass) at the Old Vic.

The first is a parabolic homiletic scene which in F is dominated largely by Lord Bardolph and the Archbishop of York (in Q both their parts are curtailed: see below, pp. 85–8). The last two scenes are shared with the royal party spearheaded by Westmorland and John of Lancaster, and result in the rebels' ignominious undoing. The parley in 4.1 and 4.2 between Westmorland and the Archbishop's party highlights the stark fact that it is not only the temporal powers, the politicians, whom Bolingbroke has alienated, but also the church. The Archbishop, the 'saintly' prelate from Holinshed, whom the people of York revered as a martyr after his execution, emphasizes that his leading the rebellion (which he apologetically calls 'these ill-beseeming arms') is inspired by the welfare of the commonwealth (4.1.93–4), whereas Mowbray delves again back into his own immediate family's circumstances and their suffering at the hands of Bolingbroke, as a reason for opposing the King.

It is the Archbishop's integrity and the sanctity of his office ('Supposed sincere and holy in his thoughts'), mooted by Morton in 1.1.189–209 and appealed to in the name of peace by both Westmorland (4.1.30–52) and Prince John (4.1.230–56), which make the Archbishop a formidable and charismatic opponent. The same virtues also render him vulnerable in a contest with a determined 'politician'. When Mowbray warns against trusting the King, the Archbishop reassures him by noting that the King's friends and foes are 'so enrooted' together that plucking up the one is bound to loosen the other:

> So that this land, like an offensive wife
> That hath enraged him on to offer strokes,
> As he is striking, holds his infant up,
> And hangs resolved correction in the arm
> That was upreared to execution.
>
> (4.1.208–12)

The peace thus achieved will, the Archbishop believes, 'like a broken limb united, | Grow stronger for the breaking'. His faith in a patriarchal and organic society, modelled jointly on the nuclear family and the human body, proves to be a naive misconception. It is as much a 'rhetoric of illusion' (Humphreys, p. lxv) under the new order as Richard II's was, and it proves to be no match for Prince John's equivocations.

Bolingbroke's reign is autogenous rather than born into existence, hence its disregard for the kind of political philosophy propounded by the Archbishop, at least as long as such a doctrine is espoused in the service of rebellion. The reconciliation of father and son and the dying King's eager desire to see the crown lineally descended demonstrates that in the end even Bolingbroke seems to endorse (albeit for pragmatic reasons) a hierarchically ordered view of the world.

'The audience feels no compulsion to take the side of law and order; indeed the tragic themes predominate in reading, but on the stage this is Falstaff's play.'[1] As at Shrewsbury, where Falstaff kept a bottle in his pistol holster, so at Gaultres the world of food, drink, and sex catches up with the grim reality of war, and is remarkably undeterred by it. Falstaff may not be the military hero that some writers have construed him to be, but he refuses to be intimidated by Prince John's contempt for him. Although he does not tender

---

[1] M. C. Bradbrook (in Bloom, 1987), p. 82.

his mischievous advice to the Prince, that he should entrust himself to the beneficent effects of 'good sherry-sack', to his face, he has the last word in the scene, in the form of a tongue-in-cheek Silenic homily (4.2.83–120).

Prince John's resolute refusal to be drawn by Falstaff is subtly mediated through his declining to speak anything other than verse in 4.2, and it is not a coincidence that the last line in the play (before the Epilogue) is one of his several hemistichs. The relentless exercise of control through language is not of course unique to this play and there are far more ambitiously manipulative and sinister rhetoricians in Shakespeare (such as Richard III) than John of Lancaster. But he perhaps best illustrates the tension in this play between its two modes of dramatic speech, and a deliberate strategy in deploying them. His is also one of the most functional and public uses of the language.

By contrast Bolingbroke's verse can achieve a rare intensity which is mediated through plain and intimate directness, as in his final interview with Hal in 4.3, or by a startling use of imagery. His powerful vision of stormy gales curling the heads of the waves and hanging them in harried, immaterial clouds (3.1.20–4) reveals glimpses of an imagination as developed as Richard II's, the difference being that Bolingbroke's is carefully reserved for moments of private contemplation, not public consumption. When he switches to a public persona after Warwick's and Surrey's joining him in the same scene, his tone becomes more philosophical ('the revolution of the times...'), but not controlled enough to suppress a surge of poetry (3.1.44 ff.) which echoes the Ovidian rhetoric of Shakespeare's own Sonnet 64, 'When I have seen by time's fell hand defaced'. It is as if the self-imposed restraints by the dying King were crumbling in anticipation of 4.3.

The verse of the play is at its most searing in its private and domestic scenes, as in the reactions in 1.1 to the news from Shrewsbury by Northumberland, Morton (ll. 170–9) and Lord Bardolph (ll. 180–6), and Kate's supplicatory elegy in 2.3. By comparison, the rhetoric of politics and war is largely formal and expository and serves to advance, and signal shifts in the direction of, the main plot. Mowbray, Morton, Hastings, Lord Bardolph, and the Archbishop try to shape history, but rarely interact dramatically as characters or personalities. There is not the time for it, because the 'high' plot is rushed along and is allocated a smallish proportion only of the total play. Its imaginative interest is out of kilter with its historical importance. Shakespeare seems almost more interested in the rhetorical pyrotechnics of the outrageously intertextual Pistol, and the egregious malapropisms of Mistress Quickly, than in the wider geopolitical movements of the warring factions.

Throughout the play 'high' (H) and 'low' (L) scenes of predominantly verse and prose respectively balance one another, as the following table shows:

1.1: Verse (H)
1.2: Prose (HL)
1.3: Verse (H)
2.1: Prose (L)
2.2: Prose (HL)
2.3: Verse (H)
2.4: Prose (L)
3.1: Verse (H)
3.2: Prose (HL)
4.1: Verse (H)
4.2: Prose & Verse (HL)
4.3: Verse (H)
5.1: Prose (HL)
5.2: Verse (H)
5.3: Prose (HL)
5.4: Prose (L)
5.5: Verse (H)

Out of seventeen scenes (eight prose scenes, eight verse scenes, and one prose–verse scene) in two cases, 2.1/2.2 and 5.3/5.4, a prose scene is succeeded by another prose scene, although in each instance one of the pair is a high–low scene, so that a general pattern of alternating verse and prose scenes is established.

What such regularity, which is itself significant, disguises, however, is the scale and impact of individual scenes. Thus 4.3 is clearly a vastly more important verse scene than 1.3 or 2.3. Its necessarily late placing in the play—since the King's death must be closely followed by the coronation which ends *2 Henry IV*—also helps to counter the imaginative sway of the low plot which has split into two different sites in the city and the country: the Boar's Head in London's Eastcheap, the setting for the great tavern scene in 2.4, and Gloucestershire, where Falstaff and Shallow recall their student days in London and enjoy the timeless leisure of the country. In this play from Shakespeare's prose period,[1] in which a considerable amount of space is granted to comedy characters, the solemnity of the deathbed scene is set in special relief.

But the irreverent convergence of the solemn and the ridiculous in the fluid world of this play does not allow us to grieve over Bolingbroke, and it achieves this denial through the effective cross-scenic rhyming echo of 'lie'—'die'—'pie'. Henry IV's last words, 'In that Jerusalem shall Harry die' (4.3.370), are followed at once on stage by Shallow's complex phrase 'By cock and pie, sir . . .' (5.1.1) which glancingly alludes, through punning, to the two traditional enemies of death and tragedy, sex and food. Commenting on the similar structural counterpoint of Doll Tearsheet in 2.4 with the grieving widow of Hotspur, M. C. Bradbrook described it as one of the play's 'telling silent strokes'.[2]

Now that Bolingbroke's reign is over, Shakespeare is eager to move away from the subjects of death and sickness. In his sights is the coronation, the happy climax of this tragicomic history play. Like Hal's victory over Hotspur, his coronation will mark an interim moment of triumph, the third stage of a journey which started with the usurpation and murder of Richard II, and which will conclude like a romantic comedy in a marriage, the union of Katherine of France and Henry of England. The sub- or 'low' plot (itself a comedy device) in *2 Henry IV* differs significantly from that in *1 Henry IV* by splitting into city and country, London and Gloucestershire. However much the two works structurally mirror each other, to the point of 'revealing more similarity between plays than one can find elsewhere in Shakespeare' (Bevington, p. 831; see below, p. 82 n.), the extension of 'below stairs' to country and rusticity widens the scope of Falstaff's influence now that he is deprived of Hal's presence. It also taps the 'garden of England' imagery that Shakespeare had already deployed in a much more abstract and allegorical fashion in *Richard II* (3.4), and was to do

---

[1] *Textual Companion*, pp. 120–1. Spevack calculates that just over half, 52 per cent of the play, is in prose.

[2] In Bloom (1987, p. 79). Greenblatt similarly notes that Falstaff's 'The undeserver may sleep, when the man of action is called on' is echoed cross-scenically in Bolingbroke's insomnia in 3.1 (ibid., p. 146).

again in *All is True*, when Thomas Cranmer, the Archbishop of Canterbury, prophesies that under Elizabeth I

> every man shall eat in safety
> Under his own vine what he plants, and sing
> The merry songs of peace to all his neighbours.
> *(All is True* 5.4.33–5)

A more realistic and adulterated version of this pastoral would seem to be the experience of Shallow's 'goodly dwelling and rich' in Gloucestershire, with its orchard, apples, and dinners at which old men reminisce, brag, and drink too much sack, while others, in their cups perhaps, indulge in songs about lads and lasses, women and wine. Shallow's garden is no Jonsonian Penshurst. The pippins he offers to Falstaff are of his own grafting.[1] He has toiled for them, and unfortunately seems to be ignorant of Falstaff's dislike of apples (or is it only wintering apple-johns that he execrates?), a nice ironic touch which may serve to remind us of the incompatibility of these two old men.

The placing of the pre-dinner and orchard scenes, immediately after the old King's death and before the scene of the as-yet-uncrowned Henry V's pledging his loyal faith to the Lord Chief Justice, may carry a long-range symbolic charge, arising from Shakespeare's collocation in time of the advent of peace and Henry IV's death. Shakespeare pointedly synchronizes the deceptively reassuring Englishness of the scene with the evolving politics at Court. But just as at Court there are apprehensions at first about the new regime, so all is far from idyllic in the country. It turns out that in time of peace the countryside remains as troubled as it was during the wars when Shallow aided and abetted Falstaff's venal recruiting. It may not quite be a case of death lurking even in Arcadia, but petty corruption is rife in the shamefully partisan adjudication between William Visor of Won'cot and Clement Perks o'th' Hill, prompted by Davy's friendship with the guilty party. It is a matter of considerable irony that it should be Falstaff who points out that 'degree' is neglected in Shallow's household, and that this exposes to exploitation the dispensation of justice.

---

[1] Kerrigan (p. 28) notes that *Part 2* was written against the 'background of deep recession' and a severe shortage of grain so that 'Shallow's farm' would have been seen at the time as a working estate, 'a venture of immediate interest'.

As much as anything, Shallow in his orchard represents a microcosm of the malaise that has subtly spread throughout the realm, from the stews of Eastcheap to the inner reaches of the country, to the point where Falstaff can almost legitimately cast himself as moral arbiter over it. These are the consequences of Bolingbroke's reign in the heartlands of England. Falstaff concludes that men should 'take heed of their company' (5.1.69). One can hear Hal's 'I do; I will' (*1 Henry IV* 2.5.486). It is a lesson that Shallow and Davy might consider as they lord it dishonourably over their petty fiefdom, unredeemed by its superficial bonhomie. One must hope that Clement Perks will be able to appeal to the severe but fair figure of the Lord Chief Justice if Shallow loses his status as a Justice of the Peace for insolvency after Falstaff's fleecing him of £1,000. Shallow presumably parted from this sum under the delusion that a friend at court 'is better than a penny in purse' (5.1.27).

Stanley Wells has remarked that ' "Ordinary" people play a much greater part in these plays than in the earlier histories' (Wells, 1994, p. 142), and the forty-nine-strong cast of *2 Henry IV* includes nearly twenty of them, and refers to colourfully named others, notably Samson Stockfish, William Cook, the three Nightworks, and the two off-stage Gloucestershire litigants. These latter are individuated to the point of being given real life addresses (see 5.1.32–3) in an area of the country that seems to have been familiar to Shakespeare.

If the world of Shallow's Gloucestershire is portrayed as something akin to a rural antimasque (if not exactly as a *Walpurgisnacht*), a worse fate befalls the tavern-alias-brothel denizens whom Falstaff left on a note of tenderness at the end of 2.4. Now, in a scene which is frequently omitted in performances of the play, perhaps because it sits uneasily with the impending coronation (see below, p. 64), Doll and Mistress Quickly are carried off for a whipping at Bridewell. They may even face the gallows if it is proven that 'There hath been a man or two killed about her' (5.4.5–6). While Hal is on his way to becoming Henry V, his beadles clear the stews, as if an Angelo or a Prince John rather than a Henry had acceded to the throne.

The 'pleasant days' of unbridled debauchery forecast by Pistol in the last line of the preceding scene start with a purge. To remove the scene from the play misses the toughness and denial of sentimentality that informs Shakespeare's vision of the new reign, however much creative energy he invested in the tavern scenes and their inhabitants. Moreover, the scene is dramatically needed to allow Falstaff some time (however short) to get to London from deepest Gloucestershire. That the rejection of Falstaff should have caused so much heartache among his admirers is predicated on a failure to differentiate between the imaginative appeal of Falstaff as a larger-than-life figure and his role in the social and political fabric of the play. As it is, he gets off rather lightly, and the Epilogue's promise of more Falstaff to come makes us anticipate that he may yet carve a niche for himself in the future; and maybe after all the King will send for him in due course. It is precisely Falstaff's stand-aloneness which can make Shakespeare lift him out of the Lancastrian period and transport him to Elizabethan Windsor.

The Play in Performance[1]

The last recorded references to the theatrical history of *2 Henry IV*, or of parts of the play, before the publication of the First Folio, or indeed for the rest of the seventeenth century, relate to the 1612–13 performance at Whitehall (see above, p. 42) and the Dering manuscript of early 1623, which conflates the two parts of *Henry IV*, with the emphasis largely on *Part 1*. As George Walton Williams and G. Blakemore Evans demonstrate, Dering omitted 11 per cent of *Part 1*, cut 75 per cent of *Part 2*, and jettisoned most of its comic material, while retaining the substance of the royal scenes, but without the Lord Chief Justice.[2] The Dering text has no independent textual authority and was intended for private performances. Whatever Dering's original intentions may have been with regard to *2 Henry IV*, the final version puts the emphasis on the politics of the concluding days of Bolingbroke's reign. When re-

[1] In this section I am throughout indebted particularly to the following indispensable studies: Barbara Hodgdon, *Henry IV, Part Two: Shakespeare in Performance* (1993); Charles B. Hogan, *Shakespeare in the Theatre, 1701–1750*, vol. i (1952), and *Shakespeare in the Theatre, 1751–1800*, vol. ii (1957); W. Van Lennep *et al.* (eds.), *The London Stage, 1660–1800*, 11 vols. (1964–8); George C. D. Odell, *Shakespeare from Betterton to Irving*, 2 vols. (1921); S. L. Williamson and James E. Person, Jr. (eds.), *Shakespearean Criticism*, vol. 14 (1991).

[2] George Walton Williams and G. B. Evans (eds.), *William Shakespeare, 'The History of King Henry the Fourth', As Revised by Sir Edward Dering* (1974). See also Shaaber (pp. 645–50).

corded performances surface again on the English stage, the emphasis will have shifted in a diametrically opposite direction.

By virtue of being the most sequel-esque of Shakespeare's plays, *2 Henry IV* cannot easily stand alone. When it was revived in the post-Restoration period, its fortunes were initially inextricably bound up with *Part 1*, which enjoyed a large measure of independence by comparison. Whereas *2 Henry IV* does not appear to have been performed between the closure of the theatres in 1642 and 1704, *1 Henry IV* was put on by Thomas Killigrew's King's Company at Gibbons's Tennis Court in Vere Street on 8 November 1660. It was seen there by Pepys on 31 December 1660. In his *Diary* Pepys records seeing the play no fewer than four times (compared to five *Hamlets*), and expresses his admiration for William Cartwright's Falstaff. The popularity of Falstaff is reflected further in the 1662 engraving which is the frontispiece for Francis Kirkman's *The Wits, or Sport upon Sport*, which shows a dandyish, albeit bulky, Falstaff holding out a goblet to Mistress Quickly who shares the foreground of the picture with him. It may well have been the continuing interest in Falstaff,[1] as well as the enduring popularity of *1 Henry IV*, which led to a revival of the sequel.

Such was the appeal of *1 Henry IV* that, apart from *Hamlet*, it was the only play in the repertory to be performed almost uninterruptedly in the next century which, on 9 November 1704, saw the first recorded single performance of *2 Henry IV* for ninety-two years, at Lisle's Tennis Court in Lincoln's Inn Fields. The driving force behind the revival was Thomas Betterton, who twenty years earlier, when he was in his forties, had been a famous Hotspur. He had revived *1 Henry IV* 'with Alterations' in 1710, and advertised the play as containing 'the humours of Sir John Falstaff', whereas Shakespeare's title-page instead referred to 'the humorous conceits of Sir Iohn Falstaffe'. Betterton's Falstaff was hugely acclaimed. As a contemporary remarked, the 'revived humour of Sir John Falstaff in Henry IV . . . has drawn all the town more than any new play'.[2]

This was almost certainly the trigger for the 1704 revival of a much changed *2 Henry IV* by Betterton. Whereas *1 Henry IV* was

---

[1] Cf. Leonard Digges's commendatory contribution to the 1640 edition of Shakespeare's *Poems* (Oxford, p. xlvi), and Sir Thomas Palmer's commendatory poem in the 1647 Beaumont and Fletcher Folio: see Bevington (1987, p. 69).

[2] S. B. Hemingway, ed., *Henry the Fourth. Part 1*, New Variorum Shakespeare (Philadelphia, 1936), p. 479.

mostly cut pragmatically with an eye to performance, *2 Henry IV* was more drastically rearranged. The text of this performance is probably the one which was printed, after Betterton's death (1710), in 1719:

The Sequel of Henry the Fourth: | With the Humours of | Sir John Falstaffe, and Justice Shallow. | As it is Acted by | His Majesty's Company of Comedians, | At the | Theatre-Royal in Drury-Lane | Alter'd from Shakespear, by the late Mr | Betterton.

Although this 'altered' version would never quite displace Shakespeare's in the way Nahum Tate's *King Lear* (1681) did the original, it proved to be an influential, theatrically intelligent, and popular work for several decades. It cuts the Induction with Rumour's reconnecting *2 Henry IV* with *Part 1* and compounds this severing of the links with its predecessor by excising 1.1 and 2.3, that is the entire Northumberland connection. If the loss of Kate Percy's lines about Hotspur seems unimaginable to a modern audience or student of the play, the removal of the Northumberlands and their family nevertheless enables *Part 2* to stand on its own more easily. As the performance history of *2 Henry IV* from Betterton in 1704 to Terry Hands in 1975 demonstrates, many of the lines and scenes that attract producers' and directors' scalpels are material where Q and F differ.

The Betterton 'adaptation' starts with Falstaff. He is an instantly recognizable figure, and one who is guaranteed to fill the house. An audience who had seen him three days earlier in *1 Henry IV* could be relied on to be there because they wanted to see more of him, and the novice audience could be expected to cheer at the sight of this legend they were at last encountering. It is perhaps for comic effect, to show that the Lord Chief Justice is so unworldly as to mistake Falstaff for just another fat man, that Shakespeare (whom Betterton here follows) identifies Falstaff for us:

LORD CHIEF JUSTICE *(to his Servant)* What's he that goes there?
SERVANT Falstaff, an't please your lordship.
LORD CHIEF JUSTICE He that was in question for the robbery?
SERVANT He, my lord; but he hath since done good service at Shrewsbury, and, as I hear, is now going with some charge to the Lord John of Lancaster.

By drastically shortening 1.3, and by transposing 3.1, the King's insomniac meditations, to Act 4, Betterton offers a play which is overwhelmingly a Falstaff prose comedy. Thus, in the 1719 edition Act 1 consists of Shakespeare's 1.2, a shortened 1.3, and is followed by a Falstaff-in-the-tavern Act 2 (Shakespeare's 2.2 and 2.4). This is in turn followed by 3.2, a scenic arrangement which echoes the identical transition from the tavern to Shallow's magisterial district in 1600 QA. The transposition of 3.1 into close collocation with the deathbed scene (4.3) points to a different theatrical conception from that current in Shakespeare's time when high- and low-life could happily co-exist side by side. Betterton starts his Act 5 with the rejection of Falstaff, but his play does not end with the coronation of Henry V. It proceeds instead into *Henry V* territory and includes shortened versions of Canterbury's Salic Law speech, the tennis balls taunt, and the Scrope and Cambridge conspiracy (*Henry V* 1.2, 2.2), before ending on the line 'No King of *England*, if not King of *France*'.

Between 1704 and 1735 Betterton's adaptation held its own, first at Drury Lane until 1732, and then at Drury Lane and the Haymarket in 1733 and 1734. Whereas the first performances of the Betterton *2 Henry IV* in 1704 followed hard on the heels of a performance of *1 Henry IV* (6 November) and were thus provided with a natural continuity in the persons of the actors as much as of the characters, *Part 2* became increasingly independent. Thus in 1727, for instance, when there were five performances of *2 Henry IV* at Drury Lane, there were none of *1 Henry IV*, and in 1730, when both plays were performed in the same theatre, *Part 2* preceded *Part 1*. In 1734 there were three consecutive performances at the Haymarket (3, 4, 5 June) of a play called 'The Humours of Sir John Falstaff, Justice Shallow, And Ancient Pistol'. This play may well be Betterton's 'altered' version, with the playbill trying to cash in on what must have been by then the best known parts of the revived *2 Henry IV*. Above all, James Quin's Falstaff, a role which he occupied for over thirty years, and Colley Cibber's Shallow (Cibber is first recorded in that role in 1720) had been joined by the maverick Pistol of Cibber's son Theophilus.

In 1736 Drury Lane, for the first time in the eighteenth century, put on Shakespeare's *2 Henry IV*. Its five performances were succeeded in the two years which followed by a further five at Drury Lane, as well as by three at Covent Garden in 1738. To

ensure that the Covent Garden play should not be confused with
the Betterton adaptation, the playbill stated that 'The Above Play
of King Henry IV. is the Genuine Play of Shakespeare, and not that
alter'd by Mr. Betterton, and so frequently acted at the other
Theatre'.

Perhaps to test the waters, the following year Drury Lane again
put on Betterton's version while Covent Garden staged the original. Both versions played for one performance each. But the days
of Betterton's text were numbered. In 1744, while the original
played on five occasions at Covent Garden, Drury Lane performed
Betterton's *2 Henry IV* just once. It was the last time that it was
staged. It was also the last time for ten years that either *Henry IV*
play was seen at Drury Lane. Covent Garden now took over, and *2*
Henry IV played there every year (except 1747 and 1748) till
1751. Altogether in this period, out of eighty-five recorded
performances of *2 Henry IV* forty-five are of Betterton's adaptation
and forty of Shakespeare's play. Notwithstanding its famous
Falstaffs and Pistols, *2 Henry IV* never matched the popularity of
1 Henry IV, which, out of thirty-four plays performed during the
period, comes fourth, after *Othello* and before *Merry Wives*,
whereas *2 Henry IV* is at number sixteen, after *Timon of Athens*
and before *Measure for Measure*. But the picture was to change in
the years which followed, and both *Henry IV* plays slid down the
popularity scale, *1 Henry IV* to number twelve (out of twenty-nine
plays considered), and *2 Henry IV* to twenty-two, behind *A*
Midsummer Night's Dream and before *The Comedy of Errors*.

By the mid 1750s there were two versions of the play, but only
one, the 'original' one, was regularly performed. The second was a
free-wheeling two-act farcical collage (probably by Theophilus
Cibber), which consisted of 2.4 and 3.2 and first played at Drury
Lane under the title of 'The Humourists' in 1754. This was even-
tually followed by a third acting version of the play cut on lines
very reminiscent of Betterton's. It misses the Induction, 1.1, 2.3,
and parts of 1.3, 2.2, 2.4, 3.1, and 4.1 in which it replaces the
pruned material with the retained parts of 3.1 (Henry IV's soliloquy). It transposes material in Act 5, but keeps the arrest of
Quickly and Doll, omits the Epilogue, and does not trespass on
Henry V territory. Whereas the farce only enjoyed a single
performance, this new revised version of the play, the second in
the century, was in 1770 put on at Drury Lane, where it played

three times. It was subsequently published by John Bell in 1773 in his acting edition of the plays which printed eighteen prompt-books from Drury Lane, including the 1770 altered *2 Henry IV*, and six from Covent Garden (Odell, ii. 42).

Drury Lane was fully back in business by 1758 staging *2 Henry IV*, no doubt because the theatre accepted that it was Shake-speare's original play which was now in demand. Although it briefly experimented with the farce and the Bell version, it gener-ally offered an orthodox *2 Henry IV* fare, with only minor altera-tions at most, such as the adding in its 1762 season of a handful of minor characters while at the same time deleting Shadow. In fact, from 1754 up to 1784, the date of the last recorded performance of the play before the end of the century, Drury Lane and Covent Garden between them played the original *2 Henry IV* sixty times, Bell's theatrical adaptation three times, and 'The Humourists' just once.

It is worth recording also that on two occasions excerpts from the play were included as part of a 'School of Shakespeare' evening at the Haymarket (1781), and that the period saw the publication of a sequel to the sequel, '*Falstaff's Wedding*, | A comedy being A Sequel to the Second | Part of the Play of King Henry The Fourth | Written in Imitation of Shakespeare, | By Mr. Kenrick'. This 1760 comedy, which is dedicated by the author to James Quin in grati-tude for giving so much pleasure as Falstaff, is set in the aftermath of Falstaff's rejection. It generates its plot from loose ends trailed by Shakespeare in *2 Henry IV*, such as Mistress Ursula (see 1.2.234 n.) and Poins's sister (cf. 'Be not too familiar with Poins, for he misuses thy favours so much that he swears thou art to marry his sister Nell'), who is here introduced as Eleanor Poins, having formerly been the new king's mistress. The play's portrayal of Falstaff was fulsomely praised by Garrick (as Kenrick reports in his 1766 'Preface'), and *Falstaff's Wedding* is indeed an enjoyable romp of wish fulfilment.

The reversion to Shakespeare's *2 Henry IV*, after its absence for nearly four decades during which it was a Falstaff play, spelt the re-emergence of the play as a dramatized political history. The assumption of the role of Henry IV in 1758 by David Garrick, and his subsequent tenure of that part for over a decade, almost certainly contributed to the shift of emphasis away from the humorists and their leader to the world of power and politics.

The drift of new readings was spelt out in Richard Valpy's 'Advertisement' which prefaces '*The Second Part of King Henry The Fourth,* | *Altered From Shakespeare,* | *As It Was Acted* | *At Reading School* | *in October, 1801*':

... This Play in the original is disfigured not only with indelicate speeches, but with characters, that cannot now be tolerated on [*sic*] a public theatre, much less in a classical exhibition ... The general moral of the story, the excellent instructions of a dying father to his son, and the reformation of a dissipated Prince ... render this Play admirably calculated for youth.

While the sternly patriarchal quality of tone may reflect the needs for hierarchy and solidarity of a society at war (as England then was), it also captures a moment in theatrical history. From being a post-Restoration Falstaff comedy the play had in the second half of the century become a political and historical work, with Garrick in the lead. Now, in the wake of the French Revolution and the emergence of Napoleon in Europe, the theatre was expected to toughen the moral fibre of the nation. As well as being a brilliant educationalist and Headmaster of Reading School, Valpy was also rumoured to be 'one of the hardest floggers of his day'.

The Induction and 2.3 are cut completely, but the rest of the play follows Shakespeare's text closely, including 3.1, which is left in its proper place. Like many versions of the play, it misses out the arrest of Doll and Quickly in 5.4. Above all, it rewrites Falstaff's arrest of Coleville at Gaultres. Coleville's name is changed to Morton, and the scene of the arrest, 4.2, becomes farcical. It derives its inspiration partly from Hal's meeting with Falstaff at Shrewsbury (*1 Henry IV* 5.3.40–61). When Falstaff is challenged by Morton, he '*Pulls out his bottle*' and retreats. The entry at that point of Bardolph and the Page confers strength in numbers on the royalist party, and Morton surrenders. Falstaff-the-coward, whom the 'Advertisement' calls 'the Knight of the mirthful countenance', is here denied his second unexpected moment of glory in battle.

If the continuing war against France did indeed leave its mark on the first nineteenth-century acting version of this English history play, the two theatrical editions which followed suggest that Valpy's text may have been rather more zealous and austere than was required. Thus an 1807 text of the play, printed by Mrs Inchbald from a Theatre Royal Covent Garden prompt-book, reverts to an almost Bettertonian rearranging of the play's scenes and emphasizes the role of Falstaff in it, while John Philip Kemble's revised version of the play, published in the year of Waterloo, 'As It Is Performed At The Theatre Royal' (1815), follows a very similar structure, but differs from its predecessor by reporting Falstaff's arrest of Coleville rather than showing it.

The grandest production of the century, with William Charles Macready as Henry IV and Charles Kemble (John Philip's younger brother) as Hal, was not far off. The Theatre Royal's predilection for lavish staging and historically accurate settings and costumes (fostered by John Philip Kemble) achieved its apotheosis on 25 June 1821, when the play was performed to anticipate the coronation of George IV, who had acceded to the throne the year before on 29 January 1820 and was crowned on 19 July 1821. On that day the performance was repeated, and the theatre was commanded by the King 'to be opened gratuitously to the public'.[1] With the exception of *All is True* (4.1) no other Shakespeare play contains an English coronation as part of its dramatic action,[2] and this production was determined, through the play's invitation to royal ritual, to capitalize on the serendipity of contemporary history. After a restructured fifth Act which leads up to the reconciliation of the Lord Chief Justice and Henry V, there follows what the printed text calls 'The Grand Coronation', which consists of four text-less apocryphal scenes of pageantry: (i) 'The Platform leading to the Abbey. Order of the Procession'; (ii) 'Westminster Abbey'; (iii) 'The Cloisters of the Abbey'; (iv) 'The Grand Banquet, The Royal Throne, The Champion'. The scale of the orchestration and its reflected glory on the production as a whole was greatly admired at the time. This highly elaborate performance was repeated at Drury Lane on 14 May 1834 as a form of *Gesamtkunstwerk*,[3] verging on the operatic with its paraphernalia of '*Airs, Duets, Trios, Chorousses &c.* . . .'.

If circumstances in 1821 directly focused attention on the royal and political history of *2 Henry IV*, Falstaff nevertheless staged a

---

[1] Shaaber (p. 659).

[2] Even so in both plays the coronations themselves happen off-stage. But in Bill Alexander's 1983–4 RSC production of *Richard III*, which starred Antony Sher, an entire coronation scene (without words) was inserted after 4.1.

[3] The concept of 'total work of art' comes from Richard Wagner's aesthetic theory and describes a work in which the different strands of the performing arts such as drama and music are harmoniously integrated.

comeback in the person of Samuel Phelps who opened his third season at Sadler's Wells in 1846 with *1 Henry IV*. After playing Hotspur initially, he moved on to Falstaff, a role in which he would continue to appear at regular intervals for nearly thirty years, and most memorably during the tercentenary of Shakespeare's birth in 1864. On that occasion he repeated his feat of 17 March 1853 by playing Falstaff in *1 Henry IV* and both the King and Shallow in *Part 2*. In this respect he anticipated Olivier's virtuoso crossing of plays of 1945 (see below, p. 68). Phelps's 1864 version differed little from Bell's 1773, and was 'made largely with an eye to the single purpose of displaying the remarkable versatility of Phelps' (Odell, ii. 300).

During the second half of the nineteenth century, the *Henry IV* plays faded into the background, perhaps because Victorian audiences cavilled at their robust prose and their presenting, without overtly judging them, outrageous low-life characters such as Falstaff and Doll Tearsheet. It was only with Herbert Beerbohm Tree in 1896 that Falstaff and the *Henry IV* plays reappeared on the London stage to a mixed reception, while at Stratford-upon-Avon the wider political implications of the single drama in the context of its companion pieces were shortly to result in a complete reconceptualizing of Shakespeare's histories.

In the meantime the Falstaff of *2 Henry IV* had crossed the Atlantic, first to the Chestnut Street Theatre in Philadelphia (1815), and then to the Park Theatre in New York where the Covent Garden pageant was offered during an 1822 production. By 1832 the American actor James Henry Hackett played Falstaff at the Arch Street Theatre in Philadelphia. He was to become one of the most acclaimed Falstaffs in the nineteenth century, and played the part for thirty-seven years. His total immersion in the role, of which he took a very tough and anti-idealized view, earned him the nickname 'Falstaff Hackett'.

But the most significant change in the perception of *2 Henry IV* was about to be initiated in England, even though it would be another fifty years (1951) before it was fully to bear fruit. This was the advent of 'cyclicality'. It was Frank Benson, the manager of the Memorial Theatre at Stratford-upon-Avon, who produced *2 Henry IV* on its own in 1894, before including it with *King John*, *Richard II*, *Henry V*, *2 Henry VI*, and *Richard III* in the 1901 'Week of Kings' at Stratford. The 'cycle' of plays (which had been cut and structurally adjusted to performance needs, and which was not staged in chronological order) was repeated for the next five years, and *1 Henry IV* joined it at last in 1905. Among other achievements Benson's productions featured strong performances from Doll Tearsheet in *2 Henry IV*. This caused a certain amount of dismay. In the course of one of the 1894 shows in which Constance Benson played Doll opposite George Weir's Falstaff, schoolgirls were marched out of the theatre during the second tavern scene (2.4); and a letter to Constance Benson ended with the words 'I could never watch you again as "Juliet", knowing to what depths you can sink'.[1]

The two *Henry IV* plays were played together on the same day on Shakespeare's birthday in 1921 by the Birmingham Repertory Theatre, and at the Memorial Theatre at Stratford in 1932. But the outstanding twentieth-century productions in England all come after the Second World War, when the play was either performed or filmed during every decade. They are John Burrell's 1945 production of both *Henry IV* plays at the New (now Albery) Theatre; the famous 1951 Lancastrian tetralogy at the Shakespeare Memorial Theatre, co-directed by Anthony Quayle, John Kidd, and Michael Redgrave; the 1955 production by Douglas Seale of both plays at the Old Vic; the double tetralogy at the Royal Shakespeare Theatre in 1964 directed by Peter Hall, John Barton, and Clifford Williams; Terry Hands's RSC 1975 production of *2 Henry IV* as part of a Lancastrian trilogy which included the *Henry IV* plays and *Henry V* (but not *Richard II*); the 1982 RSC production of both plays, directed by Trevor Nunn to start off the Company's first season at their new London home in the Barbican; the 1986–7 English Shakespeare Company's (*passim* ESC) production of all three *Henrys* under Michael Bogdanov and Michael Pennington; and the 1991 RSC *1 Henry IV* and *2 Henry IV* directed by Adrian Noble. During this period Shakespeare was avidly filmed, and the second tetralogy has delivered two cinematic masterpieces: Olivier's *Henry V* (1944) and Orson Welles's *Chimes at Midnight* (1965), which, among others, influenced the 1979 BBC/ Time-Life Shakespeare series production, directed by David Giles and which featured Jon Finch as Henry IV, David Gwillim as Hal, Anthony Quayle as Falstaff, and Robert Eddison as Shallow. In

[1] Sprague (p. 74).

1995 the BBC screened an inventively spliced production of *Henry IV* directed by John Caird and produced by Annie Castledine.

The 1945 version of *2 Henry IV* distanced itself from the world of politics to the point where it appeared that Shakespeare 'lost interest in the nobles and became absorbed in the character of Falstaff', and there was 'more poetry and magic in any of their prose sentences than in fifty lines of the stock blank verse given to the noblemen'.[1] The same Olivier who in *Part 1* had turned in an inspired performance as a stammering Hotspur (which Michael Redgrave recalled to good effect six years later) now played Shallow in a mellow autumnal orchard setting. Kenneth Tynan rated these as among his greatest moments in the theatre, and wrote that 'The keynote of the performance is old-maidishness, agitated and pathetically anxious to make things go with a swing: a crone-like pantomime dame, you might have thought, were it not for the beady delectation that steals into his eyes at the mention of sex.'[2] The production's nostalgia, even sentimentality, in Joyce Redman's portrayal of Doll as a whore with a heart of gold, or Ralph Richardson's intelligent and even wise Falstaff, may be attributable partly to a feeling of inwardness now that the war was over.

This was a star-studded, inventive but restrained production (it also included Sybil Thorndike as Mistress Quickly), with its emphasis on comedy rather than history. It was worthily succeeded by the Quayle–Redgrave 1951 tetralogy, which coincided with the Festival of Britain, whose upbeat national themes seemed particularly appropriate to a cycle of plays which concludes with the conquest of France and the consolidation of military victory through a marriage. Redgrave followed Olivier's doubling in crossing play boundaries, and acted the parts of both Richard II and Hotspur, speaking the latter's lines in a northern accent (which Kate Percy recalls at *2 Henry IV* 2.3.24). He cut the play of echoic material (which would not be needed in the third play of four so long as the plays were performed in the right order), and pruned the comic parts, while leaving the political plot virtually intact. The production was clearly conceived as a historical drama, and Redgrave's understanding of *2 Henry IV* reflected the thinking behind contemporary writing on the plays. This tended to cast

---

[1] Stephen Potter, *New Statesman and Nation*, 13 October 1945.

[2] Tynan, *A View of the English Stage* 1944–63 (1975), pp. 33–4.

them as the dramatization of a homogeneous mythic history with a clearly defined national destiny.[1] The tilt towards a political play at the expense of the low-life tavern world was signalled early on in the strain between Quayle's Falstaff and Richard Burton's charismatic Hal. This was developed further in a powerful deathbed scene and the apotheosis of the coronation, the most elaborate staging of the ceremony since the 1821 Covent Garden pageant. The effort to portray the shaping of heroic nationhood resulted in a very masculine production which rather sidelined its female characters.

Four years later *1 Henry IV* and *2 Henry IV* were produced by Douglas Seale at the Old Vic in London (1955) with Paul Rogers as Falstaff and Robert Hardy (who had played the Archbishop of York in the Redgrave Stratford production) as Hal. This was nicely calibrated and sensitive ensemble-playing which was much admired by the critics for its tact, and because it put 'Shakespearian production in general on the right realistic track'.[2] By comparison the 1964 RSC cycle of plays, which included versions of all the works in the two tetralogies, proposed a radical revisiting of Shakespeare's histories which owed much to the theatrical iconography of Brecht's *Mother Courage* and to the then influential ideas of Jan Kott, who saw the history plays as dramatizing the horror of war rather than celebrating the destiny of English nationhood. The retrenching from the nineteenth-century lavish use of scenery and stage props which had been set in motion by Quayle in 1951 was completed here in the metallic minimalism of the sets provided for Hall by his designer, John Bury. The actor and his speech were now central, and his relationship with space and sets on a thrust stage was to remain a major preoccupation in the years to come.

A year later Orson Welles's *Chimes at Midnight* (1965) was released in England (and distributed in the USA in 1966 as *Falstaff*).[3] It followed two previous adaptations by Welles of Shakespeare's histories: *Five Kings* (Theatre Guild, 1938) in which he acted Falstaff, and *Chimes at Midnight* which played in Belfast and Dublin for a month in 1960. It developed the earlier attempts'

---

[1] As expounded by E. M. W. Tillyard in *Shakespeare's History Plays* (1944).

[2] Tynan (p. 154).

[3] The script is conveniently reproduced in the Rutgers Films in Print series, *Chimes at Midnight*, ed. Bridget Gellert Lyons (1988).

presentation strategies such as the use of a narrator, while retaining roughly the same selected material from *1 Henry IV* and *2 Henry IV*. With respect to Shakespeare's texts, the filmed version differs from Welles's play collage by using *1 Henry IV* as its basic narrative and *2 Henry IV* to consolidate the material.[1] The film also drew on *Henry V* for Falstaff's death, and it borrowed some details from *Richard II* and *Merry Wives*. Welles himself played Falstaff, and he was partnered by a star cast, including John Gielgud as Henry IV, Margaret Rutherford as Mistress Quickly, Jeanne Moreau as Doll Tearsheet, and Fernando Rey as Worcester.

By one of the film's many strokes of genius, the three monologic passages of narration from Holinshed's *Chronicles* (including the last lines we hear before the show ends) were spoken by Ralph Richardson, who twenty years earlier had famously played Falstaff as a sympathetic figure in a production the spirit of which most closely anticipated that of Welles's film (see above, p. 68). Falstaff may be dead at the end of the play, but in another incarnation, as Richardson, he lives on to tell the tale, larger than life and bigger than death. This is one of several long-range and semi-private ironies in the film, not entirely dissimilar to the gentle self-parody of Jeanne Moreau's caressing Orson Welles–Jack Falstaff with 'Thou whoreson little tidy Bartholomew boar-pig', where (surely wittingly) 'whoreson' and 'Orson' become indistinguishable in the actress's Gallic pronunciation of English.[2]

From the opening shot, and before even the credits start scrolling, as the audience peers at a snowbound landscape and watches two figures, Falstaff and Shallow, slowly moving across it, it is clear that this is the cinematic world of Bergman rather than the ideological one of Brecht's theatre. Welles's dazzling deployment of cinematic techniques in the film to explore what he considered to be the 'story of the betrayal of a friendship' is amply documented elsewhere, but some reference to it here is required. Among the most important ways of communicating and controlling emotions in the film is its haunting soundtrack. In spite of being 'wretchedly post-synchronised', it displays the 'breadth and delicacy' of Welles's approach in the

---

[1] See Robert Hapgood, '*Chimes at Midnight* from Stage to Screen: The Art of Adaptation', *ShS* 39 (1987), 41–2.

[2] Samuel Crowl, 'The Long Goodbye: Welles and Falstaff', *SQ* 31 (1980), 369–80.

transitions ... between the cavernous sound of the court scenes [set in Windsor and filmed in the Spanish cathedral at Cardonna] and the festive overlapping music and dialogue in Eastcheap and more generally in Falstaff's scenes; or the distance from which we hear Shallow's thoughts on his dead friends and grand past ... or the transition from clangour to silence in the extraordinarily filmed battle.[1]

Welles's Shrewsbury battle scene has been compared to the greatest scenes by Griffith, Ford, Eisenstein, and Kurosawa.[2] It is the complete antithesis of Olivier's Agincourt, and it is angled to make the audience empathize with Falstaff's scepticism, if not cowardice. The tavern world presided over by Falstaff is regarded here with undisguised affection: it is warm, boisterous, it has women in it, and there is a prominent lavatory which is visited by the various characters, as if to signal that this is a world which comprises all human life in a single 'natural' embrace. The amount of wood in the tavern has similarly been favourably contrasted with the unadorned and cold masonry of Windsor.[3] Welles called Falstaff 'the greatest conception of a good man, the most completely good man, in all drama' (*Chimes at Midnight*, 1988, p. 261). Fittingly therefore the last close-up of a white-bearded Falstaff makes him look like King Lear, more sinned against than sinning; and our last view of the glory that was Falstaff is of his huge coffin being wheeled off for burial in the snowy plain. This is also the final shot of the film. To the purist Welles's tragicomic conception of Falstaff may appear unduly sentimental, and certainly hardly justified by Shakespeare's texts. But it proved that, in the hands of a master, Shakespeare's plays, which had been designed for the theatre, could on film become the vehicle for a magnificently conveyed imaginative vision. *Chimes at Midnight* is arguably the outstanding 'performance' interpretation of *2 Henry IV* in the context of its tetralogy partners. It also demonstrated that 'Falstaff' interpretations of the *Henry IV* plays remained as viable in the twentieth century as they had been in the first half of the eighteenth.

With Terry Hands's 1975 trilogy of *1 Henry IV*, *2 Henry IV*, and *Henry V* (*Richard II* was not done) at the Royal Shakespeare

---

[1] Peter Swaab, *CQ* 16 (1987), 174.

[2] Pauline Kael, *The New Republic*, 24 June 1967.

[3] Anthony Davies, *Filming Shakespeare's Plays. The adaptations of Laurence Olivier, Orson Welles, Peter Brook, and Akira Kurosawa* (1988), p. 126.

Theatre history and politics were firmly back in the saddle, as were the purists, in more senses than one. In spite of the performance during that season of the 'other' Falstaff play, *Merry Wives*, this was not a Falstaff cycle. The pellucid clarity of the production, which critics commended, resulted from the interaction of Hands's Brookian approach to theatrical space, his astute choreography, and a careful streamlining of the acting text. Although the production was praised for its authenticity and faithfulness to the original (and there was no modern dress), its prompt-book shows that the text was cut substantially: some 650 lines were removed at a time when the company's practice was to cut an average of 350 to 400.[1] Interestingly, some of Hands's cuts, like the ones affecting Luke's parable and the Archbishop of York in 1.3, echo those in the 1600 quarto edition of the play.

The cast included Alan Howard as Hal, Brewster Mason as Falstaff, Emrys James as Henry IV, Charles Dance as Prince John, Sydney Bromley as Shallow, and Trevor Peacock as both Poins and Silence. The decision to start the run with *Henry V* must have come as a surprise, although the gamble, if that is what it was, paid off handsomely: Alan Howard's electrifying and sublimely disdainful performance of Henry V in particular rendered this the most acclaimed *Henry V* for a generation. To move back into *2 Henry IV*, as Hands suggested, and then into *1 Henry IV*, was bound to confer on the trilogy something of a three-play psychomachia relentlessly focused on Henry and Hal. But the two *Henry IV* plays hardly provide auspicious material for tracing character development. Partly through the inverse structuring of the performance schedule, the three plays took on a novelistic character to the extent that *1 Henry IV* and *2 Henry IV* were bound to be seen to dramatize the audience's quest for the sources of Henry V's power; and for his secret 'other' life with a legendary figure, whose death was reported in *Henry V*, and who seemed to arouse passion and compassion among his followers, and who died babbling of green fields (according to Shakespeare as hypothesized by Theobald). In the light of this royalist approach, the odds were rather stacked against Falstaff when the audience was treated to *2 Henry IV*. Irving Wardle called the play another 'instalment' in 'the Alan Howard show ... the Eastcheap scenes are played as an elegiac

[1] Hodgdon (p. 71).

echo'.[1] Where Harold Hobson saw a death-haunted Falstaff, Michael Coveney rather more irenically detected warmth and dignity in the ageing knight.[2] By all accounts Mason's Falstaff was an understated, rather genial figure, whose cunning was 'pragmatic, not malicious, and we sense that, when his ship comes home and Hal is king, he plans genuinely to repay his friends'.[3]

Terry Hands's *Henrys* opened in Stratford during the centenary of the Royal Shakespeare Theatre. The tradition of these English history plays connecting with political and artistic English history in time was duly observed in 1982, when Trevor Nunn's *Henry IV* plays inaugurated the opening of the RSC's new London base at the Barbican. Gerard Murphy played Hal, while the part of Falstaff was taken by Joss Ackland. The rest of the cast included Robert Eddison as Shallow (a part he had played two years earlier in the BBC Shakespeare), Mike Gwilym as Pistol, Miriam Karlin as Mistress Quickly, Gemma Jones as Doll Tearsheet, and Patrick Stewart as Henry IV. Trevor Nunn's spectacular adaptation of *Nicholas Nickleby* two years earlier loomed over the production. This was the case particularly with John Napier's hugely crowded, and hydraulically operated, versatile set. It generated a busy, bric-a-brac Dickensian atmosphere which suited the Eastcheap scenes perfectly, and it provided a natural habitat for gargoyles such as Silas Wegg or, as here, a psychotic Pistol brandishing a gun.

Nunn's attention to detailed theatrical nuances, his legendary inventiveness, and his determination to render the text self-sufficient, combined to score a number of triumphs, notably in the use of a double prologue. The first one had a street theatre troupe dramatize the detail of Hal's boxing the Lord Chief Justice's ear from *Famous Victories*, an incident which is twice referred to in the play itself and would otherwise be unintelligible to audiences no longer versed in Hall, Holinshed, or Stow. This bold concession to narrative continuity (perhaps not entirely surprisingly from the adaptor for the theatre of a sprawling Dickensian novel) was followed by Rumour's Prologue. In a gesture towards Hands's

---

[1] Wardle, *Times*, 25 June 1975.

[2] Hobson, *Sunday Times*, 29 June 1975; Coveney, *Financial Times*, 30 January 1976.

[3] John Elsom, *Listener*, 3 July 1975.

1975 Prologue (where parts of single lines were shared out between different actors), it was delivered by a number of hooded actors holding candles, who fanned out all over the set and watched the entire play as an on-stage choric audience.

Nunn was eager to offer an intelligible as well as an authentic version of *2 Henry IV*. Hence his use of *Famous Victories*, as well as a careful, almost scholarly scrutiny of the performance text. As his prompt-book demonstrates, he cut wherever lines seemed redundant, duplicatory, or narratively retrospective. His approach coincides at times almost with that of the textual scholar: where his basic text, the New Penguin, misses out the lines 'O, if this were seen ... sit him down and die' from 3.1 (following Folio rather than QB: see 3.1.52–5 n.), Nunn restores these lines in the playing text. At the same time he inexplicably cut Falstaff's lines about Hal's chin not being 'yet fledge' down to his comic regret about the barber's never earning sixpence out of Hal's face, when the lines would have applied with great force to Gerard Murphy's regressive, almost adolescent Hal. Nunn's pruning might have been expected simply to remove the references to the boxing of the Lord Chief Justice's ears rather than just inserting an 'Interlude'. He retained it because his conception of the play focuses on its son–fathers relationships, between Hal and Falstaff, Henry IV, and the Lord Chief Justice.

But while Ackland's Falstaff was much admired, and even described as 'irresistible', Gerard Murphy's Hal acted the part in a manner that was extrovert to the point of appearing oblivious of his royal blood. This Hal was a 'physically unprepossessing boy with a mop of greasy blond hair, and a wide untrustworthy mouth opening into fatuous toothy smiles',[1] a 'hippy Prince ... who had dropped out without much liking the alternative society'.[2] He sat on Falstaff's lap and mopped up the mess Falstaff had made of his breakfast, thus signalling an emotional dependency which is almost inconceivable in Shakespeare's controlled protagonist who never lets us forget that he is the king-in-waiting. Murphy's intimacy-craving and vulnerable boy could hardly have differed more from Alan Howard's prince. To Howard's dangerously energized and manipulative character the domestic situation in the

[1] Irving Wardle, *Times*, 10 June 1982.
[2] Nicholas Shrimpton, *ShS* 39 (1983), 149–55.

Henry IV plays was ultimately adjunctive to the royal politics, whereas Murphy was throughout in search of a father and not a kingdom. It would have been hard to imagine him proceeding to France and, at Agincourt, walking amongst his men at night, burdened by the inherited guilt of usurpation, and fearful about the responsibility of the morrow. Nunn did not produce *Henry V* in this season.

In 1986 the Old Vic witnessed an iconoclastic production of the *Henry* plays. The English Shakespeare Company under Bogdanov and Pennington pledged to take Shakespeare back to the people. Their anti-elitist hostility to alleged establishment appropriation of Shakespeare translated into what was virtually an agitprop conception of the plays, which were performed as a sequential trilogy.[1] They succeeded in their intention to shock middle-class audiences by a series of inventive gimmicks, such as Falstaff, played magnificently by John Woodvine, relieving himself offstage (while the audience sat in enforced silence), or the execution on-stage by a cynical military machine of the rebels, who are cast as foolish amateurs. This was a subversive and urgently political production, rooted in a time of severe, nationwide retrenchment of the arts in Britain. But its irreverence was also extremely funny, and it repeatedly managed to be acutely alert to the fine-tuning of the text, and the requirements of the dramatic narrative demanded by the fact that *2 Henry IV* is a sequel. Taking its inspiration from Welles's *Chimes at Midnight* ('one of the best Shakespeare films ever made'), Bogdanov reversed the two parts of the last scene of *1 Henry IV* to leave Hal at odds with his father, who believes Falstaff's account of Hotspur's death. The result 'was electric. It left the story wide open, with the audience buzzing with excitement to know what followed'.[2]

By comparison, Adrian Noble's 1991 RST view of the *Henry IV* plays marked a return to the mainstream. This production, which

---

[1] The establishment view, as Bogdanov saw it, was embodied in Michael Billington's review of the production in which Billington was 'still tilting with Tillyard'. After quoting the review's objection 'to the bias that constantly emphasises Hal's ruthlessness at the expense of his humanity', Bogdanov remarks that Billington 'must be thinking of another *Henry IV*. Pirandello's, perhaps' (Michael Bogdanov and Michael Pennington, *The English Shakespeare Company. The Story of 'The Wars of the Roses' 1986–89* (1990), pp. 50–1).

[2] Bogdanov and Pennington (pp. 54–5).

inaugurated Noble's Artistic Directorship of the company, featured Julian Glover as Bolingbroke, Michael Maloney as Hal, and Robert Stephens as Falstaff. The text of *Part 2* was cut by 500 lines (as opposed to 300 for *Part 1*). While Albie Woodington's manic Pistol was both spectacular and a triumph, the production offered one of the most intelligently ambiguous *2 Henry IVs* in a long time, due partly to a finely judged performance by Robert Stephens.

The BBC 1995 production of *Henry IV* was a daringly conflated version of *Part 1* and *Part 2*, with some reference, at the beginning, to the deposition of Richard II, and a grafting on to the end of the lament for Falstaff by Mistress Quickly (*Henry V* 2.3.9–25). From our first views of Hotspur and Hal as childhood friends and rivals, who witness the deposition of Richard II, the production signalled its intent to use this relationship as a structuring principle of its political plot. As a consequence, the rebellion from *Part 2* (arguably the weakest part of Shakespeare's script) was submerged in

Figure 8. James Grout as Silence, Paul Eddington as Shallow, and director John Caird in the 1995 BBC production of *Henry IV*.

the Hotspur uprising, and the battle at Shrewsbury was amalgamated with Gaultres. Individual performances were inspiring, notably David Calder's complex, and largely sympathetic, Falstaff (he wants to do what is right, but invariably does the opposite), Ronald Pickup's robust Bolingbroke, Jonathan Firth's clinical and chillingly orthodontic Prince of Wales, and Paul Eddington's moving performance of a benevolent and ailing Shallow.

But the overwhelming interest of the production was the sheer ingenuity of its editing and the telling superimpositions of speaking heads which are impossible to achieve in the theatre. Thus for instance Bolingbroke's soliloquy from *2 Henry IV* 3.1 was shifted to come after the Gad's Hill robbery in *Part 1*, while other material from the same scene (his lines on the 'revolution of the times') was made to follow the tavern scene from *Part 1*. Falstaff's clash with the Lord Chief Justice in 1.2 of *Part 2* alternated, through a series of 'cuts', with Hal's first encounter with his father in *1 Henry IV* 3.2. This was neither a political nor a Falstaffian interpretation, but a brilliantly executed collage, which gave equal weight to both. It resisted Falstaff's bid for imaginative usurpation by defining the political stakes of the composite play exclusively in terms of Hotspur versus the Lancastrians. It will never be a purist's *Henry IV*, but it made the two plays and their contexts readily accessible to contemporary mass audiences.

Performances of *2 Henry IV* reflect the oscillating movement of a double plot which pits the anarchic energy of comedy against the authority of the state in the framing context of English history. In times of national crisis or triumph the emphasis has tended to be on the play's dynastic struggles because, like *Henry V*, the two parts of *Henry IV* have been perceived to articulate something special about Englishness, responsibility, and fathers and sons; and in the twentieth century the play has tended to be interpreted increasingly in terms of its ideology.

Since World War II politically inspired interpretations have led to productions of *Part 2* alongside not just *Part 1* but the rest of the plays which make up the Lancastrian cycle. But Falstaff, who occurs only in the two middle plays of the tetralogy, has not therefore been displaced in dramatic or other readings of a text (witness *Chimes at Midnight*) which in terms of rhetoric and stage presence belongs to him. What distinguishes *Part 2* from the first play, and what indeed confers a degree of autonomy on it, is precisely the fact that it is above all a Falstaff play; and that more than anything is what constituted its claim to fame in the early seventeenth century (see above, p. 42). In the theatre the role of Falstaff is easily the greatest part in the tetralogy, and will always be coveted by actors. Just as there have been famous Hamlets so there have also been outstanding Falstaffs, because the role encompasses the whole gamut of emotion, from cynicism and cruelty to necessary scepticism and tenderness. English literature without Falstaff is unthinkable, and therefore the greatest Falstaff play, *2 Henry IV*, will continue to entertain us in the theatre, even though it will probably never be entirely uncoupled from *Part 1*.

The Texts of '2 Henry IV'

The Control-Text. There are two early editions of *2 Henry IV*, the quarto of 1600, which exists in two substantively different issues (QA and QB), and the Folio of 1623, which has significant differences from both issues of the quarto. The quarto, printed from Shakespeare's holograph (see below), lacks information about staging present in F, whose copy, however, has been adulterated by statute, compositors, copyist, and sophistication. Modern editions are bound to draw on all three versions. For reasons explained below, the present edition is based on QA except for 3.1, based on QB, and eight passages unique to F.

Q was set up in Valentine Simmes's printing house by his Compositor A.[1] Twenty-one copies survive, ten of QA, eleven of QB, which makes it the commonest of extant Shakespeare first quartos.[2] The two issues are identical in all essentials with the exception of 3.1. This self-contained scene of the ailing, sleepless Bolingbroke is found in QB (and in F: see also 3.1.52–5 n.), but not in QA. Sigs. E3–4ᵛ from QA (Q TLN 1228–1494) are cancelled in QB by a new four-leaved sheet containing sigs. E3–6ᵛ. Q, issue A, collates A–K⁴, L² (A⁴–D⁴, E⁴, F⁴–K⁴, L²) while Q, issue B, collates A⁴–D⁴, E⁶, F⁴–K⁴, L². In order to insert the new scene of

---

[1] Ferguson (pp. 27–30), and Williams (pp. 173–4).

[2] Greg (1955, p. 274); see Berger (p. vi): Berger includes the fragment BL3 (B & P 325) among QAs and therefore counts eleven QAs. He also lists an indeterminate copy MH (B & P 340).

107 lines, the compositor needed to reset parts of the surrounding text, from 2.4.337 (Q TLN 1228: 'MISTRESS QUICKLY No, I warrant you') to 2.4.385.1 (Q TLN 1276), and from 3.2.0.1 (Q TLN 1392) to 3.2.101 (Q TLN 1494: 'good-limbed fellow, young, strong'), a total of 165 lines. In doing so, he introduced seven variant substantive readings as well as a large number of accidentals.[1] If the same proportion of errors were applied to a setting of the whole of Q's 3,300 lines, Simmes's Compositor A would have materially erred an estimated 140 times; and that would be if he set from print, as he did with the text surrounding the cancel. But Q was certainly set from manuscript, which means that the number of variants from the source is likely to be considerable.[2]

Act 3, Scene 1: QA, QB, F. The length of the 'omitted' scene 3.1 (or 'added', depending on its perceived status) may be significant to bibliographical enquiry about QA and QB. Analysis of Shakespeare's hand in Addition II.D of *Sir Thomas More* shows that he wrote about fifty lines per side of foolscap.[3] This in turn suggests that 3.1 would have taken up both sides of a sheet of paper, assuming the scene to be written on a new sheet rather than spilling over from a previous one. If, as Jowett has argued, the scene constitutes a foul-paper revision after Shakespeare had finished 'writing the play (or at least that part of the play where the scene appears)', then Shakespeare would almost certainly

---

[1] One for every reset line, a total of 165: see Humphreys (p. xii).

[2] Humphreys (pp. lxxxiii–lxxxiv); Williams (p. 174) estimates that Compositor A is 'probably responsible for introducing nearly two hundred corruptions by varying from his copy'.

[3] Pollard (1920, p. 680) noted that Shakespeare's way of writing as in *More* was, from the point of view of paper, 'rather unusually expensive'. From Shakespeare's apparent expansiveness in Hand D (he counts an average of 49 lines for Hand D in *More*) Melchiori (p. 200) generates a highly speculative argument about the relationship between the two *Henry* plays. He suggests that *2 Henry IV* 1.2.90–166 (76 lines) and 2.2.1–65 (65 lines) show signs of being an insertion from the 'ur-*Henry IV*' play, and that this is revealed by the speech-prefix *Old.* at 1.2.117 and by the entrance of *Sir Iohn Russel* at 2.2. He argues that the speech-prefixes in the quarto version of 1.2 confirm this: up to 85 and again after 181 the speech-prefix is *Iohn.* or *sir Iohn.*, but from 91 to 161 it is *Falst.*, except for one *sir Iohn.* at 100 and one *Old.* at 117. The Lord Chief Justice is *Iustice* or *Iust.* from his first speech at 55 to 159, while from 173 on he becomes *Lo.* or *Lord.* This points towards a different origin, and that section, according to Melchiori, 'would fill one side of a manuscript leaf' in Shakespeare's handwriting.

have started on a new sheet of paper.[1] Conversely, it is possible that the scene was written out on a single sheet on both sides from the start, and was mislaid during the first printing of Q.

But the problem with 3.1 is not entirely, or even primarily, a bibliographical one. Just under half of the material in this scene is of a political nature, and takes the shape of a long restrospective reference to the usurpation of Richard II. It should therefore be viewed in some important ways as on a par with four of the eight Folio-only passages (see below, p. 85), which are assumed to be missing from both QA and QB because of their allegedly inflammatory character. In fact, in Q the name 'Richard' occurs exclusively in 3.1.[2]

Whereas Jowett and Taylor (p. 50) view 3.1 as the first step by Shakespeare in a 'two-stage process of authorial expansion . . . emphasizing the links with his own earlier history plays . . . the beginning of a unified and conscious process of revision which culminated in the addition of six other passages of a similar nature', these lines might equally well have stood in the foul papers in 1596, when the play was first written. After all, as Jowett and Taylor (p. 39) also note, without 3.1 what F calls Acts 2 and 3 would only have 68 lines of 'main' plot, and 'the heart of the play is in Q(a) given over to a succession of comic scenes'. The succession in QA of the Boar's Head scene (2.4: 385 lines predominantly of prose) by the scene at Shallow's (3.2: 317 lines of prose) creates a block of some 702 lines which are focused on, or built around, Falstaff. Out of a total of about 3,300 lines in modern edited texts, 21.6 per cent are allocated to these scenes, at a crucial structural juncture in the play. In QA that proportion is higher (through the absence of all F-only passages and 3.1) and rises to 23.5 per cent.

Although it has never seriously been suggested that QA here should take precedence over QB in a modern edited version, a case could be made, on the basis perhaps of dramatic fluidity, for the transition in QA between the end of 2.4 and the beginning of 3.2, as the following indicates:

---

[1] *Textual Companion*, p. 351; Jowett and Taylor (pp. 49–50).

[2] In the composite text of *2 Henry IV*, 'Richard' occurs eight times: 1.1.205 (F-only); 1.3.98, 101 (F-only); 3.1.57, 63, 66 (id.), 87 (QB, F); 4.1.58 (F-only).

MISTRESS QUICKLY O, run, Doll, run; run, good Doll; come. She comes
blubbered. Yea, will you come, Doll? *Exeunt*

3.2 *Enter Justice Shallow and Justice Silence*
SHALLOW Come on, come on, come on! Give me your hand, sir, give me
your hand, sir. An early stirrer, by the rood! And how doth my good
cousin Silence?[1]

Furthermore, in the QA version alone does Shakespeare 'take up
the King's role at exactly the point where it is taken up in the
source [Daniel's *Civil Wars*] which most influenced his presentation of the King'.[2] The absence of 3.1 from QA, we are meant to
infer, originally resulted from Shakespeare's following too closely
his main source for the portrayal of the King, causing a moment-
ary obliviousness to the wider shaping demands of his play. This
was then set right in a first revision (3.1), to be followed later by a
reconceptualizing of the play in a wider tetralogical context, which
ultimately resulted in the copy for 1623 F (see below).

But neither this surmised tripping up of Shakespeare by his
source, nor the fact that the thrice-repeated phrase 'come' (in Q,
but not in F) is cross-scenically picked up by Shallow in QA (cf.
similarly 5.1.1 n.), provides adequate support for the hypothesis
that QA is an *Ur-2 Henry IV*, or that 3.1 constitutes an instance of
revision. Both need to be offset by the realization that if 3.1 does
not intervene between 2.4 and 3.2, then Falstaff will on stage have
moved from Eastcheap to Shallow's in Lincolnshire (later Gloucestershire) with disconcerting speed; and this would be even more
unsettling in the theatre than in the study. Moreover, a grave
breach of both imaginative credibility and dramatic construction
is caused by the absence of the King from the main plot during
these important moments in the political action. In QA the first
appearance of Henry IV occurs at 4.3, when he enters as an invalid
whose main concern is with the succession of his wayward son.
But in QB and in F he is briefed about the progress of the civil
war, and he is furthermore portrayed as a resourceful figure.
Above all, without 3.1 two major scenes of Falstaff, both in prose

[1] Pope (1725) was the first to argue that the F-only passages were Shakespeare's
revisions, but Johnson thought that the passages 'may be probably supposed rather
to have been dropped...than added...of the author' (cf. Shaaber, p. 476).

[2] Jowett and Taylor (p. 36).

and including the longest scene in the play, are juxtaposed in a manner which would be unique in Shakespeare. It would be even more surprising in this play, because it almost systematically balances verse and prose, history and comedy, and thereby mirrors *1 Henry IV* where scenes of royalty and rebellion (or robbery) alternate.[1]

The evidence so far would seem to suggest that 3.1 is as likely to have been written at the same time as the rest of the play as that it is an eleventh-hour revision. For a reason that we can at best speculate about, 3.1 was at first omitted from the printing of Q, and this, rather than a last-minute revision, accounts for its presence in QB, the text printed after QA. Was its omission an accident, or had censorship interfered? W. W. Greg (1955, p. 274) suggested that the play may not have been submitted to ecclesiastical censorship at all, for the Stationers' Register records its entry under the hands of the Wardens only. He stressed the fact that 3.1 passed muster, and that therefore the absence from Q of the other Ricardian F-only passages could not be attributed to censorship on those grounds. He (rightly) dismissed the idea that the printers would have surreptitiously inserted 3.1 after licence, and noted that the sheer number of copies of the quarto to survive may instead bear witness to the fact that it was never suppressed. This may well be true, but it is a fact that the *Henry IV* plays had already attracted the opprobrium of the Office of the Revels, and the question needs to be asked therefore whether there is any reason to surmise that the very temporary absence from the printed text in Q of 3.1 could result from action by another censor.

Since the Ricardian material in *2 Henry IV* refers back specifically to the history dramatized by Shakespeare in *Richard II* (which unlike *2 Henry IV* went through multiple reprints (Q2–Q5)

[1] The structural affinity between the two *Henry IV* plays is striking. Shaaber (1948, pp. 221–2) noted that *Part 2* was 'almost a carbon copy of the first play' and he stressed the importance of the fact that 'the sequence of scenes developing the historical plot and that of the comic scenes is almost exactly the same'. In view of this one may wonder whether 3.1 should not analogically have been (or maybe originally was?) a scene featuring the rebels preparing for Gaultres, and that Shakespeare either decided against it, or jettisoned an *Ur*-3.1 with the rebels because he needed to introduce the King at last. (This idea was put to me in a private communication by George Walton Williams. It has the twin merits of being both imaginative and alert to the problems surrounding 3.1.)

between the first quarto in 1597 and the 1623 F),[1] it is worth briefly considering that text here for the light it may throw on the question of censorship and the way it may have affected the textual history of *2 Henry IV*, *if* it did.

In *Richard II* the 'deposition scene' (4.1.145–308) does not appear until Q4 in 1608, and in some copies of Q4 the title-page draws attention to the fact that this text comes with 'new additions of the Parlia-|ment Sceane, and the deposing | of King Richard, | As it hath been lately acted by the Kinges | Maiesties seruantes, at the Globe'. The Q4 title-page could of course be signalling that the play was earlier not performed in its entirety rather than suggesting that it contains newly written material. To advertise the additions as new would not only be shrewder from a marketing point of view, it would also be safer, because the company might have been unwise to announce publicly that these were formerly suppressed wares, even if that is exactly what they were. There would seem to be no more of a prima facie political case for rescinding the deposition scene from the copy for the original printing of *Richard II* (either foul papers or a transcript of them) in 1597 than there would be for reinstating it in, or adding it to, the 1608 version, the first one to be printed after the Queen's death in 1603. But the fact remains that the scene does not appear in the first quarto, or in the two which appeared the following year.

Both with and without the Q4/F lines, 4.1 is perfectly viable from the point of view of dramatic narrative, which may further point to a situation that is in parts analogous with 3.1 in *2 Henry IV*, not least in that both sections are self-contained units. What is missed by the omission of 4.1.145–308 in *Richard II* is the powerful ritualistic iconography of the process of abdication in the theatre, its on-stage (rather than reported) swapping of the emblems of kingship. In the Q4/F-only lines Richard is deposed in public. The audience already knows well before the missing lines that Richard has renounced his throne, and that Bolingbroke has become 'Henry, of that name the fourth !' (4.1.98–103). But the usurper insists that Richard should come in person 'that in common view | He may surrender' (ll. 146–7).

---

[1] Publication of the first quarto of *Richard II* followed a similar pattern to that of *2 Henry IV*. It was entered in the Stationers' Register by Andrew Wise on 29 August 1597 and was printed for Wise by Valentine Simmes in an edition dated 1597.

It is unlikely that Shakespeare's foul papers did not contain the scene in 1595 when he completed the play. But the period between the writing of *Richard II* in 1595 and its first printing in 1597 in part coincides with the Cobhams' tenure of the Lord Chamberlain's office and the ensuing Oldcastle débâcle. The revised Epilogue to *2 Henry IV* makes it clear that by early 1597 the company was keen to comply with, if not mollify, the authorities. The reason for the absence of the deposition scene in Q1 to Q3 of *Richard II* may well be due to self-censorship by Shakespeare's company in the wake of their recent brush with the Lord Chamberlain's office. It is conceivable that, since 3.1 of *2 Henry IV* touches on the identical monarchical crisis, similar restraints decided them at first to withhold (or mark for cancellation) 3.1 in the foul papers of *Part 2*. They then reconsidered, or were advised that the passage was innocuous enough to pass muster with the 'correctors of the press', who acted as licensers of printed material on behalf of the Privy Council, the Bishop of London, the Archbishop of Canterbury, and the Lord Chamberlain (then George Carey, the second Lord Hunsdon).[1]

If the printing of 3.1 in QB *2 Henry IV* indicates that it may be the authorities (rather than the company or Shakespeare) who unexpectedly gave the green light to the historically retrospective material in the scene, they may well have regretted this almost immediately. A mere five weeks into the new year the Earl of Essex made his doomed bid for power. *Richard II* was put on at the Globe on 7 February 1601, and thus became publicly identified with the seeds of sedition. But the embarrassment that this undoubtedly caused the company was probably not one of the reasons why *2 Henry IV*, complete with 3.1, failed to be reissued during Shakespeare's lifetime, since the offending play *Richard II* was itself printed again in 1608, and this time it included the controversial deposition lines.

The F-only passages. Although 3.1 slipped into the text of Q, issue B, this is not the case with the other four references to Richard II

[1] Williams (pp. 175, 177) argues that 3.1 was omitted from QA 'by human failure', and that the reason why the scene supplies the only reference in Q to Richard is 'because the leaf containing the reference was misplaced at the time the political cuts were made in the quarto'.

which are F-only. But as regards the story of the usurpation and the fate of King Richard, these are *not* generically different from 3.1. If they stood in Shakespeare's papers alongside 3.1, it is hard to see that direct (or indirect) political pressure should have forced one set of Ricardian references, the F-specific ones, to go underground while allowing another (3.1) to proceed into print.

The eight F-only passages divide into two groups. The first, and the more homogeneous of the two, I would style the 'political' group, the second the 'dramatic' group. The 'political' group contains the four Ricardian references and a debate about rebellion, which is set invariably against the backdrop of the successful, but morally dubious and politically ambiguous, bid by Bolingbroke for power dramatized in *Richard II*.

The content of the 'political' group of passages occurring only in the Folio can be summarized as follows:

(a) 1.1.189–209: Morton reassures his fellow conspirators that the Archbishop will help them succeed where Hotspur failed, because the Archbishop holds the power from Richard and from God to turn 'insurrection to religion'.

(b) 1.3.85–108: The Archbishop (abstractly) berates the mob for its fickleness in first overthrowing Richard for Bolingbroke and now tiring of the new king. Implicit in his harangue is a keen and dangerous awareness of the fact that the people can make and unmake kings.

(c) 4.1.55–79: The Archbishop compares the present unrest in the kingdom to the 'disease' which caused the death of Richard II. He justifies his role in the insurrection by stating that grievances of the rebels outweigh the offences their arms may cause.

(d) 4.1.101–37: Westmorland and Mowbray argue about the implications of the aborted duel, dramatized at the beginning of *Richard II*, between Bolingbroke and Mowbray's father.

Three of these four passages, totalling seventy lines, reportedly (once), as well as directly (twice), implicate in the rebellion the Archbishop of York, 'the primate of England', and holder of the most important ecclesiastical office (after the Archbishopric of Canterbury) in the land. Their absence from Q inevitably means that the Archbishop's role is severely curtailed by comparison with F.[1]

[1] Cf. Prosser (p. 34).

85

The import of the Ricardian material in these F-only passages is not distinctly different from 3.1, nor had *Richard II*, or material relating to the events it dramatizes (except the deposition in 4.1), as yet attracted official opprobrium by the time of printing Q. It may follow therefore that what rendered these passages suspect per se to the licenser for the press was precisely their enlisting of the Archbishop of York on the side of rebellion.[1] If this is correct, if the problem with parts of the text arises primarily from its relation to archiepiscopal rather than Ricardian matters, then (d), the heated exchange between Westmorland and Mowbray, becomes a 'floater' and should probably be moved into the second of the two groups of F-only passages. It is substantially no different from the four 'dramatic' F-only passages, all of which occur before the end of Act 2:[2]

(e) 1.1.166–79: Morton's remonstrating with Northumberland on his strategy which adversely affected the fate of Hotspur.

(f) 1.3.21–4: Four lines by Lord Bardolph enlarging on his caution against proceeding without the help of Northumberland.

(g) 1.3.36–55: Through a lengthy architectural analogy Lord Bardolph likens rebellion to the building of a house. This particular passage could also be described as a potential 'floater' between the two groups.

(h) 2.3.23–45: Lady Percy's elegy for her dead husband Hotspur. The eight F-only passages are unevenly spread across three of the first four acts of the play, as the following brief survey demonstrates:

1.1: thirty-five almost consecutive lines (166–79; 189–209) spoken by Morton (16.3 per cent of the scene). The lines are split between the political and dramatic groups.

---

[1] Clare (p. 68) claims that the fact that in *2 Henry IV* 'the rebellion gains respectability from the leadership of a righteous Archbishop would have been an immediate reason for the censor's intervention'. It is worth noting also that the Dering manuscript, which conflates Shakespeare's two *Henry IV* plays, has nothing about the Archbishop while also playing down the rebellion. Dering's 1623 collage anticipates the 1995 BBC TV collation of the two parts of *Henry IV* which similarly jettisoned the Scrope conspiracy.

[2] Cf. Walker (p. 96) who endorses Hart's view that four of the 'cuts' were of lines which have 'poetical and amplificatory rather than dramatic value'. She attributes them ('possibly') to the book-keeper or transcriber: 'The fact that all these cuts occur before the end of the Second Act suggests that the book-keeper deferred the problem of shortening the play for acting, perhaps until a transcript made the business easier.'

1.3: forty-eight lines (21–4; 36–55; 85–108) equally divided
between Lord Bardolph and the Archbishop of York (43.6 per
cent of the scene). The lines divide evenly between the political and
dramatic groups. If, however, 36–55 are viewed as political, then
the F-only lines in this scene belong overwhelmingly to that group.
2.3: twenty-three lines (23–45) by Kate Percy (33.8 per cent of
the scene).
4.1: sixty-two lines (55–79; 101–37) by the Archbishop of York
and Westmorland and Mowbray (17.7 per cent of the scene), all of
them from the political group.

The fact that there is no F-only material after 4.1.137 may
lend support to the view that the absence of some of the F-only
passages is due to political interference with parts of Shakespeare's text, because it is at Gaultres in Act 4 that the rebellion is finally squashed so that the play is politically 'safe' from
there on.[1]

If there is reason to believe that a censor meddled with the text of
the play, what are we then to make of the four 'dramatic' F-only
passages? The very short second passage, (f), is so slight that it can
probably be safely disregarded for the time being, which leaves two
Hotspur-related passages, (e) and (h), and (g), Lord Bardolph's
architectural simile. Although Lord Bardolph's lines as well as
(d) above have been identified as possible 'floaters' between the
two groups, the distribution of the F-only material across the text
suggests that this was not how they would have been perceived. In
fact, in each case these lines are found in close proximity to
material that seems to have been censored.

In 1.3 Lord Bardolph's homiletic lines anticipate the Archbishop's unctuous (and posed?) indignation about the state of
affairs in the realm. As yet the rebels have to tread carefully, and
their circumspect phrasing reflects this. But this did not go un-
noticed by whoever licensed the play for printing. Dangerous
company and very close proximity to another political passage
may similarly have affected Morton's lines in 1.1.166–79. What
by itself may appear like a politically innocuous general remonstrating with Northumberland may become a contaminated

---

[1] Jowett and Taylor (p. 49) argue that 'all the additions come in the play's first
2000 lines (out of 3300), before John of Lancaster's entrance at Gaultree. From this
point on, the play can look to the future: the defeat of the rebels . . .'

backformation through the same speaker's views ten lines on, starting with 'The gentle Archbishop of York'. Whoever cut the reference to the Archbishop may well have cut the earlier lines as well.[1]

This leaves Kate Percy's twenty-three lines about Hotspur. There is no obvious reason for cutting them, notwithstanding the reference in line 42 to the 'Marshal and the Archbishop' which could easily be removed.[2] The gain in acting time is in itself insignificant, and needs to be balanced against the dramatic damage incurred by the scene through the removal of the F-only lines. It is in response to Kate's urgency that Northumberland agrees to stay away from the battle. Without the F-only lines, however, Kate's speech lacks momentum. The respective transitions in Q and F starkly demonstrate this.

Q:

KATE   He was indeed the glass
Wherein the noble youth did dress themselves.
NORTHUMBERLAND   Beshrew your heart,
Fair daughter, you do draw my spirits from me
With new lamenting ancient oversights.

F:

KATE
Had my sweet Harry had but half their numbers,
Today might I, hanging on Hotspur's neck,
Have talked of Monmouth's grave.
NORTHUMBERLAND   Beshrew your heart,
Fair daughter, you do draw my spirits from me
With new lamenting ancient oversights.

In Folio it is Kate's passionate lament, her plea to Northumberland

---

[1] Melchiori (p. 199) notes that Morton, 'a fictional character introduced in the play more in the role of the historian . . . than in that of the traditional messenger', may have been cut to release the actor for another role (he suggests that the same actor played Morton and the Archbishop of York).

[2] Since, however, two of the F-only passages, (a) and (h), concern Hotspur, one may wonder whether this is a coincidence. Nothing obvious is gained dramatically by the excision of the first passage, and the flow of the verse is impeded by removing the second. Was whoever removed these two passages keen to ensure that there should not be a perceived North–South split of allegiances in the past history of the kingdom (the Archbishop of York and the Percies of Northumberland versus London and the Court), in addition to an East–West one (Eastcheap versus Westminster)?

> Never, O never do his ghost the wrong
> To hold your honour more precise and nice
> With others than with him

and the intense image of her arms around Hotspur which prompt his father's desertion of the rebels' cause. In Q, instead, he would be seen to respond to a static reminiscence of his son as a kind of abstract Hamlet figure, a man who is moreover remembered primarily for his sartorial elegance. The martial context of the scene, and the audience's assumed recollection of Hotspur (evident elsewhere in the play), and therefore also of Kate, jointly argue that the F-only lines are essential. If Shakespeare had added them, with a view perhaps to capitalizing in the sequel on the success of Hotspur in the first play,[1] he would probably have done a more thorough recycling job. The dramatic rhythm of the scene as well as the metre—the F version yields a perfect pentameter for the line of dialogue shared by Kate and Northumberland—suggests that the F-only lines stood in Shakespeare's text all along.[2]

It is the argument of this edition therefore that Folio recovers (rather than rewrites or revises) lines that were written as an integral part of the play from the beginning. While Q is the control-text for this edition, Folio is the sole authority for some 168 lines without which the play is significantly impoverished. Furthermore, Folio 3.1, printed from a manuscript, differs fourteen times from QB; four of these variants (3.1.18 'mast'; 22 'billows'; 26 'thy'; 27 'sea-boy') are accepted in this edition from Folio.

There are fourteen Q-only passages, mostly consisting of single lines. But four are longer. They are

(a) Falstaff's rumination on his unappreciated merits in 1.2.208–14.
(b) Prince Henry's ironic question about the salvation of Poins's offspring in 2.2.22–6.
(c) Bolingbroke's prediction in 3.1.52–5 that the 'happiest youth' on reading his future fate would die of horror.

---

[1] The importance of Hotspur in *1 Henry IV* is acknowledged in both the Stationers' entry (see above, p. 10) and on the title-page of Q1.

[2] Greg (1955, p. 267) notes that the eight F-only passages are evidently cuts, 'for they sometimes leave the transition harsh and the metre defective. They do little to shorten the play as a whole . . .'

(d) Falstaff's enlarging on his mockery of Shallow's sexuality in
 3.2.299–304.

A number of reasons for their absence from F have been advanced,
including the problems arising from errors in casting off copy
which led to repeated miscalculating of the space for *2 Henry IV*
in Folio (see below, pp. 92–3), or suspected obscenity and profanity
(passage (b)). Before proceeding to the question of the copy for F, it
is necessary to consider Q.

Quarto 1600. There is considerable evidence to suggest that Q was
set from Shakespeare's holograph or 'foul papers'. Its stage directions and speech-prefixes are frequently imprecise, inconsistent, or
descriptive as in '*Enter Rumour painted full of Tongues.*' No fewer
than eight different names, including the generic description
'*Whoore*', are used for Doll Tearsheet, six for Mistress Quickly
(the generic term '*hostess*', or abbreviations of it, are used four
times), and four different speech-prefixes to describe each of the
Lord Chief Justice and Falstaff. Characters are named and then
forgotten, as in the mute parts of Fauconbridge, Kent, Sir John
Umfrevile (mentioned in the text of both Q and F at 1.1.34, and by
Q's speech-heading at 1.1.161) and Sir John Russell, none of
whom appears in F. Entries are given to Sir John Blunt (who
does not speak in the play) at 3.1.31.1 and at 5.2.41.1 where he
is not required. He enters, unnamed, with Prince John at 4.2.23.1,
and is sent off by him to guard Coleville. Surrey similarly does not
speak. At 5.4.0.1 the actor John Sincklo is mentioned by name
rather than by the part he plays (one of the beadles), and the
reference to his thinness has been taken as proof that Shakespeare
was exploiting the striking appearance of an actor for whom he
may have written the part expressly.[1] Furthermore, Q preserves
the (surmised) characteristic Shakespearian spellings of 'Scilens'
for Silence, 'mas' for mass, 'on' for one, 'yeere' for ear,[2] and lacks a
great number of entries and exits that would be expected in a
prompt-book (or even a fair copy). The many loose ends in Q,
and the further fact that in a single stage direction Q provides the

[1] Greg (1955, p. 266); Shaaber (pp. 433–4, 492) lists other thin man parts that
Shakespeare may have written with this particular actor in mind. Shaaber supports
the view that Sincklo's presence in Q points to foul papers rather than prompt-book
as Pollard (1909, p. 44) maintained.

[2] Humphreys (p. lxxvi n.) takes this last to be a modernization in F.

irrelevant information that the scene is set '*within the forrest of Gaultree*', point to 'the writer's work-desk' (Greg, 1955, p. 266), or, in Humphreys's summing up of the most widely held position on Q, 'It is clear that Shakespeare's manuscript was not used as the prompt-copy, and that the printer received it, apart from the cuts, in an interestingly original condition' (Humphreys, p. lxx).

The copy for Folio. In the 1623 Folio, *2 Henry IV* (occupying signatures f6^v–^{x}gg8, pages 74–102) was set by Compositor B at case y, and either A or J at case X,[1] as follows:

1623 F	*Hinman TLN*
B:	
f6^v–g4	1–988
^{x}gg1	1613–1742
^{x}gg2^{v}b	2081–2115
^{x}gg5–^{x}gg7^v	2643–3322
B?: ^{x}gg8	3323–3350
A?(J?):	
g4^v–g6^v	989–1612
^{x}gg1^v–^{x}gg2^{v}a	1743–2080
^{x}gg2^{v}c–^{x}gg4^v	2116–2642[2]

F *2 Henry IV* is curiously mispaginated on ^{x}gg2, where pages 91 and 92 should in fact be 89 and 90. The erroneous pagination in F is therefore 88, 91 [89], 92 [90], 91. The compositors' stints, in sequential order across the pages, are distributed as follows. B set pages 74–81, 87, 95–101, and a fraction of 92 [90], a total of just over sixteen pages, whereas A?(J?) set 82–6, 88–91 [89], most of 92 [90], and 91–4, a total of almost twelve pages. Of the two compositors it is B who will most closely engage our attention (see below).

Both *1 Henry IV* and *2 Henry IV*, which in Folio are wedged between *Richard II* and *Henry V*, were printed later than *Henry V*. Printing of *2 Henry IV* may well have been delayed through

---

[1] Taylor (1993, p. 245). Hinman was the first reliably to identify five compositors, A, B, C, D, and E. The case for additional compositors is made in *Textual Companion* (pp. 148–9), but in the Second Edition of the Norton Facsimile of the 1623 Folio (1996, p. xxxvi), Peter W. M. Blayney accepts only Compositors A and B for *2 Henry IV*.

[2] I am following *Textual Companion* (p. 153) here.

problems over *Richard II* or *1 Henry IV*, or perhaps copy for *2 Henry IV* was simply not ready.[1] Whatever the reason, space had to be left for the two *Henry IV* plays. This space was badly miscalculated, and the printers had to insert an extra quire (^{x}gg), interpolated into the standard signature of the Folio and having an extra sheet as well (a quire in eights rather than a quire in sixes, the norm for the volume). Whereas the two *Henry* plays should have been allocated just over two normal quires each (a total of about fifty pages), they run to an expansive, and costly, fifty-five pages in Folio.

The reason surmised for this by Prosser in her important study of the text of the play is that the last nine pages for *Richard II*, which include the controversial deposition scene in 4.1 (d2), remained to be printed, and that originally only four quires (d, e, f, g) were allocated for the entire space between the end of quire c, *Richard II* (TLN 1739), and the beginning of quire h, *Henry V*.[2] This would have meant that the two *Henry IV*s would be allowed a mere thirty-six pages of F text after the outstanding formes of *Richard II* (which include the first three pages of *1 Henry IV*, numbered 46, 49, 50) were set.

A decision must have been taken well before the setting of *2 Henry IV* to use an extra quire so that, if the quire was 'normal', then the two *Henry IV*s would now be accommodated on fifty-one pages (thirty-nine + the extra quire). If Prosser is right, awareness of the additional quire (after the casting off of *1 Henry IV*) resulted in the overly generous setting at first of *1 Henry IV*, which comes to twenty-six pages of F text, thus leaving only twenty-five for *2 Henry IV*. But *2 Henry IV* (TLN 3350) is longer than *1 Henry IV* (TLN 3180) and would have run to nearly thirty F pages if it had consistently been set on the lines of *1 Henry IV*. It was therefore decided, after setting of *2 Henry IV* had begun, exceptionally to use a four-sheet quire. Prosser's hypotheses offer a brilliant account of the problems F's compositors faced in this scenario of respective congestions and compensations of space, and she demonstrates how the solutions of Compositor B particularly can be made to bear on the textual authority, or lack of it, of F.

---

[1] The rights to both *Richard II* and *1 Henry IV* were held by the bookseller Matthew Law, by assignment from Andrew Wise. Greg (1956) notes that Law 'seems to have made difficulties over the use of his copies that held up the printing of the volume till the publishers came to terms'.

[2] Prosser (p. 74).

If the printers' first mistake may have been to forget that parts of *Richard II* remained to be set, did the second miscalculation of the space for *2 Henry IV* arise from the fact that there was additional material to go into F? And not just the 160 F-only lines, but also the 107 QB lines for 3.1? That the copy for F was influenced by QA (though at one remove at least) and not QB is suggested among others by the fact that QA and F agree against QB in the reset material around 3.1. QB was not used as copy for F.

However the space for *2 Henry IV* was estimated, the submerged presence in F of QA, a text which is some 267 lines shorter than F, may have contributed to the kind of confusion about length that bedevilled the setting of this text. If a copy of QA was used *initially* (before MS C became available: see below, p. 99) to provide rough guidance about the number of quires that would be needed for setting the play, then one can more easily imagine a scenario in which space was wrongly estimated, on the two counts of the remaining pages of *Richard II* and the discrepancy between QA of *2 Henry IV* and the copy used for printing. Once the copy for F was assembled or delivered (in time for the setting itself), QA was no longer in the picture.

The fact is that the printers encountered serious problems with the setting of the Folio text of *2 Henry IV*, and these can be traced, if not perhaps as confidently interpreted as Prosser does, in the see-saw pattern of compressed pages of text like g2, g2^v, and g3 (pp. 77, 78, 79), and in the lavish use of full pages for the 'Epilogue' (in large type) and 'The Actors' Names' (pages 101 and 102 respectively). Folio supplies 'The Actors' Names' on six occasions elsewhere; and only in the problematic case of *Timon of Athens* does it accord a similarly generous treatment to 'The Actors' Names', which are there followed by a blank page.[1]

The 1623 F text of the play has act and scene divisions, and is purged of profanity either by omitting Q's 'God' or by substituting 'H/heaven'. It expands many of Q's abbreviated forms such as

---

[1] In *Timon* the problem arose because *Timon* occupies the space that was originally allocated to the longer play *Troilus* for which copyright could not be secured on time. In the other five cases where the actors' names (i.e. parts) are given, *The Tempest* (side-by-side with the Epilogue), *The Two Gentlemen of Verona*, *Measure for Measure*, *The Winter's Tale*, and *Othello*, the parts mostly occupy a small proportion only of each page.

be thought on. There is no honesty in such dealing, vnles
a woman should be made an Asse and a Beast, to beare e-
uery Knaues wrong.   *Enter Falstaffe and Bardolfe.*
Yonder he comes, and that arrant Malmesey-Nose *Bardolfe* with him, Do your Offices, do your offices: M. *Fang,*
& M. *Snare,* do me, do me, do me your Offices.

  Fal. How now? whose Mare's dead? what's the matter ?
  Fang. Sir *Iohn,* I arrest you, at the suit of Mist. *Quickly.*
  Falst. Away Varlets, draw *Bardolfe* : Cut me off the
Villaines head: throw the Queane in the Channel.
  Host. Throw me in the channell? Ile throw thee there.
Wilt thou? wilt thou? thou bastardly rogue. Murder, mur-
der, O thou Hony-suckle villaine, wilt thou kill Gods of-
ficers, and the Kings? O thou hony-feed Rogue, thou art
a honyfeed, a Man-queller, and a woman-queller.
  Falst. Keep them off, *Bardolfe.*   *Fang.* A rescu, a rescu.
  Host. Good people bring a rescu. Thou wilt not? thou
wilt not? Do, do thou Rogue: Do thou Hempseed.
  Page. Away you Scullion, you Rampallian, you Fustil-
lirian: Ile tucke your Catastrophe.   *Enter. Ch. Iustice.*
  Iust. What's the matter? Keepe the Peace here, hoa.
  Host. Good my Lord be good to mee. I beseech you

Figure 9. Part of
sig. g3 recto of the
1623 Folio,
illustrating the
crowding of text.

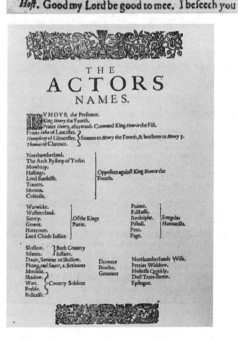

Figure 10. The
last page of the
1623 Folio 2
Henry IV.

'hee's' to 'he is' or 'ile nere' to 'I will neuer', generally turns its archaisms and colloquialisms into more standard usage (for instance 'A calls me enow' to 'He call'd me euen now'), offers a tauter punctuation, reallocates a few speeches, and elides mute or ghost characters. In its more pragmatic stage directions and speech-prefixes, F names characters more functionally and consistently. Some of these features, as well as its restructuring of the drawers in 2.4, the use of a telling block entry at the beginning of 3.2 (*Enter Shallow and Silence*: *with Mouldie, Shadow, Wart, Feeble, Bull-calfe.*), and the cutting of one of three rush-strewers and of one of the two coronation processions in 5.5, may well reflect a theatrical influence, like a prompt-book, on F.[1] Moreover, the stage is cleared seventeen times in the play after the Induction, and Folio provides all but one of the exits, compared to Q, which signals only six of them. On the other hand, F omits many essential exits and entrances which would probably not be the case if the copy for it originated entirely in a prompt-book.[2] Also, there is no record to show that the play had been performed for several years before 1620 so the prompt-book may no longer have been available.[3] Furthermore, since a 'good' quarto was available, albeit in a single edition published over twenty years earlier and missing a number of crucial lines, it would have made sense for the Folio syndicate to use it, *if* it was available.

---

[1] Humphreys (p. lxxv). Prosser (pp. 19–50) disputes that F's stage directions reflect stage practice more effectively than Q's, and she describes the massed entry at Folio 3.2 as 'literary', the expedient act of a scribe unfamiliar with the requirements of a playscript.

[2] Jowett and Taylor (p. 39) note that 'No text [in Folio] was certainly set from a prompt-book, though prompt-books were clearly consulted in order to supplement some of the plays reprinted from earlier editions'; see also Taylor (1993, pp. 65–6).

[3] Davison (p. 291). This argument, however, is not a strong one. Absence of record of performance does not imply absence of performance (cf. *As You Like It*, *Coriolanus*, and *Antony*). A seven-year-long performance lull (as, probably, in this case) does not necessarily imply that therefore the prompt-book would no longer be available. It could rather suggest that Shakespeare's company carefully hoarded its precious dramatic investments, whether in the form of foul papers or prompt-books. No fewer than eight plays in the 1623 Folio were set from foul papers, all of them more than a decade and a half old (the last 'foul paper' play in Folio wholly by Shakespeare is *Antony and Cleopatra*, dated *c.*1606). That there was a performance of *2 Henry IV* in 1612 is suggested by a scrap of paper from the Revels Office (1619) which refers to '... nd Part of Falstaff | ... laid theis 7. yeres', which is commonly taken to state that *2 Henry IV* was last staged in *c.*1612.

That there were problems with the setting of the *Henry* plays is evident from the bibliographical characteristics of the quires in the Folio, and it has already been suggested that this may have been as a result of extra text needing to be accommodated, or for copyright reasons, or both. The evidence for determining the exact nature of the relationship between Q and F of *2 Henry IV* points in opposite directions: that they are interdependent, and that they are in fact independent of each other.

The presence of possible QF common verbal errors such as, for example, 'hole' (Ind. 35), 'inuincible' (3.2.299), and 'rage' (4.1.34), need not necessarily prove the case for dependency, any more than common errors of punctuation and metrically erroneous elisions, since they might be traceable to a common source.[1] More intriguing is the absence of single lines after 4.1.92 and 93 from some copies of Q and from F,[2] and idiosyncratic spellings shared by Q and F at 4.3.163–4, where 'downy' and 'down' are spelt 'dowlny' (Q) and 'dowlney' (F), and 'dowlne' (QF) respectively. If these point to relatedness of the two texts, it is also the case that in the same scene at 4.3.309 Q has 'win' where F has 'ioyne'. F's version cannot conceivably originate in Q's text at this point. Rather, F's version looks suspiciously like misread manuscript, perhaps of 'winne'.[3] Here therefore, in the same scene, the evidence argues both ways. Additional 'proof' against Q, and in

[1] Walker (pp. 113–16). Walker's claim that 2.2.108 can be used to demonstrate dependency of Folio on Q is no more tenable than her argument about the punctuation of 3.2.75–8 from which she deduces that Folio had access to the cancel in QB (Walker, p. 107). Greg (1955, p. 270) instead endorses Shaaber's view (p. 511) that Q and F do not appear to share the 'similarities of spelling, punctuation, and typographical style' that could be expected if F were printed directly from Q.

[2] The omitted lines ('And consecrate commotion's bitter edge?...To brother born an household cruelty,') were deleted from the text during the printing of the quarto with the result that ten surviving copies have the lines and ten do not (Berger, p. viii). That these lines were cut from, rather than added to, Q is demonstrated by the fact that in the corrected state 'the type-page is two lines shorter than normal without them' (Shaaber, p. 468). But Walker (pp. 104–5) argues that the 'correction' constitutes a serious error, in that the lines which were meant to be removed were Mowbray's two and a half lines also starting with 'And' and 'To', which follow shortly after the present cut and immediately precede the excision of Westmorland's and Mowbray's exchange:

[MOWBRAY] And suffer the condition of these times

  To lay a heavy and unequal hand

  Upon our honours?

[3] Humphreys (p. lxxviii).

favour of manuscript, is provided by variants such as F's Basing-stoke (Q: Billingsgate) and Sure-card (Q: Soccard),[1] and by the fact that there are no common errors of lineation.

Furthermore, Taylor (1993, pp. 245–7) has offered a close and cogent analysis of the setting of round brackets by Compositor A?(J?) which strongly supports the manuscript hypothesis. In his stints on the play (just under twelve pages), Compositor A?(J?) set 136 pairs of round brackets, only twenty of which coincide with brackets in Q.[2] In other words, he would have added 116 if he set directly from Q. But his practice in *1 Henry IV* and elsewhere suggests that he tended to follow his copy rather closely with regard to round brackets. Taylor concludes therefore that we can 'be honourably confident that Folio *2 Henry IV* was set from manuscript copy'; and we may also surmise that the 'scribe' of the manuscript for F favoured extensive use of round brackets (as Ralph Crane did).

The two positions about the source of F are not mutually exclusive. In 'A Definitive Text of Shakespeare', Bowers (p. 26) has argued that the 'answer must logically be that for some reason an annotated quarto was transcribed to form a manuscript which was used as printer's copy for the Folio'. But annotating Q to the extent where it becomes the copy for Folio would be a near impossible task, as Prosser notes when reporting her own failed attempt at collating Q and F on a copy of Q.[3] Prosser instead endorses Humphreys's basic position that the copy for F was a transcript which collated QA and a manuscript. It is from this manuscript that 3.1 is retrieved by F. The question then arises about the nature of the manuscript. Humphreys cautiously suggests a prompt-book, whereas Prosser surmises that it is foul papers, and that 'the transcript was prepared for a reader of exclusively literary tastes. It was not prepared to serve as copy

---

[1] Humphreys divides these variants into trivial and significant groups. The former includes (Q mentioned in parenthesis): Whitsun (Wheeson), Henrie (Harrie), Germane (Iarman), Cotsall (Cotsole), Double (Dooble), Bezonian (Besonian), Fang (Phang), Gowre (Gower), Pointz (Poynes); the latter: Stamford (Samforth), Hinckley (Hunkly), Dombledon (Dommelton), Dombe (Dumbe), Bare (Barnes), Amurah (Amurath), Couitha (Coueta). All these latter variants 'would seem to be set up from manuscript rather than print' (p. 78).

[2] Walker (p. 107) notes 'the abundance of *some 260 parentheses in the F text* of the play' as opposed to some 40 in Q.

[3] Prosser (p. 197 n. 17).

for the Folio, an inference that seems self-evident in light of the unique sophistication of the text.'[1]

But what this hypothesis implicitly plays down is the fact that literary manuscripts and printed books were not subject to the restrictions of the 1606 'Profanity Act', the 'Acte to restraine Abuses of Players'.[2] There would therefore be no prima facie case for the purging of the copy which, according to Prosser, became the copy for Folio. But if the manuscript was a prompt-book, or if at least a prompt-book played an important part in its genesis, then it would show signs of being purged if this prompt-book post-dated 1606. As Bevington (1987, pp. 94–5) points out, in 'other First Folio plays excision of profanity is normally associated with the consultation of a manuscript of prompt-book authority perhaps reflecting either changes in performance after 1606, or anticipation of a stage revival'. It may appear then that the copy for Folio was a carefully prepared literary manuscript collating QA and a post-1606 expurgated prompt-book, which corresponds in all essentials to an emended version of the original prompt-book in which Falstaff had already been substituted for Oldcastle.[3] This prompt-book is the source for the eight F-only passages.

If this argument about the prompt-book is correct, it would suggest that *2 Henry IV* continued to be popular on the stage after 1606 (it was almost certainly performed at Court in the winter of 1612–13: see above, p. 42), notwithstanding the fact that it was not *reprinted* between 1600 and 1623. Furthermore, it would indicate that the cutting of the text in Q may reflect a temporary difficulty with the printing of this play which did not

---

[1] Prosser (p. 17). That a fair copy of foul papers underlies the manuscript collated with Q was argued earlier by Walker (p. 109), and Williams (pp. 179–80) cuts Q out altogether and proposes an early fair copy of foul papers (of *c.*1598) as the printer's copy for the Folio text of *2 Henry IV*.

[2] 3 Jac. I, c. 21: 27 May 1606. Taylor (1993, p. 64) notes that 'with the probable exception of the omission of "zounds" in three plays set from annotated quarto copy, all of the Folio expurgation of profanity can be attributed to theatrical practice...profanity had been outlawed from public performances, not private manuscripts or printed texts'; cf. also Greg (1955, p. 151).

[3] Taylor (1993, p. 69) cuts QA out altogether from the process of transmission: 'The Folio text of *2 Henry IV* may therefore derive from a transcript of a late, expurgated prompt-book. That transcript almost certainly went much further in the expurgation of mild profanity than the prompt-book itself; it also cleaned the text of much vulgarity (sexual and otherwise) and colloquialism.'

make the company change the performance text in the prompt-book. From 1600 to 1623 therefore the performed text in the theatre differed from the text printed in Q. From the beginning, performances of *2 Henry IV* included the material that was later found to be objectionable, and *continued* to include it on the stage after the objections were enshrined through cuts in the first printed copies of the play in 1600.

A summary of the textual history of *2 Henry IV* (as it is interpreted in this edition) would look as follows:

(1) Shakespeare's 'foul papers', MS *A1* (1596), are copied to produce a prompt-book, MS *B1* (1596).

(2) (a) MS *B1* is submitted for licensing to the Office of the Revels, and Oldcastle is altered to Falstaff in time for the performances at Court during the 1596–7 season. This altered copy of the original prompt-book is MS *B2*. It remains the company's acting version until 1606. It is then purged of profanities and becomes MS *B3*, the post-1606 prompt-book of the play.

(b) The Epilogues in Q and F suggest that Oldcastle is altered to Falstaff in foul papers during the 1596–7 season, at the same time as in the first prompt-book (MS *B1*). Altering foul papers at a later stage, for the printing of 1600 quarto for example, would have required a rescinding of the Epilogue's promise to revive Falstaff, because by 1600 he had been reported dead in *Henry V* (1598–9). The alterations in foul papers appear to have been carried out rather hurriedly on the original copy, hence the surviving Oldcastle speech-prefix in 1.2. This Falstaff version of foul papers is MS *A2*.[1]

(3) 1600 Q (issues A and B) prints MS *A2* from which a number of lines have been cut to satisfy the licensers of printed matter. Q remains the only printed text of the play for twenty-three years.

(4) QA and MS *B3* are collated in a private, 'literary' transcript to become MS *C*.

(5) Folio prints MS *C* in 1623.

[1] It is also argued here (see above, pp. 14–16) that it is at this stage that Oldcastle is changed to Falstaff in *Part 1*. Rather than showing that Shakespeare created a different Sir John for *Part 2* in the wake of a brush with the authorities over *Part 1*, the evidence may suggest that the same retrospective change was demanded of both plays simultaneously after the submission for licensing of the prompt-book for *Part 2*.

EDITORIAL PROCEDURES

THE text of this edition is modernized in accordance with the principles set out by Stanley Wells and Gary Taylor in *Modernizing Shakespeare's Spelling, with Three Studies in the Text of Henry V* (1979), Taylor's *Henry V* (1982), pp. 75–81, and Wells's *Re-Editing Shakespeare for the Modern Reader* (1984).

I have used broken brackets in stage directions and speech-prefixes to signal editorial decisions which are not universally accepted, and all these are collated. With the exception of addresses such as '(*to Northumberland*)', or visualizing parentheses such as '(*drinking*)' at 4.1.299 (which follows the collated stage direction *He drinks* at 4.1.298.1), all stage directions are fully collated. Among the editorial tradition, the stage directions in this edition are indebted particularly to the Oxford *Complete Works* edited by Stanley Wells, Gary Taylor, *et al.*, although I have generally been more conservative in my pointing of the theatrical action than the Oxford editors. In other respects my text differs significantly from theirs for reasons fully set out in 'The Texts of 2 *Henry IV*' (above, pp. 78–99).

The Oxford *Complete Works* is the source for all quotations from Shakespeare unless otherwise indicated, as for instance in the gloss on *Galloway nags* (2.4.188), where the relevant phrase from *Antony*, 'Yon ribaudred Nagge of Egypt', is quoted from the 1623 Folio.

All quotations from the Bible are from the widely available Geneva Bible (1560) rather than the Bishops' Bible of 1568, which was the text read in church in Shakespeare's time. Shakespeare draws on both in his plays, and although the scholarly consensus favours Geneva over the Bishops' as Shakespeare's Bible, Andrew Gurr has recently shown that for *Henry V* Shakespeare seems to have preferred the Bishops' Bible (*Henry V* (1992), p. 29 n. 1), and in *Henry IV, Part 1* (1987, p. 117) David Bevington also uses the Bishops'.

Rather than simply referring to the passages from Scripture by chapter and verse, I have offered the text as well. Only where space did not permit this, as in the case of Luke 15: 11–32, have I refrained from doing so. The modern editor of Shakespeare can no longer take a knowledge of the Bible for granted in readers of the plays. Similar considerations decided me to quote lines from Shakespeare whenever a point in question could be illuminated particularly well by a Shakespearian cross-reference.

Shakespeare's *2 Henry IV* is heavily indebted to Holinshed's *Chronicles*, but it did not seem practical or useful to offer large, but necessarily excerpted, chunks of Holinshed as an appendix. Shakespeare's use of his main source is as revealing in what he leaves out as in what he incorporates. Bevington's inspired solution of annotating the entire text of the play with reference to Holinshed in a Shakespeare–Holinshed appendix (1987, pp. 287–97) is an attractive strategy. I decided against it in the end, however, because it spreads annotations relevant to Holinshed across three different parts of the edition, the Introduction, the Commentary, and an appendix. No ideal solution short of printing the entire reign of Henry IV from Holinshed suggests itself. To do so would in turn overshadow the importance of other material, such as *Famous Victories*, and distort Shakespeare's eclectic use of his sources. It is the policy of this edition therefore to enshrine as much detailed information as possible about historical source material in the Introduction, and to cross-refer from the Commentary to the Introduction as much as is consonant with clarity and ease of use. All references to Holinshed (and other sources) are, unless otherwise indicated, to Geoffrey Bullough's *Narrative and Dramatic Sources of Shakespeare*.

The texts listed under *Abbreviations and References* (other than editions of the *Works* and of *2 Henry IV*) are deemed to be of general importance for the study of *2 Henry IV*, as well as particularly relevant to the concerns of this edition. Full bibliographical references for other sources are given in the footnotes to the Introduction and in the Commentary.

All differences of lineation between control-text and Folio are collated where they occur. I agree with the Oxford *Complete Shakespeare* in writing Glyndŵr (where Bevington retains 'Glendower'), but I follow Gurr (pp. 63, 92) in retaining 'ancient' for Oxford's 'ensign' to denote Pistol's rank, and for much the same reasons. The case for 'ensign' (adopted by Taylor in *Henry V*) has not been generally accepted and, as Gurr demonstrates, using modernized 'ensign' rather than 'ancient' could in fact be misleading, since contemporary and Elizabethan usage of 'ensign' do not exactly match. 'Ancient' is, as *OED* demonstrates, a corruption of 'ensign' through forms such as *'ensyne'* / *'ancien'*; both 'ensign' and 'ancient' were current in the period, but Shakespeare chose to write 'ancient', which alone generates important structures of ambiguities which are exploited by Shakespeare both here (as Gurr shows) and particularly in *Othello*.

My Act and Scene divisions follow Folio (which treats the Induction as Scene 1), except in Act 4, where I follow Capell in creating a separate 4.2 which involves Falstaff, Coleville, and John of Lancaster.

In the collations, Qa denotes uncorrected Quarto, while Qb and Qc record known press corrections in Quarto. Fa and Fb similarly signal uncorrected and corrected F.

Abbreviations and References

EDITIONS OF SHAKESPEARE

Q	1600 quarto
QA	First Issue of Q
QB	Second Issue of Q
F, F1	The First Folio, 1623
F2	The Second Folio, 1632
F3	The Third Folio, 1663
F4	The Fourth Folio, 1685
Alexander	Peter Alexander, *Complete Works* (1951)
Berger	Thomas L. Berger, *The Second Part of King Henry The Fourth 1600* (Oxford, 1990)
Betterton	Thomas Betterton, *The Sequel of Henry the Fourth* (1721)
Bevington	David Bevington, *Complete Works* (Glenview, Ill., 1980)
Bevington 1987	David Bevington, *Henry IV, Part 1* (Oxford, 1987)
Cambridge	W. G. Clark and W. A. Wright, *Works*, 9 vols. (Cambridge, 1863–6)
Cambridge 1893	W. A. Wright, *Works*, 9 vols. (Cambridge, 1891–3)
Capell	Edward Capell, *Works of Shakespeare* (1768)
Collier	John Payne Collier, *Works of Shakespeare* (1844)
Collier 1858	John Payne Collier, *Works* (1858)

Collier 1876	John Payne Collier, *Works* (1876)
Cowl	R. P. Cowl, *The Second Part of King Henry the Fourth*, The Arden Shakespeare (1923)
Craig	W. J. Craig, *Works of Shakespeare* (1891)
Davison	P. H. Davison, *The Second Part of King Henry The Fourth*, The New Penguin Shakespeare (Harmondsworth, 1977)
Deighton	K. Deighton, *Henry IV, Second Part* (1893)
Delius	N. Delius, *Shakespeares Werke* (Elberfeld, 1854)
Dyce	Alexander Dyce, *Works of Shakespeare* (1857)
Gurr	Andrew Gurr, *Henry V*, The New Cambridge Shakespeare (Cambridge, 1992)
Hanmer	Thomas Hanmer, *Works of Shakespeare* (Oxford, 1744)
Hemingway	S. B. Hemingway, *The Second Part of King Henry IV*, The Yale Shakespeare (New Haven, Conn., 1921)
Hinman	Charlton Hinman, *The First Folio of Shakespeare* (New York, 1968)
Humphreys	A. R. Humphreys, *The Second Part of King Henry IV*, The Arden Shakespeare (1966)
Humphreys 1960	A. R. Humphreys, *The First Part of King Henry IV*, The Arden Shakespeare (1960)
Johnson	Samuel Johnson, *Plays of Shakespeare* (1765)
Keightley	Thomas Keightley, *Plays of Shakespeare* (1864)
Kittredge	George Lyman Kittredge, *Complete Works* (Boston, 1936)
Knight	C. Knight, *Works of Shakespeare* (1838–43)
Malone	Edmond Malone, *Plays and Poems of Shakespeare* (1790)
Melchiori	Giorgio Melchiori, *The Second Part of King Henry IV*, The New Cambridge Shakespeare (Cambridge, 1989)
Munro	John Munro, *The London Shakespeare*, 6 vols. (1958)
Oliver	H. J. Oliver, *The Merry Wives of Windsor*, The Arden Shakespeare (1971)
Oxford	Stanley Wells, Gary Taylor, *et al.*, *The Complete Works* (Oxford, 1986)
Pope	Alexander Pope, *Works of Shakespeare* (1725)
Pope 1728	Alexander Pope, *Works of Shakespeare* (1728)
Rann	Joseph Rann, *Dramatic Works of Shakespeare* (Oxford, 1786–94)

Ridley	M. R. Ridley, *Henry IV, Second Part*, The New Temple Shakespeare (1934)
Riverside	G. Blakemore Evans, *The Riverside Shakespeare* (Boston, 1974)
Rowe	Nicholas Rowe, *Works of Shakespeare* (1709)
Rowe 1714	Nicholas Rowe, *Works of Shakespeare* (1714)
Shaaber	Matthias A. Shaaber, *The Second Part of Henry the Fourth*, The New Variorum Shakespeare (Philadelphia, 1940)
Singer	S. W. Singer, *Dramatic Works of Shakespeare* (Chiswick, 1826)
Singer 1856	S. W. Singer, *Dramatic Works* (1856)
Sisson	C. J. Sisson, *Complete Works* (1954)
Staunton	Howard Staunton, *Plays of Shakespeare* (1858)
Steevens	Samuel Johnson and George Steevens, *Plays* (1773)
Steevens 1778	Samuel Johnson and George Steevens, *Plays* (1778)
Steevens–Reed	Samuel Johnson, George Steevens, and Isaac Reed, *Plays* (1785)
Steevens–Reed 1793	George Steevens and Isaac Reed, *Plays* (1793)
Taylor	Neil Taylor, *Henry IV, Part Two* (1992)
Theobald	Lewis Theobald, *Works of Shakespeare* (1733)
Theobald 1740	Lewis Theobald, *Works* (1740)
Warburton	William Warburton, *Works of Shakespeare* (1747)
Wilson	John Dover Wilson, *The Second Part of the History of Henry IV*, The New Shakespeare (Cambridge, 1946)
Winstanley	L. Winstanley, *Henry IV, Part 2* (New York, 1918)

OTHER ABBREVIATIONS

Abbott	E. A. Abbott, *A Shakespearian Grammar*, third edition (1870)
AEB	*Analytical and Enumerative Bibliography*
AUMLA	*Journal of the Australasian Universities Language and Literature Association*
Ax	Hermann Ax, *The Relation of Shakespeare's Henry IV to Holinshed* (Freiburg-im-Breisgau, 1912)

B & P	H. C. Bartlett and A. W. Pollard, *A Census of Shakespeare's Plays in Quarto: 1594–1709* (New Haven, 1939)
Baigent	F. J. Baigent and J. E. Millard, *The History of the Ancient Town and Manor of Basingstoke* (Basingstoke, 1889)
Bale	John Bale, *A Brief Chronicle concerning the Examination and Death of the Blessed Martyr of Christ, Sir John Oldcastle, the Lord Cobham* (1544)
Bate	Jonathan Bate, 'Shakespeare Nationalised, Shakespeare Privatised', *English*, 42 (1993), 1–18
Berger and Williams	Thomas L. Berger and George Walton Williams, 'Variants in the Quarto of Shakespeare's *2 Henry IV*', *The Library*, 6th series, 3 (1981), 109–18
Berry	Ralph Berry, 'The Scenic Language of *Henry IV*', in *Elizabethan Theatre XII*, ed. A. L. Magnusson (1993), 181–91
Bevington 1986	David Bevington (ed.), *Henry IV, Parts 1 and 2, Critical Essays* (New York and London, 1986)
Bloom 1987	Harold Bloom (ed.), *William Shakespeare's Henry IV, Part 2* (New York, 1987)
Bloom 1992	Harold Bloom (ed.), *Falstaff* (New York, 1992)
Booth	Stephen Booth, *The Book Called Holinshed's Chronicles: An account of its inception, purpose, contributors, contents, publication, revision and influence on William Shakespeare* (San Francisco, 1968)
Bowers	Fredson Bowers, 'A Definitive Text of Shakespeare: Problems and Methods', in *Studies in Shakespeare*, ed. Arthur D. Matthews and Clark M. Emery (Coral Gables, Fla., 1953)
Bradley	A. C. Bradley, 'The Rejection of Falstaff', *Oxford Lectures on Poetry* (1909), 247–75
Bullough	Geoffrey Bullough, *Narrative and Dramatic Sources of Shakespeare*, vol. 4 (1962)
Capell 1774	Edward Capell, *Notes and Various Readings to Shakespeare*, Part the first (1774)
Chambers 1923	E. K. Chambers, *The Elizabethan Stage*, 4 vols. (Oxford, 1923)
Chambers 1930	E. K. Chambers, *William Shakespeare*, 2 vols. (Oxford, 1930)

Clare	Janet Clare, '*Art made tongue-tied by authority*': *Elizabethan and Jacobean Dramatic Censorship* (Manchester, 1990)
Corbin	Peter Corbin and Douglas Sedge (eds.), *The Oldcastle controversy: Sir John Oldcastle, Part 1 and The Famous Victories of Henry V* (Manchester, 1991)
CQ	*The Cambridge Quarterly*
CW	Samuel Daniel, *Civil Wars* (1595), Bullough, pp. 282–6
Davison 1977	Peter Davison, 'The Printing of the Folio Edition of *2 Henry IV*', *The Library*, 32 (1977), 256–51
Dent	R. W. Dent, *Shakespeare's Proverbial Language: An Index* (1981)
Dering	The Dering MS, *William Shakespeare*, '*The History of King Henry the Fourth*', *As Revised by Sir Edward Dering, Bart.*, ed. George Walton Williams and G. Blakemore Evans (Charlottesville, Va., 1974)
DNB	*The Dictionary of National Biography*
Donno	Elizabeth Story Donno, 'Some Aspects of Shakespeare's Holinshed', *HLQ* 50 (1987), 229–48
Dutton 1991	Richard Dutton, *Mastering the Revels: The Regulation and Censorship of English Renaissance Drama* (1991)
Dutton 1993	'Marlowe and Shakespeare: Censorship and Construction', *The Yearbook of English Studies*, 23 (1993), 1–29
EC	*Essays in Criticism*
ELR	*English Literary Renaissance*
Everett	Barbara Everett, 'The Fatness of Falstaff: Shakespeare and Character', *Proceedings of the British Academy*, 76 (1990), 109–28
Fehrenbach	Robert J. Fehrenbach, 'When Lord Cobham and Edmund Tilney "were att odds": Oldcastle, Falstaff, and the Date of *1 Henry IV*', *SSt* 27 (1986), 87–101
Ferguson	W. Craig Ferguson, *Valentine Simmes: Printer to Drayton, Shakespeare . . . and other Elizabethans* (Charlottesville, Va., 1968)
FV	Anon., *The Famous Victories of Henry the Fifth* (1598), Bullough, pp. 299–343
Gira	Catherine Gira *et al.*, *Henry IV, Parts 1 and 2: An Annotated Bibliography* (New York, 1994)

Goldberg	Jonathan Goldberg, *Sodometries: Renaissance Texts, Modern Sexualities* (Stanford, 1992), 145–75
Greenblatt	Stephen Greenblatt, 'Invisible Bullets: Renaissance Authority and Its Subversion', in Bloom 1987, 125–50
Greg 1942	W. W. Greg, *The Editorial Problem in Shakespeare. A Survey of the Foundations of the Text* (Oxford, 1942)
Greg 1950	W. W. Greg, 'The Rationale of Copy-Text', *SB* 3 (1950), 19–36
Greg 1955	W. W. Greg, *The Shakespeare First Folio: Its Bibliographical and Textual History* (Oxford, 1955)
Greg 1956	W. W. Greg, *Some Aspects and Problems of London Publishing Between 1550 and 1650* (1956)
H & S	*The Works of Ben Jonson*, ed. C. H. Herford and Percy and Evelyn Simpson, 11 vols. (1925–52)
Hart	Alfred Hart, 'Was the Second Part of *King Henry the Fourth* censored?' in *Shakespeare and the Homilies* (1934), 154–218
Hinman	Charlton Hinman, *The Printing and Proof-Reading of the First Folio of Shakespeare*, 2 vols. (Oxford, 1963)
HLQ	*Huntington Library Quarterly*
Holinshed	Raphael Holinshed, *The Third Volume of Chronicles*, second edn. (1587)
Honigmann	E. A. J. Honigmann, 'Sir John Oldcastle: Shakespeare's martyr', in *'Fanned and Winnowed Opinions': Shakespearean Essays Presented to Harold Jenkins*, ed. John W. Mahon and Thomas A. Pendleton (1987), 118–32
Hotson	J. Leslie Hotson, *Shakespeare versus Shallow* (1931)
Hunter	G. K. Hunter, 'Religious Nationalism in Later History Plays', in *Literature and Nationalism*, ed. A. Thorpe (Liverpool, 1991), 88–97
Huntley	Richard Webster Huntley, *A Glossary of the Cotswold (Gloucestershire) Dialect* (1868)
Jacob	E. F. Jacob, *The Fifteenth Century 1399–1485*, The Oxford History of England VI (Oxford, 1961)
Jenkins	Harold Jenkins, *The Structural Problem in Shakespeare's 'Henry the Fourth'* (1956)
Jowett	John Jowett, 'Cuts and Casting: Author and Book-Keeper in the Folio text of 2 *Henry IV*', *AUMLA*, 72 (1989), 275–95

Jowett and Taylor	John Jowett and Gary Taylor, 'The Three Texts of 2 *Henry IV*', *SB* 40 (1987), 31–50
Kastan	David Scott Kastan, '"Killed with Hard Opinions": Oldcastle, Falstaff, and the Reformed Text of *1 Henry IV*' (forthcoming)
Kerrigan	John Kerrigan, '*Henry IV* and the Death of Old Double', *EC* 40 (1990), 24–53
Knowles	Richard Knowles, 'Unquiet and the Double Plot of *2 Henry IV*', *SSt* 2 (1966), 133–40
Lee	Sidney Lee and C. T. Onions, *Shakespeare's England: An Account of the Life and Manners of his Age*, 2 vols. (Oxford, 1916)
Linthicum	M. Channing Linthicum, *Costume in the Drama of Shakespeare and his Contemporaries* (Oxford, 1936)
Madden	D. H. Madden, *The Diary of Master William Silence. A Study of Shakespeare and of Elizabethan Sport* (1907)
McKeen	David McKeen, *A Memory of Honour: The Life of William Brooke, Lord Cobham*, 2 vols. (Salzburg, 1986)
MSR	Malone Society Reprints
N & Q	*Notes and Queries*
Noble	Richmond Noble, *Shakespeare's Biblical Knowledge* (1935)
OED	*The Oxford English Dictionary*, second edition (Oxford, 1989)
Onions	C. T. Onions, *A Shakespeare Glossary* (Oxford, 1911; revised Robert D. Eagleson, 1986)
Palmer	Roy Palmer, *The Folklore of Gloucestershire* (Tiverton, Devon, 1994)
Partridge	Eric Partridge, *Shakespeare's Bawdy* (1947; second edn., repr. 1993)
Patterson	Annabel Patterson, *Reading Holinshed's Chronicles* (1994)
Pendleton	Thomas A. Pendleton, '"This is not the man": On Calling Falstaff Falstaff', *AEB* 4 (1990), 59–71
Pollard 1909	A. W. Pollard, *Shakespeare Folios and Quartos* (1909)
Pollard 1920	A. W. Pollard, 'Variant Settings in *II Henry IV*', *TLS*, 21 October 1920, p. 680
Prosser	Eleanor Prosser, *Shakespeare's Anonymous Editors: Scribe and Compositors in the Folio Text of '2 Henry IV*' (Stanford, 1981)

Rackin	Phyllis Rackin, *Stages of History : Shakespeare's English Chronicles* (New York, 1990)
RES	*Review of English Studies*
RSC	Royal Shakespeare Company
SB	*Studies in Bibliography*
Schmidt	Alexander Schmidt, *Shakespeare Lexicon and Quotation Dictionary*, third edn., revised Gregor Sarrazin (Berlin, 1871)
Schoenbaum	S. Schoenbaum, *William Shakespeare : Records and Images* (1981)
Scoufos	Alice-Lyle Scoufos, *Shakespeare's Typological Satire: A Study of the Falstaff–Oldcastle Problem* (Athens, Ohio, 1979)
SEL	*Studies in English Literature*
Shaaber 1948	Matthias A. Shaaber, 'The Unity of *Henry IV* ', *Joseph Quincy Adams Memorial Studies*, ed. James G. McManaway *et al.* (1948), 217–27
Sharpe	Robert Boies Sharpe, *The Real War of the Theatres. Shakespeare's Fellows in Rivalry with the Admiral's Men, 1594–1603. Repertoires, Devices, and Types* (Baltimore, 1935)
ShS	*Shakespeare Survey*
Smith	A. H. Smith, *The Place Names of Gloucestershire* (Cambridge, 1964)
Spevack	Marvin Spevack, *Complete and Systematic Concordance to the Works of Shakespeare* (1968–80)
Sprague	Arthur C. Sprague, *Shakespeare's Histories: Plays for the Stage* (1964)
SQ	*Shakespeare Quarterly*
SSt	*Shakespeare Studies*
Stow 1580	John Stow, *Chronicles of England* (1580)
Stow 1592	John Stow, *Annales of England* (1592)
Stow 1603	John Stow, *A Survey of London* (1603), 2 vols. (repr. 1908)
subs.	substantively
Sugden	Edward Sugden, *A Topographical Dictionary to the Works of Shakespeare and His Fellow Dramatists* (Manchester, 1925)
Taylor 1985	Gary Taylor, 'The Fortunes of Oldcastle', *ShS* 38 (1985), 85–100

Taylor 1987	Gary Taylor, 'William Shakespeare, Richard James, and the House of Cobham', *RES*, NS 38 (1987), 334–54
Taylor 1993	Gary Taylor, ''Swounds Revisited: Theatrical, Editorial, and Literary Expurgation', in Gary Taylor and John Jowett, *Shakespeare Reshaped 1606–1623* (Oxford, 1993), 51–106
Textual Companion	Stanley Wells, Gary Taylor, *et al.*, *William Shakespeare: A Textual Companion* (Oxford, 1987)
Thirlby	Styan Thirlby, whose manuscript annotations of contemporary editions (such as Pope's 1725) influenced Theobald's (1733) and Johnson's
Tilley	M. P. Tilley, *A Dictionary of the Proverbs in England in the Sixteenth and Seventeenth Centuries* (Ann Arbor, 1950)
TLS	*The Times Literary Supplement*
Tyrwhitt	Thomas Tyrwhitt, *Observations and Conjectures upon Some Passages of Shakespeare* (1766)
Vaughan	H. B. Vaughan, *New Readings and Renderings of Shakespeare's Tragedies*, 3 vols. (1878–86)
Vickers	Brian Vickers, *The Artistry of Shakespeare's Prose* (1968)
Walker	Alice Walker, *Textual Problems of The First Folio* (Cambridge, 1953)
Waugh	W. T. Waugh, 'Sir John Oldcastle', *English Historical Review*, 20 (1905), 434–56 and 637–58
Wells 1979	Stanley Wells, 'Modernizing Shakespeare's Spelling', in Stanley Wells and Gary Taylor, *Modernizing Shakespeare's Spelling, With Three Studies in the Text of 'Henry V'* (1979)
Wells 1984	Stanley Wells, *Re-Editing Shakespeare for the Modern Reader* (Oxford, 1984)
Wells 1994	Stanley Wells, *Shakespeare. A Dramatic Life* (1994)
Williams	George Walton Williams, 'The text of *2 Henry IV*: facts and problems', *SSt* 9 (1976), 173–82
Williams 1994	Gordon Williams, *A Dictionary of Sexual Language and Imagery in Shakespearean and Stuart Literature*, 3 vols. (1994)
Wilson 1943	John Dover Wilson, *The Fortunes of Falstaff* (Cambridge, 1943)

Yeandle   Laetitia Yeandle, 'The Dating of Sir Edward Dering's Copy of "The History of King Henry the Fourth"', *SQ* 37 (1986), 224–6

The History of King Henry the Fourth,
Part 2

THE PERSONS OF THE PLAY

RUMOUR, the Presenter

KING HENRY IV
PRINCE HENRY, later KING HENRY V
PRINCE JOHN of Lancaster   } sons of King Henry IV
Humphrey, Duke of GLOUCESTER
Thomas, Duke of CLARENCE

Earl of WARWICK
Earl of SURREY
Earl of WESTMORLAND   } of King Henry IV's party
HARCOURT
Sir John Blunt

Scrope, ARCHBISHOP OF YORK
LORD BARDOLPH
Thomas, Lord MOWBRAY, the Earl Marshal   } rebels
Lord HASTINGS
Sir John COLEVILLE

Percy, Earl of NORTHUMBERLAND
LADY NORTHUMBERLAND, his wife
Kate, LADY PERCY, Hotspur's widow   } rebels
TRAVERS, Northumberland's servant
MORTON, messenger from Shrewsbury
Northumberland's PORTER

LORD CHIEF JUSTICE
SERVANT of the Lord Chief Justice
GOWER, a messenger

Sir John FALSTAFF
PAGE, Falstaff's servant
BARDOLPH
PISTOL   } 'irregular humorists'
POINS
PETO

MISTRESS QUICKLY

DOLL TEARSHEET

Robert SHALLOW }
SILENCE   } country justices
DAVY, Shallow's servant

Ralph MOULDY ⎫
Simon SHADOW ⎪
Thomas WART   ⎬ country recruits
Francis FEEBLE ⎪
Peter BULLCALF ⎭

FANG } two sergeants
SNARE

FRANCIS ⎫
WILLIAM ⎬ drawers at the Boar's Head
SECOND DRAWER ⎭

Musicians

FIRST BEADLE

FIRST GROOM
SECOND GROOM

Page to the King

MESSENGER

Soldiers, Attendants, Beadles

EPILOGUE

The Second Part of Henry the Fourth, Continuing to his Death, and Coronation of Henry the Fifth

Induction   *Enter Rumour painted full of tongues*
RUMOUR

Open your ears; for which of you will stop
The vent of hearing when loud Rumour speaks?
I from the orient to the drooping west,
Making the wind my post-horse, still unfold
The acts commencèd on this ball of earth.   5
Upon my tongues continual slanders ride,
The which in every language I pronounce,
Stuffing the ears of men with false reports.
I speak of peace, while covert enmity
Under the smile of safety wounds the world;   10
And who but Rumour, who but only I,
Make fearful musters, and prepared defence,

Title *Continuing . . . Fifth*] Q; *Containing his Death: and the coronation of King Henry the Fift.* F
    Induction] F (*Actus Primus. Scaena Prima.* | INDVCTION.); *not in* Q   0.1 *painted . . . tongues*]
    not in F   1 RUMOUR] CAPELL; *not in* QF   6 tongues] Q; Tongue F   8 men] Q; them F

Induction This denoting of Rumour's lines
first appears in F, which also introduces
Act and Scene divisions; there are
none in Q. In Shakespeare the phrase
usually signals the first steps of an enterprise as in *Richard III* 1.1.32 and *1 Henry
IV* 3.1.2. Its presence here may reflect F's
desire for structural tidiness, to balance
the Epilogue, which is formally identified
as such by both Q and F. F counts the
Induction as Scene 1. Rumour's lines
35–7 localize the scene as the Percies'
stronghold, Warkworth Castle in Northumberland.

0.1 *Rumour . . . tongues* The iconography of
Rumour's appearance as 'full of tongues'
was well established by the early sixteenth century (cf. Knowles, p. 134),
and in 1553 the Revels Office paid for a
coat and cap to be painted with 'Ies [eyes]
tonges and eares for fame'. The passage
which Shakespeare recalls here is Virgil's

portrayal of 'Fama' (i.e. Rumour) in *Aeneid*, where 'Rumour is fleet of foot, and
swift are her wings; she is a vast, fearful
monster, with a watchful eye miracu-
lously set under every feather which
grows on her, and for every one of them
a tongue in a mouth which is loud of
speech, and an ear ever alert' (*Aeneid* 4.
180–3; trans. W. F. Jackson Knight,
1956).

3 **drooping** because the sun declines
('droops') in there

4 **post-horse** a horse kept at a post-house or
inn for the use of postriders, or for hire by
travellers (*OED*)
still always, continually

5 **acts** actions, with a pun on the 'acts' of a
play, because Rumour is here cast as
presenter ('unfold') of the drama.

12 **fearful . . . defence** enrolment of troops
and readied defences inspired by fear

117

Whiles the big year, swoll'n with some other grief,
Is thought with child by the stern tyrant war,
And no such matter? Rumour is a pipe,   15
Blown by surmises, Jealousy's conjectures,
And of so easy and so plain a stop
That the blunt monster with uncounted heads,
The still-discordant wav'ring multitude,
Can play upon it. But what need I thus   20
My well-known body to anatomize
Among my household? Why is Rumour here?
I run before King Harry's victory,
Who in a bloody field by Shrewsbury
Hath beaten down young Hotspur and his troops,   25
Quenching the flame of bold rebellion
Even with the rebels' blood. But what mean I
To speak so true at first? My office is
To noise abroad that Harry Monmouth fell
Under the wrath of noble Hotspur's sword,   30
And that the King before the Douglas' rage
Stooped his anointed head as low as death.
This have I rumoured through the peasant towns
Between that royal field of Shrewsbury

13 Whiles] Q; Whil'st F   grief] Q; griefs F   16 Jealousy's conjectures] Q (Iealousies coniectures); ~, ~ F   19 wav'ring] Q; wauering F   27 rebels'] THEOBALD 1740; rebels QF   34 that] Q; the F

13 **big** pregnant, i.e. full of uncomfortable business ('grief')

15 **pipe** recorder, a small wind instrument like a 'vertical' flute or flageolet

16 **Jealousy** suspicion (rather than 'envy': *OED* 5)

17 **so...stop** Either (a) its vents so easily mastered, or (b) its vents themselves are so easy ('plain') as not to require any mastery in the playing. A 'stop' on a recorder is a vent-hole through which the notes are produced. Shaaber (p. 13) thinks that 'stop' here denotes the act of stopping the vents, but refers to *Hamlet* as illustrating the meaning of 'stop' = vent (cf. *Hamlet* 3.2.68–9: 'That they are not a pipe for Fortune's finger | To sound what stop she please', and 3.2.345–7 'Govern these ventages with your fingers and thumb, give it breath with your

mouth, and it will discourse most excellent music').

18 **blunt** dull, insensitive, obtuse (*OED a.* 1)
monster...heads Cf. the proverb 'A multitude of people is a beast of many heads' (Dent M1308).

19 **still-discordant** forever at odds

22 **household** audience (both inside the play and in the theatre)

23 **King Harry's victory** The Battle of Shrewsbury, won by the forces of Henry IV and dramatized in *1 Henry IV*, Acts 4–5.

29 **Monmouth** Prince Henry (Hal) was born at Monmouth in 1387, hence the surname.

33 **peasant** country, rustic. The term is used pejoratively and suggests that lowly people are credulous and easily duped by Rumour.

And this worm-eaten hold of raggèd stone,   35
Where Hotspur's father, old Northumberland,
Lies crafty-sick. The posts come tiring on,
And not a man of them brings other news
Than they have learned of me. From Rumour's tongues
They bring smooth comforts false, worse than true
   wrongs.   *Exit*   40

I.I   *Enter Lord Bardolph at one door*

LORD BARDOLPH
Who keeps the gate here, ho? Where is the Earl?

35 hold] THEOBALD; hole QF   36 Where] F; When Q   40 *Exit*] F; *exit Rumours.* Q
I.I.O.I *Enter ... door*] Q (*Enter the Lord Bardolfe at one doore.*); *Enter Lord Bardolfe, and the Porter.* F

35 **hold** fortress (cf. stronghold). Both Q and F have 'hole', and I follow Theobald in changing <e> to <d>, which are easily confused in secretary hand. Shaaber (p. 15) retains 'hole', but concedes (p. 509) that an <e>/<d> confusion did occur here in the text of F as a result of F being set from a manuscript rather than from Q. Davison (p. 166) rejects the surmised iterative linkage of 'worm-eaten', 'hole' and 'raggèd' by pointing out that 'worm-eaten' could denote arrow-slits in the walls and 'raggèd' the usual castellations of a fortified place.

37 **crafty-sick** feigning illness. Northumberland's sickness is not attributed to subterfuge in *1 Henry IV* 4.4.14 ('the sickness of Northumberland'), or in Holinshed (Bullough, p. 186) and Daniel (*CW*, 3. 97).
   tiring on (a) exhausting themselves and their horses; (b) in tearing haste

I.I.O.I **Lord Bardolph** He is listed by Holinshed (Bullough, p. 270) among the main conspirators who, with Northumberland, Scrope, Mowbray *et al.*, rose against the King in the summer of 1405, the historical date of this scene (although at 3.1.59 Shakespeare seems to think it should be 1407, because of King Henry's reference to 1399 as 'eight years since'). Bardolph is Northumberland's partner in the later insurrection which culminates in the Battle of Bramham Moor (1408) where Northumberland was 'slaine outright' while Bardolph was 'sore wounded, so that he

shortlie after died of the hurts' (Bullough, p. 275); see Introduction, p. 30.

O.I **at one door** It is usually assumed that three different points of entry are required for the rapid succession of dialogue by Lord Bardolph, the Porter, and Northumberland. Oxford posits a balcony (*Enter Porter [above]*) for the Porter's entry, while other editors (Shaaber, Humphreys, Davison, Melchiori) acknowledge that there is a problem, but do not clarify the positioning of the doors. Q provides no wholly reliable guidance for the Porter's entry or that of Northumberland. Its specifying '*one door*' suggests that Shakespeare visualized at least one *other* door (the one through which Northumberland enters), but its omission of an entry for the Porter may be deliberate. It may be as natural for the Porter here to speak from within as it is for the Porter in *Macbeth* 2.3 to be 'without' (i.e. on-stage) while responding to knocking inside. This hypothesis would seem to be supported by the dialogue, with the Porter instructing Lord Bardolph to knock at the gate and Lord Bardolph's reply 'Here comes the Earl' (I.I.6). This line might seem redundant if the Porter and Lord Bardolph were both on stage together, but natural if the Porter were out of sight. As well as identifying the Earl for the audience, Lord Bardolph tells the Porter that his further services are not now required.

I **here** i.e. at Warkworth Castle in Northumberland

PORTER ⌈*within*⌉
  What shall I say you are?
LORD BARDOLPH   Tell thou the Earl
  That the Lord Bardolph doth attend him here.
PORTER ⌈*within*⌉
  His lordship is walked forth into the orchard.
  Please it your honour knock but at the gate,   5
  And he himself will answer.
        Enter the Earl of Northumberland as sick, with a crutch
        and coif
LORD BARDOLPH   Here comes the Earl.
NORTHUMBERLAND
  What news, Lord Bardolph? Every minute now
  Should be the father of some stratagem.   *effort, Straining]*
  The times are wild; contention, like a horse
  Full of high feeding, madly hath broke loose   10
  And bears down all before him.
LORD BARDOLPH   Noble Earl,
  I bring you certain news from Shrewsbury.
NORTHUMBERLAND
  Good, an God will.
LORD BARDOLPH   As good as heart can wish.
  The King is almost wounded to the death,
  And, in the fortune of my lord your son,   15
  Prince Harry slain outright; and both the Blunts

2, 4 *within*] This edition; *not in* QF   6 *Enter . . . coif*] Q (*Enter the Earle Northumberland.*); *Enter Northumberland.* F   *as . . . coif*] OXFORD; *not in* QF   7 Every] Q; Eu'ry F   13 God] Q; heauen F

---

4 **orchard** garden (*OED* 1a *obs.*)
6 *coif* nightcap
8 **stratagem** a violent and bloody deed (rather than the modern meaning of 'plot')
10 **Full of high feeding** too richly fed (*OED*, *high*, *a.* 8 = luxurious, of food and drink); cf. the 'soilèd horse' in *Lear* 4.5.120.
12 **certain** definite (*OED a.* 3)
15 **in . . . son** as far as your son's predicament is concerned
16–17 **both . . . Douglas** Sir Walter Blunt '*disguised as the King*' is killed by Douglas in *1 Henry IV* 5.3.13 at the Battle of Shrewsbury. Shakespeare does not men-

tion another Blunt, nor does Holinshed (who, however, relates Sir Walter Blunt's death twice: Bullough, p. 191). In *Civil Wars* 3.111–12 (Bullough, pp. 214–15), however, Daniel records that 'Another of that forward name and race' was killed, and he identifies him in the margin as 'Another Blunt which was the kings Standard bearer' (Bullough, p. 215). A Blunt is referred to in the text at 2 *Henry IV* 4.2.72, and a Sir John Blunt appears as a non-speaking member of the council in the Q version of 3.1.31.1. Also in the Q version (but not in F) of 5.2.41.1 a Blunt enters as the Prince's companion.

Killed by the hand of Douglas; young Prince John
And Westmorland and Stafford fled the field,
And Harry Monmouth's brawn, the hulk Sir John,   *Falstaff*
Is prisoner to your son. O, such a day,   20
So fought, so followed, and so fairly won,
Came not till now to dignify the times
Since Caesar's fortunes.

NORTHUMBERLAND   How is this derived?
Saw you the field? Came you from Shrewsbury?

LORD BARDOLPH

I spake with one, my lord, that came from thence,   25
A gentleman well bred and of good name,
That freely rendered me these news for true.
          Enter Travers

NORTHUMBERLAND

Here comes my servant Travers, who I sent
On Tuesday last to listen after news.

LORD BARDOLPH

My lord, I overrode him on the way,   30
And he is furnished with no certainties

27.1 *Enter Travers] as here* CAPELL; *opposite l. 25* Q; *after l. 29* F   28 who] Q; whom F

18 **Stafford fled** Rumour is (deliberately?) mistaken. The Earl of Stafford was one of those dressed in the King's clothes and armour at Shrewsbury, and was killed in battle: cf. *1 Henry IV* 5.3.7-9.

19 **brawn** boar fattened for the table
hulk commonly used of large ships, hence (as here) a big unwieldy person

21 **So…won** This recalls Julius Caesar's famous 'Veni, vidi, vici' ('I came, I saw, I overcame') which Falstaff quotes at 4.2.40-1, and which is referred to by 'Caesar's fortunes' at line 23.

23 **fortunes** success (*OED, fortune, sb.* 4)

27 **freely** of his own accord
these news In Elizabethan usage news can be both singular and plural (Shaaber, p. 22).

28 **who** whom (Abbott, §274)

30 **overrode** outrode (Humphreys, p. 9; Davison, p. 169). Melchiori (p. 62) retains Q's Sir *Iohn Vmfrevile* at line 34, and prefers to interpret as 'overtook' (*OED, override, v.* 4). While the context renders a reading of 'overtook' almost impossible,

the imagined action is complex. Lord Bardolph learns from a 'gentleman well bred' (l. 26) that the rebels have won at Shrewsbury. With this report he hastens towards Warkworth Castle. On the way there he encounters Northumberland's post Travers, hastily passes the good (but false) news to him, and at once proceeds on his journey. Travers, who is less well horsed, falls behind (outridden by Bardolph) and is in turn overtaken by a frantic post from Shrewsbury. This (unidentified) gentleman imparts the *true* news of the rebels' defeat to Travers who, on Bardolph's heels, continues his rush back to Warkworth Castle. Shakespeare envisages no fewer than four messengers with the news from Shrewsbury—two (one wrong and one right) from the battlefield, and two (Bardolph and Travers) relaying their news to Northumberland—to underline the chaos and confusion of the battle's aftermath, and the way in which historical fact is distorted in the reporting even as it happens.

More than he haply may retail from me.

NORTHUMBERLAND

Now, Travers, what good tidings comes with you?

TRAVERS

My lord, Lord Bardolph turned me back
With joyful tidings, and being better horsed   35
Outrode me. After him came spurring hard
A gentleman, almost forspent with speed,
That stopped by me to breathe his bloodied horse.
He asked the way to Chester, and of him
I did demand what news from Shrewsbury.   40
He told me that rebellion had bad luck,
And that young Harry Percy's spur was cold.
With that he gave his able horse the head,
And, bending forward, struck his armèd heels
Against the panting sides of his poor jade   45
Up to the rowel-head; and starting so,
He seemed in running to devour the way,
Staying no longer question.

NORTHUMBERLAND   Ha? Again:

33 with] Q; frō F   34 Lord Bardolph] OXFORD; sir Iohn Vmfreuile QF, CAPELL   36 hard]
Q; head F   41 bad] Q; ill F   44 forward] Q; forwards F   armèd] Q; able F

34 **Lord Bardolph** Following Capell and
Oxford I have changed Q's and F's 'Sir
John Umfrevile' (retained by Shaaber,
Humphreys, Davison, Melchiori) to
'Lord Bardolph', notwithstanding the
awkward rhythm of 'My lord, Lord Bardolph' and the creation of an octosyllabic
line. Shaaber (p. 24) wonders why no
editor (including himself) has changed
the reading of the line, and approvingly
cites Chambers's hypothesis that 'Lord
Bardolph has replaced Sir John Umfreville through a belated historical correction, not fully carried out'. As a Lord
Robert Umfrevile is mentioned by Holinshed (Bullough, p. 271) among the
King's party at Gaultres, it would have
been historically inaccurate to have an
Umfrevile on the rebels' side, let alone
Umfreviles on both sides. At line 161 Q
attributes 'This...lord' to Umfrevile
(only Shaaber's among major editions
retains this), while F misses the line out
altogether. Working on the assumption
that Bardolph and Umfrevile merged in

Shakespeare's conception of the play, but
that he failed systematically to rectify this
'error' in his foul papers, as indeed happened with a number of other slips,
names, mute parts, and other blemishes
in the copy for Q, I have removed Umfrevile completely from the text of this edition, and given the Q-only line 161 to
Lord Bardolph.

37 **forspent** worn out

38 **bloodied** lacerated (by the pricking of
spurs)

42 **spur...cold** Cf. l. 50.

43 **able** Rather than 'powerful', the usual
gloss, it here means more something
akin to 'recovered enough' to proceed.
The horse is described as 'poor jade' (l.
45), i.e. it has been reduced to a 'spent'
hack by the rider's relentless spurring on.

46 **rowel-head** the spiky wheel of a spur

48 **Staying...question** not waiting for
further conversation: cf. *Merchant*
4.1.343: 'I'll stay no longer question',
i.e. I'll expect no further determining of
my claim.

Said he young Harry Percy's spur was cold?
Of Hotspur, Coldspur? That rebellion   50
Had met ill luck?
LORD BARDOLPH   My lord, I'll tell you what:
If my young lord your son have not the day,
Upon mine honour, for a silken point
I'll give my barony, never talk of it.
NORTHUMBERLAND
Why should that gentleman that rode by Travers   55
Give then such instances of loss?
LORD BARDOLPH   Who, he?
He was some hilding fellow that had stol'n
The horse he rode on, and, upon my life,
Spoke at a venture. Look, here comes more news.
        Enter Morton
NORTHUMBERLAND
Yea, this man's brow, like to a title-leaf,   60
Foretells the nature of a tragic volume.
So looks the strand whereon the imperious flood
Hath left a witnessed usurpation.
    Say, Morton, didst thou come from Shrewsbury?
MORTON
I ran from Shrewsbury, my noble lord,   65
Where hateful death put on his ugliest mask
To fright our party.
NORTHUMBERLAND   How doth my son, and brother?
Thou tremblest, and the whiteness in thy cheek
Is apter than thy tongue to tell thy errand.
Even such a man, so faint, so spiritless,   70
So dull, so dead in look, so woebegone,

55 that gentleman] Q; the Gentleman F   59 Spoke] Q; Speake F   a venture] Q; aduenture
F   59.1 *Enter Morton*] F; *opposite l.* 59 Q   62 whereon] Q; when F

53 **point** a lace for tying a garment, hence a
very trivial item
57 **hilding** worthless
59 **at a venture** at random
60 **like...title-leaf** For an example of the
title-page of an Elizabethan publication
advertising its contents as 'a tragic volume', see the title-page of Q1 of *Lear*
which prominently refers to the tragic
actors of both main and sub-plots.
63 **witnessed usurpation** The tide at ebb
leaves behind evidence of its encroaching
on the beach, whose lined aspect is here
compared to the frowning human brow.

Drew Priam's curtain in the dead of night
And would have told him half his Troy was burnt;
But Priam found the fire ere he his tongue,
And I my Percy's death ere thou report'st it.   75
This thou wouldst say: 'Your son did thus and thus,
Your brother thus; so fought the noble Douglas',
Stopping my greedy ear with their bold deeds;
But in the end, to stop my ear indeed,
Thou hast a sigh to blow away this praise,   80
Ending with 'brother, son, and all are dead'.
MORTON
Douglas is living, and your brother yet;
But for my lord your son—
NORTHUMBERLAND   Why, he is dead.
See what a ready tongue suspicion hath.
He that but fears the thing he would not know   85
Hath by instinct knowledge from others' eyes
That what he feared is chanced. Yet speak, Morton.
Tell thou an earl his divination lies,
And I will take it as a sweet disgrace,
And make thee rich for doing me such wrong.   90
MORTON
You are too great to be by me gainsaid,
Your spirit is too true, your fears too certain.
NORTHUMBERLAND
Yet for all this, say not that Percy's dead.
I see a strange confession in thine eye.

79 my] Q; mine F   83 dead.] F; ~? Q   88 an] Q; thy F

72 **Drew ... night** There is no such account
in either Homeric epic or in Virgil's account of the sack of Troy, but Shakespeare may be recalling the apparition
to Aeneas of Hector in *Aeneid* 2.268 ff.,
when Hector warns Aeneas that the
Greeks are sacking the city while he is
still asleep.
curtain bed-curtain
74 **found the fire** discovered the conflagra-
tion
78 **Stopping** filling
79 **to stop ... indeed** to prevent me ever

hearing again, i.e. to strike me dead with
bad news
87 **is chanced** has happened
88–9 **Tell ... disgrace** 'Tell me that my
conjecture is an untruth, and I shall construe your statement as a soothing insult.' Usually giving a nobleman the lie
was a serious offence, but this time it
would be most welcome because it
would mean that Northumberland's son
was still alive.
92 **spirit** instinct, intuition (*OED sb.* 12)
94 **strange** reluctant

Thou shak'st thy head, and hold'st it fear or sin   95
To speak a truth. If he be slain, say so;
The tongue offends not that reports his death;
And he doth sin that doth belie the dead,
Not he which says the dead is not alive.
Yet the first bringer of unwelcome news   100
Hath but a losing office, and his tongue
Sounds ever after as a sullen bell
Remembered tolling a departing friend.

LORD BARDOLPH

I cannot think, my lord, your son is dead.

MORTON (*to Northumberland*)

I am sorry I should force you to believe   105
That which I would to God I had not seen;
But these mine eyes saw him in bloody state,
Rend'ring faint quittance, wearied and out-breathed,
To Harry Monmouth, whose swift wrath beat down
The never-daunted Percy to the earth,   110
From whence with life he never more sprung up.
In few, his death, whose spirit lent a fire
Even to the dullest peasant in his camp,
Being bruited once, took fire and heat away
From the best-tempered courage in his troops;   115

---

96 say so] F; *not in* Q   103 tolling] Q; knolling F   106 God] Q; heauen F   109 Harry]
Q; *Henrie* F

95–8 **sin . . . dead** Cf. the proverb 'To belie
the dead is a sin' (Dent D124.1).
101 **losing office** a duty that results in
loss
102 **sullen** mournful (at funerals). Cf. Sonnet 71: 'No longer mourn for me when I
am dead | Than you shall hear the surly
sullen bell'.
108 **quittance** lit. requital, repayment;
hence return of blows
out-breathed put out of breath
109–11 **To Harry . . . up** It is Shakespeare
who first (unhistorically) credits Hal
with the death in battle of Hotspur in *1*

Henry IV 5.4.75.2–3: *The Prince killeth
Hotspur*. Shakespeare may be developing
a suggestion by Daniel in *Civil Wars*, that
at Shrewsbury 'shall young Hotspur with
a fury led | Meet with thy forward son as
fierce as he' (*CW* 3.97). Holinshed and
Stow (Bullough, p. 191) record Hotspur's
death at the (unspecified) hands of the
royal army.
112 **In few** in short
his death the death of him
114 **bruited** noised abroad
115 **best-tempered** compounded of the
finest mingling of (martial) attributes

For from his metal was his party steeled,
Which once in him abated, all the rest
Turned on themselves, like dull and heavy lead;
And, as the thing that's heavy in itself
Upon enforcement flies with greatest speed,   120
So did our men, heavy in Hotspur's loss,
Lend to this weight such lightness with their fear
That arrows fled not swifter toward their aim
Than did our soldiers, aiming at their safety,
Fly from the field. Then was that noble Worcester   125
So soon ta'en prisoner; and that furious Scot
The bloody Douglas, whose well-labouring sword
Had three times slain th'appearance of the King,
Gan vail his stomach and did grace the shame
Of those that turned their backs; and in his flight,   130
Stumbling in fear, was took. The sum of all
Is that the King hath won, and hath sent out
A speedy power to encounter you, my lord,

---

116 metal] Q (mettal); Mettle F   126 So] Q; Too F

116 **metal** Although 'metal' and 'mettle' were not clearly differentiated, Q's reading is here preferred to F's 'mettle', because of the imagery of chemical elements which extends from 'best-tempered' (l. 115) through 'metal' (116) and 'steeled' (116) to 'abated' (117, i.e. blunted; cf. *Richard III* 5.8.35: 'Abate the edge of traitors...') and 'heavy lead' (118). F's 'mettle' loses the suggestive specificity of Q in which the movement of Hotspur's troops on the battlefield is visualized in terms of his varying inner constitution.

120 **Upon enforcement** under compulsion

121 **heavy in** saddened by

123 **fled** i.e. flew (*OED, flee, v.* 6). The unusual, but possible, past participle construction here welds into one the flying arrows and the fleeing troops, as does 'Fly' (l. 125) for 'Flee'. Shakespeare's syntactic choice ensures that the speed of the men's flight is not merely compared to the flight of arrows, but equated with it so that the two become indistinguishable.

127–8 **The bloody Douglas... King** According to Holinshed (Bullough, p. 191)

Douglas killed three men at Shrewsbury who were 'apparelled in the kings sute' (cf. *1 Henry IV* 5.3.7–8, 19–28; 5.4.25–7), and Hal rescues his father from Douglas with 'The spirits | Of valiant Shirley, Stafford, Blunt, are in my arms' (5.4.39–40). This suggests that, according to Shakespeare, the third of the King's 'Hydra's heads' (5.4.24) or 'shadows' (5.4.29) was Shirley who is reported slain at Shrewsbury by Holinshed and Daniel ('valiant Shorly': *CW* 3.111–13). See also notes 16–17 and 18 above.

129 **Gan** did (aphetic form of 'began': *OED, gin, v.*[1])
    vail his stomach lower his courage (an aphetic form of obs. 'avail': *OED, vail, v.*[2], I. *trans.* 1)

131 **Stumbling ... took** The capture and 'ransomless' release by Hal of Douglas after the latter's 'falling from a hill' is related in *1 Henry IV* 5.5.17–32. Holinshed (Bullough, p. 191) records Douglas's 'falling from the crag of an high mountain' and his subsequent release by the King (not Hal).

133 **power** armed force

Under the conduct of young Lancaster
And Westmorland. This is the news at full.   135

NORTHUMBERLAND

For this I shall have time enough to mourn.
In poison there is physic, and these news,
Having been well, that would have made me sick,
Being sick, have in some measure made me well;
And, as the wretch whose fever-weakened joints,   140
Like strengthless hinges, buckle under life,
Impatient of his fit, breaks like a fire
Out of his keeper's arms, even so my limbs,
Weakened with grief, being now enraged with grief,
Are thrice themselves.

⌜*He throws away his crutch*⌝
                         Hence therefore, thou nice crutch !   145
A scaly gauntlet now with joints of steel
Must glove this hand.

⌜*He snatches off his coif*⌝
                         And hence, thou sickly coif!
Thou art a guard too wanton for the head
Which princes fleshed with conquest aim to hit.
Now bind my brows with iron, and approach   150
The ragged'st hour that time and spite dare bring
To frown upon th'enraged Northumberland !

---

137 these] Q; this F   143 keeper's] QF (keepers)   145 *He ... crutch*] This edition; *not in*
QF   147 *He ... coif*] OXFORD; *not in* QF

137 **physic** medicine
137–9 **these news ... well** The news of
    Hotspur's death is the 'poison' which
    would have made Northumberland ill, if
    he had been well. As it is, he is ill, and
    therefore the news acts as a medicine by
    galvanizing his sick body into action
    through a desire for revenge ('now en-
    raged with grief', l. 144). The inverted
    construction of 'Having ... sick' (138)
    combines with the line which follows
    (139) to produce a taut chiasmus.
141 **under life** under the weight of the liv-
    ing body

142 **Impatient ... fit** not able to endure a
    paroxysm of lunacy (while being re-
    strained)
143 **keeper** nurse
145 **nice** unmanly
146 **scaly** made of small overlapping plates
    of armour
147 **coif** nightcap
148 **wanton** effeminate
149 **fleshed with conquest** their appetites
    whetted for more bloodshed by the taste
    of victory
150 **approach** i.e. let them approach
151 **ragged'st** harshest and most discordant

Let heaven kiss earth, now let not nature's hand
Keep the wild flood confined! Let order die,
And let this world no longer be a stage   155
To feed contention in a ling'ring act;
But let one spirit of the first-born Cain
Reign in all bosoms, that each heart being set
On bloody courses, the rude scene may end,
And darkness be the burier of the dead!   160

LORD BARDOLPH

This strainèd passion doth you wrong, my lord.

MORTON

Sweet Earl, divorce not wisdom from your honour.
The lives of all your loving complices
Lean on your health, the which, if you give o'er
To stormy passion, must perforce decay.   165
You cast th'event of war, my noble lord,

155 this] Q; the F   161 LORD BARDOLPH] POPE; *Vmfr⟨euile⟩*. Q   This...lord] Q; *not in* F
162 MORTON] WILSON (*conj.* Daniel); *Bard⟨olf⟩*. Q; *L⟨ord⟩*. *Bar⟨dolf⟩*. F   164 Lean on your] F
(Leane-on ~); Leaue on you Q   164–5 o'er...passion,] F; ~, ... ~∧ Q   166–79 You...
be] F; *not in* Q

153–60 **Let...dead** Northumberland's cry of despair takes the form of a universal curse of chaos and fratricide, when in fact it is his family who by their rebellion first sanctioned the upheaval in nature and the body politic which costs Hotspur his life and, unnaturally, leaves his father outliving his son. Northumberland's rhetoric here anticipates Lear's ravings in *Lear* 3.2.1–9, but it sounds a morally much more discordant note, because it emanates from a traitor (cf. 'Let order die...', l. 154) in an English history play rather than from the maddened king in the (partly) de-historicized world of *Lear*.

156 **To...act** to sustain strife in a long-drawn-out struggle. 'Act' here means action (including legal action), but also continues the world-as-stage metaphor launched by 'stage' (l. 155) and concluded by 'rude scene' (159).

157 **one** the same
Cain His killing of his brother Abel was the first murder.

159 **rude scene** harsh action (of life, when everyone is a murderer at heart)

161–3 **LORD BARDOLPH...complices** This edition follows Pope in changing Q's speech-prefix *Vmfre*. (Sir John Umfrevile) to Lord Bardolph (see note 34). F misses 161 out altogether, and both Q and F give 162 to Lord Bardolph, and 163 to Morton. Commenting on his decision to retain the Q-only line, Pope (1728) remarked that 'it is spoken by Umfreville, who speaks no where else. It seems necessary to the connection'. Several modern editions (Humphreys, Davison, Riverside, and this edition) view the comma which in Q ends 162 as evidence of a close link between 162 and the lines which follow it, and therefore attribute the entire (largely F-only) speech from 'Sweet Earl' (l. 162) to 'like to be' (179) to Morton (but cf. Bevington, 1980, p. 837; Oxford, p. 577; and Melchiori, pp. 68–9, 197–9); see further Introduction, p. 90.

161 **passion** passionate speech

163 **complices** confederates

166 **cast th'event** calculated the outcome

And summed the account of chance, before you said
'Let us make head'. It was your presurmise
That in the dole of blows your son might drop.
You knew he walked o'er perils, on an edge,   170
More likely to fall in than to get o'er.
You were advised his flesh was capable
Of wounds and scars, and that his forward spirit
Would lift him where most trade of danger ranged.
Yet did you say 'Go forth'; and none of this,   175
Though strongly apprehended, could restrain
The stiff-borne action. What hath then befall'n?
Or what hath this bold enterprise brought forth
More than that being which was like to be?

LORD BARDOLPH

We all that are engagèd to this loss   180
Knew that we ventured on such dangerous seas
That if we wrought out life 'twas ten to one;
And yet we ventured for the gain proposed,
Chokèd the respect of likely peril feared,
And since we are o'erset, venture again.   185
Come, we will all put forth, body and goods.

---

178 brought] F2; bring FI   182 'twas] Q; was F   183 ventured∧ ... proposed,]
QF; ~, ... ~∧ CAPELL

---

167 **summed . . . chance** reckoned the
  likelihood of success
168 **make head** raise an army
169 **dole** Either (a) distribution (*OED sb.¹*
  5b), or (b) destiny (i.e. the chance of
  war: *OED sb.¹* 4) (cf. *1 Henry IV* 2.2.74:
  'happy man be his dole'). A pun on 'dole'
  meaning 'sorrow' may also be intended:
  cf. 'weighing delight and dole' (*Hamlet*
  1.2.13).
170-1 **he walked . . . o'er** he was in the
  habit of crossing over dangers on peri-
  lously narrow bridges, and the probabil-
  ity was that he would fall to perdition
  rather than safely get across to the other
  side. Humphreys (p. 16) argues that
  'edge' (which can be metonymic for
  'sword' as in *Coriolanus* 5.6.113: 'Stain
  all your edges on me') suggests the
  sword-bridges of medieval romance, because Shakespeare may recall *1 Henry IV*
  1.3.189-91 when Worcester, talking to

Hotspur, notes that the matter of rebellion is 'As full of peril and adventurous
spirit | As to o'erwalk a current roaring
loud | On the unsteadfast footing of a
spear'. That crossing a ravine on a very
narrow bridge could be a sign not only of
foolhardiness as in Hotspur, but of
madness and possession, is suggested by
Poor Tom's riding 'on a bay trotting-
horse over four-inched bridges' (*Lear*
3.4.53).
172 **advised** aware
172-3 **capable | Of** susceptible to
174 **trade of** trafficking in
177 **stiff-borne** stubbornly pursued
180 **engagèd to** involved in
182 **wrought out life** came through alive
184 **respect** consideration
185 **o'erset** overwhelmed
186 **all put forth** (a) stake everything; (b) set
  out all of us (to go to battle)

MORTON

'Tis more than time ; and, my most noble lord,
I hear for certain, and dare speak the truth,
The gentle Archbishop of York is up
With well-appointed powers. He is a man   190
Who with a double surety binds his followers.
My lord your son had only but the corpse,
But shadows and the shows of men, to fight ;
For that same word 'rebellion' did divide
The action of their bodies from their souls,   195
And they did fight with queasiness, constrained,
As men drink potions, that their weapons only
Seemed on our side ; but for their spirits and souls,
This word 'rebellion', it had froze them up,
As fish are in a pond. But now the Bishop   200
Turns insurrection to religion ;
Supposed sincere and holy in his thoughts,
He's followed both with body and with mind,
And doth enlarge his rising with the blood
Of fair King Richard, scraped from Pomfret stones ;   205
Derives from heaven his quarrel and his cause ;
Tells them he doth bestride a bleeding land

188 dare] Q; do F   189–209 The...him] F; *not in* Q   201–2 religion;...thoughts,]
ROWE; Religion,...Thoughts: F

189 **gentle** well born
  Archbishop of York Richard Scrope
who 'bears hard | His brother's death at
Bristol' (*1 Henry IV* 1.3.264–5) at the
hands of Bolingbroke. Shakespeare follows Holinshed in making the Archbishop of York and William Scrope
brothers when historically they were dis-
tant cousins. Unlike Holinshed, Shakespeare telescopes history by bringing
forward Scrope's rebellion from May
1405 to the immediate aftermath of the
Battle of Shrewsbury (21 July 1403): see
Introduction, pp. 19–20.
191 **double surety** both spiritual and temporal authority
192 **the corpse** the bodies of men (without
their souls or hearts)
193 **But** mere
196–7 **constrained, | As . . . potions** exhi-
biting the same reluctance with which

men take medicine. With this very compressed simile for 'like men when they
drink potions', Shaaber (p. 47) compares
'Till that his passions, like a whale on
ground' (*2 Henry IV* 4.3.40) and suggests
that short allusive similes such as these
are characteristic of the *Henry IV* plays.
202 **Supposed sincere** since he is considered to be sincere. Most editors (*pace* Melchiori, p. 69) agree that 'Supposed'
(which does not imply scepticism here)
refers to the Archbishop's disposition,
and this would seem to be the main burden of the passage which sets out his
'double surety' claim to succeed where
Hotspur failed.
204 **enlarge** enhance; extend the range or
scope of (*OED v.* 3a)
205 **Pomfret** Richard II was murdered at
Pomfret (i.e. Pontefract) Castle.
206 **Derives from** traces back to

Gasping for life under great Bolingbroke;
And more and less do flock to follow him.
NORTHUMBERLAND
I knew of this before, but, to speak truth,   210
This present grief had wiped it from my mind.
Go in with me, and counsel every man
The aptest way for safety and revenge.
Get posts and letters, and make friends with speed,
Never so few, and never yet more need.   *Exeunt*   215

I.2   *Enter Falstaff, and his Page bearing his sword and
buckler*

FALSTAFF Sirrah, you giant, what says the doctor to my
water?

PAGE He said, sir, the water itself was a good healthy
water, but, for the party that owed it, he might have
more diseases than he knew for.   5

FALSTAFF Men of all sorts take a pride to gird at me. The
brain of this foolish-compounded clay, man, is not able to
invent anything that intends to laughter more than I
invent, or is invented on me. I am not only witty in
myself, but the cause that wit is in other men. I do here   10
walk before thee like a sow that hath overwhelmed all

---

215 and] Q; nor F
1.2.0.1–2 *Enter . . . buckler*] Q (*Enter sir Iohn alone, with . . . buckler.*); *Enter Falstaffe, and Page.*
F   I FALSTAFF] *throughout this edition for 'Sir Iohn', 'Iohn', 'Old.', and 'Falst.' in* QF   3 PAGE] QF
and throughout for Q's *'Boy', 'boy'*   5 more] Q (moe)   7 foolish-compounded] POPE; foolish
compounded QF   clay, man] POPE (-clay, Man); clay-man QF   8 intends] Q; tends F

---

208 **Bolingbroke** Henry IV's surname before he became king.
209 **more and less** greater and lesser, persons of all ranks
212 **counsel every man** let each man consider
1.2.0.1–2 *Enter . . . buckler* Unlike F's perfunctory *Enter Falstaffe, and Page*, Q has
Falstaff entering alone, with his page
bearing his sword and buckler. The use
of 'alone' here probably indicates that
the page follows Falstaff at a respectful
distance, a comically appropriate defer-
ence to the supposed vanquisher of
Hotspur at Shrewsbury who is now
accompanied by the sword and buckler,
emblems of heroic manhood. The visual-

theatrical character of Q's stage direction
is characteristic of holograph copy, and a
similar usage of 'alone' occurs at 3.1.0.1
where QB's 'alone' is applied to the
King's entry with a page in tow.
 I **giant** ironically, because the page is of
very small stature
to concerning
 2 **water** urine
 4 **party** person (not the facetious modern
use of 'party')
owed owned
 5 **knew for** was aware of (*OED, know, v.*
17)
 6 **gird at** taunt
 7 **foolish-compounded** composed of folly
 8 **intends** inclines (*OED, intend, v. intr.* 24)

her litter but one. If the Prince put thee into my service
for any other reason than to set me off, why then I have
no judgement. Thou whoreson mandrake, thou art fitter
to be worn in my cap than to wait at my heels. I was   15
never manned with an agate till now, but I will inset you
neither in gold nor silver, but in vile apparel, and send
you back again to your master for a jewel—the juvenal
the Prince your master, whose chin is not yet fledge. I
will sooner have a beard grow in the palm of my hand   20
than he shall get one off his cheek, and yet he will not
stick to say his face is a face-royal. God may finish it
when He will, 'tis not a hair amiss yet. He may keep it
still at a face-royal, for a barber shall never earn sixpence
out of it; and yet he'll be crowing as if he had writ man   25
ever since his father was a bachelor. He may keep his
own grace, but he's almost out of mine, I can assure him.

14 judgement. Thou] F; ~∧ thou Q   15 heels.] F; ~∧ Q   16 inset] Q; sette F   19 fledge]
Q; fledg'd F   21 off] Q; on F   and yet] Q; yet F   22 God] Q; Heauen F   23 'tis] Q; it is F
25 he'll] Q; he will F   27 he's] Q; he is F

13 **set me off** render me conspicuous by
contrast (*OED, set, v.*[1] 147 e (*a*))

14 **whoreson** Used humorously here to
mean 'confounded' rather than in the
commonly abusive sense of 'vile', 'abominable' (*OED* b).
    mandrake A plant with emetic and nar-
cotic properties whose forked root is
thought to resemble the human form. It
was fabled to utter a deadly shriek when
plucked up from the ground; see also
below, 3.2.300–1.

14–15 **thou . . . heels** The page is so small
that he should be worn as one of his
master's hat ornaments rather than follow in his steps.

16 **manned with** attended by (*OED, man, v.*
3a)
    agate Used figuratively here to denote a
diminutive person, after the small figures
cut in agate for seals.

17 **vile** mean (in rank and condition)

17–18 **send . . . jewel** Falstaff jokingly offers
to return the page to the prince as a badly
turned out ornament (cf. 2.2.66–8: 'the
boy that I gave Falstaff . . . Christian, and
look if the fat villain have not trans-
formed him ape').

18 **juvenal** Affectionate word for 'youth':
the near-homophony with 'jewel' points
up Falstaff's otherwise seamless chiastic
rhetoric ('master . . . jewel . . . juvenal . . .
master'). Throughout this passage (ll.
6–29) the prose is highly stylized while
conveying the impression of natural
speech (cf. Introduction, pp. 41–2).

19 **fledge** covered with down

22 **stick** hesitate (*OED v.*[1] 15)
    face-royal a first class face (in spite of its
manly—i.e. beardless—imperfections).
'Face-royal' here means a royal face,
but the phrase also puns on the coin
known as 'royal' which carried the
king's picture stamped on it and was
worth ten shillings, or half a pound sterling.

22–3 **God . . . yet** A witty paradox. Falstaff
claims that no detail in Hal's face is imperfect because everything in it is wholly
imperfect: there is no hair amiss, because
there is no hair. There is also a quibble on
hair meaning 'one iota'.

25 **writ man** called himself a man (*OED,
write, v.* 11b (*b*))

27 **grace** (a) title ('Your grace'); (b) favour

What said Master Dommelton about the satin for my
short cloak and my slops?

PAGE He said, sir, you should procure him better assurance   30
    than Bardolph. He would not take his bond and yours;
    he liked not the security.

FALSTAFF Let him be damned like the glutton! Pray God his
    tongue be hotter! A whoreson Achitophel, a rascal yea-
    forsooth knave, to bear a gentleman in hand and then   35
    stand upon security! The whoreson smoothy-pates do
    now wear nothing but high shoes and bunches of keys at
    their girdles; and if a man is through with them in
    honest taking-up, then they must stand upon security.
    I had as lief they would put ratsbane in my mouth as offer   40

28 Dommelton] Q; *Dombledon* F   29 my slops] Q; Slops F   31 bond] F, Q (band)   33 Pray
God] Q; may F   34 rascal∧] Q (rascall:); Rascally F   36 smoothy-pates] Q; smooth-pates
F   40 lief] Q (liue), F (liefe)

28 **Dommelton** The name probably quib-
    bles on 'dummel', a dialectic usage of
    the time meaning 'stupid, dull'.
29 **short cloak** Probably fashionable in Eli-
    zabethan times rather than specifically in
    the Lancastrian period, although Hum-
    phreys (p. 20) quotes Stow's *Annales* to
    show that in the reign of Henry IV there
    was 'exceeding pride in garments, gowns
    with drape and broade sleeves'. Falstaff is
    guilty of vanity as well as being a glutton.
    slops baggy breeches
33 **glutton** An allusion to the parable of
    Dives and Lazarus from Luke 16,
    prompted by the foppish clothing ima-
    gery and by the look of Bardolph's red
    nose. In Luke the glutton or rich man
    (Latin '*Dives*') is 'clothed in purple and
    fine linen' before going to hell and
    damnation. Falstaff evokes the same
    story in *1 Henry IV* 3.3.30–2 in direct
    response to Bardolph's face, and refers
    to it again at 4.2.25–7. This, and the
    parable of the Prodigal Son from Luke
    15: 12–31 (cf. 2.1.141 and *1 Henry IV*
    4.2.34), are the two biblical stories most
    deeply lodged in his mind: see Introduc-
    tion, p. 42.
34 **hotter** Cf. Luke 16: 24: 'Then he [Dives]
    cryed, and said, Father Abraham, haue
    mercie on me, and send Lazarus that he
    may dippe ye typ of his finger in water,
    and coole my tongue; for I am tormented
    in this flame'.

34 **Achitophel** One of King David's coun-
    sellors who betrayed him and supported
    Absalom's conspiracy. When his counsel
    was rejected by the rebels, he hanged
    himself, like Judas Iscariot (2 Samuel
    16–17).
34–5 **a...knave** Alludes to the self-con-
    sciously mild oaths favoured by obse-
    quious London tradesmen at the time.
    Most editions (e.g. Davison, Humphreys,
    Oxford) prefer F here, but Prosser (p.
    140) defends Q's 'a rascall: yea forsooth
    knave' and suggests punctuating 'a ras-
    call—yea forsooth, knave!—...'
35 **bear...hand** lead on with false expecta-
    tion
36 **stand upon** insist on (*OED, stand, v.* 78m)
    smoothy-pates with   their   short-
    cropped hair. Falstaff refers to the predi-
    lection of Puritan tradesmen for the fash-
    ionably short hairstyles, which in 1641
    produced the tag 'round-head' for the
    Puritan Parliamentary party.
37 **high...keys** Indicative of dandyish pre-
    tension and a vulgar show of self-impor-
    tance.
38–9 **if...taking-up** if one has completed
    an honest purchase from them. 'To be
    through with' = to have finished or
    completed (*OED, through*, II. *adv.* 3b);
    'take up' = 'to purchase wholesale, buy
    up; to borrow (at interest)' (*OED v.* 93d).
40 **I...lief** I would as happily
    ratsbane rat poison

to stop it with security. I looked a should have sent me
two and twenty yards of satin, as I am a true knight, and
he sends me 'security'! Well, he may sleep in security, for
he hath the horn of abundance, and the lightness of his
wife shines through it—where's Bardolph?—and yet   45
cannot he see, though he have his own lanthorn to
light him.

PAGE He's gone in Smithfield to buy your worship a horse.

FALSTAFF I bought him in Paul's, and he'll buy me a horse
in Smithfield; an I could get me but a wife in the stews, I   50
were manned, horsed, and wived.

---

41 a] Q; hee F   42 a] Q; *not in* F   45 it—where's Bardolph?] Q; it, F   47 him] Q; him.
Where's *Bardolfe?* F   48 in] Q; into F   50 an] *throughout for* QF *'and' meaning 'if'*   an] Q; If
F   but a] Q; a F

---

41 **looked** expected (*OED, look, v.* 3c)
a he

43 **he ... 'security'** he asks for payment in
advance

44–5 **horn of abundance ... through it** the
horn of plenty or cornucopia, with a pun
on the cuckold's horn. Falstaff's tailor
has 'security' (i.e. wealth) in his plentiful
progeny, but this is false security because
through his wife's 'lightness' (infidelity)
his children are not his. Throughout the
passage Falstaff quibbles on the various
meanings of 'security' which can also
mean, as here, misplaced confidence or
complacency. A further play on 'horn'
meaning 'the side of a lantern' (*OED, sb.*
11a) is intended and spelt out in the
phrase 'lanthorn to light him', i.e. his
wife's cheating is glaringly obvious because of his cuckold's horn. This edition
retains the archaic form 'lanthorn' for
modern lantern to preserve the wordplay
in the original (cf. Wells, 1979, p. 16).

45 **it—where's Bardolph?—** Q's text here
offers a more interesting theatrical reading than F which places the question
after Bardolph at the end of the sentence
(cf. Prosser, p. 130, who construes the
internal placing of this stage direction as
'typical' of Falstaff's 'breaks in thought').
Q captures the nimbly associative character of Falstaff's lines as it jumps from
'light' to Bardolph, whose red nose attracted ample attention in *1 Henry IV*
where Falstaff called him 'the Knight of
the Burning Lamp' and whose face invariably reminded him of 'hell-fire and

Dives that lived in purple ... burning,
burning' (*1 Henry IV* 3.3.30–2).

48 **in** Used commonly for 'into' in this period
(Abbott §159).
Smithfield i.e. west Smithfield (originally 'Smoothfield'), an open space of between five and six acres in the City of
London. It served as a horse and cattle
market as well as the site of the annual
Bartholomew Fair (24 August) from the
Middle Ages to the middle of the nineteenth century. By the end of the sixteenth century the area had become
notorious for fighting and duelling and
was known as 'Ruffians' Hall'.
buy ... horse Horses bought in Smithfield had a bad reputation: in *London and
the Covntrey Carbonadoed and Quartered
into seuerall Characters* (1632), pp. 36–
7, D. Lupton reports that 'he that lights
vpon a Horse in this place, from an olde
Horse-Courser, sound both in wind and
limbe, may light of an honest Wife in the
Stews: here's many an old Iade, that trots
hard for't ... '; see also next note.

50–1 **I could ... wived** In the middle aisle of
St Paul's known as 'Duke Humphrey's
Walk' or 'Paul's Walk' out-of-work servants looked for new masters. Falstaff
here alludes to the proverbial saying of
the time that a man must not choose a
wife in Westminster, nor a servant in St
Paul's and a horse in Smithfield lest he
choose 'a whore, a knave, and a jade'
(Dent W276).

50 **stews** brothels

Enter the Lord Chief Justice and his Servant

PAGE Sir, here comes the nobleman that committed the
    Prince for striking him about Bardolph.

FALSTAFF Wait close, I will not see him.

LORD CHIEF JUSTICE (*to his Servant*) What's he that goes   55
    there?

SERVANT Falstaff, an't please your lordship.

LORD CHIEF JUSTICE He that was in question for the robbery?

SERVANT He, my lord; but he hath since done good service
    at Shrewsbury, and, as I hear, is now going with some   60
    charge to the Lord John of Lancaster.

LORD CHIEF JUSTICE What, to York? Call him back again.

SERVANT Sir John Falstaff!

FALSTAFF Boy, tell him I am deaf.

PAGE (*to the Servant*) You must speak louder; my master is   65
    deaf.

LORD CHIEF JUSTICE I am sure he is, to the hearing of any-
    thing good. (*To the Servant*) Go pluck him by the elbow; I
    must speak with him.

SERVANT Sir John!   70

FALSTAFF What, a young knave and begging! Is there not
    wars? Is there not employment? Doth not the King lack
    subjects? Do not the rebels need soldiers? Though it be a
    shame to be on any side but one, it is worse shame to beg
    than to be on the worst side, were it worse than the name   75
    of rebellion can tell how to make it.

51.1 *Enter ... Servant*] OXFORD; *Enter Lord chiefe Iustice.* Q; *Enter Chiefe Iustice, and Seruant.* F
55 LORD CHIEF JUSTICE] *throughout this edition for 'Iustice', 'Iust.', 'Lo.', 'Lord' in* Q *and 'Ch. Iust.' in*
F   71 begging] Q; beg F   73 need] Q; want F

51.1 *Enter ... Justice* See Introduction,
    pp. 21-2.
    Servant The tipstaff who attends the
    Lord Chief Justice.
53 **for striking him** See Introduction, p. 21.
54 **Wait close** wait concealed, i.e. let us
    withdraw out of sight
58 **in question** Either (a) under judicial ex-
    amination, or (b) referred to, talked
    about.
59 **good service** The irony here suggests that
    Shakespeare fully expects his audience to
    be familiar with the account in *Part 1* of
    Shrewsbury and the desecration of Hot-
    spur's body.

60-1 **some charge** Probably 'troops' rather
    than 'a certain military command'.
62 **York** At the end of *1 Henry IV* 5.5.36-7
    Lancaster and Westmorland are dis-
    patched to York against Northumber-
    land and Scrope, whereas in Holinshed
    (Bullough, p. 192) it is the King who
    proceeds straight to York after the victory
    at Shrewsbury. Shakespeare here follows
    his own imaginative history rather than
    Holinshed's chronicle: see Introduction,
    pp. 19-21.
71-2 **Is ... wars** Singular and plural accords
    are possible in the English of the period
    (Abbott, §333).

SERVANT You mistake me, sir.

FALSTAFF Why, sir, did I say you were an honest man? Setting my knighthood and my soldiership aside, I had lied in my throat if I had said so.　　　　80

SERVANT I pray you, sir, then set your knighthood and your soldiership aside, and give me leave to tell you you lie in your throat if you say I am any other than an honest man.

FALSTAFF I give thee leave to tell me so? I lay aside that　　85
which grows to me? If thou gettest any leave of me, hang me. If thou takest leave, thou wert better be hanged. You hunt counter. Hence, avaunt!

SERVANT Sir, my lord would speak with you.

LORD CHIEF JUSTICE Sir John Falstaff, a word with you.　　90

FALSTAFF My good lord! God give your lordship good time of day. I am glad to see your lordship abroad. I heard say your lordship was sick. I hope your lordship goes abroad by advice. Your lordship, though not clean past your youth, have yet some smack of an ague in you, some relish　　95
of the saltness of time in you; and I most humbly beseech your lordship to have a reverent care of your health.

---

85 me∧ so?] F; ~, ~∧ Q　　91 God] Q; *not in* F　　92 of] Q; of the F　　95 have] Q; hath F　an ague] Q; age F　　96 time in you] Q; time F

79 **Setting . . . aside** even if I were to relinquish my civil and military honour (and were thus capable of telling a lie)

80 **in my throat** deliberately. The expression 'To lie in one's throat' (Dent T268) is proverbial.

86 **grows to** is an integral part of (*OED*, *grow*, *v*. 3b)

87–8 **You hunt counter** (a hunting term) you are on the wrong trail

92 **abroad** out of doors (*OED adv*. 3)

94 **advice** doctor's recommendation (*OED* 5)

95 **ague** malarial fever, or the shivers it causes. I have preferred Q's reading to F's 'smack of age' because of the references to sickness which precede. Falstaff's snide allusion to the judge's age (cf. below: 'You that are old . . .') follows in the next line and would effectively duplicate F's version. It is in any case not easy (*pace* Shaaber, p. 66, Davison, p.

181) to explicate the train of thought behind F's reading of 'not . . . age in you' which would require an awkward reading on the lines of 'you're not entirely old yet, but have nevertheless a taste of old age about you'. The contrast between the two halves of the proposition is not strong enough to justify a formal antithesis of the 'youth versus age' order.

96 **saltness of time** In view of the taste imagery of 'smack' and 'relish' this means, probably, something like 'time which is artificially preserved from going off by being salted like meat in brine'. Falstaff has to tread warily while sniping at the Lord Chief Justice, and this insult is carefully wrapped in enough ambiguity to pass as an innocent enquiry after the judge's declining health and years.

97 **reverent** very respectful

LORD CHIEF JUSTICE Sir John, I sent for you before your
    expedition to Shrewsbury.

FALSTAFF An't please your lordship, I hear his majesty is   100
    returned with some discomfort from Wales.

LORD CHIEF JUSTICE I talk not of his majesty. You would not
    come when I sent for you.

FALSTAFF And I hear, moreover, his highness is fallen into
    this same whoreson apoplexy.   105

LORD CHIEF JUSTICE Well, God mend him! I pray you, let me
    speak with you.

FALSTAFF This apoplexy, as I take it, is a kind of lethargy,
    an't please your lordship, a kind of sleeping in the blood,
    a whoreson tingling.   110

LORD CHIEF JUSTICE What tell you me of it? Be it as it is.

FALSTAFF It hath it original from much grief, from study,
    and perturbation of the brain. I have read the cause of his
    effects in Galen, it is a kind of deafness.

LORD CHIEF JUSTICE I think you are fallen into the disease,   115
    for you hear not what I say to you.

---

98 for] Q; *not in* F   100 An't] Q; If it F   106 God] Q; heauen F   you] Q; *not in* F
108 as ... is] Q (as I take it? is); is (as I take it) F   109 an't ... of] Q; a F   in] Q; of F

---

101 **discomfort from Wales** Falstaff appears to conflate two different expeditions
in Wales by Henry IV: (a) the 1403 campaign after Shrewsbury (cf. *1 Henry IV*
5.5.40–1 and Note 62 on York, above),
and (b) in 1405, anachronistically for
Falstaff, after his defeat of Northumberland and the winning of Warkworth
Castle, the King proceeded again to
Wales with disastrous consequences.
(Cf. Holinshed, 1587, iii. 530: 'Thus
hauing quieted the north parts, he tooke
his iournie directlie into Wales, where he
found fortune nothing fauourable unto
him, for all his attempts had euill
successe, insomuch that losing fiftie of
his cariages through abundance of raine
and waters, he returned ... ')

105 **whoreson** vile
    apoplexy paralysis. Falstaff may allude
to the leprosy which Henry IV was rumoured to have contracted for the murder of Richard II, or the executing of the

Archbishop of York (see Jacob, pp. 99–
100). Falstaff, however, covers his tracks
by correctly defining the symptoms of
'apoplexy' as those of the palsy which
affected Henry IV towards the end of his
life, and by attributing it to Henry IV's
onerous duties and the cares of kingship
('It ... deafness', ll. 112–14).

111 **What** why

112 **it** its. Although it was used repeatedly
by Shakespeare, the modern form of this
possessive pronoun was not common in
the period (Abbott, §228), as Shakespeare's use of 'his' in the next sentence
demonstrates.
    original origin

114 **Galen** Galen of Pergamum (AD 129–c.
199), a famous physician whose pathol-
ogy was founded on the doctrine of the
four humours. He was still regarded as
the supreme authority on medicine in the
sixteenth century.

FALSTAFF Very well, my lord, very well. Rather, an't please
you, it is the disease of not listening, the malady of not
marking, that I am troubled withal.

LORD CHIEF JUSTICE To punish you by the heels would   120
amend the attention of your ears, and I care not if I do
become your physician.

FALSTAFF I am as poor as Job, my lord, but not so patient.
Your lordship may minister the potion of imprisonment
to me in respect of poverty; but how I should be your   125
patient to follow your prescriptions, the wise may make
some dram of a scruple, or indeed a scruple itself.

LORD CHIEF JUSTICE I sent for you when there were matters
against you for your life, to come speak with me.

FALSTAFF As I was then advised by my learned counsel in 130
the laws of this land-service, I did not come.

LORD CHIEF JUSTICE Well, the truth is, Sir John, you live in
great infamy.

FALSTAFF He that buckles himself in my belt cannot live in
less.   135

---

117 FALSTAFF] F (*Fal.*); *Old.* Q   121–2 do become] Q; be F   134 himself] Q; him F

117 **FALSTAFF** On this speech-prefix, see Introduction, pp. 7, 36.
120 **punish...heels** put in irons or the
stocks, i.e. imprison; also 'lay by the
heels'
123 **as poor as Job...patient** Proverbial
(Dent J60; J59).
125 **in...poverty** because I am poor (i.e.
too poor to pay the required fine and
therefore jailed)
126–7 **make...itself** entertain a very slight
doubt, or indeed a real doubt. Falstaff
plays with the literal and conceptual
significance of 'scruple', which, firstly
(after Latin '*scrupulus*'), means a small
sharp or pointed stone and therefore the
smallest division of weight, while 'dram'
also signifies a very small quantity (one
sixteenth of an ounce avoirdupois weight
to be precise). The point is that Falstaff
could be saying that wise (i.e. intelligent
and fair-minded) men might just be very
slightly doubtful about the judge's wisdom in jailing him. If this is the case, then
the first scruple means doubt (*OED, scruple, sb.*² 2b), while the second denotes the
smallest weight (with 'scruple = doubt'
needing to be supplemented), i.e. a scru-

ple of a scruple. This version would be the
more politic one for Falstaff; the other,
where scruple denotes doubt in both
cases, constitutes impudent banter. Falstaff's entire verbal exchange with the
Lord Chief Justice consists of covertly
abusive double-talk.
128–9 **matters . . . life** a capital charge
against you
131 **land-service** Specifically denotes military service on land as opposed to at
sea, and technically refers therefore to
the campaign which ended at Shrewsbury during which Falstaff could not leg-
ally be summoned by the civil
authorities. But it is also the case that
Falstaff again cocks a snook at the judge
because the phrase could also be a euphe-
mism for the robbery on Gad's Hill.
134–5 **He...less** This is usually read as Falstaff pretending to mistake 'infamy' for
an item of clothing; maybe all he means
is that because of his huge girth everything about him, even infamy, is necessarily large and therefore the judge's
charge need not carry much moral
weight.

LORD CHIEF JUSTICE　Your means are very slender, and your
　　waste is great.

FALSTAFF　I would it were otherwise, I would my means
　　were greater and my waist slender.

LORD CHIEF JUSTICE　You have misled the youthful Prince.　　　140

FALSTAFF　The young Prince hath misled me. I am the
　　fellow with the great belly, and he my dog.

LORD CHIEF JUSTICE　Well, I am loath to gall a new-healed
　　wound. Your day's service at Shrewsbury hath a little
　　gilded over your night's exploit on Gad's Hill. You may　　145
　　thank th'unquiet time for your quiet o'erposting that
　　action.

FALSTAFF　My lord?

LORD CHIEF JUSTICE　But since all is well, keep it so. Wake not
　　a sleeping wolf.　　　150

FALSTAFF　To wake a wolf is as bad as smell a fox.

LORD CHIEF JUSTICE　What! You are as a candle, the better
　　part burnt out.

FALSTAFF　A wassail candle, my lord, all tallow; if I did say
　　of wax, my growth would approve the truth.　　　155

136 are] Q; is F　137 is] Q; *not in* F　139 greater] QF; great BETTERTON　waist] QF (waste)
slender] Q; slenderer F　146 th'unquiet] Q; the vnquiet F　151 bad as] Q; bad as to F

141–2 **I...dog** Probably an unexplained
topical reference the main burden of
which is that, according to Falstaff, the
expected roles are reversed: the dog is
master, and the master is dog. The joke
is in the double-take, because it is the
deliberate wrongness of Falstaff's pre-
mises that creates the twist: it is of course
not the Prince of Wales who is the dog
but Falstaff, so that the dog misleading
his master is exactly what Falstaff does. It
is his love of role reversal which, reck-
lessly, makes him assume the guise of the
King (*1 Henry IV* 2.5.401–41).

143 **gall** irritate

146–7 **your quiet...action** having your
offence quietly passed over

149–50 **Wake...wolf** Cf. the proverb 'It is
evil (ill, not good) waking of a sleeping
dog' (Dent W7).

151 **smell a fox** become suspicious; cf. 'to
smell a rat'

154 **wassail candle** large candle used at a
feast
　tallow A form of hard animal fat used in
candles, soaps, etc., applied ironically by

Falstaff to himself here because he is full
of lard.

155 **wax** Produced by bees (cf. 'beeswax')
and therefore not suitable to the 'tallow-
catch' Falstaff (*1 Henry IV* 2.5.232), who
proceeds to pun on the meanings of 'wax'
= to grow.
　my growth...truth the fact that I have
grown (i.e. 'waxed') so huge would prove
('approve') the truthfulness of my statement. It may be that Shakespeare was
irresistibly tempted by the rather poor
'wax'/'growth' pun, but the train of
thought suggests otherwise, and reveals
a degree of acute calculation. Wax was a
much rarer and more refined commodity
than tallow, and Falstaff may well have
this in mind when replying to the judge's
'the better part'. He concedes that he
would be largely 'burnt out' as a tallow
candle, but since he is a *wax* candle he
waxes (grows) rather than declines. Falstaff pretends that he considers himself to
be a noble specimen of humanity who is
in the prime of life.

LORD CHIEF JUSTICE There is not a white hair in your face
    but should have his effect of gravity.
FALSTAFF His effect of gravy, gravy, gravy.
LORD CHIEF JUSTICE You follow the young Prince up and
    down like his ill angel.   160
FALSTAFF Not so, my lord. Your ill angel is light, but I hope
    he that looks upon me will take me without weighing;
    and yet in some respects, I grant, I cannot go. I cannot
    tell. Virtue is of so little regard in these costermongers'
    times that true valour is turned bearherd; pregnancy is   165
    made a tapster, and his quick wit wasted in giving reck-
    onings; all the other gifts appertinent to man, as the
    malice of this age shapes them, are not worth a goose-
    berry. You that are old consider not the capacities of us
    that are young. You do measure the heat of our livers   170
    with the bitterness of your galls; and we that are in the

---

156 in] Q; on F   160 ill] Q; euill F   165 times] Q; *not in* F   bearherd] Q (Berod), F (Beare-
heard)   166 and] Q (&); and hath F   168 this] F; his Q   them, are] F (them)ₐ ~); the one
Q   170 do] Q; *not in* F

---

158 **gravy** sweat, used punningly because of
    Falstaff's gluttony
161 **Your ... light** Puns on the dual signif-
    ication in the period of 'angel' and, con-
    nectedly, on the two meanings of 'light'.
    An 'angel' was an Elizabethan gold coin
    which portrayed the archangel Michael
    slaying the dragon. It was sometimes
    fraudulently clipped and thus lightened
    of its gold content. But 'angel' also means
    the fallen angels and particularly Satan
    ('Lucifer': lit. 'carrier of light'), and the
    phrase as used here may specifically echo
    2 Corinthians 11: 14, 'And no marueile;
    for Satan himself is transformed into an
    Angel of light'. The point is that Falstaff
    cannot be, according to his own logic,
    the Prince's ill angel because he is far
    from light.
162 **take** accept
163 **I cannot go** (a) I will not be able to pass
    as honest money, or (b) I cannot comfor-
    tably travel on foot (because I'm not in
    good health). A submerged bawdy mean-
    ing ('capable of having sex') may be in-
    tended, by analogy with *Lear* 4.5.120

('the soilèd horse goes to't') and *Antony*
1.2.57–8 ('a woman that cannot go':
see also Williams, 1994, pp. 605–6).
164–5 **costermongers' times** materialistic
    (and therefore mean-spirited) times. A
    costermonger originally meant a street
    hawker selling costard apples from his
    barrow.
165 **bearherd** The profession of keeping
    tame bears for exhibition was held in
    low esteem, but now, Falstaff implies,
    the mercenary climate of the time has
    reduced courage to that sort of lame ex-
    ercise.
    pregnancy quick intellect (*OED sb.*[1] 3a
    fig.)
166–7 **tapster ... reckonings** The tapster's
    only intellectual activity consists of pro-
    ducing the bills for the drinks.
168–9 **not ... gooseberry** Cf. similarly
    'proved not worth a blackberry' (*Troilus*
    5.4.11), and the locution 'not worth a
    fig' (cf. also 5.3.117).
170 **livers** The liver was considered to be the
    seat of passion.
171 **galls** the secretion of the liver, bile

vanguard of our youth, I must confess, are wags too.

LORD CHIEF JUSTICE Do you set down your name in the scroll
of youth, that are written down old with all the characters of age? Have you not a moist eye, a dry hand, a   175
yellow cheek, a white beard, a decreasing leg, an increas-
ing belly? Is not your voice broken, your wind short,
your chin double, your wit single, and every part about
you blasted with antiquity? And will you yet call yourself
young? Fie, fie, fie, Sir John!   180

FALSTAFF My lord, I was born about three of the clock in
the afternoon with a white head, and something a round
belly. For my voice, I have lost it with hallowing and
singing of anthems. To approve my youth further, I will
not. The truth is, I am only old in judgement and under-   185
standing; and he that will caper with me for a thousand
marks, let him lend me the money, and have at him! For

---

172 vanguard] Q (vaward)   178 your chin double,] Q; *not in* F   179 yet] Q; *not in* F
181–2 about... afternoon] Q; *not in* F   184 further] Q, F (farther)   187 him! For] F (~.
~); him‸ for Q

172 **vanguard . . . youth** forefront of our
  youth, i.e. in its early stages, rather
  than, as Davison (p. 185) suggests, in
  early middle age which would mitigate
  Falstaff's provocative counterpoint between his extreme 'youth' and the Lord
  Chief Justice's hoary agedness
    wags full of high spirits, with (perhaps)
  an ominous innuendo. *OED* (*wag, sb.* 2)
  records that wag may originally be a
  shortening of 'waghalter', i.e. someone
  who is likely to end up hanged.
174–5 **characters** (a) letters; (b) characteristics
175 **moist** rheumy (because he is old)
    dry hand As opposed to a moist one
  which was thought to be typical of
  youth; cf. *Othello* 3.4.36–47.
176 **decreasing leg** his legs shrink in the
  hams
178 **single** poor, weak
181–2 **about . . . afternoon** (Possibly) a
  meta-theatrical joke by Falstaff, claiming
  that he was born during the time of theatrical performance which in this period
  meant the afternoon, i.e. he pretends to
  exist solely as a product of the dramatic
  imagination; or, he may mean that he

was born mature, as the middle of the
  afternoon can denote the later stages of
  life (cf. *Richard III* 3.7.175–6: 'A beauty-
  waning and distressèd widow | Even in
  the afternoon of her best days'); on the
  absence of the phrase from F, cf. Introduction, pp. 89–90.
182 **something a** somewhat
183 **hallowing** (a) shouting aloud (*OED vbl.
  sb.* and *ppl. a.*, from 'hallow' *v.*² 3 *trans.*);
  (b) shouting to hounds to urge them on
  (*OED v.*² 2 *intr.*); (c) honour as holy,
  especially in prayer (*OED v.*¹ 3). Falstaff
  may be alluding to Ephesians 5: 18–19,
  where St Paul warns against drunken-
  ness and recommends the 'Speaking
  vnto your selues in psalmes, and
  hymns, and spiritual songs . . . making
  melodie to the Lord in your hearts'.
184 **singing of anthems** Cf. *1 Henry IV*
  2.5.132–3: 'I would I were a weaver—I
  could sing psalms, or anything.'
186 **caper with me** compete with me in
  dancing
187 **marks** A mark was valued at two-thirds
  of £1.
    have at him have a go at him

the box of th'ear that the Prince gave you, he gave it like
a rude prince, and you took it like a sensible lord. I have
checked him for it, and the young lion repents—⌈*aside*⌉   190
marry, not in ashes and sackcloth, but in new silk and
old sack.

LORD CHIEF JUSTICE Well, God send the Prince a better companion!

FALSTAFF God send the companion a better prince! I can-   195
not rid my hands of him.

LORD CHIEF JUSTICE Well, the King hath severed you and
Prince Harry. I hear you are going with Lord John of
Lancaster against the Archbishop and the Earl of North-
umberland.   200

FALSTAFF Yea, I thank your pretty sweet wit for it. But look
you pray, all you that kiss my lady Peace at home, that
our armies join not in a hot day; for, by the Lord, I take
but two shirts out with me, and I mean not to sweat
extraordinarily. If it be a hot day and I brandish anything   205
but a bottle, I would I might never spit white again.
There is not a dangerous action can peep out his head
but I am thrust upon it. Well, I cannot last ever, but it
was alway yet the trick of our English nation, if they have
a good thing, to make it too common. If ye will needs say   210

---

188 th'ear] F; the yeere Q   193 God] Q; heauen F   195 God] Q; Heauen F   197–8 and
Prince Harry] F; *not in* Q   201 Yea] Q; Yes F   203 by the Lord,] Q; if F   205 and] Q (&); if
F   206 a] Q; my F   bottle,] F; bottle. Q   I would] Q; would F   208–14 but it...motion]
Q; *not in* F

188 **box of th'ear** Cf. above, ll. 52–3.
189 **sensible** (a) capable of physical sensa-
    tion (*OED a.* 1d), with a pun on (b) 'rea-
    sonable' (*OED a.* 7c)
190 **checked** rebuked (*OED*, *check*, *v.*[1] 11)
    lion On the association between royalty
    and the lion as king of the beasts, cf. 1
    Henry IV 2.5.274–5 and 3.3.147–8.
191–2 **not in . . . old sack** Sackcloth and
    ashes are the proper emblems of repen-
    tance, but Falstaff twists this through
    punning on the other meanings of
    'sack' = a sweet white wine from Spain
    or the Canaries (*OED sb.*[3] 1a); the expres-
    sion 'To mourn in sack and claret' is
    proverbial (Dent S13).
197–8 **and Prince Harry** See Introduction,
    pp. 89–90.

201 **I...it** Probably a mildly sarcastic gen-
    eral remark, meaning something like
    'Thank you for so shrewdly reminding
    me of what is all too obvious to me',
    rather than a specific connecting of the
    Lord Chief Justice's severing of Falstaff
    and Hal, or his commission.
206 **bottle** Cf. 1 *Henry IV* 5.3.54.1–2 where
    Hal draws a bottle of sack from Falstaff's
    pistol holster.
    spit white Most modern editions agree
    that this means 'to spit clean', i.e. in a
    manner pertaining to health rather than
    disease.
208–14 **but it...motion** See Introduction,
    pp. 89–90.

I am an old man, you should give me rest. I would to God
my name were not so terrible to the enemy as it is. I were
better to be eaten to death with a rust than to be scoured
to nothing with perpetual motion.

LORD CHIEF JUSTICE Well, be honest, be honest, and God   215
bless your expedition.

FALSTAFF Will your lordship lend me a thousand pound to
furnish me forth?

LORD CHIEF JUSTICE Not a penny, not a penny. You are too
impatient to bear crosses. Fare you well. Commend me to   220
my cousin Westmorland.

Exeunt Lord Chief Justice and his Servant

FALSTAFF If I do, fillip me with a three-man beetle. A man
can no more separate age and covetousness than a can
part young limbs and lechery; but the gout galls the one
and the pox pinches the other, and so both the degrees   225
prevent my curses. Boy!

PAGE Sir?

FALSTAFF What money is in my purse?

PAGE Seven groats and two pence.

FALSTAFF I can get no remedy against this consumption of   230
the purse. Borrowing only lingers and lingers it out, but
the disease is incurable. (*Giving letters*) Go bear this letter
to my lord of Lancaster; this to the Prince; this to the

---

215 God] Q; heauen F   221.1 *Exeunt . . . Servant*] OXFORD; *not in* QF   223 a] Q; he F
232 (*Giving letters*)] OXFORD; *not in* QF

212–14 **I . . . perpetual motion** Falstaff pro-
tests that his good offices as a heroic soldier are exploited by overuse: he is
rendered 'too common' by 'perpetual
motion'. He would prefer 'rest' (after all
the Lord Chief Justice claims that he is 'an
old man') and a quiet decay at the corro-
sive hands of 'rust' (old age); cf. the proverb 'It is better to wear out than rust
out' (Dent W209).

220 **crosses** A quibble on 'cross' meaning
coin (because a cross was stamped upon
one side of the coin—*OED sb.* 20). Far
from granting him a facetiously demanded thousand pound, the Lord Chief
Justice tells Falstaff that he is not even to
be trusted with coins; but he also means
that Falstaff complains too much about
his lot.

222 **fillip** strike smartly
three-man beetle a huge sledgeham-
mer with three handles for driving
wedges and ramming paving stones
222–4 **A man . . . lechery** Cf. the proverb
'Old men are covetous by nature' (Dent
M568).
225 **pinches** torments
225–6 **both . . . curses** both age and youth
anticipate (lit. 'come before'—*OED, prevent, v.* 1c) my curses (because they have
their intrinsic diseases, they obviate the
need for Falstaff's imprecations)
229 **groats** A groat is a four-pence piece.
230–1 **consumption of the purse** Cf. the
proverb 'He is purse-sick and lacks a physician' (Dent P263).
233 **this . . . Prince** Delivered by Bardolph
at 2.2.94.

Earl of Westmorland; and this to old Mistress Ursula
whom I have weekly sworn to marry since I perceived   235
the first white hair of my chin. About it; you know
where to find me.   ⌜*Exit Page*⌝
A pox of this gout, or a gout of this pox, for the one or
the other plays the rogue with my great toe. 'Tis no
matter if I do halt; I have the wars for my colour,   240
and my pension shall seem the more reasonable. A
good wit will make use of anything. I will turn diseases
to commodity.   *Exit*

1.3   *Enter the Archbishop of York, Thomas Mowbray the*
           Earl Marshal, Lord Hastings, and Lord Bardolph

ARCHBISHOP OF YORK
    Thus have you heard our cause, and known our means,
    And, my most noble friends, I pray you all
    Speak plainly your opinions of our hopes;
    And first, Lord Marshal, what say you to it?

MOWBRAY
    I well allow the occasion of our arms,   5
    But gladly would be better satisfied
    How in our means we should advance ourselves
    To look with forehead bold and big enough
    Upon the power and puissance of the King.

---

236 of] Q; on F   237 *Exit Page*] CAPELL; *not in* QF   239 the other] Q; th'other F   'Tis] Q; It
is F   243 *Exit*] CAPELL; *Exeunt* F; *not in* Q
    1.3.0.1–2 *Enter … Bardolph*] CAPELL (subs.); *Enter th'Archbishop, Thomas Mowbray (Earle
Marshall) the* | *Lord Hastings, Fauconbridge, and Bardolfe.* Q; *Enter Archbishop, Hastings,
Mowbray, and* | *Lord Bardolfe.* F   1 cause] Q; causes F   known] Q; kno F

234 **Ursula** At 2.1.85–91 Mistress Quickly
     claims that sitting in her Dolphin cham-
     ber on a Wednesday in Whitsun week
     Falstaff promised to marry her. In *Henry
     V* 2.1.17 she is called 'Nell Quickly' and
     is married to Pistol (after an earlier
     betrothal to Nym). It would appear
     therefore that 'old Mistress Ursula' may
     be another woman unscrupulously
     courted by Falstaff (cf. his similar, but
     more comically presented, philandering
     in *Merry Wives*, and see Introduction, p.
     63). His use of the epithet 'old' might
     suggest that this is a rich elderly widow
     whose fortunes might replenish his hae-
     morrhaging purse.
240 **halt** limp
     colour pretext (*OED sb.*[1] 12b)

243 **commodity** profit
1.3.1 **cause** matter in dispute
4 **Lord Marshal** Thomas Mowbray, the
   son of the identically named first Duke
   of Norfolk who was banished in perpe-
   tuity by Richard II, at the same time as
   Henry Bolingbroke's ten-year exile was
   announced. The courtesy title of Earl
   Marshal had been bestowed on Westmorland, but the Mowbrays continued to
   claim it as theirs.
5 **allow** grant
7 **in** within
8 **forehead … big** Cf. the proverb 'To have
   an impudent (etc.) forehead' (Dent
   F590).
9 **puissance** power, strength

HASTINGS

Our present musters grow upon the file   10
To five-and-twenty thousand men of choice,
And our supplies live largely in the hope
Of great Northumberland, whose bosom burns
With an incensèd fire of injuries.

LORD BARDOLPH

The question then, Lord Hastings, standeth thus: 15
Whether our present five-and-twenty thousand
May hold up head without Northumberland?

HASTINGS

With him we may.

LORD BARDOLPH   Yea, marry, there's the point;
But if without him we be thought too feeble,
My judgement is we should not step too far
Till we had his assistance by the hand;   20
For in a theme so bloody-faced as this,
Conjecture, expectation, and surmise
Of aids incertain should not be admitted.

ARCHBISHOP OF YORK

'Tis very true, Lord Bardolph, for indeed
It was young Hotspur's cause at Shrewsbury.   25

LORD BARDOLPH

It was, my lord; who lined himself with hope,
Eating the air and promise of supply,
Flatt'ring himself in project of a power
Much smaller than the smallest of his thoughts;   30
And so, with great imagination
Proper to madmen, led his powers to death,
And winking leapt into destruction.

---

18 Yea] Q; I F   21–4 Till... admitted] F; *not in* Q   26 cause] Q; case F   28 and] Q; on
F   29 in] Q; with F

10 **upon the file** on the roll (*OED, file, sb.*² 3c)
11 **men of choice** picked troops
12 **supplies** reinforcements (*OED sb.* 5)
   largely plentifully
26 **cause** matter of concern
27 **lined** fortified (*OED v.*¹ 2)
28 **air and promise** Cf. 'I eat the air, pro-mise-crammed' (*Hamlet* 3.2.90–1). Hot-spur fed on a promise of reinforcements

as insubstantial as air: cf. the proverb 'A man cannot live on air like a chameleon' (Dent M226).
29 **project of a power** anticipation of an armed force
30 **Much smaller** which turned out to be much smaller
33 **winking** shutting his eyes. Cf. the story of Caesar's daring Cassius to 'Leap' into the 'angry flood' (*Julius Caesar* 1.2.102–11).

HASTINGS

    But, by your leave, it never yet did hurt
    To lay down likelihoods and forms of hope.   35

LORD BARDOLPH

    Yes, if this present quality of war—
    Indeed the instant action, a cause on foot—
    Lives so in hope, as in an early spring
    We see th'appearing buds, which to prove fruit
    Hope gives not so much warrant as despair   40
    That frosts will bite them. When we mean to build,
    We first survey the plot, then draw the model;
    And when we see the figure of the house,
    Then must we rate the cost of the erection,
    Which if we find outweighs ability,   45
    What do we then but draw anew the model
    In fewer offices, or, at least, desist
    To build at all? Much more in this great work—
    Which is almost to pluck a kingdom down
    And set another up—should we survey   50
    The plot of situation and the model,
    Consent upon a sure foundation,
    Question surveyors, know our own estate,
    How able such a work to undergo,
    To weigh against his opposite; or else   55
    We fortify in paper and in figures,
    Using the names of men instead of men,
    Like one that draws the model of an house

36–55 Yes...else] F; *not in* Q   36–7 war—... action,...foot—] F (~,...~: ~,)   57 instead] F, Q (in steed)   58 one] F, Q (on)   an] Q; a F

36–41 **Yes...them** These F-only lines (cf. Introduction, pp. 86–7) are among the most complex in the play. They could be paraphrased as follows: 'Yes, it does hurt [to plan in this fashion] if the present state of war—this imminent action, the matter that is now afoot—has as little hope of success as the new buds of spring which are more likely to be nipped by the frost than to produce fruit' (lit. in the case of which the hope that they will achieve full maturity is less justified than the despairing anticipation that the frost will destroy them).

41–62 **When . . . tyranny** Adapted from

the Parable of the Builder in Luke 14: 28–30: 'For which of you minding to buylde a towre, sitteth not downe before, and cou[n]teth the cost, whether he haue sufficient to performe it, Lest that after he hathe laid the fundation, and is not able to performe it, all that beholde it, beginne to mocke him, Saying, This man began to buylde, and was not able to make an end.'

43 **figure** design

44 **rate** calculate (*OED v.*[1] 2)

45 **ability** i.e. ability to pay

47 **offices** rooms

55 **opposite** adverse circumstances

Beyond his power to build it, who, half-through,
Gives o'er, and leaves his part-created cost   60
A naked subject to the weeping clouds,
And waste for churlish winter's tyranny.

HASTINGS

Grant that our hopes, yet likely of fair birth,
Should be stillborn, and that we now possessed
The utmost man of expectation,   65
I think we are a body strong enough,
Even as we are, to equal with the King.

LORD BARDOLPH

What, is the King but five-and-twenty thousand?

HASTINGS

To us no more, nay, not so much, Lord Bardolph;
For his divisions, as the times do brawl,   70
Are in three heads: one power against the French,
And one against Glyndŵr, perforce a third
Must take up us. So is the unfirm King
In three divided, and his coffers sound
With hollow poverty and emptiness.   75

LORD BARDOLPH

That he should draw his several strengths together
And come against us in full puissance
Need not be dreaded?

HASTINGS   If he should do so,
He leaves his back unarmed, the French and Welsh
Baying him at the heels; never fear that.   80

LORD BARDOLPH

Who is it like should lead his forces hither?

HASTINGS

The Duke of Lancaster and Westmorland;

66 a] F; so Q   71 Are] F; And Q   78 not] F; not to Q   79 He...Welsh] F (He leaues his backe vnarm'd, the French, and Welch); French and Welch he leaues his back vnarmde, they Q; To *French*, and *Welsh*, he leaves his back unarm'd, | They CAPELL

60 **his part-created cost** the incompletely achieved object of his expenditure
65 **The utmost...expectation** every last man that we could expect
70 **as...brawl** in these times of strife
81 **Who...hither** At 1.1.131–5 Morton already announced to Northumberland in Lord Bardolph's presence that the royal forces were led by 'young Lancaster

| And Westmorland'.
82 **Duke of Lancaster** The title properly belongs to Hal (who inherited it from Bolingbroke) and not to his brother John, even though John was born at Lancaster and is called 'the lord Iohn of Lancaster' by Holinshed. If not to Hal, then the title should belong to his second brother Thomas (see Stow, 1592, p. 513).

Against the Welsh, himself and Harry Monmouth;
But who is substituted against the French
I have no certain notice.

ARCHBISHOP OF YORK   Let us on,   85
And publish the occasion of our arms.
The commonwealth is sick of their own choice;
Their over-greedy love hath surfeited.
An habitation giddy and unsure
Hath he that buildeth on the vulgar heart.   90
O thou fond many, with what loud applause
Didst thou beat heaven with blessing Bolingbroke,
Before he was what thou wouldst have him be!
And being now trimmed in thine own desires,
Thou, beastly feeder, art so full of him   95
That thou provok'st thyself to cast him up.
So, so, thou common dog, didst thou disgorge
Thy glutton bosom of the royal Richard;
And now thou wouldst eat thy dead vomit up,
And howl'st to find it. What trust is in these times?   100
They that when Richard lived would have him die
Are now become enamoured on his grave.
Thou that threw'st dust upon his goodly head,
When through proud London he came sighing on
After th'admirèd heels of Bolingbroke,   105
Cri'st now, 'O earth, yield us that king again,
And take thou this!' O thoughts of men accursed!
Past and to come seems best; things present, worst.

---

84 against] Q; 'gainst F   85–108 ARCHBISHOP . . . worst] F; *not in* Q

84 **substituted** delegated (*OED, substitute,*
   v. 1c)
85 **notice** information
89–90 **An habitation . . . heart** Echoes
   Luke 6: 49: 'But he that heareth and
   doeth not, is like a man that buylt an
   house vpon ye earth without funda-
   cio[n], against which the flood did beat,
   and it fel by and by: and the fall of that
   house was great.'
91 **fond** foolish
   many multitude
94 **trimmed** furnished
99 **eat . . . up** The proverbial expression
   that a dog returns to its vomit (Dent

D455) is biblical in origin; compare
'As . . . foolishness' with Proverbs 26:
11: 'As a dogge turneth againe to his
owne vomite, so a foole turneth to his
foolishness'; see also 2 Peter 2: 22: 'But
it is come vnto them, according to the
true prouerbe, The dogge is returned to
his owne vomit: and, The sowe that was
washed, to the wallowing in the myer.'
103–5 **Thou . . . Bolingbroke** Cf. *Richard II*
   5.2.1–40, and particularly 5.2.6 and 30.
108 **seems** On the use of the singular accord
   with a plural subject, see above, 1.2.71–
   2.

⌈MOWBRAY⌉

Shall we go draw our numbers and set on?

HASTINGS

We are time's subjects, and time bids be gone.   *Exeunt*   110

2.1   *Enter Mistress Quickly, the hostess of a tavern, and*
Fang, an officer, ⌈followed by⌉ Snare, another officer

MISTRESS QUICKLY Master Fang, have you entered the action?

FANG It is entered.

MISTRESS QUICKLY Where's your yeoman? Is't a lusty yeoman? Will a stand to't?   5

FANG Sirrah!—Where's Snare?

MISTRESS QUICKLY O Lord, ay, good Master Snare.

SNARE Here, here.

FANG Snare, we must arrest Sir John Falstaff.

MISTRESS QUICKLY Yea, good Master Snare, I have entered   10
him and all.

SNARE It may chance cost some of us our lives, for he will
stab.

---

109 MOWBRAY] F; *Bish⟨op⟩*. Q   110 *Exeunt*] Q (*ex.*); *not in* F

2.1.0.1–2 *Enter . . . another officer*] This edition; *Enter Hostesse of the Tauerne, and an Officer or two*. Q; *Enter Hostesse, with two Officers, Fang, and Snare*. F   1 MISTRESS QUICKLY] *throughout for* Q '*Hostesse*', '*Host*.', '*Quickly*', '*Qui*.', '*host*.', '*Ho*.' *Fang*] Q (*Phang*), F   4 Is't] Q; Is it F   5 a] Q; he F   to't] Q; to it F   7 O Lord, ay] Q (O Lord I); I, I F   10 Yea] Q; I F   12 for] Q; *not in* F

---

109 **draw our numbers** assemble our troops (Schmidt, i. 334)

2.1.0.2 *Fang . . . Snare* The sergeant and his yeoman respectively. Names for the sheriff's officers were common in the period (as e.g. in Sergeant Ambush and his yeoman Clutch in Dekker's and Webster's *Westward Ho!*). With Doll's abusive comments about the physical appearance of the first beadle, 'Nut-hook' (5.4.7), compare Middleton's and Webster's 'Flesh-hook' in *Anything for a Quiet Life* which also features a yeoman called 'Counter-buff'; 'fang' describes 'the act or fact of catching or seizing' (*OED sb*. I).

1 **Master** An inappropriate form of address for a mere constable. Mistress Quickly

similarly blunders by elevating characters in rank when she addresses the Lord Chief Justice as 'your grace', a title for which he does not qualify, and Pistol as 'captain'. Her folly and malapropisms are everywhere in evidence. She is not likely to be sycophantic here (*pace* Cowl, p. 43; Humphreys, p. 38).

1–2 **entered the action** begun the law-suit (*OED*, *enter*, *v*. 22a)

5 **stand to't** apply himself manfully to the task in hand (*OED v*. 76c); with a bawdy pun on becoming erect: see Williams, 1994, pp. 1305–9.

10–11 **entered him** brought a suit against him

MISTRESS QUICKLY Alas the day, take heed of him; he
    stabbed me in mine own house, most beastly, in good   15
    faith. A cares not what mischief he does; if his weapon be
    out, he will foin like any devil, he will spare neither man,
    woman, nor child.
FANG If I can close with him, I care not for his thrust.
MISTRESS QUICKLY No, nor I neither; I'll be at your elbow.   20
FANG An I but fist him, an a come but within my
    view—
MISTRESS QUICKLY I am undone by his going, I warrant
    you; he's an infinitive thing upon my score. Good Master
    Fang, hold him sure; good Master Snare, let him not   25
    scape. A comes continuantly to Pie Corner—saving your
    manhoods—to buy a saddle, and he is indited to dinner

15–16 most...A] Q; and that most beastly: he F   16 does] Q; doth F   21 An] Q; If F   an]
Q; if F   a] Q; he F   22 view] Q; Vice F   23 by] Q; with F   24 you] Q; *not in* F   he's] Q; he
is F   26 A] Q; he F   continuantly] F; continually Q

14–19 **he stabbed...thrust** A string of
unwitting bawdy double-entendres on
stabbed, weapon, foin ('to make a thrust
with a pointed weapon', *OED*; cf. also
below, l. 30), and cf. 'thrust to the wall'
(*Romeo* 1.1.15).
19 **close** grapple with (*OED v.* 13)
21 **fist** strike with the fist
22 **view** Fang's reading 'Vice' (i.e. firm grip) is
preferred in some editions, perhaps because Fang has just expressed a wish to
'close' with Falstaff. The Fang of F specifically continues the idea launched in l.
19, whereas in Q he embarks on a new
lateral train of thought which amounts
to a hyperbolical statement of his san-
guine threat against Falstaff.
24 **infinitive** infinite. Mistress Quickly's
usage is either archaic or malapropistic.
It is worth noting that the first recorded
usage in *OED* dates from John Hardyng's
Chronicle (1470). Two sixteenth-century
editions were printed (1543), and, unlike
Holinshed, Hardyng directly accuses
Northumberland of acting in bad faith
towards Hotspur: 'His father came not
out of Northumberland, | But failed

hym foule without witte or rede' (see
Gilian West, 'Hardyng's *Chronicle* and
Shakespeare's Hotspur', *SQ* 41 (1990),
348–51).
26 **continuantly** F's reading (Q has 'continually') is Mistress Quickly's version of
(probably) 'continuately', i.e. continually. Humphreys, Melchiori, and others
follow Delius's interpretation of it as a
blunder for 'incontinently' = 'at once,
immediately'.
26–7 **Pie Corner—...saddle** 'The corner
of Giltspur St. and Cock Lane in W.
Smithfield, London. It was so called
from the cooks' shops which stood
there, at which pigs were dressed during
Bartholomew Fair' (Sugden, p. 411). It
had a reputation for foul smells and it is
here that Face first met Subtle, 'at *pie-
corner*, | Taking your meale of steeme
in, from cookes stalls' (Ben Jonson's *The
Alchemist* 1.1.25–6, H & S v.).
27 **indited** i.e. invited. The slip is alliterative
(followed by 'dinner' and 'Head') and
occurs in anticipation of Mistress
Quickly's 'legal exion' (l. 29).

to the Lubber's Head in Lombard Street to Master
Smooth's the silk-man. I pray you, since my exion is
entered, and my case so openly known to the world, let   30
him be brought in to his answer. A hundred mark is a
long one for a poor lone woman to bear, and I have
borne, and borne, and borne, and have been fobbed off,
and fobbed off, and fobbed off, from this day to that day,
that it is a shame to be thought on. There is no honesty in   35
such dealing, unless a woman should be made an ass and
a beast, to bear every knave's wrong.

Enter Falstaff, Bardolph and the Page

Yonder he comes, and that arrant malmsey-nose knave
Bardolph with him. Do your offices, do your offices,
Master Fang and Master Snare, do me, do me, do me   40
your offices.

29 pray you] Q; pra'ye F   34 and fobbed off] Q; *not in* F   37.1 *Enter . . . Page*] OXFORD; *En-*
ter sir Iohn, and Bardolfe, and the boy. Q (*after l.* 41); *Enter Falstaffe and Bardolfe.* F   38 knave]
Q; *not in* F

28 **Lubber's** A Quicklyism for Libbard's or
Leopard's. The joke lies partly in the pho-
nic confusion of Lubber's and Libbard's
with the former denoting 'a big, clumsy,
stupid fellow' who is also lazy, a fitting
description of Falstaff. The surmised lost
meaning of the word in French 'lober'
('to sponge upon') may still have been
available in a submerged form given the
context here. In support of the leopard's
head as a fitting sign for a silkman's shop,
Shaaber (p. 109) quotes Sherwood's
1632 *Dictionary*: 'A Libbards head (on
the knees or elbowes of old fashioned
garments)'.
Lombard Street Runs from Mansion
House to Gracechurch Street and is
named after the Lombard merchants
who settled here in the thirteenth century. It contained a number of inns
which were identified by signs, such as
'The Lamb', 'The Pelican', 'The Phoe-
nix', 'The Flower-de-Luce', and 'The
George' (cf. Sugden, p. 312).
29 **exion** i.e. action, used here perhaps to
reflect a comically affected pronunciation
by Mistress Quickly
30 **case** For a similar sexual use of the
phrase, cf. Mistress Quickly's indignation
over 'Jinny's case' in response to the
Latin genitive plurals '*horum, harum,*

horum' (*Merry Wives* 4.1.61). According
to *OED* (*a.* 2) 'Genitive' denoted 'pertain-
ing to generation' until 1656.
31 **A hundred mark** The equivalent of £66,
a great deal of money in Shakespeare's
time; see below, ll. 144, 149–50.
31–2 **a long one** Perhaps a loan that almost
over-stretches her resources. The use of a
spatial adjective rather than of a quan-
tifier may be because she collapses the
debt with a hundred yard mark at archery (Hemingway, 1921).
33 **borne** patiently endured (*OED ppl. a.* 1a)
fobbed off put off deceitfully (*OED, fob, v.*¹
3a)
38 **arrant** 'notorious, downright, unmiti-
gated' (*OED a.* 3)
malmsey-nose i.e. his nose is as red as the
colour of malmsey, a strong sweet wine
from the Mediterranean
40 **do me** The ethical dative is used colloquially for emphasis in the period (Abbott, §220), but 'do' also means 'coit
with' (Williams, 1994, pp. 395–8), and
the bawdy meaning may be intended
here; the 'ethical dative' is the dative
when used 'to imply that a person,
other than the subject or object, has an
indirect interest in the fact stated' (*OED,*
ethical, a. 3).

FALSTAFF How now, whose mare's dead? What's the
  matter?

FANG Sir John, I arrest you at the suit of Mistress Quickly.

FALSTAFF Away, varlets! Draw, Bardolph, cut me off the   45
  villain's head, throw the quean in the channel.

MISTRESS QUICKLY Throw me in the channel? I'll throw thee
  in the channel. Wilt thou, wilt thou, thou bastardly
  rogue? Murder, murder! Ah, thou honeysuckle villain,
  wilt thou kill God's officers and the King's? Ah, thou   50
  honeyseed rogue, thou art a honeyseed, a man-queller,
  and a woman-queller.

FALSTAFF Keep them off, Bardolph.

FANG A rescue, a rescue!

MISTRESS QUICKLY Good people, bring a rescue or two. Thou   55
  wot, wot thou, thou wot, wot ta? Do, do, thou rogue, do,
  thou hempseed!

PAGE Away, you scullion, you rampallian, you fustilarian!
  I'll tickle your catastrophe!

---

44 Sir John] F; *not in* Q   Mistress‸ Quickly] Qb (~ Quickly), F (Mist. *Quickly*); ~, ~ Qa
48 in the channel] Q; there F   49 Ah] Q; O F   50 Ah] Q; O F   54 FANG] F; *Offic⟨er⟩*.
Q   55 or two] Q; *not in* F   55–6 Thou . . . ta] Q; Thou wilt not? thou wilt not? F
59 tickle] Q; tucke F

---

42 **whose . . . dead** Proverbial for 'why the
  fuss?'; cf. Dent M657.

45 **varlets** Acutely appropriate to Fang and
  Snare: the word means both sergeant
  (*OED, varlet,* 1d) and 'a person of a low,
  mean, or knavish disposition' (*OED* 2).

46 **quean** a harlot, strumpet (*OED* 1)
  channel gutter

48 **bastardly** Either (a) counterfeit, i.e. false
  to his vows, promises, and bonds (*OED a.*
  2), or (b) a running together of 'bastard'
  and 'dastardly'. In view of the catachresis
  which follows (b) has probably a stronger
  claim.

49–51 **honeysuckle . . . honeyseed** Instead
  of 'homicidal' and 'homicide'.

51 **man-queller** killer of men (*OED, quell,* v.¹
  1: to kill, slay, put to death)

54–5 **rescue . . . or two** Fang's exclamation may be a panic-stricken reference to
  Bardolph's restraining two officers from
  arresting Falstaff (*OED, rescue, sb.* 2),
  while Mistress Quickly seems to want the
  officers ('Good people') to go and get rein-

forcements; **bring . . . two** may be a forced
  usage of 'rescue' rather like 'guard' or
  'rear'. She is certainly in a state of high
  excitement and seems to be daring Falstaff
  and his page to strike at her.

55–6 **Thou wot . . . wot ta** You will . . . will
  ye?

57 **hempseed** Another variation on 'homicide'.

58 **scullion** An abusive epithet for a menial.
  rampallian ruffian, villain, scoundrel
  (sometimes applied to women as well as
  men)
  fustilarian *OED* suspects a nonceword,
  perhaps a comic formation on 'fustilugs'
  = 'a person, esp. a woman, of gross or
  corpulent habit; a fat, frowzy woman'.
  The page may be wishing to taunt Mistress Quickly by parodying her linguistic
  abuses.

59 **tickle . . . catastrophe** A quip current at
  the time and meaning 'make your back-
  side smart' (*OED, catastrophe,* 2b = 'the
  posteriors').

Enter the Lord Chief Justice and his men

LORD CHIEF JUSTICE

  What is the matter? Keep the peace here, ho! 60

    ⌈*Fang* ⌉ *seizes Falstaff*

MISTRESS QUICKLY Good my lord, be good to me. I beseech
you, stand to me.

LORD CHIEF JUSTICE

  How now, Sir John? What, are you brawling here?

  Doth this become your place, your time and business?

  You should have been well on your way to York. 65

  ⌈*To Fang* ⌉ Stand from him, fellow; wherefore hang'st
    thou upon him?

MISTRESS QUICKLY O my most worshipful lord, an't please
your grace, I am a poor widow of Eastcheap, and he is
arrested at my suit.

LORD CHIEF JUSTICE For what sum? 70

MISTRESS QUICKLY It is more than for some, my lord, it is for
all I have. He hath eaten me out of house and home. He
hath put all my substance into that fat belly of his; (*to
Falstaff*) but I will have some of it out again, or I will ride
thee a-nights like the mare. 75

FALSTAFF I think I am as like to ride the mare, if I have any
vantage of ground to get up.

59.1 *Enter . . . men*] Q (~ *the . . .*); *Enter. Ch. Iustice.* F   60 What is] Q; What's F
60.1 *Fang . . . Falstaff*] OXFORD; *not in* QF   66 thou] Q; *not in* F   72 all] Q; all: all F
75 a-] Q; o' F

---

62 **stand to** side with, help, back, support
(*OED v.* 76h), with a bawdy allusion to
being erect (see above, l. 5).

68 **grace** See above, l. 1.
Eastcheap The street runs from the
junction of Cannon and Gracechurch
Streets to Great Tower Street and was
the site of the Boar's Head tavern. In his
Survey of London Stow (1603, i. 217)
records how 'In the yeare 1410. the 11.
of *Henrie* the fourth . . . the kings sonnes,
Thomas and *Iohn*, being in *Eastcheape* at
supper, (or rather at breakefast, for it was
after the watch was broken vp, betwixt
two and three of the clock after midnight)
a great debate happened betweene their
men, and other of the Court, which lasted
one houre, till the Maior and Shiriffes
with other Citizens appeased the same:
for the which afterwards the said Maior,

Aldermen and shiriffes, were called to
answere before the King, his sonnes,
and diuerse Lordes being highly mooued
against the Citie. At which time *William
Gascoyne* chiefe Iustice required the
Maior and Aldermen, for the Citizens, to
put them in the kings grace: whereunto
they aunswered, that they had not
offended, but (according to the law) had
done | their best in stinting debate, and
maintaining of the peace: vpon which
aunswere the king remitted all his ire,
and dismissed them.'

72 **eaten . . . home** Proverbial (Dent H784).

76 **ride . . . mare** pursue you at night like a
nightmare (*OED*, *mare*, n.² 1). In his
reply Falstaff twists this phrase to give
an obvious sexual meaning.

77 **vantage** 'position or opportunity likely to
give superiority' (*OED sb.* 3a)

LORD CHIEF JUSTICE How comes this, Sir John? What man of
   good temper would endure this tempest of exclamation?
   Are you not ashamed, to enforce a poor widow to so   80
   rough a course to come by her own?
FALSTAFF (*to the Hostess*) What is the gross sum that I owe
   thee?
MISTRESS QUICKLY Marry, if thou wert an honest man, thyself, and the money too. Thou didst swear to me upon a   85
   parcel-gilt goblet, sitting in my Dolphin chamber, at the
   round table, by a sea-coal fire, upon Wednesday in
   Wheeson week, when the Prince broke thy head for
   liking his father to a singing-man of Windsor—thou
   didst swear to me then, as I was washing thy wound,   90

---

78 Sir John] Q; Sir *Iohn*? Fy F   man] Q; a man F   85 upon] Q; on F   88 Wheeson]
Q; Whitson F   89 liking] Q; lik'ning F   his father] Q; him F

---

79 **temper** disposition
86 **parcel-gilt** 'Partly gilded; *esp.* of silver
ware, as bowls, cups, etc., having the
inner surface gilt' (*OED a.*) The image of
Falstaff vowing to marry Mistress Quickly
on something of considerable value may
be intended as a comic travesty of the
mass and its sacraments. Oaths are
usually taken on the Bible (cf. below, l.
101), but the tavern is Falstaff's place of
worship and so a goblet is a fitting substitute.
   Dolphin chamber It was a common practice to name inn-rooms, as in 'Half-
moon' (l. 27) and 'Pomegranate' (ll.
36–7) in *1 Henry IV* 2.5. The fact that
Falstaff promises marriage in the Dolphin
chamber may suggest that, like Antony
whose delights are dolphin-like, Falstaff
imagines that his back also transcends
the elements he inhabits, notably the tavern.
87 **sea-coal** mineral coal from the coast (as
distinguished from the cheaper inland
charcoal)
88 **Wheeson** A north-country and midland
form for Whitsun, and pronounced
'Whisson'.
89 **liking** likening (*OED, like, v.²* 1b = 'To
represent as like *to*')
   singing-man of Windsor Probably a
reference to John Magdalen, 'a priest
one of king Richards chappele' (see Bullough, vol. 3, 1960, p. 413 and Humphreys, pp. 234–5) who closely

resembled the former king in appearance. During the 1400 conspiracy at
Brentford led by Aumerle, the Duke of
York and the Abbot of Westminster
(when the King was at nearby Windsor
for Christmas), the rebels dressed Magdalen up like King Richard to lend credibility to their claim that he had escaped.
Although Magdalen is not specifically
called a 'singing-man', Shakespeare
may have associated the chaplain with
choristers at St George's Chapel in Windsor. That a 'singing-man' was widely
known to have been a pretender during
the Lancastrian reign is clear from Sidney's *Discourse to the Queen's Majesty*
(1580), when he urges the Queen to consider former pretenders' bids for power:
'Lett the singing man in Henry IVths
time, Perkin Warbeck in your grand-
fathers...' (quoted by Humphreys, p.
243). Falstaff's comparison of Henry IV
to Magdalen would imply that the King
was a fake or an impostor, which in a
sense he is (cf. 4.3.313–15). In 'Falstaff's
"Singing-Man of Windsor": 2 Henry IV
II.i.', *SQ* 39 (1988), 58–9, Elizabeth
Schafer argues instead that the reference
is to 'a notorious singing-man of Windsor, well-known to Shakespeare's contemporary audience: William Wolner',
a famous glutton (he died of eating a
raw eel) who was called 'a singing-man
of Windsor' in a contemporary jest-book.

to marry me, and make me my lady thy wife. Canst thou
deny it? Did not goodwife Keech the butcher's wife come
in then and call me Gossip Quickly?—coming in to borrow a mess of vinegar, telling us she had a good dish of
prawns, whereby thou didst desire to eat some, whereby   95
I told thee they were ill for a green wound? And didst
thou not, when she was gone downstairs, desire me to be
no more so familiarity with such poor people, saying
that ere long they should call me madam? And didst
thou not kiss me, and bid me fetch thee thirty shillings?   100
I put thee now to thy book-oath, deny it if thou canst.

FALSTAFF My lord, this is a poor mad soul, and she says up
and down the town that her eldest son is like you. She
hath been in good case, and the truth is, poverty hath
distracted her. But for these foolish officers, I beseech you   105
I may have redress against them.

LORD CHIEF JUSTICE Sir John, Sir John, I am well acquainted
with your manner of wrenching the true cause the false
way. It is not a confident brow, nor the throng of words
that come with such more than impudent sauciness from   110
you, can thrust me from a level consideration. You have,
as it appears to me, practised upon the easy-yielding
spirit of this woman, and made her serve your uses
both in purse and in person.

MISTRESS QUICKLY Yea, in truth, my lord.   115

LORD CHIEF JUSTICE Pray thee, peace. (*To Falstaff*) Pay her
the debt you owe her, and unpay the villainy you have

---

97 thou not] Q; not thou F   98 more so] Q; more F   familiarity] Q; familiar F   102 mad] Q
(made), F   111–12 You...me] Q; I know you ha' F   113–14 and...person] Q; *not in* F
115 Yea, in truth] Q; Yes in troth F   116 Pray thee] Q; Prethee F

---

92 **Keech** An appropriate name for a
   butcher, because 'keech' means 'a lump
   of congealed fat' (*OED sb.* 1); cf. also *All is
   True* 1.1.55, where Cardinal Wolsey, a
   butcher's son, is called 'a keech'.
93 **Gossip** A familiar form of address between female neighbours and friends.
94 **mess** 'a quantity (of meat,...etc.) sufficient to make a dish' (*OED sb.* 1c)
95 **whereby** whereupon
96 **green** (of a wound) recent, unhealed
   (*OED a.* 10a)

98 **familiarity** Malapropism for 'familiar',
   which is also F's reading.
99 **madam** An appellation befitting the wife
   of a knight.
101 **book-oath** oath on the Bible
104 **in good case** Perhaps meaning in good
   physical condition (*OED, case, sb.*¹ 5);
   well off.
117 **unpay** 'undo, make good' (*OED v.*²)

done with her. The one you may do with sterling money,
and the other with current repentance.

FALSTAFF My lord, I will not undergo this sneap without   120
reply. You call honourable boldness impudent sauci-
ness; if a man will make curtsy and say nothing, he is
virtuous. No, my lord, my humble duty remembered, I
will not be your suitor. I say to you I do desire deliverance
from these officers, being upon hasty employment in the   125
King's affairs.

LORD CHIEF JUSTICE You speak as having power to do
wrong; but answer in th'effect of your reputation, and
satisfy the poor woman.

FALSTAFF Come hither, hostess.   130
          She joins him.
          Enter Gower, a messenger

LORD CHIEF JUSTICE Now, Master Gower, what news?

GOWER
     The King, my lord, and Harry Prince of Wales,
     Are near at hand; the rest the paper tells.
          [Lord Chief Justice studies the paper]

FALSTAFF As I am a gentleman!

MISTRESS QUICKLY Faith, you said so before.   135

FALSTAFF As I am a gentleman! Come, no more words of it.

MISTRESS QUICKLY By this heavenly ground I tread on, I
must be fain to pawn both my plate and the tapestry of
my dining-chambers.

---

118 with her] Q; her F   122 make] Q; *not in* F   123 my humble] Q; your humble F
124 do] Q; *not in* F   128 th'effect] Q; the effect F   130.1 *She ... him.*] This edition; *not in*
QF   130.2 *Enter ... messenger*] OXFORD; *enter a messenger* Q (*after l.* 131); *Enter M. Gower* F
132 The King, my lord,] Q (The King, my Lord,), F (The King (my Lord)) Harry]
Q; Henrie F   133.1 *Lord ... paper*] This edition; *not in* QF   135 Faith] Q; Nay F

---

119 **current** 'sterling, genuine, authentic:
opposed to *counterfeit*' (*OED a.* 5). The
numismatic usage continues the train of
thought launched by 'Pay' and 'unpay'.

120 **sneap** snub, rebuke

125 **hasty** requiring haste

128 **in ... reputation** as befits the good report you claim

137 **heavenly ground** conflates two different
oaths, 'by heavenly light' and 'by this
ground'.

138 **fain** 'glad or content to take a certain
course ... as the lesser of two evils' (*OED
a.* 2)

FALSTAFF Glasses, glasses, is the only drinking; and for thy   140
walls, a pretty slight drollery, or the story of the Prodigal,
or the German hunting in waterwork, is worth a thousand of these bed-hangers and these fly-bitten tapestries.
Let it be ten pound if thou canst. Come, an 'twere not for
thy humours, there's not a better wench in England. Go,   145
wash thy face and draw the action. Come, thou must not
be in this humour with me. Dost not know me? Come,
come, I know thou wast set on to this.

MISTRESS QUICKLY Pray thee, Sir John, let it be but twenty
nobles; i'faith, I am loath to pawn my plate, so God save   150
me, la!

FALSTAFF Let it alone; I'll make other shift. You'll be a fool
still.

MISTRESS QUICKLY Well, you shall have it, though I pawn
my gown. I hope you'll come to supper. You'll pay me all   155
together?

142 German] Q (Iarman), F (Germane)   143 -hangers] Q; hangings F   tapestries] F; tapes-
trie Q   144 ten pound] Q (X.£), F (tenne pound)   an 'twere] Q; if it were F   145 there's]
Q; there is F   146 the] Q; thy F   147 Dost ... me] Q; *not in* F   147–8 Come, come]
Q; Come F   149 Pray thee] Q; Prethee F   150 i'faith] Q; *not in* F   I am] Q; I F
150–1 so ... me] Q; in good earnest F   154 though] Q; although F

140 **Glasses** Glass, particularly from Venice, was becoming very fashionable in
  the later sixteenth century and started to
  supersede gold, silver, and pewter for
  drinking vessels.
141 **drollery** 'A comic picture or drawing; a
  caricature' (*OED* 2b). These genre paint-
  ings, which featured low-life scenes, originated with Dutch painters towards the
  end of the sixteenth century.
  story ... Prodigal See Luke 15: 11–32, a
  popular subject for wall hangings and
  one of the leitmotifs of the *Henry IV*s.
142 **German hunting** i.e. a hunting scene,
  perhaps featuring a wild boar (cf. *Cymbeline* 2.5.16–17). The phrasing suggests
  that the audience is expected to recognize
  the motif. Rather than specifically denoting a legendary German hunter (such as
  St Hubert: Shaaber, p. 125), the phrase
  may be used adjectivally to point to the
  Continental (German and Dutch) origins
  of the scene.
  waterwork 'A kind of imitation tapestry,
  painted in size or distemper' (*OED* 4). But
  'water-colours' has also been suggested,
  perhaps because the phrase seems to be

  used here in opposition to tapestry.
143 **bed-hangers** A phrase applied con-
  temptuously to tapestries, i.e. as little
  more than curtains. This certainly
  seems to be the meaning of the F variant
  'bed-hangings'; but 'bed-hangers' could
  be a neutral word for tapestry (*OED*,
  hanger, n.² 2a = 'a piece of tapestry hanging'), although the context collocates
  'bed-hangers' with 'fly-bitten tapestries'.
144 **ten pound** Far from repaying his debt
  immediately as instructed, Falstaff en-
  gages in hugely increased borrowing
  from the thirty shillings (£1.50) of
  Whitsun.
145 **humours** moods
146 **draw** withdraw
149–50 **twenty nobles** As well as being
  given to malapropisms, Mistress Quickly
  is comically innumerate. A noble was
  worth 10 shillings (and by Shakespeare's
  time there were 20 shillings to the
  pound), so that the sum which she feels
  prepared to part from (instead of the one
  demanded by Falstaff) is exactly equivalent to his ten pounds; see 3.2.213–14.
155 **pay** repay

FALSTAFF Will I live? (*To Bardolph and the Page*) Go with
  her, with her; hook on, hook on.
MISTRESS QUICKLY Will you have Doll Tearsheet meet you at
  supper?   160
FALSTAFF No more words; let's have her.
  Exeunt Mistress Quickly, Fang, Snare, Bardolph, and
              the Page
LORD CHIEF JUSTICE (*to Gower*) I have heard better news.
FALSTAFF What's the news, my lord?
LORD CHIEF JUSTICE (*to Gower*) Where lay the King tonight?
GOWER At Basingstoke, my lord.   165
FALSTAFF (*to Lord Chief Justice*) I hope, my lord, all's well.
  What is the news, my lord?
LORD CHIEF JUSTICE (*to Gower*) Come all his forces back?
GOWER
  No, fifteen hundred foot, five hundred horse,
  Are marched up to my lord of Lancaster   170
  Against Northumberland and the Archbishop.
FALSTAFF (*to Lord Chief Justice*)
  Comes the King back from Wales, my noble lord?
LORD CHIEF JUSTICE (*to Gower*)
  You shall have letters of me presently.
  Come, go along with me, good Master Gower.

161.1–2 *Exeunt . . . Page*] OXFORD (*subs.*); *exit hostess and sergeant.* Q (*after l.* 158); *not in* F
162 better] Q; bitter F 163 my lord] Q; my good Lord F 164 tonight] Q; last night F
165 Basingstoke] F; Billingsgate Q

158 **hook on** hang on to her, i.e. do not let
her out of sight while she is in this humour (*OED, hook, v.* 5, 'To attach oneself
or be attached with or as with a hook; to
be coupled') ·
159 **Doll Tearsheet** Doll was a name for a
prostitute, as in Doll Common in *The Alchemist*. 'Tearsheet' has been read as a
misprint for 'Tearstreet' (i.e. street-
walker) in the light of Hal's anticipating
to meet 'some road' (2.2.158), but a
'sheet-walker' or 'tearer' is equally plausible, in view particularly of Beaumont's
and Fletcher's *Valentinian* 3.1.340–1,
where Maximus says 'If my wife for all
this should be a whore now, | A kind of
kicker out of sheets' (*The Dramatic Works
in the Beaumont and Fletcher Canon*, ed.
Fredson Bowers, vol. 4, 1979).

164 **tonight** last night (*OED adv.* 3)
165 **Basingstoke** At this time a market
town in Hampshire, some 46 miles
south-west of London. Q's inexplicable
'Billingsgate', London's fishmarket, may
result from a foul-paper misreading by
the compositor. F, which probably prints
a collated version of a (foul-paper pedigree) prompt-book and QA (see Introduction, pp. 98–9), makes better sense, even
though there is no historical evidence to
connect the King to Basingstoke (there
are no recorded royal visits to the town
between King Henry III's visit in 1230
and that of Henry VII in 1499: Baigent,
p. 78). The possibility remains that both
may be wrong guesses at the same original, but F's is the only acceptable one.
173 **presently** immediately

FALSTAFF My lord!   175
LORD CHIEF JUSTICE What's the matter?
FALSTAFF Master Gower, shall I entreat you with me to
    dinner?
GOWER I must wait upon my good lord here. I thank you,
    good Sir John.   180
LORD CHIEF JUSTICE Sir John, you loiter here too long, being
    you are to take soldiers up in counties as you go.
FALSTAFF Will you sup with me, Master Gower?
LORD CHIEF JUSTICE What foolish master taught you these
    manners, Sir John?   185
FALSTAFF Master Gower, if they become me not, he was a
    fool that taught them me. (*To Lord Chief Justice*) This is
    the right fencing grace, my lord—tap for tap, and so part
    fair.
LORD CHIEF JUSTICE Now the Lord lighten thee; thou art a   190
    great fool.   *Exeunt*

2.2 *Enter Prince Henry and Poins*
PRINCE HENRY Before God, I am exceeding weary.
POINS Is't come to that? I had thought weariness durst not
    have attached one of so high blood.
PRINCE HENRY Faith, it does me, though it discolours the
    complexion of my greatness to acknowledge it. Doth it
    not show vilely in me to desire small beer?

179–80 I...John] Q; I...here. | I...*Iohn* F   181–2 Sir...go] F; Sir...long, |
Being...vp | In...go. Q   182 counties] Q; Countries F   191 *Exeunt*] F; *not in* Q
    '**2.2.**0.1 *Enter...Poins*] ROWE; *Enter the Prince, Poynes, sir Iohn Russel, with other.* Q; *Enter
Prince Henry, Pointz, Bardolfe, and Page.* F   1 Before God] Q; Trust me F   2 Is't] Q; Is it F
4 Faith, it does] Q; It doth F

---

181 **being** 'it being the case that, seeing that,
    since' (*OED, be, v.* B. 3)
182 **take...up** levy, raise, enlist (troops)
    (*OED, take, v.* 93j)
    counties But his journey north would
    hardly take Falstaff through Glouceste-
    shire: see Introduction, p. 12.
2.2.0.1 On the presence in Q of *sir Iohn Rus-
    sel*, see Introduction, p. 29.
3 **attached** Used in the legal sense here,

meaning 'Arrested, seized under warrant
    of attachment' (*OED ppl. a.* 1).
4–5 **discolours the complexion** i.e. he
    blushes
6 **small beer** thin beer. A longing for it may
    show 'vilely' because it proves that the
    Prince is just like everybody else. That
    thin beer may have been used to counter
    hangovers is suggested by Humphreys,
    p. 49.

POINS Why, a prince should not be so loosely studied as to
remember so weak a composition.

PRINCE HENRY Belike then my appetite was not princely got,
for, by my troth, I do now remember the poor creature   10
small beer. But indeed, these humble considerations
make me out of love with my greatness. What a disgrace
is it to me to remember thy name! Or to know thy face
tomorrow! Or to take note how many pair of silk stockings thou hast—videlicet these, and those that were thy   15
peach-coloured ones—or to bear the inventory of thy
shirts—as one for superfluity, and another for use? But
that the tennis-court keeper knows better than I, for it is
a low ebb of linen with thee when thou keepest not
racket there, as thou hast not done a great while, be-   20
cause the rest of thy low countries have made a shift to
eat up thy holland. And God knows whether those that

10 by my troth] Q; in troth F   15 hast—videlicet] F (hast? (Viz.)); ~∧ with Q   16 ones]
F; once Q   17 another] Q; one other F   19 keepest] Q; kept'st F   21 thy] F; the Q
made...to] F; *not in* Q   22–6 And...strengthened] Q; *not in* F

7 **loosely studied** versed in immoral or
dissolute pursuits
10 **creature** For a similar inanimate usage,
cf. *Othello* 2.3.302: 'Good wine is a good
familiar creature' (*OED* 1 c & 1 d).
12–13 **What . . . name** Noblemen prided
themselves on 'forgetting' the names of
commoners: cf. Coriolanus' forgetting
the name of the 'poor man' who once in
Corioles used him 'kindly' (*Coriolanus*
1.10.81–90).
14–16 **silk stockings . . . peach-coloured** A
fashionable item and colour of clothing
usually associated with gallants and
would-be courtiers. The colour was probably symbolic of 'diminished riches, lost
courage, little nobleness' (Linthicum,
p. 40), and it may therefore have
prompted laughter in comic scenes.
15 **videlicet** F's phrase, more pointedly
than Q's 'with', draws attention to the
truly impecunious state of Poins's flashy
wardrobe: he owns only two pairs of
socks (one of which has lost its deep
pink colour, presumably through repeated washing) and two shirts. Q's
'with' may result from a ⟨th⟩ for ⟨z⟩ deciphering error.
16 **bear** bear in mind
18–20 **it . . . racket there** it is a sign of your

running out of shirts when you don't
play tennis (because players changed
their shirts often)
21–2 **the rest . . . holland** your other low-
life habits (i.e. vices) have contrived to
devour your linen. 'Holland' is a linen
fabric named after the province of Holland in the Netherlands (cf. *1 Henry IV*
3.3.70–1). There are several puns and
double-entendres here in (a) 'low countries' meaning the genital area, the
stews, and of course the Netherlands;
(b) 'shift' meaning change of shirt, but
also, here, contrivance; (c) 'eat up thy
holland' in which both the fabric and
the province are meant, and the political
tension between the low countries and
Holland may be alluded to as well (Humphreys, p. 50). Hal's rhetorical pyrotechnics display a degree of self-conscious, if
not self-indulgent, wit.
22–6 **And . . . strengthened** These Q-only
lines may have been removed from the
prompt-book, the source text for F, by the
Master of the Revels on account of their
profanity, particularly if the play was first
performed during the 1596–7 Christmas
season.
22–3 **those that bawl** i.e. Poins's bastards
begotten in the stews

bawl out the ruins of thy linen shall inherit his kingdom,
but the midwives say the children are not in the fault;
whereupon the world increases, and kindreds are migh-   25
tily strengthened.

POINS How ill it follows, after you have laboured so hard,
you should talk so idly. Tell me, how many good young
princes would do so, their fathers being so sick as yours
at this time is?   30

PRINCE HENRY Shall I tell thee one thing, Poins?

POINS Yes, faith, and let it be an excellent good thing.

PRINCE HENRY It shall serve among wits of no higher breeding than thine.

POINS Go to, I stand the push of your one thing that you   35
will tell.

PRINCE HENRY Marry, I tell thee it is not meet that I should
be sad now my father is sick; albeit I could tell to thee, as
to one it pleases me, for fault of a better, to call my friend,
I could be sad, and sad indeed too.   40

POINS Very hardly, upon such a subject.

PRINCE HENRY By this hand, thou thinkest me as far in the
devil's book as thou and Falstaff, for obduracy and per-
sistency. Let the end try the man. But I tell thee, my heart
bleeds inwardly that my father is so sick; and keeping   45
such vile company as thou art hath, in reason, taken
from me all ostentation of sorrow.

POINS The reason?

---

29 being] Q; lying F   30 at this time] Q; *not in* F   32 faith] Q; *not in* F   35–6 you will]
Q; you'l F   37 Marry] Q; Why F   42 By this hand] Q; *not in* F

---

23 **out** out of
 shall . . . kingdom After Matthew 25: 34:
 'Then shal the King say to them on his
 right hand, Come ye blessed of my
 Father: inherite ye ye kingdome prepared
 for you fro[m] the fundations of the
 worlde'; see also Mark 10: 14: 'But
 when Iesus sawe it, he was displeased,
 and said to them, Suffre the litle chil-
 dre[n] to come vnto me, and forbid
 them not: for of suche is the kingdome
 of God'.
25–6 **kindreds . . . strengthened** family

bonds are considerably reinforced (perhaps intended sarcastically)
27–8 **after . . . idly** after such verbal gym-
nastics you have so little substance to
communicate
35 **stand the push** stand up to
41 **Very hardly** with great difficulty
44 **Let . . . man** Cf. the proverb 'The end tries
(proves, etc.) all' (Dent E116.1).
46 **in reason** on reflection (*OED, reason, sb.*[1]
13b)
47 **ostentation** outward show

PRINCE HENRY What wouldst thou think of me if I should
      weep?   50
POINS I would think thee a most princely hypocrite.
PRINCE HENRY It would be every man's thought, and thou
      art a blessed fellow to think as every man thinks. Never a
      man's thought in the world keeps the roadway better
      than thine. Every man would think me an hypocrite   55
      indeed. And what accites your most worshipful thought
      to think so?
POINS Why, because you have been so lewd, and so much
      engrafted to Falstaff.
PRINCE HENRY And to thee.   60
POINS By this light, I am well spoke on; I can hear it with
      mine own ears. The worst that they can say of me is that I
      am a second brother, and that I am a proper fellow of my
      hands, and those two things I confess I cannot help.
            Enter Bardolph and the Page
      By the mass, here comes Bardolph.   65
PRINCE HENRY And the boy that I gave Falstaff. A had him
      from me Christian, and look if the fat villain have not
      transformed him ape.
BARDOLPH God save your grace.
PRINCE HENRY And yours, most noble Bardolph.   70
POINS (*to Bardolph*) Come, you virtuous ass, you bashful
      fool, must you be blushing? Wherefore blush you now?

---

59 engrafted] Q (engraffed), F (ingraffed)   61 By this light] Q; Nay F   spoke on] Q; spoken of
F   64.1 *Enter . . . Page*] This edition; *Enter Bardolfe and boy.* Q (*after l.* 65); *Enter Bardolfe.* F
(*after l.* 68)   65 By the mass] Q; Looke, looke F   66 A] Q; he F   67 look] Q; see F
69 God save] Q; Saue F   71 virtuous] Q; pernitious F

56 **accites** excites, i.e. induces (*OED v.* 3).
   The legal meaning of 'accite' = to summon (*OED* 1) (cf. 5.2.140) is quibbled on
   as Hal's mocking address 'worshipful
   thought' shows (he pretends to mistake
   Poins for a magistrate).
58 **lewd** common, low (*OED a.* 3)
59 **engrafted** closely attached (*OED v.* 2b)
63 **a second brother** a younger brother and
   therefore needing to fend for himself in
   the days of primogenitive laws
63–4 **of my hands** a doughty fighter (proverbial: cf. Dent M163)

71–2 **virtuous . . . blushing**   F's 'pernitious' cannot be attributed to revision
   (*pace* Shaaber, p. 506). It almost certainly reflects misread copy, and 'virtuous' is the correct deciphering. See also
   Dent B480: 'Blushing (bashfulness) is
   virtue's colour (is a sign of grace)'. The
   joke is about Bardolph's complexion
   which is permanently rubicund from al-
   coholic over-indulgence.

What a maidenly man-at-arms are you become! Is't
such a matter to get a pottle-pot's maidenhead?

PAGE A calls me e'en now, my lord, through a red lattice,   75
and I could discern no part of his face from the window.
At last I spied his eyes, and methought he had made
two holes in the ale-wife's petticoat and so peeped
through.

PRINCE HENRY (*to Poins*) Has not the boy profited?   80

BARDOLPH Away, you whoreson upright rabbit, away!

PAGE Away, you rascally Althea's dream, away!

PRINCE HENRY Instruct us, boy; what dream, boy?

PAGE Marry, my lord, Althea dreamt she was delivered of a
firebrand, and therefore I call him her dream.   85

PRINCE HENRY A crown's-worth of good interpretation!
(*Giving him money*) There 'tis, boy.

POINS O, that this blossom could be kept from cankers!
Well, there is sixpence to preserve thee.

[*He gives the Page money*]

BARDOLPH An you do not make him hanged among you,   90
the gallows shall have wrong.

PRINCE HENRY And how doth thy master, Bardolph?

---

73 Is't] Q; Is it F   75 A] Q; He F   calls] Q; call'd F   e'en now] Q (enow); euen now F
78 ale-wife's] Q (alewiues), F (Ale-wiues)   petticoat] Q; new Petticoat F; red petticoat
MONRO   so] Q; *not in* F   80 Has] Q; Hath F.   81 rabbit] F; rabble Q   87 *Giving . . . money*]
OXFORD (*before* 'A crown'); *not in* QF   'tis] Q; it is F   88 blossom] Q; good blossom F
90 An] Q; If F   hanged] Q; be hanged F   91 have wrong] Q; be wronged F

---

74 **get . . . maidenhead** Lit. to possess a pot
of ale, but used here with a sexual innuendo. This was an accepted idiom at
the time and one frequently used in the
drama; a pottle-pot is a two-quart pot or
tankard of ale.

75 **red lattice** The lattice-work windows of
alehouses and inns were usually painted
red (and Bardolph's face blends in so
completely as to become indistinguishable).

78 **the . . . petticoat** The image of Bardolph
peeping out (albeit only in the page's
imagination) from the (probable) prostitute's petticoat is suggestive of strange
sexual activities.

82 **Althea's dream** The page confuses
Althea with Hecuba, who before the
birth of Paris dreamt that she was delivered of a firebrand that consumed Troy

(Ovid, *Heroides* 16; and cf. *Troilus*
2.2.109: 'Our firebrand brother, Paris').
After the birth of her son Meleager,
Althea was told by the Fates (*Moirai*)
that he would live until a brand which
was then on fire was consumed. She at
once quenched it. But when she learnt
that he had killed her brothers, after an
argument over the spoils of the Calydonian boar (it had been rightly adjudged to
Atalanta), she burnt the brand and thus
killed him. The tale is related in Ovid's
Metamorphoses 8.425–525, and Shakespeare clearly expects at least part of his
audience to recognize the deliberate confusion, which allows Hal ironically to
compliment the page on his 'good interpretation'.

89 **sixpence . . . thee** Perhaps alluding to the
cross on Elizabethan sixpence coins.

BARDOLPH Well, my lord. He heard of your grace's coming
to town. There's a letter for you.

POINS Delivered with good respect. And how doth the   95
Martlemas your master?

BARDOLPH In bodily health, sir.

POINS Marry, the immortal part needs a physician, but that
moves not him; though that be sick, it dies not.

PRINCE HENRY I do allow this wen to be as familiar with me   100
as my dog, and he holds his place, for look you how he
writes.

⌈*He shows Poins the letter*⌉

POINS 'John Falstaff, knight'—Every man must know that
as oft as he has occasion to name himself; even like those
that are kin to the King, for they never prick their finger   105
but they say 'There's some of the King's blood spilt.'
'How comes that?' says he that takes upon him not to
conceive. The answer is as ready as a borrower's cap: 'I
am the King's poor cousin, sir.'

PRINCE HENRY Nay, they will be kin to us, or they will fetch 110
it from Japhet. But the letter. (*Reads*) 'Sir John Falstaff,
knight, to the son of the King nearest his father, Harry
Prince of Wales, greeting.'

93 my] Q; my good F   101 how] Q; *not in* F   102.1 *He ... letter*] This edition; *not in* QF
103 POINS 'John ... knight'—Every] Q (~ ~ ... ~, ~), F (*Poin. Letter. Iohn ... Knight:* (Euery);
John ... Poins. Every SISSON   John] QF; Sir John CAPELL   104 has] Q; hath F   106 There's]
Q; there is F   108 conceive.] F (conceiues?); ~∧ Q   borrower's] THEOBALD (*conj.* Warburton); borowed QF (*subs.*)   110 or] Q; but F   111 the] Q; to the F   (*Reads*)] This edition; *not*
in QF

95 **good respect** Used ironically about Bardolph's unceremonious delivery of the
letter.
96 **Martlemas** Martinmas is the feast of St
Martin (11 November) and is used here
as a derisive appellation (*OED* 2) for Falstaff who is in the autumn of his life, but
who is well matched by girth, lard, and
temperament to a season associated with
the slaughter of animals for winter festiv-
ities. Hal's fondness for applying lopsided
seasonal references to Falstaff is evident
from his earlier apostrophe to him as 'the
latter spring ... All-hallown summer' (*1*
Henry IV 1.2.156–7).
100 **wen** 'A lump or protuberance on the
body, a knot, bunch, wart' (*OED* n.¹ 1a)

107–8 **takes upon ... conceive** pretends not
to understand
108 **borrower's** Warburton's conjecture
for QF 'borrowed' has gained almost universal acceptance. Just as a borrower will
always act in the most complaisant manner, so the self-styled kin of the king are
forever eager for a chance to trumpet
their relation with royalty.
110 **fetch** derive (*OED* v. 6a)
111 **Japhet** The third son of Noah and
thought to be the father of all Europeans
(Genesis 10: 1–5). The point is that if
they cannot prove their close kinship
with the king, they will if necessary re-
trace their common ancestry with him
back to the Ark.

POINS Why, this is a certificate!

PRINCE HENRY Peace!—'I will imitate the honourable   115
    Romans in brevity.'

POINS He sure means brevity in breath, short winded.

[PRINCE HENRY] 'I commend me to thee, I commend thee,
    and I leave thee. Be not too familiar with Poins, for he
    misuses thy favours so much that he swears thou art to   120
    marry his sister Nell. Repent at idle times as thou mayst,
    and so, farewell.

    Thine by yea and no—which is as much as to say, as
    thou usest him—Jack Falstaff with my familiars, John
    with my brothers and sisters, and Sir John with all   125
    Europe.'

POINS My lord, I'll steep this letter in sack and make him eat
    it.

PRINCE HENRY That's to make him eat twenty of his words.
    But do you use me thus, Ned? Must I marry your   130
    sister?

POINS God send the wench no worse fortune, but I never
    said so.

PRINCE HENRY Well, thus we play the fools with the time,
    and the spirits of the wise sit in the clouds and mock us.   135
    (*To Bardolph*) Is your master here in London?

116 Romans] QF; Roman WARBURTON   117 He sure] Q; Sure he F   118 PRINCE HENRY]
THEOBALD; *not in* QF   124 familiars] F; family Q   125 sisters] Q; Sister F   127 I'll] Q; I
will F   132 God . . . wench] Q; May the wench haue F

114 **certificate** a licence issued to a subject
    by the king. For a letter Falstaff's form of
    address is patently wrong. He should
    start with the addressee rather than him-
    self, and ought to be more respectful
    when addressing the Prince of Wales.
116 **Romans** Warburton's conjecture
    'Roman' for QF plural is attractive be-
    cause the tripartite clause structure of
    the next sentence, 'I . . . thee', recalls
    Caesar's famous 'Veni, vidi, vici', quoted
    by Falstaff at 4.2.40–1.
118 **commend me to thee** recommend me
    to your kindly remembrance (*OED, com-
    mend, v.* 5)
121 **mayst** canst
123 **yea and no** The mildest expletive con-
    forming to Matthew 5: 34–7: 'But I say
    vnto you, Sweare not at all, nether by
    heaue[n], for it is ye throne of God . . . But
    let your communication be, Yea, yea:

Nay, nay. For whatsoeuer is more
the[n] these, commeth of euil.' It is here
(probably) intended as a parody of a Puritan's oath, although Shallow also uses
the expression at 3.2.8.
129 **twenty** 'used vaguely or hyperbolically
    for a large number' (*OED adj.* 1d); cf.
    Venus and Adonis 575.
134 **play . . . time** probably 'act like fools as
    befits the time'
135 **the spirits . . . us** Perhaps, as Shaaber
    suggests, 'Shakespeare's image of the
    spirits of the wise sitting in the clouds
    would appear to have been suggested by
    the use in Masques of scenic machinery
    representing clouds' (p. 149); but the
    play is rather early for that, and Psalm
    2: 4 may be a better guess: 'But he that
    dwelleth in the heauen shal laugh: the
    Lord shal haue the[m] in derisio[n].'

BARDOLPH Yea, my lord.

PRINCE HENRY Where sups he? Doth the old boar feed in the
old frank?

BARDOLPH At the old place, my lord, in Eastcheap.   140

PRINCE HENRY What company?

PAGE Ephesians, my lord, of the old church.

PRINCE HENRY Sup any women with him?

PAGE None, my lord, but old Mistress Quickly and Mistress
Doll Tearsheet.   145

PRINCE HENRY What pagan may that be?

PAGE A proper gentlewoman, sir, and a kinswoman of my
master's.

PRINCE HENRY Even such kin as the parish heifers are to the
town-bull. Shall we steal upon them, Ned, at supper?   150

POINS I am your shadow, my lord; I'll follow you.

PRINCE HENRY Sirrah, you, boy, and Bardolph, no word to
your master that I am yet come to town. (*Giving money*)
There's for your silence.

BARDOLPH I have no tongue, sir.   155

PAGE And for mine, sir, I will govern it.

PRINCE HENRY Fare you well; go.

Exeunt Bardolph and the Page

This Doll Tearsheet should be some road.

137 Yea] Q; Yes F   153 come to] Q; in F   *Giving money*] OXFORD; *not in* QF   157 you]
Q; ye F   157.1 *Exeunt . . . Page*] CAPELL (*subs.*); *not in* QF

138–9 **old boar . . . frank** Cf. the proverb 'He
feeds like a boar in a frank' (Dent B483);
a frank is a sty. The line almost certainly
alludes to the Boar's Head tavern in Eastcheap, and is the only such reference in
either of the *Henry IV* plays. Several taverns of that name existed in the London
of Shakespeare's time. This one was located on the north side of Great Eastcheap where it abutted at the back on St
Michael's in Crooked Lane. Although no
tavern of that name stood on this site
during the reign of Bolingbroke, when
the area was full of cookshops, a tene-
ment of that name did exist there in the
late fourteenth century, when the street
was reputed as a place for food and
drinks. (See Sugden, p. 66; Lee ii. 172.)
142 **Ephesians** boon companions (*OED sb.* 2)
the old church Rather than 'the prime

church' of Ephesus whose purity of life
conformed to St Paul's instructions and
provided a model for the Puritans (Humphreys). But the allusion may be to Ephesians 4: 22–4, which urges the casting off
the 'olde man, which is corrupt through
the deceiuable lustes' and the putting on
the new man. The page probably means
'his usual unregenerate company'.
146 **pagan** prostitute (*OED sb.* 2b)
147 **proper** respectable, worthy (*OED a.* 8b)
150 **town-bull** 'a bull formerly kept in turn
by the cow-keepers of a village; hence *fig.*
of a man' (*OED, town, sb.* 10)
158 **road** i.e. whore; cf. 'As common as
the cartway (etc.)' (Dent C109), an expression which already occurs in
Piers Plowman Passus 3.127: '. . . As
comyn as the cart-wei to knaves and to
alle'.

POINS I warrant you, as common as the way between Saint
    Albans and London.   160

PRINCE HENRY How might we see Falstaff bestow himself
    tonight in his true colours, and not ourselves be seen?

POINS Put on two leathern jerkins and aprons, and wait
    upon him at his table as drawers.

PRINCE HENRY From a god to a bull? A heavy descension! It 165
    was Jove's case. From a prince to a prentice? A low
    transformation that shall be mine, for in everything the
    purpose must weigh with the folly. Follow me, Ned.

                                                    Exeunt

2.3   *Enter the Earl of Northumberland, Lady*
        Northumberland, and Lady Percy

NORTHUMBERLAND

    I pray thee, loving wife and gentle daughter,
    Give even way unto my rough affairs;
    Put not you on the visage of the times
    And be like them to Percy troublesome.

LADY NORTHUMBERLAND

    I have given over; I will speak no more.   5
    Do what you will; your wisdom be your guide.

NORTHUMBERLAND

    Alas, sweet wife, my honour is at pawn,
    And, but my going, nothing can redeem it.

LADY PERCY

    O yet, for God's sake, go not to these wars.

163 leathern] Q; leather F   164 as] Q; like F   165 descension] Q; declension F
166 prince] F; pince Q   167 everything] F; enery thing Q

2.3.0.1–2 *Enter . . . Percy*] Q (*Enter Northumberland his wife, and the wife to Harry Percie.*); *Enter Northumberland, his Ladie, and Harrie Percies Ladie.* F   1 pray thee] Q; prethee F   2 even] Q; an euen F   9 God's] Q; heauens F

159–60 **the way . . . London** The main
    route from London to the Midlands, and
    the first stretch of the Great North Road,
    was very busy.
161 **bestow himself** behave, acquit himself
164 **drawers** A drawer is a tapster at a ta-
    vern.
165–6 **From . . . Jove's case** Jove trans-

formed himself into a bull to seduce
    Europa (Ovid, *Metamorphoses* 2.846–
    75).
165 **heavy descension** a serious (i.e. pain-
    ful?) descent
2.3.2 **Give . . . affairs** grant me as smooth a
    passage as you can through this difficult
    business

The time was, father, that you broke your word   10
When you were more endeared to it than now,
When your own Percy, when my heart's dear Harry
Threw many a northward look to see his father
Bring up his powers; but he did long in vain.
Who then persuaded you to stay at home?   15
There were two honours lost, yours and your son's.
For yours, the God of heaven brighten it;
For his, it stuck upon him as the sun
In the grey vault of heaven, and by his light
Did all the chivalry of England move   20
To do brave acts. He was indeed the glass
Wherein the noble youth did dress themselves.
He had no legs that practised not his gait,
And speaking thick, which nature made his blemish,
Became the accents of the valiant;   25
For those that could speak low and tardily
Would turn their own perfection to abuse
To seem like him. So that in speech, in gait,
In diet, in affections of delight,
In military rules, humours of blood,   30
He was the mark and glass, copy and book,
That fashioned others. And him—O wondrous him!
O miracle of men!—him did you leave,
Second to none, unseconded by you,
To look upon the hideous god of war   35
In disadvantage, to abide a field

10 that] Q; when F   11 endeared] F; endeere Q   12 heart's dear] Q; heart-deere F
17 the God of heaven] Q; may heauenly glory F   23–45 He...grave] F; *not in* Q   32 wondrous him!] ROWE; ~! ~, F

11 **endeared** bound by gratitude and honour
19 **grey** Often used in conjunction with
   'bright', as in 'the morn is bright and
   grey' (*Titus* 2.2.1), or dawn as in 'the
   grey cheeks of the east' (Sonnet 132.6),
   hence coming to mean 'light-blue'.
21 **glass** i.e. mirror; cf. 'The glass of fashion'
   (*Hamlet* 3.1.156), hence 'model' to follow and imitate as in *The Mirror for Magistrates*
23–45 **He...grave** F-only lines: see Introduction, pp. 88–9.
24 **thick** Cf. *OED adv.* 3, 'quickly, fast',
   which quotes from Fuller's *Holy and Pro-*

fane State, 'Great talkers discharge too
thick to take always true aim' (1642).
The meaning 'thick and fast' was available. There is nothing in the chronicles
about Hotspur's speech, but Shakespeare
may already touch on this in *1 Henry IV*
3.1.125–31, in Hotspur's professed dislike of 'mincing poetry' (while using
some magnificent rhetoric himself).
29 **affections of delight** likings of pleasure
30 **humours of blood** capriciousness
31 **mark** guiding pattern
36 **abide a field** face a battle

Where nothing but the sound of Hotspur's name
Did seem defensible; so you left him.
Never, O never do his ghost the wrong
To hold your honour more precise and nice   40
With others than with him. Let them alone.
The Marshal and the Archbishop are strong.
Had my sweet Harry had but half their numbers,
Today might I, hanging on Hotspur's neck,
Have talked of Monmouth's grave.

NORTHUMBERLAND   Beshrew your heart,   45
Fair daughter, you do draw my spirits from me
With new lamenting ancient oversights.
But I must go and meet with danger there,
Or it will seek me in another place,
And find me worse provided.

LADY NORTHUMBERLAND   O fly to Scotland,   50
Till that the nobles and the armèd commons
Have of their puissance made a little taste.

LADY PERCY
If they get ground and vantage of the King,
Then join you with them like a rib of steel,
To make strength stronger; but, for all our loves,   55
First let them try themselves. So did your son.
He was so suffered. So came I a widow,
And never shall have length of life enough
To rain upon remembrance with mine eyes,
That it may grow and sprout as high as heaven   60
For recordation to my noble husband.

NORTHUMBERLAND
Come, come, go in with me. 'Tis with my mind
As with the tide swelled up unto his height,
That makes a still-stand, running neither way.
Fain would I go to meet the Archbishop,   65

38 **defensible** capable of offering protection
   (*OED*, *defensive*, *a.* 1b parallels 'defensible' and is so cross-referenced)
44–5 **I . . . grave** See Introduction, p. 89.
45 **Beshrew** A gentle and playful use of an
   imprecatory phrase, perhaps to signal ex-
   asperation.
47 **new** newly

52 **taste** trial
57 **suffered** allowed
   came became
59 **To . . . eyes** to water the plant of remembrance (i.e. rosemary) with my tears
61 **recordation** commemorative account
   (*OED* 3 *Obs.*)
64 **still-stand** i.e. standstill

But many thousand reasons hold me back.
I will resolve for Scotland. There am I
Till time and vantage crave my company.   *Exeunt*

2.4   *Enter Francis, a Drawer, [followed by] Second Drawer
[with a dish of apple-johns]*

FRANCIS What the devil hast thou brought there—apple-
johns? Thou knowest Sir John cannot endure an apple-
john.

SECOND DRAWER Mass, thou sayst true. The Prince once set
a dish of apple-johns before him, and told him there were   5
five more Sir Johns; and, putting off his hat, said 'I will
now take my leave of these six dry, round, old, withered
knights.' It angered him to the heart. But he hath forgot
that.

FRANCIS Why then, cover, and set them down; and see if   10

2.4.0.1–2 *Enter . . . apple-johns*] This edition; *Enter a Drawer or two.* Q; *Enter two Drawers.* F
1 FRANCIS] Q; 1. *Drawer* F   the devil] Q; *not in* F   4 SECOND DRAWER] F; *Draw.* Q   Mass]
Q; *not in* F   10 FRANCIS] Q; 1. *Draw.* F

2.4.1–20 The speech-prefixes here follow Q,
which have three drawers, while F, which
cuts 'Dispatch . . . straight', has two. Q
names the first drawer Francis, but does
not give the second drawer a name, while
apparently intending 'Will' ('William' in
this edition) to be the third (he is called
'Third Drawer' by Alexander). The Q-
only lines ought to be spoken by a character who has newly entered with additional information and announces the
imminent arrival of several characters
who are as yet off-stage and whom he
has just preceded. I have therefore
moved William's entry from its placing
in Q (before l. 19, 'By the mass . . .') to l.
12.1 so that it is William who speaks
'Dispatch . . . straight'. Referring to the
stage direction '*Enter Will Kemp*' in Q2
Romeo (4.4.127.2), another foul-paper
text, Greg (1955, p. 273) wonders
whether William here designates Will
Kemp rather than the part of a drawer
called 'William'. Kemp was the company's leading comic actor and an accomplished dancer, and is a very likely
candidate for the role of Falstaff. As a
dancer he may have spoken the Epilogue

(see Introduction, p. 14) which may
therefore, intriguingly, be spoken by Falstaff, just as the Epilogue to *As You Like It*
is spoken by its main character, Rosalind.
His leaving the company in 1599 may be
relevant to Shakespeare's writing him
out of *Henry V*. If it is indeed Falstaff
who, without speaking, crosses the
stage (after l. 12 in Q), it may well be for
comic effect: he is urgently on his way to
empty his bladder, as his first line in the
scene appears to confirm (cf. Wilson, p.
157). It is worth noting also that Kemp is
repeatedly listed for Dogberry in the
quarto (of foul-paper pedigree) of *Much
Ado* 4.2 (*Kemp, Ke.*, *Kem.*), which was
entered with *2 Henry IV* in the Stationers'
Register; cf. Chambers, 1923, ii. 325–7,
and Wilson, 1943, pp. 124–5.

1–2 **apple-johns** 'a kind of apple said to
keep two years, and to be in perfection
when shrivelled and withered' (*OED*).
The reason for Falstaff's dislike of them
is clear from the context and from
Falstaff's acute awareness of looking
like a withered 'old apple-john' (*1 Henry
IV* 3.3.4).

10 **cover** spread the tablecloth

thou canst find out Sneak's Noise. Mistress Tearsheet
would fain hear some music.

    Enter William

[WILLIAM] Dispatch! The room where they supped is too
hot; they'll come in straight.

FRANCIS Sirrah, here will be the Prince and Master Poins   15
anon, and they will put on two of our jerkins and aprons,
and Sir John must not know of it. Bardolph hath brought
word.

[WILLIAM] By the mass, here will be old utis! It will be an
excellent stratagem.   20

SECOND DRAWER I'll see if I can find out Sneak.   *Exeunt*

    Enter Mistress Quickly and Doll Tearsheet

MISTRESS QUICKLY I'faith, sweetheart, methinks now you
are in an excellent good temperality. Your pulsidge
beats as extraordinarily as heart would desire, and your
colour, I warrant you, is as red as any rose, in good truth,   25
la; but i'faith, you have drunk too much canaries, and
that's a marvellous searching wine, and it perfumes the
blood ere one can say 'What's this?' How do you now?

DOLL TEARSHEET Better than I was—hem!

---

12 hear] Q; haue F   12.1 *Enter William*] Q (*Enter Will., after l.* 18); *not in* F   13 WILLIAM]
This edition; *not in* QF; ALEXANDER *reads* THIRD DRAWER (*conj.* Ridley)   13–14 Dispatch . . .
straight] Q; *not in* F   15 FRANCIS] Q; 2. *Draw.* F   19 WILLIAM] This edition; *not in* QF; ALEX-
ANDER *reads* THIRD DRAWER By the mass] Q; Then F   old] Qb; oll Qa   21 SECOND DRAWER]
F; *Francis* Q   Exeunt] ROWE; *exit* Q; Exit. F   21.1 *Enter . . . Tearsheet*] Q; *Enter Hostesse, and
Dol.* F   22 I'faith] Q (Yfaith); *not in* F   25–6 in . . . la] Q (law); *not in* F   26 i'faith] Q
(yfaith); *not in* F   28 one] Q; wee F   29 DOLL TEARSHEET] *throughout for* Q 'Tere.', 'Doll',
'Dorothy', 'Dol', 'Teresh.', 'Doro.', 'Dol.', 'Whoore'

---

11 **Noise** band. The fact that its leader is
called 'Sneak' may reflect a prevailing
opprobrious view of such companies
(but cf. Humphreys, p. 63). The word
'noise' is also used in *FV* VI.539, when
Henry V wishes to be provided with
'three Noyse of Musitians'.

19 **old utis** old high larks, with 'old' acting
as an intensifier. Humphreys, p. 63,
notes that 'utis' may be a Midlands dialectical use (meaning 'noise, confusion,
din'), or at least a variant of 'utas' =
'period of festivity' (*OED* n.¹ c). Either
reading points in the direction of noisy
Eastcheap revels.

23–4 **temperality . . . pulsidge . . . extra-**

ordinarily Three Quicklyisms for temper,
pulse, and ordinarily.

26 **canaries** i.e. canary wine

27 **searching** 'That finds out weak points,
keen, sharp, "piercing"' (*OED ppl. a.*
1b), used here to mean 'heady'

perfumes A malapropism (probably) for
'perfuses', i.e. suffuses, or diffuses
through.

29 **hem** Probably used to denote a hiccup,
appropriately here since Doll is recover-
ing from a hangover. It was also a beck-
oning signal by whores, and Shallow
('Hem, boys') used it as a drinking
watchword (see 3.2.209–10).

MISTRESS QUICKLY Why, that's well said. A good heart's   30
worth gold.

Enter Falstaff

Lo, here comes Sir John.

FALSTAFF (*sings*) 'When Arthur first in court'—empty the
jordan!—(*Sings*) 'And was a worthy king'—how now,
Mistress Doll?   35

MISTRESS QUICKLY Sick of a calm, yea, good faith.

FALSTAFF So is all her sect; an they be once in a calm, they
are sick.

DOLL TEARSHEET A pox damn you, you muddy rascal! Is
that all the comfort you give me?   40

FALSTAFF You make fat rascals, Mistress Doll.

DOLL TEARSHEET I make them? Gluttony and diseases make
them; I make them not.

FALSTAFF If the cook help to make the gluttony, you help to
make the diseases, Doll. We catch of you, Doll, we catch   45
of you; grant that, my poor virtue, grant that.

DOLL TEARSHEET Yea, joy, our chains and our jewels.

30 that's] Q; that was F   31.1 *Enter Falstaff*] F (*after l. 32*); enter sir Iohn. Q (*after l. 32*)
32 Lo] Q; Looke F   36 good faith] Q; good-sooth F   37 an] Q; if F   39 A...you] Q; *not in*
F   42–3 make them] F; make Q   44 help to] Q; *not in* F   46 you;] F (you:); ~∧ Q
47 Yea, joy] Q; I marry F; Yea, Jesu OXFORD (*conj.* Ridley); Yea, Mary's joys DAVISON

30–1 **A good...gold** Cf. the proverb 'A
good name is better than riches' (Dent
N22).

33–4 **When ... king** Falstaff's inaccurately
quoted version of the opening lines of the
ballad *Sir Launcelot du Lake*: 'When
Arthur first in court began | And was
approved king'.

34 **jordan** chamber-pot

36 **calm** She means its homophone 'qualm'
= a sudden fit.

37 **sect** (a) sex; (b) profession

37–8 **an ... sick** Playing on the Quicklyism
of calm/qualm. Falstaff jokes that (a)
women are unwell when they are quiet,
and (b) prostitutes sicken if they cannot
ply their trade.

39 **muddy** dirty

41 **fat rascals** Falstaff picks up Doll's phrase
(as he did Mistress Quickly's) and plays
on the meaning of 'rascal' as 'lean' when
applied to deer (cf. also 5.4.8, 30). He
tells her that she renders lean deer
gross and bloated, presumably through
venereal disease (as her reply further suggests).

47 **joy** Probably a term of endearment, but
F's 'I [ay] marry' points perhaps to an
oath suppressed in an acting version. Davison (pp. 207–9) offers an imaginative
(but far-fetched), allegorical reading,
'Yea, Mary's joys', where Doll's 'joys'
are seen as (perhaps) a Mary Magdalen's
version of the five canonical Joys of the
Virgin.

our ... jewels those are the things that
you catch from us

FALSTAFF Your brooches, pearls, and ouches—for to serve
bravely is to come halting off, you know ; to come off the
breach with his pike bent bravely, and to surgery   50
bravely; to venture upon the charged chambers
bravely—

DOLL TEARSHEET Hang yourself, you muddy conger, hang
yourself.

MISTRESS QUICKLY By my troth, this is the old fashion. You   55
two never meet but you fall to some discord. You are
both, i'good truth, as rheumatic as two dry toasts ; you
cannot one bear with another's confirmities. What the
goodyear! One must bear, (*to Doll*) and that must be
you ; you are the weaker vessel, as they say, the emptier   60
vessel.

---

49 off, you know; to] OXFORD; ~ ~ ~ ∧ ~ Q; ~: ~ ~, ~ F   53–4 DOLL . . . yourself] Q; *not in* F
55 By my troth] Q; Why F   57 i'good truth] Q (ygood); in good troth F

48 **brooches, pearls, and ouches** All
three are probably outward manifesta-
tions on the skin (used here euphemisti-
cally for boils and sores) of venereal
infection; 'ouches' is 'a carbuncle or
other tumour or sore on the skin' (*OED*,
ouch, sb.[1] 3), and 'brooches' and 'pearls'
may be compared to the 'little pimples
. . . in the noses and faces . . . [which] are
called the Saphires and Rubies of
the Tauerne' in Nicholas Udall's translation of *The Apophthegmes of Erasmus*
(1564).

48–9 **for . . . bravely** Falstaff deploys a
string of military metaphors of assault
which are full of sexual innuendoes, particularly in his collocation of breach ('A
gap in a fortification made by a battery':
OED sb. 7c) and 'pike bent'; 'surgery'
quibbles on the treatment for the pox.
With 'to . . . bravely' he appears to be re-
launching the image of an attack on the
'breach', although 'charged chambers'
(usually a loaded piece of ordnance)
would be more obviously applicable to
the male sex organs than the female.
But then a cannon does have a bore
(-hole) in front of its breech, and a loaded
cannon offers a very dangerous hole—
which could be translated sexually as
'infected female genitalia'; cf. Sonnet
144.14: 'Till my bad angel fire my good
one out', where the bad angel (or 'worser

spirit') who drives out is female. In the
sonnet there is also a quibble on infecting
with venereal disease.

53 **conger** A species of large sea eel which
lives in muddy waters; often used as a
term of abuse, and here with a fairly
obvious sexual innuendo. The line is
omitted in F.

57 **rheumatic** The opposite almost of what
she intends, which is probably 'choleric'
(she uses the word 'choler' at l. 160
below), i.e. hot and dry, and therefore
they cannot rub along smoothly any
more than two dry toasts.

58 **confirmities** for 'infirmities'

58–9 **What the goodyear** A mild expletive,
perhaps from Dutch 'wat goedjaar' = 'as
I hope for a good year'.

59 **bear** put up (referring back to her preceding sentence), but also, because she
is a woman, she will have to bear
children, and men. This latter sense is
the one developed by Doll in her reply.

60–1 **weaker . . . vessel** The idea of woman
as the weaker vessel is proverbial (cf.
Tilley W655) and biblical in origin (1
Peter 3: 7: 'Likewise ye housbands,
dwel with the[m] as men of knowledge,
giuing honour vnto the woma[n], as
vnto the weaker vessel . . . '). They are
emptier vessels than men, because they
can be filled, as Doll's next line makes
clear.

DOLL TEARSHEET Can a weak empty vessel bear such a huge
full hogshead? There's a whole merchant's venture of
Bordeaux stuff in him; you have not seen a hulk better
stuffed in the hold. Come, I'll be friends with thee, Jack.   65
Thou art going to the wars, and whether I shall ever see
thee again or no there is nobody cares.

  Enter a Drawer

DRAWER Sir, Ancient Pistol's below, and would speak with
you.

DOLL TEARSHEET Hang him, swaggering rascal, let him not   70
come hither. It is the foul-mouthedest rogue in England.

MISTRESS QUICKLY If he swagger, let him not come here. No,
by my faith, I must live among my neighbours. I'll no
swaggerers. I am in good name and fame with the very
best. Shut the door; there comes no swaggerers here. I   75
have not lived all this while to have swaggering now.
Shut the door, I pray you.

FALSTAFF Dost thou hear, hostess?

DOLL TEARSHEET Pray ye pacify yourself, Sir John. There
comes no swaggerers here.   80

FALSTAFF Dost thou hear? It is mine ancient.

MISTRESS QUICKLY Tilly-fally, Sir John, ne'er tell me. And
your ancient swaggerer comes not in my doors. I was
before Master Tisick the debuty t'other day, and, as he

67.1 *a Drawer*] QF (*Drawer*) 68 Pistol's] Q; Pistol is F 72–3 No…faith] Q; *not in*
F 73 among] Q; amongst F 79 ye] Q; you F 82 ne'er] Q; neuer F And] Q; *not in* F
84 debuty] Q; Deputie F t'other] Q; the other F

62–3 **Can…hogshead** With spirit and
sarcasm Doll demonstrates the inappro-
priateness in this instance of Mistress
Quickly's stereotyping.

63–4 **merchant's . . . stuff** a shipload of
Bordeaux wine

64 **hulk** See 1.1.19.

68 **Ancient** standard-bearer, ensign, 'something like a modern sergeant-major'
(Gurr, p. 63)
Pistol Shakespeare clearly plays on the
name's near-homophony with 'pizzle'
(below, l. 159); Davison (p. 210) refers
to Italian '*pistolfo*' and John Florio's
gloss, 'a roguing beggar, a cantler, an
upright man that liveth by cozenage'.

70 **swaggering** hectoring, talking bluster-
ingly. The word itself first occurs in

1590, a few years before the play, and
describes a type of 'roaring boy' who
haunted taverns and brothels in search
of entertainment and quarrels.

79 **pacify** She is asking him to keep his
peace, i.e. to be quiet and not interrupt
her.

82 **Tilly-fally** nonsense, fiddlesticks

84 **Tisick** An obsolete and dialectical form
('tisic') for phthisic (pronounced the
same way), i.e. consumption; the deputy
is imagined as an elderly worthy racked
by a consumptive cough.
debuty A Quicklyism for 'deputy', here
someone who acts as a magistrate on
behalf of the alderman in his absence in
a City of London ward.

said to me—'twas no longer ago than Wed'sday last, 85
i'good faith—'Neighbour Quickly,' says he—Master
Dumb our minister was by then—'Neighbour Quickly,'
says he, 'receive those that are civil, for', said he, 'you
are in an ill name.' Now a said so, I can tell whereupon.
'For', says he, 'you are an honest woman, and well 90
thought on; therefore take heed what guests you receive. Receive', says he, 'no swaggering companions.'
There comes none here. You would bless you to hear
what he said. No, I'll no swaggerers.

FALSTAFF He's no swaggerer, hostess—a tame cheater, 95
i'faith. You may stroke him as gently as a puppy grey-
hound. He'll not swagger with a Barbary hen, if her
feathers turn back in any show of resistance. Call him
up, drawer. ⌈*Exit Drawer*⌉

MISTRESS QUICKLY Cheater call you him? I will bar no hon- 100
est man my house, nor no cheater, but I do not love
swaggering, by my troth, I am the worse when one says
'swagger'. Feel, masters, how I shake, look you, I warrant you.

DOLL TEARSHEET So you do, hostess. 105

MISTRESS QUICKLY Do I? Yea, in very truth do I, an 'twere
an aspen leaf. I cannot abide swaggerers.
Enter Pistol, Bardolph, and the Page

---

85 'twas] Q; it was F   Wed'sday] Q; Wednesday F   86 i'good faith] Q; *not in* F   88 said]
Q; sayth F   89 a] Q; hee F   96 i'faith] Q; hee F   97 He'll] Q; hee will F   99 *Exit Drawer*]
CAPELL; *not in* QF   102 by my troth] Q; *not in* F   106 an 'twere] Q; if it were F   107.1 *En-
ter . . . Page*] F (*Enter Pistol, and Bardolph and his Boy.*); *Enter antient Pistol, and Bardolfes boy.* Q

86–7 **Master Dumb** So called (probably)
because he lacked the necessary zeal to
gain the approbation of the Puritans who
applied the phrase 'dumb dogs' to
preachers whom they found lacking in
fervour.

89 **I . . . whereupon** I know upon what
ground

92 **companions** fellows

95 **tame cheater** tractable gamester (and
therefore hardly swaggerer)

97 **swagger** squabble
Barbary hen guinea fowl. 'Barbary'

and 'guinea' are terms applied to the
northern and western coastlines of Africa
respectively; they are frequently compounded with animals, birds, and plants
(cf. *As You Like It* 4.1.142). But Falstaff
also uses the phrase in its generic appli-
cation for 'woman', and probably (here)
'prostitute'; the phrase 'swagger with a
Barbary hen' is the equivalent of modern
'say boo to a goose'.

107 **aspen leaf** Proverbial: cf. 'He trembles
(quakes, shakes) like an aspen leaf' (Dent
L140).

PISTOL God save you, Sir John.

FALSTAFF Welcome, Ancient Pistol. Here, Pistol, I charge
you with a cup of sack; do you discharge upon mine   110
hostess.

PISTOL I will discharge upon her, Sir John, with two bullets.

FALSTAFF She is pistol-proof, sir; you shall not hardly
offend her.

MISTRESS QUICKLY Come, I'll drink no proofs, nor no bullets;   115
I'll drink no more than will do me good, for no man's
pleasure, I.

PISTOL Then to you, Mistress Dorothy! I will charge you.

DOLL TEARSHEET Charge me? I scorn you, scurvy companion. What, you poor, base, rascally, cheating, lack-linen   120
mate! Away, you mouldy rogue, away! I am meat for
your master.

PISTOL I know you, Mistress Dorothy.

DOLL TEARSHEET Away, you cutpurse rascal, you filthy
bung, away! By this wine, I'll thrust my knife in your   125
mouldy chaps an you play the saucy cuttle with me.
Away, you bottle-ale rascal, you basket-hilt stale juggler,

---

108 God] Q; *not in* F   113 pistol-proof, sir;] F (Pistoll-proofe (Sir)); pistoll proofe: sir Q   not]
Q; *not in* F   116 I'll] Q; I will F   126 an] Q; if F

109–10 **charge . . . discharge** He is offering a toast to Pistol and invites him to
pledge the hostess in return. That
'charge' could be so used is suggested by
e.g. Chapman's *The Gentleman Usher*
2.1.19 (Shaaber, p. 177). The phrase
here quibbles on Pistol's name and
launches a string of martial and sexual
doublespeak exchanges which culminate
in Pistol's offering to 'charge' Doll, who
immediately interprets it as a sexual advance: cf. ll. 121–2.

112 **discharge . . . bullets** fire at her from a
pistol or from Pistol's other 'gun'

113 **pistol-proof** cf. bullet-proof

113–14 **you . . . her** there is nothing you
can do to do her harm

115 **drink . . . no bullets** The hostess has
somewhat innocently misunderstood
the sexual drift of the preceding exchanges and seems to assume that
'proofs' (*OED, proof, sb.* 11a) and 'bullets'
are drinks.

120 **lack-linen** Cf. Poins's shortage of shirts,
and Kent's use of 'three-suited' to Oswald
as a term of abuse in *Lear* 2.2.14.

121 **mate** fellow
meat With a quibble on its homophone
'meet' (fit, proper), and punning on
'mate', as well as containing a sexual
innuendo.

125 **bung** pickpocket (*OED, sb.*² b)

126 **play . . . me** (probably) 'pull a fast one
on me'; 'cuttle' was a cant term for the
knife used by pickpockets for slicing the
strings of purses worn at the girdle.

127 **bottle-ale** Perhaps meaning cheap ale.
you . . . juggler She may be taunting
Pistol about his spurious martial appearance, and his basket-hilt sword (basket-
hilts protected the swordsman's hand).
He is as much of a fake as the tiresome
jugglers at fairs.

you! Since when, I pray you, sir? God's light, with two
points on your shoulder! Much!

PISTOL God let me not live, but I will murder your ruff for   130
this.

FALSTAFF No more, Pistol, I would not have you go off
here. Discharge yourself of our company, Pistol.

MISTRESS QUICKLY No, good Captain Pistol, not here, sweet
captain.   135

DOLL TEARSHEET Captain? Thou abominable damned cheater, art thou not ashamed to be called captain? An
captains were of my mind, they would truncheon you
out, for taking their names upon you before you have
earned them. You a captain? You slave! For what? For   140
tearing a poor whore's ruff in a bawdy-house? He a
captain? Hang him, rogue, he lives upon mouldy stewed
prunes and dried cakes. A captain? God's light, these
villains will make the word as odious as the word
'occupy', which was an excellent good word before it   145
was ill sorted; therefore captains had need look to't.

BARDOLPH Pray thee go down, good ancient.

---

128 God's light] Q; what F   130 God...but] Q; *not in* F   132-3 FALSTAFF...Pistol] Q; *not
in* F   137 An] Q; If F   143 God's light] Q; *not in* F   144 the word as] Q; the word Captaine
F   144-6 as the...sorted] Q; *not in* F   146 to't] Q; to it F

128 **Since when** i.e. how long then have you
known me? or, how long 'have you set
up as a soldier?' (Humphreys, p. 71)
129 **points** tags which fasten body armour
Much A sarcastic exclamation of won-
derment.
130 **murder** rip off
ruff Prostitutes wore big ruffs and often
had their garments shredded in brawls.
132-3 **FALSTAFF...Pistol** The absence of
these lines from F, as well as ll. 144-6
('as . . . sorted') below, suggests that
some of the sexual quibbles in the scene
may have been obvious to a censor who,
for whatever reason, did not seem to cavil
at the obscenities of the earlier exchanges
between Pistol, Falstaff, and Mistress
Quickly. On the other hand, eye-skip
may have played a part here (Davison,
p. 212).
134 **Captain** For once this may not be one of
Mistress Quickly's rhetorical infelicities,
but a quick-witted bestowing of military
rank on Pistol, to pacify him by flattery

and acceptance of his impostor's appearance.
138 **truncheon** cudgel (*OED sb.* 2)
142-3 **mouldy...cakes** He lives on scraps
from brothels and pastry-cook shops;
'stewed prunes' were commonly associated with brothels in the writing of the
period: cf. *Measure* 2.1.88 and *1 Henry IV*
3.3.112-13. Falstaff tells Mistress
Quickly that there is no more faith in
her than in a 'stewed prune'.
145 **occupy** Shakespeare had already used
the word in an 'odious' and 'ill-sorted'
fashion in *Romeo* 2.3.90-2 and may do
so again in *Othello* 3.3.362. There are
other examples in the period, and the
word is one of those singled out by Ben
Jonson for having its innocent meaning
twisted by those of impure mind: 'Many,
out of their owne obscene Apprehensions, refuse proper and fit words; as
occupie, nature, and the like...' (*Discov-
eries,* H & S viii. 610).

FALSTAFF Hark thee hither, Mistress Doll.

>   *They move aside*

PISTOL Not I! I tell thee what, Corporal Bardolph, I could
tear her! I'll be revenged of her.   150

PAGE Pray thee go down.

PISTOL

I'll see her damned first

To Pluto's damned lake, by this hand,

To th'infernal deep,

With Erebus and tortures vile also.   155

Hold hook and line, say I.

Down, down, dogs, down, faitours!

Have we not Hiren here?

148.1 *They...aside*] OXFORD (*subs.*); *not in* QF   150 of] Q; *on* F   152–8 I'll...here?] *as
verse* OXFORD; *as prose* QF   153 by this hand] Q; *not in* F   154 th'infernal] Q; the Infernall
F   155 With] Q; where F   157 faitours!] Q (faters$_\wedge$); Fates: F

---

149 **Corporal Bardolph** Bardolph is not a
corporal, but the newly elevated Pistol
pretends that he is.

152–8 **I'll...here** From this point on Pistol's rhetoric is impregnated by the fustian boasts of the Braggart in John Eliot's
Ortho-epia Gallica, *Eliots Fruits for the
French* (1593), p. 54$^\text{v}$: 'Where is Hector
that Troian Lad?... | 'Where is Alexan-
der, the great drunkard of Greece? | I will
make him drinke a carouse... | Where is
Achilles the Grig,... | Where is this
quaking-quiuering coward Iulius | Cae-
sar?' QF set out these lines as prose, but
they are almost certainly parodic verse,
alternating irregular pentameters and
three-stress lines. On Shakespeare's debt
to Eliot here and for Pistol's French in
Henry V, see J. W. Lever, 'Shakespeare's
French Fruits', *ShS* 6 (1953), 79–90.

153–5 **To...also** Echoes Muly Mahamet
from Peele's *The Battle of Alcazar* 1230–
54: 'you dastards of the night and Erybus
| ...Descend and take to thy tormenting
hell, | The mangled bodie of that traitor
king, | ...Damned let him be' (MSR,
1907, ed. W. W. Greg). Other popular
plays of the period such as *The Spanish
Tragedy*, *Locrine*, and *Tamburlaine I* may
also be alluded to.

155 **Erebus** The son of Chaos and Night who
personifies the underworld.

156 **Hold...I** Proverbial (cf. Dent H589); a
similar connection between the lake of
the underworld and angling occurs in
Lear 3.6.6–7: 'Nero is an angler in the
lake of darkness'.

157 **faitours** Faitour is obs. for 'cheat' and
'impostor' (*OED, faitour*, 1). F's 'Fates' (Q
= faters) may be a guess at the original by
someone who no longer recognized the
phrase; or it may simply be a slip.

158 **Hiren** Pistol's use of the name 'Hiren'
(Irene) probably alludes to Peele's lost
play *The Turkish Mahamet and Hyrin the
Fair Greek*, written and performed in all
likelihood two or three years earlier. His
question may well be a tag from the play,
but it is also intended as a slight to Doll
since Hiren is a prostitute. Moreover
Hiren and 'iron' are homophonic so
that the phrase could also describe Pistol's gesture of drawing his sword. But as
Capell notes (1774, p. 174), 'It is not
improbable, that the sword of some hero
or other bore this name; which we may
derive from [eirene], as who should say—
peace-maker'.

[*He draws his sword*]

MISTRESS QUICKLY Good Captain Pizzle, be quiet. 'Tis very
    late, i'faith. I beseek you now, aggravate your choler.   160
PISTOL

These be good humours indeed! Shall packhorses
And hollow pampered jades of Asia,
Which cannot go but thirty mile a day,
Compare with Caesars and with cannibals,
And Trojan Greeks?   165
Nay, rather damn them with King Cerberus,
And let the welkin roar. Shall we fall foul for toys?

MISTRESS QUICKLY By my troth, captain, these are very
    bitter words.

BARDOLPH Be gone, good ancient; this will grow to a brawl   170
    anon.

PISTOL

Die men like dogs! Give crowns like pins!
Have we not Hiren here?

MISTRESS QUICKLY O' my word, captain, there's none such
    here. What the goodyear, do you think I would deny   175
    her? For God's sake be quiet.

158.1 *He...sword*] WILSON (*subs.*); *not in* QF   159 'Tis] Q; it is F   160 i'faith] Q; *not in* F
161 These...packhorses] *as verse* POPE; *as prose* QF   162–7 And...toys?] *as verse* OXFORD;
as prose QF   163 mile] Q; miles F   164 Caesars] Q; Caesar F   165 Trojan] Q (troiant), F
(Troian)   172–3 Die...here?] *as verse* OXFORD; *as prose* QF   172 Die men] F; Men
Q   dogs!] F (Dogges;); ~ ∧ Q   174 O'] Q (A); On F   176 For God's sake] Q; I pray F

---

159 **Pizzle** Mistress Quickly's unfortunate
  pronunciation of Pistol's name, with its
  auditory pun on a bull's pizzle, was current colloquially at the time.

160 **beseek** Again the hostess either uses
  non-standard English, or this is one of
  her usual malapropisms; 'beseek' may
  be a northern or north-Midlands form of
  'beseech'; or it may be a mistake for 'beseech'.
  aggravate She means the opposite.

161 **humours** Cf. 2.3.30.

161–3 **Shall...day** A travesty of *Tamburlaine II* 4.3.1–2: 'Holla, ye pampered
jades of Asia! | What, can ye draw but
twenty miles a day?'

164–5 **Caesars...Greeks** A further echo
from *Ortho-epia Gallica*. Pistol seems to
imply that the rhetoric of Marlowe's
heroic overreacher compares poorly

with the bombast of Eliot's ranting braggart.

166 **with King Cerberus** to the company of
Cerberus, the triple-headed guard dog of
the underworld. Pistol has elevated Cerberus to royalty, displaying the same lack
of discrimination as in his preference of
Eliot over Marlowe.

167 **let...roar** A common tag: cf. *Tamburlaine I* 4.2.46 ('the welkin crack').
  Shall...toys Shall we quarrel over
trifles? (*OED, fall, v.* 87b)

172 **Die...dogs** Proverbial: cf. 'To die like a
dog (a dog's death)' (Dent D509).
  Give...pins Probably another reference
to Tamburlaine who hands out crowns
in return for pledges of loyalty (*Tamburlaine I* 4.4.115–18): cf. proverbial 'Not
worth a pin' (Dent P334).

175 **goodyear** Cf. ll. 58–9 above.

PISTOL

Then feed and be fat, my fair Calipolis.

Come, give's some sack.

Si fortune me tormente, sperato me contento.

Fear we broadsides? No, let the fiend give fire!   180

Give me some sack; and, sweetheart, lie thou there.

⌈*He lays down his sword*⌉

Come we to full points here? And are etceteras nothings?

FALSTAFF Pistol, I would be quiet.

PISTOL Sweet knight, I kiss thy neaf. What, we have seen
the seven stars!   185

DOLL TEARSHEET For God's sake, thrust him downstairs. I
cannot endure such a fustian rascal.

PISTOL

Thrust him downstairs? Know we not Galloway nags?

FALSTAFF Quoit him down, Bardolph, like a shove-groat
shilling. Nay, an a do nothing but speak nothing, a   190
shall be nothing here.

177–9 Then...*contento*] CAPELL; *as prose* QF   178 give's] Q (giues); giue me F   179 *contento*] Q; *contente* F   180–2 Fear...nothings?] *as verse* POPE; *as prose* QF   181.1 *He...sword*] JOHNSON (*subs.*); *not in* QF   182 nothings] Q; no-|thing F   186 For...thrust] Q; Thrust F   190 an a] Q; if hee F   190–1 a shall] Q; hee shall F

177 feed...Calipolis Parodies lines from
      The Battle of Alcazar 584–618: 'Hold
      thee Calypolis feede and faint no more,
      | ...Feede and be fat...' (MSR, 1907).
179 *Si...contento* 'If fortune torments me,
      hope contents me' (Humphreys, p. 75).
      The language Pistol uses (for what was a
      common motto) is primarily Italian, not-
      withstanding the garbled vowels. A 'cor-
      rect' version is provided by Melchiori (p.
      106): 'Se fortuna mi tormenta, ben sper-
      ato mi contenta'. Almost the identical
      line is Pistol's last line in the play
      (5.5.94), but vocalic confusion is there
      confined to ⟨i⟩ for ⟨e⟩ in 'Si' for 'Se', and
      'me' for 'mi'. Pistol is error-prone, and
      the mistakes are probably his.
182 Come...nothings 'Have we come to a
      full stop here?', perhaps because the
      others are trying to ignore him. His ques-
      tion after 'etceteras' and 'nothings'
      seems to be a randomly bawdy reference,
      inspired (perhaps) by the presence of
      Doll. Both phrases denote the female gen-
      italia, as in *Romeo* 2.1.38 where the com-
      monly accepted (editorial) 'open-arse' is
      'open *Et caetera*' in Q1.

184 neaf Dialectical for 'fist'; Pistol is mock-
      ingly courteous.
184–5 we...stars we have shared adven-
      tures at night: cf. Falstaff's reference to
      'the chimes at midnight' (3.2.206), and
      'we that take purses go by the moon and
      the seven stars' (*1 Henry IV* 1.2.13–14).
      The seven stars are the Pleiades.
188 Galloway nags Small but strong breed
      of horses peculiar to Galloway (*OED, Gal-
      loway*, 1a), applied here to Doll, because
      anyone may ride her: cf. 'Yon ribaudred
      Nagge of Egypt' (*Antony* 1623 Folio,
      emended by Oxford 3.10.10 to 'riband-
      red').
189 Quoit throw like a quoit
189–90 shove-groat shilling A coin from the
      reign of Edward VI used in the game of
      shove-groat or shove-board, in which a
      coin was driven down (by a blow of the
      hand) a polished board into compart-
      ments at the end of it; the modern equiva-
      lent is shove-halfpenny (ha'penny) and is
      played mostly in pubs.

BARDOLPH Come, get you downstairs.

PISTOL

What, shall we have incision? Shall we imbrue?

⌈*He snatches up his sword*⌉

Then death rock me asleep, abridge my doleful days.

Why then, let grievous, ghastly, gaping wounds   195

Untwine the Sisters Three. Come, Atropos, I say!

MISTRESS QUICKLY Here's goodly stuff toward!

FALSTAFF Give me my rapier, boy.

DOLL TEARSHEET I pray thee, Jack, I pray thee, do not draw.

FALSTAFF (*to Pistol*) Get you downstairs.   200

⌈*He takes his rapier.*⌉ A brawl

MISTRESS QUICKLY Here's a goodly tumult! I'll forswear
keeping house afore I'll be in these tirrits and frights.
So! Murder, I warrant now. Alas, alas, put up your
naked weapons, put up your naked weapons!

Exit Pistol, pursued by Bardolph

DOLL TEARSHEET I pray thee, Jack, be quiet; the rascal's   205
gone. Ah, you whoreson little valiant villain, you!

MISTRESS QUICKLY Are you not hurt i'th' groin? Methought
a made a shrewd thrust at your belly.

Enter Bardolph

FALSTAFF Have you turned him out o'doors?

193–6 What...say!] *as verse* CAPELL; *as prose* QF   193.1 *He...sword*] CAPELL (*subs.*); *not in*
QF   196 Untwine] Q (vntwinde); vntwin'd F   197 goodly] Q; good F   199 pray thee...
pray thee] Q; prethee...prethee F   200.1 *He...brawl*] This edition; *not in* QF   202 afore]
Q; before F   204.1 *Exit...Bardolph*] OXFORD; *not in* QF   205 pray thee] Q; prethee F   ras-
cal's] Q; Rascall is F   208 a made] Q; hee made F   208.1 *Enter Bardolph*] CAPELL; *not in*
QF   209 o'doors] Q; of doors F

---

193 **incision** bloodshed
     imbrue i.e. 'with blood'
194 **Then...asleep** A fragment of a song
     attributed to Anne Boleyn or her brother,
     as they awaited execution. Pistol's quot-
     ing it suggests that it was still popular
     sixty years later.
195 **grievous...wounds** An alliterative
     burlesque on the bombast rhetoric of
     plays like Kyd's *The Spanish Tragedy*.
196 **the Sisters Three** The three Fates
     Clotho, Lachesis, and Atropos, also
     known as the 'harsh Spinners'. They

either finish their spinning at man's
birth to determine his future life, or continue with the thread throughout his life
until it runs out and thus causes a natural death. The cutting of the thread is
attributed to Atropos, and Pistol rightly
associates her with violent death, even
though he seems to be otherwise under
the impression that the Fates are tied
together (cf. *Dream* 5.1.279–82; 331–6).
202 **tirrits** upsets
206 **whoreson** Used here as a term of affectionate commendation (see l. 228).

BARDOLPH Yea, sir ; the rascal's drunk. You have hurt him,   210
    sir, i'th' shoulder.

FALSTAFF A rascal, to brave me !

DOLL TEARSHEET Ah, you sweet little rogue, you ! Alas, poor
    ape, how thou sweatest. Come, let me wipe thy face.
    Come on, you whoreson chops. Ah, rogue, i'faith, I   215
    love thee. Thou art as valorous as Hector of Troy,
    worth five of Agamemnon, and ten times better than
    the Nine Worthies. Ah, villain !

FALSTAFF A rascally slave ! I will toss the rogue in a blan-
    ket.   220

DOLL TEARSHEET Do, an thou darest for thy heart. An thou
    dost, I'll canvas thee between a pair of sheets.

      Enter musicians

PAGE The music is come, sir.

FALSTAFF Let them play.—Play, sirs.

    ⌈*Music plays* ⌉

    Sit on my knee, Doll. A rascal bragging slave ! The rogue   225
    fled from me like quicksilver.

DOLL TEARSHEET I'faith, and thou followed'st him like a
    church. Thou whoreson little tidy Bartholomew boar-

---

210 Yea] Q; Yes F 211 i'th'] Q; in the F 213, 215, 218 Ah,] Q (A∧) 215 i'faith] Q; *not
in* F 219 A] F; Ah Q 221 an . . . An] Q; if . . . if F 222.1 *Enter musicians*] *enter musicke.* Q
(*after l.* 223); *Enter Musique.* F 224.1 *Music plays*] OXFORD; *not in* QF 227 I'faith, and]
Q; And F

---

214 **ape** fool

215 **chops** a person with fat or bloated
    cheeks (*OED, chop, sb.²* 3 *transf.*)

216 **Hector of Troy** The son of Priam and
    husband of Andromache. He was the
    mainstay of the Trojan defence and was
    traditionally regarded as the most hon-
    ourable of the heroes of the Trojan war.
    He was killed by Achilles in revenge for
    killing Patroclus.

217 **Agamemnon** The commander-in-chief
    of the Greek army which campaigned
    against Troy. He was murdered by his
    unfaithful wife Clytemnestra on his re-
    turn home. It was his trading of Chryseis
    for Briseis (who was Achilles' slave girl)
    which brought about Achilles' refusal to
    fight. Agamemnon's anger and Achilles'
    petulance are parodied by Shakespeare in
    Troilus.

218 **Nine Worthies** Consisting of three pa-

gans (Hector, Alexander, Julius Caesar),
three Jews (Joshua, David, Judas Macca-
beus), and three Christians (Arthur,
Charlemagne, Godfrey of Bouillon).

219–20 **toss . . . blanket** A punishment for
    cowards: cf. proverbial 'To toss like a
    dog in a blanket' (Dent D513.1).

221 **for thy heart** as if it were to save your life
    (*OED, for, prep.* 9c)

222 **I'll . . . sheets** To canvas means to toss
    in a sheet of canvas. Doll offers Falstaff a
    tossing of another kind, i.e. sex to reward
    his humiliation of Pistol.

227–8 **like a church** Perhaps alluding affec-
    tionately to Falstaff's stately girth which
    could not be more opposite to quicksilver.

228 **tidy** in good condition, fat, plump (*OED
    a.* 2)

228–9 **Bartholomew boar-pig** The feast of St
    Bartholomew (24 August) was the occa-
    sion of the great Bartholomew Fair in

pig, when wilt thou leave fighting o'days, and foining
o'nights, and begin to patch up thine old body for   230
heaven.

    Enter Prince Henry and Poins, disguised as drawers

FALSTAFF Peace, good Doll, do not speak like a death's
  head, do not bid me remember mine end.

DOLL TEARSHEET Sirrah, what humour's the Prince of?

FALSTAFF A good shallow young fellow. A would have   235
  made a good pantler; a would ha' chipped bread well.

DOLL TEARSHEET They say Poins has a good wit.

FALSTAFF He a good wit? Hang him, baboon! His wit's as
  thick as Tewkesbury mustard; there's no more conceit in
  him than is in a mallet.   240

DOLL TEARSHEET Why does the Prince love him so, then?

FALSTAFF Because their legs are both of a bigness, and a
  plays at quoits well, and eats conger and fennel, and
  drinks off candles' ends for flap-dragons, and rides the

229–30 o'days...o'nights] Q; on dayes...on nights F   231.1 *Enter...drawers*] OXFORD
(*subs.*); *Enter Prince and Poynes.* Q; *Enter Prince and Poines disguis'd.* F   234 humour's]
Q; humour is F   235–6 A would...a would] Q; hee would...hee would F   236 ha'
chipped] Q (a ~); haue chipp'd F   237 has] Q; hath F   238 wit's] Q; Wit is F   239 there's]
Q; there is F   241 does] Q; doth F   242–3 a plays] Q; hee playes F

London (see 1.2.48), when pigs were
dressed and sold; a boar-pig is a young
boar. Falstaff is hardly young, but he can
still pull off a fight and Doll will reward
him in a manner befitting an old boar
who behaves like an eager young one.

229 **foining** thrusting with a pointed
weapon (with an obvious sexual innuendo)

232–3 **death's head** figure of a skull with the
motto 'memento mori', i.e. 'remember
that you have to die'

236 **pantler** pantryman
  chipped bread well done a good job
paring bread by cutting away the crust.
Falstaff implies that the Prince would
have been perfectly suited to a menial
position in a great household. He is probably deliberately showing off in front of
Doll and the hostess by pretending to be
easily dismissive of Hal and Poins.

239 **Tewkesbury mustard** famous for its
solid consistency
  conceit imagination, wit (*OED, conceit,
sb.* 8d)

240 **mallet** a heavy wooden hammer

242 **legs...bigness** i.e. they are both of
them fops who are obsessed with fashion

243 **eats...fennel** Conger eel was notor-
iously hard to digest and fennel was
used in fish sauces. The point is that
they indulge in food which blunts the
mind, as conger was supposed to do (cf.
Beaumont and Fletcher, *Philaster*
2.2.41–2: 'fly... fresh pork, conger...
all dullers of the vital spirits', ed. Andrew
Gurr, 1969), and they are both dullards.

244 **drinks...flap-dragons** The trick is to
drink the liquor on which the flap-dragons (in this case candle-ends) float,
without swallowing the flap-dragon.
The normal sense of 'flap-dragon' is 'A
play in which they catch raisins out of
burning brandy and, extinguishing them
by closing the mouth, eat them' (*OED sb.*
1a). Falstaff accuses Poins of idle and
frivolous tavern pastimes.

244–5 **rides...mare** Cf. proverbial 'To ride
(shoe) the wild mare' (Dent M655), and
Henry V 5.2.137 ff.: 'If I could win a lady
at leap-frog...').

wild mare with the boys, and jumps upon joint-stools,   245
and swears with a good grace, and wears his boots very
smooth like unto the sign of the leg, and breeds no bate
with telling of discreet stories, and such other gambol
faculties a has that show a weak mind and an able body,
for the which the Prince admits him; for the Prince   250
himself is such another—the weight of a hair will turn
the scales between their avoirdupois.

PRINCE HENRY Would not this nave of a wheel have his ears
cut off?

POINS Let's beat him before his whore.   255

PRINCE HENRY Look whe'er the withered elder hath not his
poll clawed like a parrot.

POINS Is it not strange that desire should so many years
outlive performance?

FALSTAFF Kiss me, Doll.   260

She kisses him

PRINCE HENRY Saturn and Venus this year in conjunction!
What says th'almanac to that?

---

246 boots] Q; Boot F   249 a has] Q; hee hath F   251 a] Q; an F   252 the scales]
F; scales Q   255 Let's] Q; Let vs F   256 whe'er] Q (where); if F   260.1 *She kisses him*]
CAPELL; *not in* QF   262 th'almanac] Q; the Almanack F

---

245 **jumps upon joint-stools** i.e. he indulges
  in high jinks
246–7 **very smooth . . . leg** tightly fitting like
  the sign advertising a bootmaker's shop
  (to contrast with those who do not have
  good legs and therefore wear ruffled
  boots). Humphreys (p. 80) compares
  Marston, *Antonio and Mellida* 5.2.64–6:
  'O when I see one . . . wears a ruffled boot,
  I fear the fashion of his leg' (ed. G. K.
  Hunter, 1965).
247 **breeds no bate** provokes no row (*OED*,
  bate, *sb.*[1] *Obs.* = 'contention, strife, discord')
248 **with . . . stories** by spreading gossip
  about matters that ought to remain private ('discreet'). The point is that either
  (a) he gets away with gross indiscretion,
  because no one really takes him seriously, except the prince, or (b) he never
  gets into an argument because everyone
  is so keen to share his store of outrageous
  tales; or (c) no one gets annoyed at him

for telling modest stories (because he only
tells malicious ones which are the ones
that his audiences desire to hear).
252 **avoirdupois** weight
253 **nave of a wheel** Quibbling on Falstaff's
  rotundity (nave and hub) and knavery.
253–4 **ears cut off** A Star Chamber punishment for defaming royalty.
256 **elder** aged man, with a pun on elder
  tree (see 'dead elm' below, l. 328), i.e. a
  sapless elder. The idea may be that he is
  supporting Doll on his knee (cf. next
  note).
257 **poll . . . parrot** Doll is affectionately
  rumpling his hair, as if he were a parrot
  (with a pun on 'poll' meaning both head
  and parrot).
261 **Saturn and Venus** An appropriate comparison for the ageing Falstaff and the
  Venusian Doll. The two planets are
  hardly ever in conjunction, and this
  ironically underlines the patent absurd-
  ity of a union between Falstaff and Doll.

POINS And look whether the fiery Trigon his man be not
   lisping to his master's old tables, his notebook, his
   counsel-keeper!   265

FALSTAFF (*to Doll*) Thou dost give me flattering busses.

DOLL TEARSHEET By my troth, I kiss thee with a most constant heart.

FALSTAFF I am old, I am old.

DOLL TEARSHEET I love thee better than I love e'er a scurvy   270
   young boy of them all.

FALSTAFF What stuff wilt have a kirtle of? I shall receive
   money o' Thursday; shalt have a cap tomorrow. A
   merry song! Come, it grows late; we'll to bed. Thou'lt
   forget me when I am gone.   275

DOLL TEARSHEET By my troth, thou'lt set me a-weeping an
   thou sayst so. Prove that ever I dress myself handsome
   till thy return—well, hearken a'th' end.

FALSTAFF Some sack, Francis.

PRINCE HENRY *and* POINS (*coming forward*) Anon, anon, sir.   280

FALSTAFF Ha, a bastard son of the King's?—And art not
   thou Poins his brother?

PRINCE HENRY Why, thou globe of sinful continents, what a
   life dost thou lead!

FALSTAFF A better than thou: I am a gentleman, thou art a   285
   drawer.

---

264 master's] F (Masters‿); master, Q   267 By my troth] Q; Nay truely F   272 wilt]
Q; wilt thou F   273 o' Thursday] Q; on Thursday F   shalt] Q; thou shalt F   274 we'll]
Q; wee will F   Thou'lt] Q; Thou wilt F   276 By my troth] Q; *not in* F   thou'lt] Q; Thou wilt
F   an] Q; if F   278 a'th' end] Q; the end F   280 (*coming forward*)] CAPELL; *not in* QF

---

263 **fiery Trigon** i.e. Bardolph's face; lit. one
   of the zodiac's four trigons which consist
   of the three fiery signs: Aries, Leo, and
   Sagittarius.

264–5 **lisping . . . counsel-keeper** Bardolph
   is making love to Mistress Quickly in
   whispering tones; the phrases 'old tables'
   and 'notebook' were in the period applied
   to a woman so that all three nouns describe the hostess and Falstaff's con-
   fidante.

266 **busses** kisses

272 **kirtle** gown which consisted of a bodice
   and a skirt

278 **hearken a'th' end** only the end will tell
   (whether or not I remain faithful), with a
   quibble on the theme of 'memento mori'
   (see above, ll. 232–3); cf. proverbial
   'Remember (Mark) the end' (Dent E125).

283 **sinful continents** With a quibble on the
   various meanings of 'continent' as (a) a
   part of the world; (b) that which contains, or that which is contained, i.e.
   contents. In other words, Falstaff is a
   world of mischief.

PRINCE HENRY Very true, sir, and I come to draw you out by
the ears.

MISTRESS QUICKLY O, the Lord preserve thy grace! By my
troth, welcome to London! Now the Lord bless that   290
sweet face of thine! O Jesu, are you come from Wales?

FALSTAFF Thou whoreson mad compound of majesty! By
this light flesh and corrupt blood, thou art welcome.

DOLL TEARSHEET How, you fat fool! I scorn you.

POINS (*to Prince Henry*) My lord, he will drive you out of   295
your revenge and turn all to a merriment, if you take not
the heat.

PRINCE HENRY (*to Falstaff*) You whoreson candlemine you,
how vilely did you speak of me now, before this honest,
virtuous, civil gentlewoman!   300

MISTRESS QUICKLY God's blessing of your good heart, and so
she is, by my troth.

FALSTAFF (*to Prince Henry*) Didst thou hear me?

PRINCE HENRY Yea, and you knew me as you did when you
ran away by Gad's Hill; you knew I was at your back,   305
and spoke it on purpose to try my patience.

FALSTAFF No, no, no, not so; I did not think thou wast
within hearing.

PRINCE HENRY I shall drive you then to confess the wilful
abuse, and then I know how to handle you.   310

FALSTAFF No abuse, Hal, o'mine honour, no abuse.

PRINCE HENRY Not? To dispraise me, and call me 'pantler'
and 'bread-chipper', and I know not what?

FALSTAFF No abuse, Hal.

POINS No abuse?   315

FALSTAFF No abuse, Ned, i'th' world, honest Ned, none. I

---

289 grace] Q; good Grace F   289–90 By my troth] Q; *not in* F   290 the Lord] Q; Heauen
F   291 O Jesu Q; what F   293 light...blood] F (light, Flesh, and corrupt Blood,); ~, ~, ~ ~
~, Q   299 now] Q; euen now F   301 God's blessing] Q; 'Blessing F of] Q; on F
304 Yea] Q; Yes F   311 o'] Q; (a); on F   313 bread-chipper] Q; Bread-chopper F
316 i'th'] Q; in the F

292–3 **By...blood** Refers to Doll (as her re-
tort makes clear).

296–7 **if...heat** (probably) if you don't act
while you're angry, by analogy with

'striking while the iron is hot'

298 **candlemine** heaps of tallow

305 **Gad's Hill** See *1 Henry IV* 2.3 and
2.5.161–228.

dispraised him before the wicked (*to Prince Henry*) that
the wicked might not fall in love with thee; in which
doing I have done the part of a careful friend and a true
subject, and thy father is to give me thanks for it. No 320
abuse, Hal; none, Ned, none; no faith, boys, none.

PRINCE HENRY See now whether pure fear and entire cowardice doth not make thee wrong this virtuous gentlewoman to close with us. Is she of the wicked? Is thine
hostess here of the wicked? Or is thy boy of the wicked? 325
Or honest Bardolph, whose zeal burns in his nose, of the
wicked?

POINS Answer, thou dead elm, answer.

FALSTAFF The fiend hath pricked down Bardolph irrecov-
erable, and his face is Lucifer's privy kitchen, where he 330
doth nothing but roast malt-worms. For the boy, there is
a good angel about him, but the devil bids him too.

PRINCE HENRY For the women?

FALSTAFF For one of them, she's in hell already, and burns
poor souls. For th'other, I owe her money, and whether 335
she be damned for that I know not.

---

318 thee] Q; him F   321 faith] Q; *not in* F   325 thy] Q; the F   332 bids] This edition;
blinds Q; outbids F; binds DAVISON   334 she's] Q; shee is F   335 th'other] Q; the other F

317 **wicked** A mocking use of the phrase
which the Puritans applied to non-Pur-
itans (cf. the similar use of the Puritan
phrase 'zeal' below, l. 326).

328 **dead elm** Cf. 'withered elder' above, l.
256. The male elm tree traditionally supported the clinging female vine, but this
mock idyll collapses further when Falstaff
(though perhaps in jest) calls Doll (and
his other companions) 'wicked', as Hal
points out.

329 **pricked down** chosen; 'prick' means 'to
mark (a name, or an item) in a list by
making a "prick" through or against it'
(*OED v.* 15)

331 **malt-worms** drunkards

332 **bids** The striking differences between
Q's 'blinds' and F's 'outbids' are hard to
trace to a common original, as Shaaber
(p. 209) and Davison (pp. 220–1) note.
But 'blind' and a version of '[-]b/l/i/n/ds'
could easily be misread, as Davison's pro-

posed 'binds' also implies. It may be that
Shakespeare wrote 'bids' ('commands':
OED v. str. 10), i.e. in spite of his good
angel's offices, the boy is as lost to the
devil as Bardolph. The change to 'outbids' in F may have been caused, or
abetted, by the syntactic ambiguity of
'him': in Q and in this edition 'him' can
refer to either the boy or the angel, but in
F the devil outbids the good angel ('him')
for the soul of the boy. It is conceivable
that F's 'outbids' is not a slip so much as a
deliberate mitigation (for performance) of
the unacceptable idea of the devil com-
manding the good angel or the boy under
angelic tutelage. The idea of a tug-of-war
between divine powers and evil forces,
suggested by 'outbids', reaches back to
Job and may be more orthodox and safer.

334 **burns** i.e. infects them with venereal
disease

MISTRESS QUICKLY No, I warrant you.

FALSTAFF No, I think thou art not; I think thou art quit for
that. Marry, there is another indictment upon thee, for
suffering flesh to be eaten in thy house, contrary to the   340
law, for the which I think thou wilt howl.

MISTRESS QUICKLY All victuallers do so. What's a joint of
mutton or two in a whole Lent?

PRINCE HENRY You, gentlewoman—

DOLL TEARSHEET What says your grace?   345

FALSTAFF His grace says that which his flesh rebels against.
          Peto knocks at door ⌈within⌉

MISTRESS QUICKLY Who knocks so loud at door? Look to th'
door there, Francis.
          Enter Peto

PRINCE HENRY Peto, how now, what news?

PETO

The King your father is at Westminster,   350
And there are twenty weak and wearied posts
Come from the north; and as I came along
I met and overtook a dozen captains,
Bareheaded, sweating, knocking at the taverns,
And asking every one for Sir John Falstaff.   355

PRINCE HENRY

By heaven, Poins, I feel me much to blame
So idly to profane the precious time,

---

342 What's] Q; What is F   346.1 *Peto...within*] Q (*Peyto knockes at doore.*); *not in* F
347-8 th' door] Q; the doore F   348.1 *Enter Peto*] F; *not in* Q

---

338 **quit** forgiven (because, far from extract-
ing interest, she will not even recover her
original outlay from Falstaff)

340-3 **flesh...Lent** Falstaff plays on the
double-entendre of flesh meaning both
meat and sex, which Mistress Quickly
unwittingly develops by the cognate use
of 'a joint of mutton' (*OED*, *mutton*, n. 4
slang = 'loose woman, prostitute'; cf. also
'laced mutton', i.e. a strumpet as in *Two
Gentlemen* 1.1.94–6: 'I, a lost mutton,
gave your letter to her, a laced mutton,
and she, a laced mutton, gave me, a lost
mutton, nothing for my labour'). The
point is that Falstaff accuses her of being

a procuress or bawd, while she owns up
to a minor infringement of the 'law', the
insistent Privy Council proclamations
against meat-eating during Lent.

346 **that . . . rebels against** Falstaff is probably saying that by calling Doll a gentlewoman and by pretending to think of her
and the hostess as not 'wicked' Hal is
saying things that his sexual instincts
tell him are not so. The use of the phrase
'flesh' here immediately after the exchange between Mistress Quickly and
Falstaff may lend support to a reading
which opposes reason and sex.

When tempest of commotion, like the south
Borne with black vapour, doth begin to melt
And drop upon our bare unarmèd heads.   360
Give me my sword and cloak.—Falstaff, good night.
                 Exeunt Prince Henry and Poins
FALSTAFF Now comes in the sweetest morsel of the night,
    and we must hence and leave it unpicked.
       Knocking within. ⌈*Exit Bardolph*⌉
More knocking at the door?
       Enter Bardolph
How now, what's the matter?   365
BARDOLPH
    You must away to court, sir, presently.
    A dozen captains stay at door for you.
FALSTAFF (*to the Page*) Pay the musicians, sirrah. Farewell,
    hostess; farewell, Doll. You see, my good wenches, how
    men of merit are sought after. The undeserver may sleep,   370
    when the man of action is called on. Farewell, good
    wenches. If I be not sent away post, I will see you again
    ere I go.   ⌈*Exeunt musicians*⌉
DOLL TEARSHEET I cannot speak. If my heart be not ready to
    burst—well, sweet Jack, have a care of thyself.   375
FALSTAFF Farewell, farewell.
               Exit ⌈*with Bardolph, Peto, and the Page*⌉
MISTRESS QUICKLY Well, fare thee well. I have known thee
    these twenty-nine years come peascod-time, but an hon-
    ester and truer-hearted man—well, fare thee well.
BARDOLPH ⌈*within*⌉ Mistress Tearsheet!   380
MISTRESS QUICKLY What's the matter?
BARDOLPH ⌈*within*⌉ Bid Mistress Tearsheet come to my
    master.

---

358 south₌] QB, F (south,); ~. QA   361.1 *Exeunt . . . Poins*] Q (*exeunt Prince and Poynes.*);
Exit. F   363.1 *Knocking within*] CAPELL (*subs.*); *not in* QF   *Exit Bardolph*] HUMPHREYS; *not in*
QF   364.1 *Enter Bardolph*] CAPELL; *not in* QF   373 *Exeunt musicians*] OXFORD; *not in* QF
376.1 *Exit . . . Page*] OXFORD; *exit.* QB (*not in* QA); *Exit.* F   380 *within*] This edition; *not in*
QF   382 *within*] This edition; *not in* QF

---

358 **commotion** insurrection (*OED* 4)
    south The south wind was thought to
    bring storms and noxious fog in its wake.

366 **presently** immediately
372 **post** posthaste
378 **peascod-time** the time when peas pod

MISTRESS QUICKLY O, run, Doll, run ; run, good Doll ; come.
  She comes blubbered. Yea, will you come, Doll ?   385

                                              Exeunt

3.1   *Enter King Henry in his nightgown, with a Page*
KING HENRY *(giving letters)*

  Go, call the Earls of Surrey and of Warwick.
  But ere they come, bid them o'er-read these letters
  And well consider of them. Make good speed.

                                              Exit Page

  How many thousand of my poorest subjects
  Are at this hour asleep ! O sleep, O gentle sleep,   5
  Nature's soft nurse, how have I frighted thee,
  That thou no more wilt weigh my eyelids down,
  And steep my senses in forgetfulness ?
  Why rather, sleep, liest thou in smoky cribs,
  Upon uneasy pallets stretching thee,   10
  And hushed with buzzing night-flies to thy slumber
  Than in the perfumed chambers of the great,
  Under the canopies of costly state,
  And lulled with sound of sweetest melody ?
  O thou dull god, why li'st thou with the vile   15
  In loathsome beds, and leav'st the kingly couch

384–5 come . . . Doll] Q; *not in* F   385.1 *Exeunt*] QB, F
  3.1.0.1 *Enter . . . page*] F (*Enter the King, with a Page*.); *Enter the King in his night-gowne |
alone*. QB   3.1 *Exit page*] F (*Exit*.); *not in* QB   14 sound] QB; sounds F

384–5 **come . . . Doll** See Introduction, pp.
    80–1.
385 **blubbered** tear-stained
3.1.0.1 **Enter . . . Page** QB's *Enter . . . alone*
    does not necessarily exclude the page
    who is clearly needed to convey the let-
    ters. The use of 'alone' here is probably
    similar to Q's stage direction at 1.2.0,
    where Falstaff enters *alone, with his page*;
    the phrase may stipulate a respectful dis-
    tance for the page.
  nightgown 'A night-gown was an ankle-

length gown with long sleeves and collar
varying in size from the shawl-collar of
the men's modern dressing-gown to the
fur collar on ladies' coats. It was worn for
warmth both indoors and out' (Linthicum, p. 184).
  5 **O sleep** With this apostrophe cf. *Macbeth*
    2.2.33–8, and see Introduction, p. 48.
  9 **cribs** hovels (*OED*, *crib*, *sb.* 3a)
  10 **pallets** poor straw beds (*OED sb.* 2 1)
  13 **state** splendour (*OED sb.* 17a)
  15 **vile** mean in rank

A watch-case, or a common 'larum-bell?
Wilt thou upon the high and giddy mast
Seal up the ship-boy's eyes, and rock his brains
In cradle of the rude imperious surge,   20
And in the visitation of the winds,
Who take the ruffian billows by the top,
Curling their monstrous heads, and hanging them
With deafing clamour in the slippery clouds,
That with the hurly death itself awakes?   25
Canst thou, O partial sleep, give thy repose
To the wet sea-boy in an hour so rude,
And in the calmest and most stillest night,
With all appliances and means to boot,
Deny it to a king? Then happy low, lie down.   30
Uneasy lies the head that wears a crown.
     Enter the Earls of Warwick and Surrey

WARWICK

Many good morrows to your majesty!

---

18 mast] F; masse QB   22 billows] F; pillowes QB   24 deafing clamour] QB; deaff'ning Clamors F   26 thy] F; them QB   27 sea-boy] F; season QB   31.1 *Enter... Surrey*] F (*Enter Warwicke and Surrey.*); *Enter Warwike, Surry and sir Iohn | Blunt.* QB

17 **watch-case . . . 'larum-bell** The King may here compare himself to the wound-up mechanism in a watchcase. Watchcases with alarms were already used in Shakespeare's time: cf. 'the watch rings alarum in his pocket!' (Middleton, *A Mad World, My Masters* 5.2.240–1, vol. 3, 1885, ed. A. H. Bullen). The sense tentatively suggested by *OED* for 'watch-case', 'a place in which one must keep watch', would tend to support Hanmer's gloss: 'This alludes to the Watchman set in Garrison-towns upon some Eminence attending upon an Alarum-bell, which he was to ring out in case of fire or any approaching danger'.

21 **visitation** 'violent or destructive agency or force falling upon a people or a country' (*OED* 8)

25 **That** so that
hurly tumult

26 **partial** (a) unfair, in the sense of favour-

ing one set of persons rather than another (*OED a.* 1a); (b) kindly (*OED a.* 1b)

27 **sea-boy** Q's 'season' (for, probably, 'season') is not implausible (cf. Davison, pp. 223–4), particularly since 'sea-boy' is not recorded elsewhere in the period and may be thought rather awkwardly to echo 'ship-boy'.

31 **Uneasy . . . crown** Cf. proverbial 'Crowns have cares' (Dent C863).

31.1 **Enter ... Surrey** The King has called for Warwick and Surrey only, and there is no need to bring on Sir John Blunt (as Q does), who does not speak in either Q or F. The QF difference here may reflect disagreement between 'foul papers' (Q) and a prompt-book (F), the former suggesting that Shakespeare changed his mind as he wrote the scene, while the acting version would dispose of a ghost character. Blunt enters at 4.2.23.1–2 with Prince John (see also Introduction, p. 90).

KING HENRY

  Is it good morrow, lords?

WARWICK   'Tis one o'clock, and past.

KING HENRY

  Why then, good morrow to you all, my lords.

  Have you read o'er the letter that I sent you?   35

WARWICK We have, my liege.

KING HENRY

  Then you perceive the body of our kingdom,

  How foul it is, what rank diseases grow,

  And with what danger near the heart of it.

WARWICK

  It is but as a body yet distempered,   40

  Which to his former strength may be restored

  With good advice and little medicine.

  My lord Northumberland will soon be cooled.

KING HENRY

  O God, that one might read the book of fate,

  And see the revolution of the times   45

  Make mountains level, and the continent,

  Weary of solid firmness, melt itself

  Into the sea; and other times to see

  The beachy girdle of the ocean,

  Too wide for Neptune's hips; how chance's mocks   50

  And changes fill the cup of alteration

  With divers liquors! O, if this were seen,

---

35 letter] QB; Letters F   44 God] QB; Heauen F   52–5 O…die] QB; *not in* F

38 **rank** foul, festering (*OED a.* 14b)

42 **little** a little

45 **revolution** changes, alteration (cf. l. 51)

46 **continent** shore ('that which contains or holds', *OED sb.* 1a): see similarly *Dream* 2.1.92.

52–5 **O…die** These Q-only lines are thought by some editors to be a late manuscript addition by Shakespeare, or an interpolation (Humphreys, p. lxxxii n. 3; Davison, p. 225) so that F reflects the original text. The half-line ' 'Tis…gone' would perfectly complete 'With…liquors'. According to this scenario the text printed by Q reflects the *revised* state of foul papers when they were submitted to the printers in 1600. Conversely the lines may have been edited out of F, as

clearly happened with the stage direction and its reference to Blunt. Q's apostrophe could have been intended as the culmination of the abstract train of thought launched by 'O God…', the voicing of a feeling of almost suicidal despair at life's apocalyptic mutability; in which case the last line ('Would…die') would provide a cross-play echoic transition into the Richard II reflection, since it seems to allude to Richard's passive response, and specifically the lines 'For God's sake, let us sit upon the ground, | And tell sad stories of the death of kings' from *Richard II* 3.2.151–2. The use of a hemistich could be intended to signal the new direction now taken by the King as he moves from the general to the specific.

The happiest youth, viewing his progress through,
What perils past, what crosses to ensue,
Would shut the book and sit him down and die.   55
'Tis not ten years gone
Since Richard and Northumberland, great friends,
Did feast together; and in two year after
Were they at wars. It is but eight years since
This Percy was the man nearest my soul,   60
Who like a brother toiled in my affairs,
And laid his love and life under my foot,
Yea, for my sake, even to the eyes of Richard
Gave him defiance. But which of you was by—
(*To Warwick*) You, cousin Neville, as I may remember—   65
When Richard, with his eye brimful of tears,
Then checked and rated by Northumberland,
Did speak these words, now proved a prophecy—
'Northumberland, thou ladder by the which
My cousin Bolingbroke ascends my throne'—   70
Though then, God knows, I had no such intent
But that necessity so bowed the state
That I and greatness were compelled to kiss—
'The time shall come'—thus did he follow it—
'The time will come that foul sin, gathering head,   75
Shall break into corruption'; so went on,

58 year] QB; yeeres F   71 God] QB; Heauen F

56–9 'Tis . . . eight years See Introduction, p. 20.
65 cousin Neville There is no Earl of Warwick in *Richard II*, and the personal name of the one in this play was Richard de Beauchamp (1382–1439), while the Earl of Westmorland was Ralph Neville (1364–1425). There is, however, a Richard Neville who is Earl of Warwick in *Richard Duke of York* (3 *Henry VI*).
  cousin Often used loosely between people as a mark of intimacy rather than kinship (see below, ll. 69–76).
67–78 Then . . . amity Refers back to *Richard II* 4.1.212–42 (2 *Henry IV* l. 67) and *Richard II* 5.1.55–65 (2 *Henry IV* ll. 69–76).
67 rated berated
69–76 'Northumberland . . . corruption' Rather than being 'loosely quoted' (Humphreys, p. 93), Bolingbroke's echo

of *Richard II* 5.1.55–9 is a carefully calculated rewording of Richard's words to Northumberland and characteristic of the speaker. Richard II's 'The mounting Bolingbroke', with its subversive and sexually predatory overtones (cf. *Cymbeline* 2.5.16–17)—as if Bolingbroke's bid for power were simultaneously an act of rape—becomes a tame and intimate address, 'My cousin Bolingbroke'; and Richard's expansive and poetic 'The time shall not be many hours of age | More than it is' becomes a flat, almost banal 'The time shall come . . . | The time will come'. Bolingbroke is continuously on his guard to the point where he reinvents the past during which he played the role of usurper. That the past is deliberately rewritten here in order to control the future is clear from Warwick's reply. See Introduction, p. 48 n.

Foretelling this same time's condition,
And the division of our amity.

WARWICK

There is a history in all men's lives
Figuring the natures of the times deceased;   80
The which observed, a man may prophesy,
With a near aim, of the main chance of things
As yet not come to life, who in their seeds
And weak beginnings lie entreasurèd.
Such things become the hatch and brood of time;   85
And by the necessary form of this
King Richard might create a perfect guess
That great Northumberland, then false to him,
Would of that seed grow to a greater falseness,
Which should not find a ground to root upon·   90
Unless on you.

KING HENRY   Are these things then necessities?
Then let us meet them like necessities;
And that same word even now cries out on us.
They say the Bishop and Northumberland
Are fifty thousand strong.

WARWICK   It cannot be, my lord.   95
Rumour doth double, like the voice and echo,
The numbers of the feared. Please it your grace
To go to bed? Upon my soul, my lord,
The powers that you already have sent forth
Shall bring this prize in very easily.   100
To comfort you the more, I have received
A certain instance that Glyndŵr is dead.
Your majesty hath been this fortnight ill,
And these unseasoned hours perforce must add

---

80 natures] QB; nature F   83 who] QB; which F   84 beginnings] F; beginning QB
98 soul] QB; Life F

---

80 **Figuring . . . deceased** revealing the forms of the past
82 **the main . . . things** the most important eventuality
83 **who** which
  in their seeds Cf. *Macbeth* 1.3.56: 'the seeds of time'.

84 **entreasurèd** stored carefully (*OED*, *entreasure*, 1 *trans.*)
86 **necessary form** inevitable pattern
102 **instance** proof
  Glyndŵr . . . dead See Introduction, p. 20.
104 **unseasoned** unseasonable, late

Unto your sickness.

KING HENRY   I will take your counsel.   105
And were these inward wars once out of hand,
We would, dear lords, unto the Holy Land.   *Exeunt*

3.2   *Enter Justice Shallow and Justice Silence*

SHALLOW Come on, come on, come on! Give me your
hand, sir, give me your hand, sir. An early stirrer, by
the rood! And how doth my good cousin Silence?

SILENCE Good morrow, good cousin Shallow.

SHALLOW And how doth my cousin, your bedfellow? and   5
your fairest daughter and mine, my god-daughter Ellen?

SILENCE Alas, a black ouzel, cousin Shallow.

SHALLOW By yea and no, sir, I dare say my cousin William
is become a good scholar. He is at Oxford still, is he not?

SILENCE Indeed, sir, to my cost.   10

SHALLOW A must then to the Inns o' Court shortly. I was
once of Clement's Inn, where I think they will talk of mad
Shallow yet.

SILENCE You were called 'lusty Shallow' then, cousin.

3.2.0.1 *Enter ... Silence*] Q; *Enter Shallow and Silence: with Mouldie, Shadow,* | *Wart, Feeble,*
Bull-calfe. F   1 come on! Give] QA, F; come on sir, giue QB   8 no] Q; nay F   sir,] QA, F; ~:
QB   11 A] Q; Hee F   o'] Q (a); of F

106 **inward** domestic

3.2 On the location, see Introduction, p. 12.

0.1 There are good reasons for following Q's
stage direction rather than F's block
entry, even though the latter is prompt-
book based and can therefore be expected
to reflect theatrical practice (see *Textual
Companion*, pp. 352, 361). The text twice
implies that the recruits are off-stage: in
Falstaff's wish to see them (l. 93), and in
Shallow's 'Let them appear as I call' (96–
7). Furthermore, as Davison (p. 229)
points out, the one-by-one appearance
of the recruits provokes our laughter
(and sympathy) on each of the five occasions when they are summoned (as opposed to a single laughter shared with the
entrance of the two justices at the start of
the scene).

3 **rood** cross

7 **black ouzel** blackbird. Ellen is not fair,
but dark which was unfashionable for
women at the time. Silence is probably

just being modest about his daughter's
looks.

8 **By ... no** See 2.2.123.

9 **Oxford** The universities of Oxford and
Cambridge were often the stepping-
stones for young men preparing to attend
the London Inns of Court and Chancery.

12 **Clement's Inn** Founded in *c.*1480 and
one of the eight Inns of Chancery in existence by 1600. Along with Clifford's
and Lyon's Inns it was affiliated to the
Inner Temple. By the time Falstaff and
Shallow attended Clement's Inn, the
Chancery Inns had become preparatory
schools for students wishing to be called
to the Bar by the Inns of Court. In the
1590s, when Shakespeare wrote the
play, the Inns of Chancery were gradu-
ally taken over by attorneys and solici-
tors who were increasingly excluded
from the Inns of Court.

14 **lusty** lively; lascivious

SHALLOW By the mass, I was called anything; and I would   15
have done anything indeed, too, and roundly, too. There
was I, and little John Doit of Staffordshire, and black
George Barnes, and Francis Pickbone, and Will Squeal,
a Cotswold man—you had not four such swinge-buck-
lers in all the Inns o' Court again. And I may say to you,   20
we knew where the bona-robas were, and had the best of
them all at commandment. Then was Jack Falstaff, now
Sir John, a boy, and page to Thomas Mowbray, Duke of
Norfolk.

SILENCE This Sir John, cousin, that comes hither anon   25
about soldiers?

SHALLOW The same Sir John, the very same. I see him break
Scoggin's head at the court gate when a was a crack, not
thus high. And the very same day did I fight with one
Samson Stockfish, a fruiterer, behind Gray's Inn. Jesu,   30
Jesu, the mad days that I have spent! And to see how
many of my old acquaintance are dead.

SILENCE We shall all follow, cousin.

---

15 By the mass] Q; *not in* F   18 Barnes] Q; *Bare* F   20 o'] Q (a); of F   21 bona-robas]
F; bona robes Q   25 This . . . cousin] QA, F; Coosin, this sir Iohn QB   27 ₍Sir John,] QA, F; (~
~) QB   see] Q; saw F   28 a was] Q; hee was F   30–1 Jesu, Jesu] Q; Oh F   32 my] Q; mine
F

16 **roundly** to the full, thoroughly (*OED adv.*
2)
19 **Cotswold** If the scene is intended to be set
in Gloucestershire rather than the north
of England (see Introduction, p. 12), then
Shallow is here singling out Will Squeal
because he is a 'local' man like himself.
19–20 **swinge-bucklers** swash-bucklers
21 **bona-robas** From the Italian 'bona roba',
lit. 'good stuff', and rendered by Florio in
A Worlde of Wordes (1598) as 'a good
wholesome plum-cheeked wench'; here
meaning 'classy tarts'.
22–4 **Then . . . Norfolk** See Introduction, pp.
43–4.
27 **see** 'Complete present' tense; see Abbott,
§346.
28 **Scoggin's** A reference probably to John
Scoggin who was court jester to Edward
IV (rather than the fourteenth-century
court poet Henry Scogan). His name was

synonymous with 'buffoon' in Shakespeare's day through a mid sixteenth-
century jestbook, *Scoggin, his iestes*. The
point may be that even the young Falstaff
was always brawling with various buf-
foons. See also on 'Dagonet', below, ll.
269–75.
28 **court gate** palace gates
   crack lively, pert young lad
30 **Samson Stockfish** His heroic first name
and egregious surname (meaning dried
cod, and suggesting shrivelled dryness)
are comically ill-matched; 'stockfish' is
used by Falstaff as a term of abuse at *1
Henry IV* 2.5.249: 'you bull's pizzle, you
stock-fish' (cf. also *Measure* 3.1.373 and
Tempest 3.2.71–2).
   behind Gray's Inn in Gray's Inn Fields,
north of Gray's Inn in present-day Hol-
born

SHALLOW Certain, 'tis certain; very sure, very sure. Death,
   as the Psalmist saith, is certain to all; all shall die. How a   35
   good yoke of bullocks at Stamford Fair?

SILENCE By my troth, I was not there.

SHALLOW Death is certain. Is old Double of your town living
   yet?

SILENCE Dead, sir.   40

SHALLOW Jesu, Jesu, dead! A drew a good bow; and dead!
   A shot a fine shot. John o' Gaunt loved him well, and
   betted much money on his head. Dead! A would have
   clapped i'th' clout at twelve score, and carried you a
   forehand shaft a fourteen and fourteen and a half, that   45
   it would have done a man's heart good to see. How a
   score of ewes now?

SILENCE Thereafter as they be; a score of good ewes may be
   worth ten pounds.

SHALLOW And is old Double dead?   50

SILENCE Here come two of Sir John Falstaff's men, as I
   think.

   Enter Bardolph and ⌈the Page⌉

---

35 as...saith] Q; *not in* F   36 Stamford] F; Samforth Q   37 By my troth] Q; Truly Cousin
F   41 Jesu, Jesu, dead!] Q; Dead? See, see: F   A] Q; hee F   42 A] Q; hee F   o'] Q (a); of F
43 A] Q; hee F   44 i'th' clout] Q; in the Clowt F   45 a fourteen] Q; at foureteene F
52.1 *Enter...Page*] F (*Enter Bardolph and his Boy., after l.* 50); *Enter Bardolfe, and one with
him.* Q

34–5 **Death...saith** From Psalm 89: 'What
man liueth, & shal not se death?'.

35 **How** what price is

36 **Stamford** A town in Lincolnshire, famous
for its horse and cattle fairs held in February, Lent, and August; see Introduction, p. 12.

42 **John o' Gaunt** See Introduction, p. 43.

44–5 **clapped...half** The main burden of
the passage is that Double, according
to Shallow, was an expert shot. He
could hit the target ('clapped i'th' clout',
where 'clout' means the square of cloth
in the centre of the target) at 240
yards, and was capable of shooting over

a distance of 280 to 290 yards ('fourteen
and fourteen and a half' [score yards])
by aiming his arrow straight ahead
('forehand', lit. above the bow hand)
rather than in a high arc. This appears
to be an almost impossible feat, and its
intention may be to introduce Shallow
as a nostalgic fantasist, addicted to old
men's 'vice of lying' (l. 290), i.e. exag-
geration.

44 **you** Ethical dative, used for emphasis: cf.
above, 2.1.40.

48 **Thereafter...they be** according to their
quality

Good morrow, honest gentlemen.

BARDOLPH I beseech you, which is Justice Shallow?

SHALLOW I am Robert Shallow, sir, a poor esquire of this   55
county, and one of the King's Justices of the Peace. What
is your good pleasure with me?

BARDOLPH My captain, sir, commends him to you—my
captain Sir John Falstaff, a tall gentleman, by heaven,
and a most gallant leader.   60

SHALLOW He greets me well, sir. I knew him a good backsword man. How doth the good knight? May I ask how
my lady his wife doth?

BARDOLPH Sir, pardon, a soldier is better accommodated
than with a wife.   65

SHALLOW It is well said, in faith, sir, and it is well said
indeed, too. 'Better accommodated'—it is good; yea,
indeed, is it. Good phrases are surely, and ever were,
very commendable. 'Accommodated'—it comes of '*ac-
commodo*'. Very good, a good phrase.   70

---

53 Good] QA(b), QB; *Bardolfe.* Good QA(a); *Shal.* F   57 good] QA, F; *not in* QB   59 by
heaven] Q; *not in* F   64 accommodated] F; accommodate Q   66 in faith] Q; *not in* F
68 ever were] Q; euery where F

53 **Good ... gentlemen** F assigns the line to
Shallow. It is given to Bardolph in uncorrected QA, which cannot be right because the next speech-prefix is also
Bardolph's. Berger and Williams (p.
115) note that the speech-prefix in
QA(a) may be attracted from the line
which follows, but Berger (p. viii) later
argues that it 'is the result of erroneous
attraction from the name in the stage
direction at Q/TLN 1446'. F needed to
clarify the position for performance, and
decided to alternate the speech-prefixes
between Shallow and Silence, and most
editions give the line to Shallow. But the
evidence from corrected QA, along with
the placing of the entry in F of Bardolph
and the Page after 'And ... dead' (l. 50),
may suggest that Silence is indeed intended to speak the lines 'Here ... gentlemen'. It may be that QA's speech-prefix
slipped down (through eye-skip?) from
the stage direction (it is fully spelled out
as in the stage direction), and was then
removed by the corrector of QA working
from manuscript (QB is set from corrected
QA here). Berger (pp. vii–viii) argues that
the correction has no authority; he construes it as evidence of the corrector's
'crude attempt to make sense of the passage without consulting the manuscript', a mechanical response to a
duplicated speech-prefix.

55 **esquire** someone who belongs to the
higher order of English gentry

61–2 **backsword man** fencer at single stick,
a stick with a basketwork hilt used in
practice instead of swords (cf. Pistol's
basket-hilt sword at 2.4.127)

64 **accommodated** Apparently a modish
word at the time, as Ben Jonson noted
when he referred to 'the perfumed termes
of the time, as *Accommodation*, ...' (*Dis-
coveries*, H & S viii. 632). It may be used
here comically to underline the contrast
between town and country.

68 **phrases** A phrase could denote a single
word (*OED, phrase, sb.* 2b).

BARDOLPH Pardon, sir, I have heard the word—'phrase'
call you it?—By this day, I know not the phrase, but I
will maintain the word with my sword to be a soldier-like
word, and a word of exceeding good command, by
heaven. 'Accommodated': that is, when a man is, as   75
they say, accommodated, or when a man is being whereby a may be thought to be accommodated; which is an
excellent thing.
　　Enter Falstaff
SHALLOW It is very just. Look, here comes good Sir John. (*To
Falstaff*) Give me your hand, give me your worship's   80
good hand. By my troth, you like well, and bear your
years very well. Welcome, good Sir John.
FALSTAFF I am glad to see you well, good Master Robert
Shallow. (*To Silence*) Master Surecard, as I think?
SHALLOW No, Sir John, it is my cousin Silence, in commis-   85
sion with me.
FALSTAFF Good Master Silence, it well befits you should be
of the peace.
SILENCE Your good worship is welcome.
FALSTAFF Fie, this is hot weather, gentlemen. Have you   90
provided me here half a dozen sufficient men?
SHALLOW Marry, have we, sir. Will you sit?
FALSTAFF Let me see them, I beseech you.
　　⌈*He sits*⌉
SHALLOW Where's the roll? where's the roll? where's the

---

71 Pardon] QA, F; Pardon me QB   72 this] QA, F; this good QB   74–5 by heaven] Q; *not in*
F   77 a may be] Q; he F   78.1 *Enter Falstaff*] QA, F; *Enter sir Iohn Falstaffe.* QB   80 your
hand] F; your good hand Q   81 By my troth] Q; Trust me F   like] Q; looke F   84 Surecard]
F; Soccard Q   85, 87 Silence] QA (Scilens), QB (Silens), F   91 dozen] Q; dozen of F

---

74 **a word . . . command** a very proper
　military term
79 **just** true
81 **like** F's 'looke' is possible, but not neces-
　sary, since 'like' (*OED v.*[1] 4) means 'to be
　in good condition, to thrive'.
84 **Surecard** F's word (Q has 'Soccard')
　means a 'person certain to bring success'
　(Onions); the gloss 'boon companion'
　was suggested by Malone, but it cannot
　be corroborated by *OED*.

85 **Silence** Here and elsewhere in Q (a total of
　nine occurrences) the spelling of the
　name starts with 'Sci-' for 'Si-'. On the
　relevance of this as evidence about the
　manuscript behind Q, see Introduction,
　p. 90.
85–6 **in commission** having the authority
　(under the Great Seal) to act as a Justice
　of the Peace (*OED, commission, sb.*[1] 2c)
90–1 **Have . . . men** See Introduction, p. 45.
91 **sufficient** able

roll? Let me see, let me see, let me see. So, so, so, so, so,   95
so, so. Yea, marry, sir: Ralph Mouldy! ⌈*To Silence*⌉ Let
them appear as I call, let them do so, let them do so. Let
me see; (*calls*) where is Mouldy?
        ⌈*Enter Mouldy*⌉
MOULDY Here, an't please you.
SHALLOW What think you, Sir John? A good-limbed fellow,   100
    young, strong, and of good friends.
FALSTAFF Is thy name Mouldy?
MOULDY Yea, an't please you.
FALSTAFF 'Tis the more time thou wert used.
SHALLOW Ha, ha, ha, most excellent, i'faith. Things that   105
    are mouldy lack use. Very singular good, in faith, well
    said, Sir John, very well said.
FALSTAFF Prick him.
MOULDY I was pricked well enough before, an you could
    have let me alone. My old dame will be undone now for   110
    one to do her husbandry and her drudgery. You need not
    to have pricked me; there are other men fitter to go out
    than I.
FALSTAFF Go to, peace, Mouldy. You shall go, Mouldy; it is
    time you were spent.   115
MOULDY Spent?

---

95 let me see. So] QA, F; SO QB   95–6 so, so, so. Yea] Q; yea F   97 do∧...do∧] QB,
F; ~,...~, QA   98.1 *Enter Mouldy*] OXFORD; *not in* QF   99 an't] QA; and it QB; if it F
103 an't] Q; if it F   105 i'faith] Q; *not in* F   106 in faith] Q; *not in* F   108 FALSTAFF
Prick him] F; *Iohn prickes him.* Q   109 an] Q; if F

---

101 **friends** kin
108 **Prick him** choose him (by marking his
    name on the list). Q prints '*Iohn prickes
    him*' because the compositor mistook the
    speech-prefix and command for a stage
    direction.
109–11 **I...drudgery** Mouldy quibbles on
    the various meanings of 'pricked' as
    'chosen', 'vexed', 'turned sour' (i.e.
    mouldy). There is also a sexual innuendo
    similar to the one in Sonnet 20.13,
    where Nature is said to have 'pricked
    thee [the young man] out for women's

pleasure'. The sexual equivoque is developed further in the next sentence, particularly in 'husbandry' and 'drudgery';
'old dame' probably means wife here
rather than mother (*pace* Onions). However, at ll. 220–3 she is described as 'old'
in the way befitting an aged parent who
will be left alone without a support by
Mouldy's departure to war.
115 **spent** used up, with a probable bawdy
    innuendo (cf. Williams, 1994, pp. 1281–
    2: 'spend = shed seed')

SHALLOW Peace, fellow, peace. Stand aside; know you
where you are? For th'other, Sir John, let me see:
Simon Shadow!

FALSTAFF Yea, marry, let me have him to sit under. He's   120
like to be a cold soldier.

SHALLOW (*calls*) Where's Shadow?
⌈*Enter Shadow*⌉

SHADOW Here, sir.

FALSTAFF Shadow, whose son art thou?

SHADOW My mother's son, sir.   125

FALSTAFF Thy mother's son! Like enough, and thy father's
shadow. So the son of the female is the shadow of the
male. It is often so indeed—but much of the father's
substance!

SHALLOW Do you like him, Sir John?   130

FALSTAFF Shadow will serve for summer. Prick him, for we
have a number of shadows fill up the muster book.

SHALLOW (*calls*) Thomas Wart!

FALSTAFF Where's he?
⌈*Enter Wart*⌉

WART Here, sir.   135

FALSTAFF Is thy name Wart?

WART Yea, sir.

---

118 th'other] Q; the other F   see:] F; ~∧ Q   120 Yea] Q; I F   122.1 *Enter Shadow*]
OXFORD; *not in* QF   128 much] Q; not F   132 fill] Q; to fill F   134.1 *Enter Wart*] OXFORD;
not in QF

---

118 **other** others

119 **Shadow** Presumably a particularly
emaciated recruit, but the name also
glances at the recruiting of 'shadows'
(see below, l. 132: 'a number of shadows') for the purpose of embezzling public money.

121 **cold** (a) cool, deliberate; (b) cowardly

126–9 **Thy mother's . . . substance** Essentially a rather heavy-handed joke about
Shadow's doubtful paternity. Falstaff
agrees that he is his mother's son and
suggests either (a) that his father was
called Shadow, or (b) that he is a
shadowy reflection of his father, because
male children are often insubstantial re-
plicas of their fathers; and because his
father is called Shadow, he is the shadow
of a Shadow.

131 **serve** do well enough; be a soldier

132 **shadows . . . muster book** fictitious
troops entered in the muster roll whose
pay their commanders can claim

133 **Thomas Wart** A Thomas Warter from
Chipping Campden near Stratford-upon-
Avon appears in a list of men from Gloucestershire. He is a carpenter and is de-
clared 'fitt to serve with a Calyver' (see
Humphreys, p. 103). The carpentry, the
use of the caliver, and Warter's first
name are all paralleled in the play. Warter's age was moreover roughly the same
as Shakespeare's. The play as a whole is
full of local colour and what seem to be
specific contemporary references: see Introduction, p. 57.

FALSTAFF Thou art a very ragged wart.

SHALLOW Shall I prick him, Sir John?

FALSTAFF It were superfluous, for his apparel is built upon   140
his back, and the whole frame stands upon pins. Prick
him no more.

SHALLOW Ha, ha, ha, you can do it, sir, you can do it. I
commend you well. (*Calls*) Francis Feeble!

⌈*Enter Feeble*⌉

FEEBLE Here, sir.   145

SHALLOW What trade art thou, Feeble?

FEEBLE A woman's tailor, sir.

SHALLOW Shall I prick him, sir?

FALSTAFF You may, but if he had been a man's tailor he'd
ha' pricked you. (*To Feeble*) Wilt thou make as many   150
holes in an enemy's battle as thou hast done in a woman's petticoat?

FEEBLE I will do my good will, sir; you can have no more.

FALSTAFF Well said, good woman's tailor; well said, coura-
geous Feeble! Thou wilt be as valiant as the wrathful   155
dove or most magnanimous mouse. Prick the woman's
tailor. Well, Master Shallow; deep, Master Shallow.

FEEBLE I would Wart might have gone, sir.

FALSTAFF I would thou wert a man's tailor, that thou
mightst mend him and make him fit to go. I cannot put   160
him to a private soldier that is the leader of so many
thousands. Let that suffice, most forcible Feeble.

---

139 him] Q; him downe F   140 for his] F; for Q   144.1 *Enter Feeble*] OXFORD; *not in* QF
149–50 he'd ha'] Q (hee'd a); he would haue F

138 **ragged** (a) tattered; (b) 'full of rough
and sharp projections' (*OED a.*¹ 2), with
a pun on the plant-name 'ragwort'
(*Orchis mascula*), also known as 'priest's
pintle' (*OED n.*²), dialectal for 'penis'.
The plant was regarded as an aphrodisiac.

140–1 **his apparel . . . pins** his clothes are
precariously held together on his back
by pins (i.e. pegs) like a loose building.
The implication is that any further pricking will make the whole edifice collapse.

147–52 **woman's tailor . . . petticoat** Playing on the traditional association of 'tailor' with cowardice, effeminacy, and
sexual deviancy, which Jonson bril-

liantly exploits in the comically perverse
figure of Nick Stuffe (*The New Inn*), who
makes love to his wife dressed in the
clothes commissioned by rich ladies; but
'tailor' also signifies the male and female
organs, and this is played on in the
'man's tailor' doing the pricking.

150 **pricked** (a) clothed you (*OED, prick, v.*
20); (b) thrust you through (*OED v.* I)

151 **battle** army

156 **magnanimous** valiant

160 **fit to go** A bawdy double-entendre (i.e.
'able to copulate': see above, l. 112).

160–1 **put him to** enlist him as

162 **thousands** of lice, or warts. Wart is in-
fested with vermin.

FEEBLE It shall suffice, sir.

FALSTAFF I am bound to thee, reverend Feeble. Who is
next?   165

SHALLOW (*calls*) Peter Bullcalf o'th' Green!

FALSTAFF Yea, marry, let's see Bullcalf.
        [*Enter Bullcalf*]

BULLCALF Here, sir.

FALSTAFF Fore God, a likely fellow! Come, prick Bullcalf till
he roar again.   170

BULLCALF O Lord, good my lord captain—

FALSTAFF What, dost thou roar before thou art pricked?

BULLCALF O Lord, sir, I am a diseased man.

FALSTAFF What disease hast thou?

BULLCALF A whoreson cold, sir; a cough, sir, which I   175
caught with ringing in the King's affairs upon his coronation day, sir.

FALSTAFF Come, thou shalt go to the wars in a gown. We
will have away thy cold, and I will take such order that
thy friends shall ring for thee. Is here all?   180

SHALLOW Here is two more called than your number. You
must have but four here, sir, and so I pray you go in with
me to dinner.

FALSTAFF Come, I will go drink with you, but I cannot tarry
dinner. I am glad to see you, by my troth, Master Shal-   185
low.

163 sir] Q; *not in* F   165 next] Q; the next F   166 o'th'] Q; of the F   167 let's] Q; let us
F   167.1 *Enter Bullcalf*] OXFORD; *not in* QF   169 Fore God] Q; Trust me F   prick] Q; prick
me F   171 Lord] Q; *not in* F   172 thou art] Q; th'art F   173 Lord] Q; *not in* F   181 Here]
Q; There F   185 by my] Q; in good F

166 **Green** i.e. the village green

169–70 **Bullcalf . . . again** Cf. *1 Henry IV* 2.5.261–4, and proverbial 'To roar like a bull' (Dent B715).

176 **affairs** business

176–7 **coronation day** anniversary of the coronation

178 **gown** See 3.1.0.1, note on 'night-gown'.

181–2 **two . . . four** Shallow counts six, but only five have been seen so far. He may be

anxious to stop Falstaff from over-recruiting in his district. The point of Falstaff's shenanigans may be to increase his pickings from the supernumerary recruits buying their way out of service, as Mouldy and Bullcalf do. In the end he leaves with three (Wart, Shadow, and Feeble).

184 **tarry** stay for

SHALLOW O, Sir John, do you remember since we lay all
      night in the Windmill in Saint George's Field?

FALSTAFF No more of that, Master Shallow, no more of
      that.   190

SHALLOW Ha, 'twas a merry night! And is Jane Nightwork
      alive?

FALSTAFF She lives, Master Shallow.

SHALLOW She never could away with me.

FALSTAFF Never, never. She would always say she could   195
      not abide Master Shallow.

SHALLOW By the mass, I could anger her to th' heart. She
      was then a bona-roba. Doth she hold her own well?

FALSTAFF Old, old, Master Shallow.

SHALLOW Nay, she must be old; she cannot choose but be   200
      old; certain she's old; and had Robin Nightwork by old
      Nightwork before I came to Clement's Inn.

SILENCE That's fifty-five year ago.

SHALLOW Ha, cousin Silence, that thou hadst seen that that
      this knight and I have seen! Ha, Sir John, said I well?   205

FALSTAFF We have heard the chimes at midnight, Master
      Shallow.

SHALLOW That we have, that we have, that we have; in
      faith, Sir John, we have. Our watchword was 'Hem,
      boys!' Come, let's to dinner; come, let's to dinner.   210
      Jesus, the days that we have seen! Come, come.

                  Exeunt Shallow, Falstaff, and Silence

BULLCALF Good Master Corporate Bardolph, stand my
      friend, and here's four Harry ten shillings in French
      crowns for you. In very truth, sir, I had as lief be hanged,

189 Master] Q; good Master F   189–90 no...that] F; *not in* Q   191 'twas] Q; it was F
197 By the mass] Q; *not in* F   to th'] Q; to the F   203 year] Q; yeeres F   208 that we have;
in] Q; in F   209–10 Hem, boys!] Q (Hemboies), F (Hem-Boyes)   211 Jesus] Q; Oh F
211.1 *Exeunt...Silence*] CAPELL (*subs.*); *exeunt.* Q; *not in* F   213 here's] Q; heere is F
214 lief] Q (liue), F

188 **Windmill...Field** Probably refers to a
      brothel (rather than a tavern) in South-
      wark; see also Introduction, p. 38.
194 **away with** endure, get on with
203 **That's . . . ago** See Introduction, pp.
      43–4.
209–10 **watchword...boys** See 2.4.29.
212 **Corporate** A Quicklyism for 'corporal';
      see also l. 220.

212 **stand** act as (*OED v.* 15c)
213–14 **four Harry...crowns** The coins
      referred to are Tudor in origin, and by
      Shakespeare's time the ten-shilling piece
      had been devalued and was worth only
      five. Bullcalf is therefore offering twenty
      shillings (£1) compared to Mouldy's forty
      shillings (£2) which adds up to the £3 that Bar-
      dolph gives Falstaff at l. 235.

sir, as go. And yet for mine own part, sir, I do not care; 215
but rather because I am unwilling, and, for mine own
part, have a desire to stay with my friends; else, sir, I did
not care, for mine own part, so much.

BARDOLPH Go to, stand aside.

MOULDY And, good Master Corporal Captain, for my old 220
dame's sake stand my friend. She has nobody to do anything about her when I am gone, and she is old and
cannot help herself. You shall have forty, sir.

BARDOLPH Go to, stand aside.

FEEBLE By my troth, I care not. A man can die but once. We 225
owe God a death. I'll ne'er bear a base mind. An't be my
destiny, so; an't be not, so. No man's too good to serve's
prince. And let it go which way it will, he that dies this
year is quit for the next.

BARDOLPH Well said; thou'rt a good fellow. 230

FEEBLE Faith, I'll bear no base mind.

    Enter Falstaff, Shallow, and Silence

FALSTAFF Come, sir, which men shall I have?

SHALLOW Four of which you please.

BARDOLPH (*to Falstaff*) Sir, a word with you. I have three
pound to free Mouldy and Bullcalf. 235

FALSTAFF Go to, well.

SHALLOW Come, Sir John, which four will you have?

FALSTAFF Do you choose for me.

SHALLOW Marry, then: Mouldy, Bullcalf, Feeble, and Shadow. 240

FALSTAFF Mouldy and Bullcalf: for you, Mouldy, stay at

---

220 old] QC, F; *not in* Qa, Qb   221 has] Q; hath F   225 By my troth] Q; *not in* F   226 God] Q; *not in* F   I'll ne'er] Q; I will neuer F   An't] Q; if it F   227 an't] Q; if it F   man's] Q; man is F   serve's] Q; serue his F   230 thou'rt] Q; thou art F   231 Faith] Q; Nay F   I'll] Q; I will F   231.1 *Enter ... Silence*] Q (*Enter Falstaffe and the Iustices.*); *not in* F

220–3 **old dame's . . . herself** See above, note 109–11.

225–9 **A man ... for the next** Feeble turns out to be unexpectedly stoical and coura-geous, and quotes no fewer than three

proverbs in support of his stand. Both his sentences 'A man ... death' are pro-verbial (Dent M219 and G237), and so is 'He that dies ... next' (Dent D326).

229 **quit** free (*OED a.* 1b)

home till you are past service ; and for your part, Bullcalf,
grow till you come unto it. I will none of you.

               ⌈*Exeunt Bullcalf and Mouldy*⌉

SHALLOW Sir John, Sir John, do not yourself wrong. They
are your likeliest men, and I would have you served with   245
the best.

FALSTAFF Will you tell me, Master Shallow, how to choose
a man ? Care I for the limb, the thews, the stature, bulk,
and big assemblance of a man ? Give me the spirit, Master
Shallow. Here's Wart ; you see what a ragged appear-   250
ance it is ? A shall charge you, and discharge you, with
the motion of a pewterer's hammer, come off and on
swifter than he that gibbets on the brewer's bucket.
And this same half-faced fellow Shadow ; give me this
man. He presents no mark to the enemy ; the foeman   255
may with as great aim level at the edge of a penknife. And
for a retreat, how swiftly will this Feeble the woman's
tailor run off ! O, give me the spare men, and spare me the
great ones.—Put me a caliver into Wart's hand, Bardolph.   260

243.1 *Exeunt . . . Mouldy*] OXFORD; *not in* QF   250 Here's] Q; Where's F   251 A] Q; hee F

242 **service** (a) military; (b) domestic, either
for his wife (in which case there is a sexual quibble), or doing chores for his
mother

243 **come unto it** grow to manhood, by ceas-
ing to be a calf (and becoming a proper
bull and carrying out the duties of a bull):
see 'town-bull' above, 2.2.150.

248–9 **Care I . . . spirit** Falstaff may incidentally be parodying different contemporary manuals about recruiting (see
Humphreys, p. 108), but he is more likely
to be echoing 1 Samuel 16 : 7, when
David is chosen over his bigger brothers:
'But the Lord said vnto Samuel, Loke not
on his cou[n]tinance, nor on the height
of his stature, because I haue refused
him: for God seeth not as man seeth: for
man loketh on the outward appearance,
but the Lord beholdeth the heart.'

248 **thews** 'bodily proportions, lineaments,
or parts, as indicating physical strength'
(*OED, thew, sb.*[1] 3b)

249 **assemblance** appearance, show

251 **charge . . . discharge** load and fire

251–2 **with . . . hammer** i.e. in quick succession

252 **come . . . on** (probably) retreat and advance

253 **gibbets . . . bucket** The problem with
the phrase is that the glosses suggested
by *OED* for 'gibbet' ('To hang as on a
gibbet', *OED v.* 1. *intr.*) and 'bucket' ('a
beam or yoke on which anything may be
hung or carried', *sb.*[2]) point in the direction of readings which denote anything
but the speed which is the point of the
comparative here ('swifter than'). The
phrase seems rather to refer to the quick
act of counterbalancing the two buckets
carried on a beam on somebody's
shoulder when taking it from the vat to
the barrel (see Shaaber, p. 264).

254 **half-faced** i.e. pinched

256 **as great aim** as large a target
    level aim (*OED v.*[1] 7a)

259 **caliver** A light kind of musket; the light-
est portable firearm after the pistol.

BARDOLPH Hold, Wart. Traverse—thas, thas, thas!

FALSTAFF (*to Wart*) Come, manage me your caliver. So;
very well. Go to, very good, exceeding good. O, give me
always a little, lean, old, chopped, bald shot. Well said,
i'faith, Wart; th'art a good scab. Hold, there's a tester for   265
thee.

> [*He gives him a coin*]

SHALLOW He is not his craft's master; he doth not do it
right. I remember at Mile-End Green, when I lay at
Clement's Inn—I was then Sir Dagonet in Arthur's
show—there was a little quiver fellow, and a would   270
manage you his piece thus, and a would about and
about, and come you in and come you in. 'Ra-ta-ta!'
would a say; 'Bounce!' would a say; and away again
would a go, and again would a come. I shall ne'er see
such a fellow.   275

FALSTAFF These fellows will do well, Master Shallow. God
keep you, Master Silence; I will not use many words with
you. Fare you well, gentlemen both; I thank you. I must
a dozen mile tonight.—Bardolph, give the soldiers coats.

---

261 thas, thas, thas!] Q; thus, thus, thus F   265 i'faith] Q; *not in* F   th'art] Q; thou art
F   there's] Q; there is F   266.1 *He . . . coin*] This edition; *not in* QF   270–4 and a . . . a . . .
a . . . a . . . a . . . a come] Q; and hee . . . hee . . . hee . . . hee . . . hee . . . he come F   274 ne'er]
Q; neuer F   276 will] Q (wooll), F   276–7 God keep you] Q; Farewell F

---

261 **Traverse . . . thas** 'To go to and fro over
  or along; to cross and recross' (*OED*,
  traverse, *v.* 5), followed by (probably)
  the shouted commands of Bardolph in
  the role of drill-sergeant.

264 **chopped** dried up
  shot a musketeer; perhaps with a quibble
  on shot = 'a refuse animal left after the
  best of the flock or herd have been selected' (*OED sb.³*), even though the
  noun, unlike the verb, is not recorded
  with this meaning until much later
  (1796).

265 **scab** scoundrel, spoken here with mock
  affection, and punning on Wart's name
  tester sixpence

268 **Mile-End Green** An open field on the
  site of modern Stepney Green and formerly a favourite place of recreation for
  Londoners, as well as a drill ground for
  the London militias. It was here that Richard II met the men of Essex during the

Peasants' Revolt in 1381. By the time
Shakespeare wrote *2 Henry IV* the area
was already rapidly being encroached on
by a proliferation of new buildings.
  lay lodged

269–70 **Sir Dagonet . . . show** Sir Dagonet
  was King Arthur's fool in Malory's
  Morte Arthur; 'Arthur's show' was a popular display of archery on Mile-End Green
  by a society which took its name from
  Prince Arthur and the Knights of the
  Round Table.

270 **quiver** active, nimble

270–4 **a would manage . . . a come** After
  firing, the first line of Elizabethan mus-
  keteers rushed to the rear to reload, while
  the next line fired, thus ensuring a continuous wave of fire.

273 **'Bounce'** bang. The word may have
  come into fashion at about this time (see
  Davison, p. 238).

SHALLOW Sir John, the Lord bless you! God prosper your   280
  affairs! God send us peace! At your return, visit our
  house; let our old acquaintance be renewed. Peradven-
  ture I will with ye to the court.
FALSTAFF Fore God, would you would!
SHALLOW Go to, I have spoke at a word. God keep you!   285
FALSTAFF Fare you well, gentle gentlemen.

                              Exeunt Shallow and Silence
On, Bardolph, lead the men away.

                    Exeunt Bardolph, Feeble, Shadow, and Wart
As I return, I will fetch off these justices. I do see the
bottom of Justice Shallow. Lord, Lord, how subject we old
men are to this vice of lying! This same starved justice   290
hath done nothing but prate to me of the wildness of his
youth, and the feats he hath done about Turnbull Street;
and every third word a lie, duer paid to the hearer than
the Turk's tribute. I do remember him at Clement's Inn,
like a man made after supper of a cheese paring. When a   295
was naked, he was for all the world like a forked radish,
with a head fantastically carved upon it with a knife. A
was so forlorn that his dimensions, to any thick sight,

280 the Lord] Q; Heauen F   you! God] Q; you, and F   281 affairs! God] Q; Affaires, and
F   peace!] F (~.); ~∧ Q   At your] Q; As you F   our] Q; my F   283 ye] Q; you F   284 Fore
God, would] Q; I would F   you would!] Q; you would, Master *Shallow* F   285 God keep you]
Q; Fare you well F   286.1 *Exeunt . . . Silence*] OXFORD; *exit* Q; *Exit.* F *(after l. 285)*   287 On]
F; *Shal⟨low⟩*. On Q   287.1 *Exeunt . . . Wart*] CAPELL *(subs.)*; *not in* QF   289 Lord, Lord]
Q; *not in* F   295–6 a was] Q; hee was F   297 A] Q; Hee F

285 **I . . . word** I mean what I say
288 **fetch off** get the better of; con
289–90 **Lord . . . lying** Cf. *1 Henry IV*
   5.4.142–3 ('Lord, Lord, how this world
   is given to lying!').
292 **Turnbull Street** The most notorious
   haunt in London of thieves and prostitutes.
293–4 **duer . . . Turk's tribute** Shallow is
   more eager to tell his boastful story to
   those who listen than the Turk's subjects
   are to pay their tribute (which they do
   with the utmost alacrity for fear of savage
   reprisals on defaulting).

295–7 **like . . . knife** As a young man Shallow was so slight and insignificant that
   he had no more presence than an ab-
   stracted after-dinner carving of a
   human likeness from a rind of cheese;
   he had as little substance as a cartoon
   or a doodle. Falstaff develops this train
   of thought in the image of a split root
   ('forked') radish resembling the diminutive Shallow, whose very masculinity
   may be called in question by 'invincible'
   (see below, l. 299).
298 **forlorn** meagre (*OED a.* 5b)
   thick dull (*OED a.* 9a)

were invincible. A was the very genius of famine, yet
lecherous as a monkey, and the whores called him man-   300
drake. A came ever in the rearward of the fashion, and
sung those tunes to the overscutched housewives that he
heard the carmen whistle, and sware they were his
fancies or his good-nights. And now is this Vice's dagger
become a squire, and talks as familiarly of John o' Gaunt   305
as if he had been sworn brother to him, and I'll be sworn
a ne'er saw him but once in the Tilt-yard, and then he

299 invincible] QF; invisible ROWE   A] Q; Hee F   genius] QC, F; gemies Qa, Qb   299–
301 yet . . . mandrake] Q; *not in* F   301 A] Q; hee F   ever] F; ouer Q   301–4 and
sung . . . good-nights] Q; *not in* F   305 o' Gaunt] Q; of Gaunt F; *cf. similarly below at*
l. 309   307 a ne'er] Q; hee neuer F

299 **invincible** Both Q and F print 'invincible', but many editors prefer Rowe's
emendation 'invisible', which can be
supported by *OED*, *invincible, a.* 3: 'Cat-
achr[*esis*], or error for *invisible*'. But the
QF reading makes perfectly good sense,
and may be preferable to the blander
emendation. In the reading proposed by
QF we are meant to imagine a comic
cameo scene of short sight struggling in
vain to see anything of Shallow's crucial
(for a lecher) dimensions.
  genius archetype (*OED* 1e = 'embodied
type')
299–304 **yet . . . good-nights** These lines,
with the exception of perhaps the most
offensive of them all (*if* 'moral' censorship intervened; see 2.2.22–6 n.) are
missing from F. They may have been
removed at the insistence of the Master
of the Revels (Shaaber, p. 500) for reasons of propriety.
300–1 **mandrake** The root of the mandrake
was said by the Geneva Bible (Genesis 30:
14: marginal gloss) to have 'a certeine
likenes of ye figure of a man'. Its use here
may follow on from the anthropomor-
phic radish, but the mandrake was also
popularly supposed to be an aphrodisiac
(see also 1.2.14). Falstaff's point is that
Shallow was called the epitome of lust by
the whores.
301 **rearward of the fashion** As well as
meaning 'old-fashioned', there may be a
further dark dig here at Shallow's sexuality. Partridge notes 'perhaps he was
insatiable and monstrously perverted in
his sexual practices' (p. 173), presumably thinking of buggery; or, he muses

further, this may be an accusation of
'monosexuality' (but this would not
tally with Shallow's prurient obsession
with women).
302 **overscutched housewives** 'overscutched' may mean 'thoroughly
whipped', which is Doll's likely punishment as a whore at the end of the play.
But the more likely sense here is 'worn
out' by the job; 'housewives' = hussies,
i.e. prostitutes. The point Falstaff makes,
almost incidentally, is that Shallow has
frequented the cheapest and least desir-
able whores in town, a far cry from the
classy 'bona-roba' girls he brags about.
303–4 **carmen . . . good-nights** Carters were
famous for whistling tunes, and 'The
Carman's Whistle' was the name of a
popular Elizabethan bawdy song. The
point is that Shallow easily picked up
any old tune (preferably lascivious ones)
from the carters, and then passed them
off as his own fantasias ('fancies') and
serenades ('good-nights'); see also
Bartholomew Fair 1.4.70–81, where
Bartholmew Cokes is reported to pick up
'vile tunes' instantly from carmen, and
then sing them 'at supper, and in the
sermon-times!' (H & S vi. 29).
304 **Vice's dagger** In the Morality plays and
Tudor Interludes the Vice frantically
jumped about brandishing a thin 'dagger
of lath'. Falstaff is lampooning both Shallow's many sexual antics and his thin
appearance (*OED* *lath* stresses 'thin',
'narrow', and 'flat' in its definitions).
306 **sworn brother** bosom friend
307 **Tilt-yard** An area for tournaments near
Whitehall.

burst his head for crowding among the marshal's men. I
saw it, and told John o' Gaunt he beat his own name, for
you might have thrust him and all his apparel into an   310
eel-skin. The case of a treble hautboy was a mansion for
him, a court; and now has he land and beeves. Well, I'll
be acquainted with him if I return, and't shall go hard
but I'll make him a philosopher's two stones to me. If the
young dace be a bait for the old pike, I see no reason in   315
the law of nature but I may snap at him. Let time shape,
and there an end.   *Exit*

4.1   *Enter the Archbishop of York, Thomas Mowbray,*
        Lord Hastings, and ⌈Coleville,⌉ within the Forest of
        Gaultres

ARCHBISHOP OF YORK What is this forest called?
HASTINGS
    'Tis Gaultres Forest, an't shall please your grace.
ARCHBISHOP OF YORK
    Here stand, my lords, and send discoverers forth
    To know the numbers of our enemies.

---

310 thrust] Q; truss'd F   311 eel-skin] Qb, Qc, F; eele-shin Qa   312 has] Q; hath F   I'll]
Q; I will F   313 be] Qb, Qc, F; he Qa   and't shall] Q (and t'shal); and it shall F   314 I'll]
Q; I will F   316 him. Let] Qa, Qb, F; ~, till Qc   317 *Exit*] CAPELL; *Exeunt.* F; *not in* Q
    4.1.0.1–3 *Enter . . . Gaultres*] This edition; *Enter the Archbishop, Mowbray, Bardolfe,*
Hastings, within | the forrest of Gaultree. Q; *Enter the Arch-bishop, Mowbray, Hastings, | Westmer-*
land, Coleuile. F   2 Gaultres] Q (*Gaultree*)

309 **he . . . name** i.e. Shallow is thinner than
    is suggested by the word 'gaunt'
310–11 **thrust . . . eel-skin** Because of his
    extreme thinness: cf. *1 Henry IV*
    2.5.248, where Falstaff calls the arch-
    slim Hal 'eel-skin'. Oxford has 'elf-skin',
    but many modern editions follow Han-
    mer in writing 'eel-skin'.
311 **treble hautboy** The slenderest of the Eli-
    zabethan hautboys, the ancestor of the
    modern oboe.
312 **beeves** Archaic pl. of beef, now usually
    poetic for 'oxen, cattle'.
314 **a philosopher's two stones** The two
    stones would confer eternal youth and
    fabulous wealth respectively. It is the lat-
    ter presumably that Falstaff has in mind
    above all, and by the end of the play it has
    yielded him a not negligible £1,000.
314–16 **If . . . him** Cf. the proverb 'The great
    fish eat the small' (Dent F311).

315 **dace** a small fresh-water fish used as a
    bait
4.1.0.1–3 Q includes Lord Bardolph among
    the rebels, but according to Holinshed he
    has joined Northumberland in Scotland
    (Bullough, p. 274). F cuts Lord Bardolph
    (he is a mute character), but erroneously
    introduces Westmorland (he is again in-
    troduced at l. 24, but he cannot possibly
    appear in the rebels' camp) and Coleville,
    who is not needed until his encounter
    with Falstaff in 4.2. His place here can
    be justified on the basis of his being a
    'famous rebel' who is prominent enough
    to participate in councils of war (see also
    Textual Companion, p. 361).
2 **Gaultres** Pronounced 'Gaultree'. An an-
    cient royal forest to the north of York of
    nearly 100,000 acres.
3 **discoverers** scouts

HASTINGS

We have sent forth already.

ARCHBISHOP OF YORK   'Tis well done.   5

My friends and brethren in these great affairs,

I must acquaint you that I have received

New-dated letters from Northumberland,

Their cold intent, tenor, and substance, thus:

Here doth he wish his person, with such powers   10

As might hold sortance with his quality,

The which he could not levy; whereupon

He is retired to ripe his growing fortunes

To Scotland, and concludes in hearty prayers

That your attempts may overlive the hazard   15

And fearful meeting of their opposite.

MOWBRAY

Thus do the hopes we have in him touch ground,

And dash themselves to pieces.

    Enter a Messenger

HASTINGS   Now, what news?

MESSENGER

West of this forest, scarcely off a mile,

In goodly form comes on the enemy;   20

And, by the ground they hide, I judge their number

Upon or near the rate of thirty thousand.

MOWBRAY

The just proportion that we gave them out.

Let us sway on, and face them in the field.

    Enter the Earl of Westmorland

ARCHBISHOP OF YORK

What well-appointed leader fronts us here?   25

MOWBRAY

I think it is my lord of Westmorland.

12 could] QC, F; would Qa, Qb   18 *Enter a Messenger*] F; *Enter messenger* Q   24.1 *Enter . . . Westmorland*] F (*Enter Westmerland.*), Q (*after l. 25*)

8 **New-dated** of recent date
11 **hold sortance** accord
  quality rank
16 **opposite** adversary
17 **touch ground** i.e. crash, specifically referring to the bottom of the sea at the

point where the water becomes too shallow for a vessel to float (*OED, ground, sb.* 2b)
23 **just proportion** exact number
24 **sway on** move ahead (*OED, sway, v.* 4b *transf.*)

WESTMORLAND
        Health and fair greeting from our general,
        The Prince, Lord John and Duke of Lancaster.
ARCHBISHOP OF YORK
        Say on, my lord of Westmorland, in peace,
        What doth concern your coming?
WESTMORLAND   Then, my lord,   30
        Unto your grace do I in chief address
        The substance of my speech. If that rebellion
        Came like itself, in base and abject routs,
        Led on by bloody youth, guarded with rage,
        And countenanced by boys and beggary;   35
        I say, if damned commotion so appeared
        In his true native and most proper shape,
        You, reverend father, and these noble lords
        Had not been here to dress the ugly form
        Of base and bloody insurrection   40
        With your fair honours. You, Lord Archbishop,
        Whose see is by a civil peace maintained,
        Whose beard the silver hand of peace hath touched,
        Whose learning and good letters peace hath tutored,
        Whose white investments figure innocence,   45
        The dove and very blessèd spirit of peace,
        Wherefore do you so ill translate yourself
        Out of the speech of peace that bears such grace
        Into the harsh and boist'rous tongue of war,
        Turning your books to graves, your ink to blood,   50

30–1 Then ... | Unto ... address] F; Then ... vnto ... address Qc; Vnto ... address Qa, Qb
34 rage] QF; rags SINGER 1856 (*conj.* Walker)   36 appeared] POPE; appeare QF   45 figure]
Qc, F; figures Qa, Qb

32 **If that** if
33 **like itself** as it truly is
34 **guarded** Either 'protected' or 'trimmed'
    (*OED*, *guard*, *v.* 7).
    rage QF agree on 'rage', and although
    the conjectured emendation 'rags' has
    found favour with several editors, Q and
    F may have independent authority here,
    unless one assumes that the error oc-
    curred at source and that Shakespeare
    intended 'rags' but slipped and wrote
    'rage'. The image of rebellion protected
    by a personified figure of Rage could be

very effective (cf. a similar collocation to
'bloody youth' and 'rage' at 4.3.63,
where 'rage and hot blood' are Hal's
counsellors).

35 **by boys** by (none but) boys
45 **investments** clothes, i.e. robe
    figure symbolize
47 **translate** The Archbishop has translated
    one language (of peace) into another
    'tongue' (of war), and he has trans-
    formed himself from scholar to rebel sol-
    dier.

Your pens to lances, and your tongue divine
To a loud trumpet and a point of war?

ARCHBISHOP OF YORK

Wherefore do I this? So the question stands.
Briefly, to this end: we are all diseased,
And with our surfeiting and wanton hours   55
Have brought ourselves into a burning fever,
And we must bleed for it; of which disease
Our late King Richard, being infected, died.
But, my most noble lord of Westmorland,
I take not on me here as a physician,   60
Nor do I as an enemy to peace
Troop in the throngs of military men;
But rather show a while like fearful war
To diet rank minds sick of happiness,
And purge th'obstructions which begin to stop   65
Our very veins of life. Hear me more plainly.
I have in equal balance justly weighed
What wrongs our arms may do, what wrongs we suffer,
And find our griefs heavier than our offences.
We see which way the stream of time doth run,   70
And are enforced from our most quiet there
By the rough torrent of occasion;
And have the summary of all our griefs,
When time shall serve, to show in articles,

54 end:...diseased,] F; ~ʌ...~: Q   55–79 And...wrong] F; *not in* Q   71 there]
F; sphere HANMER; shore WILSON (*conj.* Vaughan); flow SISSON

52 **point of war** 'a short phrase sounded on
   an instrument as a signal' (*OED sb.*[1] A.
   9a)
55–79 **And ... wrong** Not in Q: see Introduction, pp. 85–7.
57 **bleed** Equivocal for (a) being bled (as a
   medical cure), and (b) shedding blood in
   battle. The entire passage (ll. 54–66) is
   predicated on an elaborate parallel between political insurrection and the
   cure of a sick body.
60 **take not on me** do not assume the part of
   (*OED, take, v.* 16a)
64 **rank** bloated
67 **justly** exactly
70 **which way ... run** The expression 'How
   runs the stream?' is proverbial (Dent
   S925); cf. also at *Twelfth Night* 4.1.59.

71 **And ... there** Probably meaning something like 'and our serenity ("most
   quiet") in the flow of time ("there" referring back to "stream of time") is brutally
   disturbed'. The Archbishop suggests that
   the rebels were peaceful members of the
   state until they were violently pushed
   ('enforced'; 'rough', l. 72). The image of
   still waters intersected by a torrent is here
   turned to their advantage by the rebels
   who cast themselves as the realm's
   physicians; as well they might since the
   legitimate king, Richard II, was overthrown by the incumbent. The river
   image is echoed in 'awe-full banks' at
   l. 174 below.
72 **occasion** events

Which long ere this we offered to the King,   75
And might by no suit gain our audience.
When we are wronged, and would unfold our griefs,
We are denied access unto his person
Even by those men that most have done us wrong.
The dangers of the days but newly gone,   80
Whose memory is written on the earth
With yet appearing blood, and the examples
Of every minute's instance, present now,
Hath put us in these ill-beseeming arms,
Not to break peace, or any branch of it,   85
But to establish here a peace indeed,
Concurring both in name and quality.

WESTMORLAND

Whenever yet was your appeal denied?
Wherein have you been gallèd by the King?
What peer hath been suborned to grate on you,   90
That you should seal this lawless bloody book
Of forged rebellion with a seal divine?

---

92 divine?] Qb, F; diuine, | And consecrate commotions bitter edge Qa

80–3 **The dangers . . . now** The Archbishop
is playing with time here, by suggesting
that the memory of the recent confrontation (Shrewsbury? the deposition of Richard II?) is inscribed in the earth in
future deaths ('yet appearing blood'),
and that it, along with countless instances of present injustices, has caused
the insurrection. The past, the present,
and the future, he argues, inspire the
rebellion.

84 **Hath** The use of the singular for the
plural was common in the speech of the
period.

90 **suborned** bribed
   grate on oppress, harass

92–4 In uncorrected Q two lines occur
which do not appear in F, the first one
after l. 92, and the second after l. 93.
They must have been marked for deletion
by Shakespeare before the prompt-book
was copied from the manuscript, and
certainly before the printing of Q three
years later. The copyist seems to have
been more careful than the compositor
(but see 'three words', below, 4.2.40),
and Simmes's proofreader spotted the

error. It is hard to see why the first one
was removed (it makes good sense), but
the second one is almost unintelligible as
it stands and suggests that at least one
other line (to which it either refers back
or which it anticipates) has also been
deleted. However, if the two lines were
erroneously removed instead of the adja-
cent ll. 99 and 100 (which start with the
same opening words 'And', 'To'—see
Introduction, p. 96), then the second
omitted line, 'To brother borne an hous-
hold cruelty,' would need to be interpreted without reference to a lost line. It
could perhaps be seen in apposition to
'commonwealth', i.e. 'commonwealth,
| To . . . cruelty', in which case a possible
paraphrase might be that the commonwealth, the mutually supportive social
fabric, has degenerated into a cruel domestic strife between brothers (i.e. civil
war rather than harmony), and it is this
situation which the Archbishop proposes
to redress. The phrase 'brother' may follow on from the Archbishop's use of
'brother general', a gesture of friendli-
ness in a realm now divided against itself.

ARCHBISHOP OF YORK

  My brother general, the commonwealth
  I make my quarrel in particular.

WESTMORLAND

  There is no need of any such redress,   95
  Or if there were, it not belongs to you.

MOWBRAY

  Why not to him in part, and to us all
  That feel the bruises of the days before,
  And suffer the condition of these times
  To lay a heavy and unequal hand   100
  Upon our honours?

WESTMORLAND   O my good Lord Mowbray,
  Construe the times to their necessities,
  And you shall say indeed it is the time,
  And not the King, that doth you injuries.
  Yet for your part, it not appears to me,   105
  Either from the King or in the present time,
  That you should have an inch of any ground
  To build a grief on. Were you not restored
  To all the Duke of Norfolk's signories,
  Your noble and right well-remembered father's?   110

MOWBRAY

  What thing in honour had my father lost
  That need to be revived and breathed in me?
  The King that loved him, as the state stood then,
  Was force perforce compelled to banish him;
  And then that Henry Bolingbroke and he,   115
  Being mounted and both rousèd in their seats,
  Their neighing coursers daring of the spur,

---

93 commonwealth] Qb, F; common wealth | To brother borne an houshold cruelty, Qa
101–37 O...King] F; *not in* Q   114 force] THEOBALD; forc'd F

100 **unequal** unjust
101–37 **Upon...King** Not in Q: see Introduction, pp. 85–7.
102 **Construe...necessities** interpret the present times in the light of inevitable circumstances
109 **signories** estates. Cf. *Richard II* 1.3; 4.1.77–80, and particularly l. 80, where Norfolk's 'lands and signories' are restored.

112 **breathed** exercised (*OED, breathed, ppl. a.* 1)
116 **rousèd** raised, lifted up (because of their heavy armours); also (probably) excited
117 **daring of the spur** i.e. very eager to change (and therefore challenging the prick of the spur)

Their armèd staves in charge, their beavers down,
Their eyes of fire sparkling through sights of steel,
And the loud trumpet blowing them together,   120
Then, then, when there was nothing could have stayed
My father from the breast of Bolingbroke—
O, when the King did throw his warder down,
His own life hung upon the staff he threw;
Then threw he down himself and all their lives   125
That by indictment and by dint of sword
Have since miscarried under Bolingbroke.

WESTMORLAND

You speak, Lord Mowbray, now you know not what.
The Earl of Hereford was reputed then
In England the most valiant gentleman.   130
Who knows on whom fortune would then have smiled?
But if your father had been victor there,
He ne'er had borne it out of Coventry;
For all the country in a general voice
Cried hate upon him, and all their prayers and love   135
Were set on Hereford, whom they doted on
And blessed and graced, indeed more than the King.
But this is mere digression from my purpose.
Here come I from our princely general
To know your griefs, to tell you from his grace   140
That he will give you audience; and wherein
It shall appear that your demands are just,
You shall enjoy them, everything set off
That might so much as think you enemies.

MOWBRAY

But he hath forced us to compel this offer,   145
And it proceeds from policy, not love.

WESTMORLAND

Mowbray, you overween to take it so.

---

137 indeed] THEOBALD (*conj.* Thirlby); and did F

---

118 **armèd . . . charge** lances ready for the charge
  beavers visors
119 **sights** visors (*OED, sight, sb.*[1] 13b *Obs.*)
123 **warder** mace or staff, held by the person who presides over a combat (cf. *Richard II*

1.3.118, which this particular *2 Henry IV* line paraphrases)
143 **set off** taken away, removed (*OED, set, v.*[1] 147a)

This offer comes from mercy, not from fear;
For lo, within a ken our army lies,
Upon mine honour, all too confident   150
To give admittance to a thought of fear.
Our battle is more full of names than yours,
Our men more perfect in the use of arms,
Our armour all as strong, our cause the best;
Then reason will our hearts should be as good.   155
Say you not then our offer is compelled.

MOWBRAY
Well, by my will we shall admit no parley.

WESTMORLAND
That argues but the shame of your offence.
A rotten case abides no handling.

HASTINGS
Hath the Prince John a full commission,   160
In very ample virtue of his father,
To hear and absolutely to determine
Of what conditions we shall stand upon?

WESTMORLAND
That is intended in the general's name.
I muse you make so slight a question.   165

ARCHBISHOP OF YORK
Then take, my lord of Westmorland, this schedule,
For this contains our general grievances.
Each several article herein redressed,
All members of our cause, both here and hence,
That are ensinewed to this action   170
Acquitted by a true substantial form
And present execution of our wills,
To us and our purposes confined

167–8 grievances.... redressed,] F (~:... ~,); ~,... ~. Q   173 our] Q; to our F   confined]
QF; confirm'd HANMER; consigned CAPELL

149 **ken** range of sight or vision (*OED sb.*¹ 2)
152 **battle** army (*OED sb.* 8a)
    names i.e. famous fighting men (*OED, name, sb.* 5a)
159 **A... handling** Proverbial: cf. 'It is a bad sack that will abide no clouting' (Dent S6).
161 **very... virtue** full authority
163 **stand** insist

164 **intended** signified (*OED, intend, v.* 20)
167 **general** common
170 **ensinewed** joined as by strong sinews
171–5 **Acquitted... peace** provided that all of us in this affair are granted a full pardon and immediate satisfaction for our demands, we will reconfine ourselves to our proper respectful bounds and work together in the cause of peace

We come within our awe-full banks again,
And knit our powers to the arm of peace.   175
WESTMORLAND (*taking the schedule*)
This will I show the general. Please you, lords,
In sight of both our battles we may meet,
And either end in peace—which God so frame—
Or to the place of diff'rence call the swords
Which must decide it.
ARCHBISHOP OF YORK   My lord, we will do so.   180

                                   Exit Westmorland

MOWBRAY
There is a thing within my bosom tells me
That no conditions of our peace can stand.
HASTINGS
Fear you not that. If we can make our peace
Upon such large terms and so absolute
As our conditions shall consist upon,   185
Our peace shall stand as firm as rocky mountains.
MOWBRAY
Yea, but our valuation shall be such
That every slight and false-derivèd cause,
Yea, every idle, nice, and wanton reason,
Shall to the King taste of this action ;   190
That were our royal faiths martyrs in love,
We shall be winnowed with so rough a wind
That even our corn shall seem as light as chaff,
And good from bad find no partition.
ARCHBISHOP OF YORK
No, no, my lord ; note this. The King is weary   195
Of dainty and such picking grievances,
For he hath found to end one doubt by death
Revives two greater in the heirs of life ;

---

174 awe-full] Q (awefull), F (awfull)   176 (*taking the schedule*)] OXFORD; *not in* QF
178 And] THEOBALD (*conj.* Thirlby); At QF   God] Q; Heauen F   180.1 *Exit Westmorland*] Q
(*after* 'decide it'); *not in* F   183 not‸ that.] F2 (~ ~,); ~, ~‸ Q, FI   187 Yea] Q; I F

---

174 **awe-full** respectful, reverential
179 **diff'rence** battle
185 **consist** insist
189 **nice** trivial
191 **were...love** even if our loyalty were

such that we died for love of the King
196 **picking** fastidious, i.e. trivial
197 **doubt** suspicion
198 **heirs of life** i.e. survivors

And therefore will he wipe his tables clean,
And keep no tell-tale to his memory   200
That may repeat and history his loss
To new remembrance; for full well he knows
He cannot so precisely weed this land
As his misdoubts present occasion.
His foes are so enrooted with his friends   205
That, plucking to unfix an enemy,
He doth unfasten so and shake a friend;
So that this land, like an offensive wife
That hath enraged him on to offer strokes,
As he is striking, holds his infant up,   210
And hangs resolved correction in the arm
That was upreared to execution.

HASTINGS
    Besides, the King hath wasted all his rods
    On late offenders, that he now doth lack
    The very instruments of chastisement;   215
    So that his power, like to a fangless lion,
    May offer, but not hold.

ARCHBISHOP OF YORK   'Tis very true;
    And therefore be assured, my good Lord Marshal,
    If we do now make our atonement well,
    Our peace will, like a broken limb united,   220
    Grow stronger for the breaking.

MOWBRAY   Be it so.

    Enter the Earl of Westmorland

    Here is returned my lord of Westmorland.

WESTMORLAND
    The Prince is here at hand. Pleaseth your lordship

221.1 *Enter ... Westmorland*] QF (*after l.* 222)

199 **tables** records
201 **history** record (*OED v.* 1 *trans.*)
203–4 **He ... occasion** i.e. he cannot root
    out every single cause of fear ('mis-
    doubts')
211 **hangs** suspends
213 **wasted** used up

217 **offer** threaten force
219 **atonement** reconciliation
220–1 **a broken ... breaking** Proverbial: cf.
    Dent B515.
223 **Pleaseth** if it please you (*OED, please,*
    v. 3)

To meet his grace just distance 'tween our armies.

MOWBRAY

Your grace of York, in God's name then set forward.   225

ARCHBISHOP OF YORK

Before, and greet his grace!—My lord, we come.
⌈*They march across the stage.*⌉
Enter Prince John ⌈*with several attendants*⌉

PRINCE JOHN

You are well encountered here, my cousin Mowbray;
Good day to you, gentle Lord Archbishop;
And so to you, Lord Hastings, and to all.
My lord of York, it better showed with you   230
When that your flock, assembled by the bell,
Encircled you to hear with reverence
Your exposition on the holy text,
Than now to see you here an iron man,
Cheering a rout of rebels with your drum,   235
Turning the word to sword, and life to death.
That man that sits within a monarch's heart
And ripens in the sunshine of his favour,
Would he abuse the countenance of the king,
Alack, what mischiefs might he set abroach   240
In shadow of such greatness! With you, Lord Bishop,
It is even so. Who hath not heard it spoken
How deep you were within the books of God,

---

225 God's] Q; heauen's F   set] Q; *not in* F   226.1–2 *They . . . attendants*] This edition; *Enter Prince Iohn and his armie.* Q (*after l.* 224); *Enter Prince Iohn.* F   234 Than] F (Then); That Q   man] F; man talking Q   243 God] Q; Heauen F

224 **just distance** halfway (cf. Holinshed: Bullough, p. 273)
226 **Before** lead on
226.1–2 *They . . . attendants* Neither Q nor F (which carefully marks its Act and Scene division) stipulates a break at this point. The action is properly continuous, and this edition follows QF here.
234 **iron** clad in armour
  man Q's 'man talking' may initially appear to recover one of Shakespeare's rejected first thoughts, before he substituted 'Cheering' in the line which follows; 'talking' would be intended to refer back to 'exposition' rather than forward to the 'rout of rebels'. But Q as well as F has 'Cheering', and one has to conclude either that Q failed to cancel 'talking', or that the copyist of the prompt-book deleted 'talking', because it produced hypermetricity. There is a third possibility, namely that 'talking' represents Shakespeare's *second* thoughts in his foul papers, after the prompt-book had been copied in the winter of 1596 and before the foul papers were printed in 1600.
236 **word to sword** Near homophones in the period: cf. *Merry Wives* 3.1.41: 'What, the sword and the Word?'
239 **countenance** favour, patronage
243 **deep . . . God** both deeply learned in Holy Scripture, and in God's grace

To us the speaker in his parliament,
To us th'imagined voice of God himself,   245
The very opener and intelligencer
Between the grace, the sanctities of heaven,
And our dull workings? O, who shall believe
But you misuse the reverence of your place,
Employ the countenance and grace of heav'n   250
As a false favourite doth his prince's name
In deeds dishonourable? You have ta'en up,
Under the counterfeited zeal of God,
The subjects of his substitute, my father,
And both against the peace of heaven and him   255
Have here upswarmèd them.
ARCHBISHOP OF YORK   Good my lord of Lancaster,
I am not here against your father's peace;
But, as I told my lord of Westmorland,
The time misordered doth, in common sense,
Crowd us and crush us to this monstrous form   260
To hold our safety up. I sent your grace
The parcels and particulars of our grief,
The which hath been with scorn shoved from the court,
Whereon this Hydra son of war is born;
Whose dangerous eyes may well be charmed asleep   265
With grant of our most just and right desires,
And true obedience, of this madness cured,
Stoop tamely to the foot of majesty.

245 th'imagined] ROWE 1714; th'imagine QF   God himself] Q; Heauen it selfe F   250 Employ] Q (*catchword and text*) (Imply), F   251-2 name_... dishonourable?] F (~,...~?); ~: ~_
Q   252 ta'en] Q; taken F   253 God] Q; Heauen F   254 his] Q; Heauens F

244 **speaker** The intermediary between the
    sovereign and members of parliament;
    here, the representative of the nation be-
    fore God.
246 **opener and intelligencer** exegete and
    informer (i.e. messenger)
247 **sanctities** holiness
248 **workings** endeavours
252 **ta'en up** levied
254 **substitute** deputy
256 **upswarmèd** raised in swarms
259 **misordered** confused
    in common sense plain for all to see
260 **monstrous** distorted, strange, unna-
    tural

262 **parcels** details (used here pleonastically
    with 'particulars')
263 **hath** On the singular/plural accord, see
    above, l. 84.
264 **Hydra** A many-headed snake whose
    heads multiplied more quickly than they
    could be cut off (Ovid, *Metamorphoses* 9.
    70-3). It was finally killed by Hercules.
265 **dangerous eyes** Another mythological
    monster, Argus, who was Juno's watch-
    man and had a hundred eyes and was
    watching over Io when he was charmed
    asleep by Mercury (Ovid, *Metamorphoses*
    1.622-721).

MOWBRAY

  If not, we ready are to try our fortunes
  To the last man.

HASTINGS   And though we here fall down,   270
  We have supplies to second our attempt.
  If they miscarry, theirs shall second them;
  And so success of mischief shall be born,
  And heir from heir shall hold his quarrel up
  Whiles England shall have generation.   275

PRINCE JOHN

  You are too shallow, Hastings, much too shallow,
  To sound the bottom of the after-times.

WESTMORLAND

  Pleaseth your grace to answer them directly
  How far forth you do like their articles.

PRINCE JOHN

  I like them all, and do allow them well,   280
  And swear here, by the honour of my blood,
  My father's purposes have been mistook,
  And some about him have too lavishly
  Wrested his meaning and authority.
  (*To the Archbishop*) My lord, these griefs shall be with
      speed redressed;   285
  Upon my soul they shall. If this may please you,
  Discharge your powers unto their several counties,
  As we will ours; and here between the armies
  Let's drink together friendly and embrace,
  That all their eyes may bear those tokens home   290
  Of our restorèd love and amity.

ARCHBISHOP OF YORK

  I take your princely word for these redresses.

⌈PRINCE JOHN⌉

  I give it you, and will maintain my word;

---

274 his] Q; this F   286 soul] Q; Life F   292–3 redresses. | ⌈PRINCE JOHN⌉ I] F; ~, | I Q

270–5 **And . . . generation** Continues the
    metaphor of multi-headed war launched
    by 'this Hydra son'.
277 **sound the bottom** measure the depth of
    (*OED, sound, v.*² 5)

278 **Pleaseth** if it please you
293–7 **PRINCE JOHN . . . captain** F must be
    right in attributing ll. 293–4 to Prince
    John, and ll. 295–7 to a member of the
    rebels' high command, since instructions

And thereupon I drink unto your grace.

⌈HASTINGS⌉ ⌈*to Coleville*⌉

  Go, captain, and deliver to the army   295

  This news of peace. Let them have pay, and part.

  I know it will well please them. Hie thee, captain.

                          Exit ⌈*Coleville*⌉

      ⌈*Drinks are poured*⌉

ARCHBISHOP OF YORK

  To you, my noble lord of Westmorland.

    He drinks

WESTMORLAND (*drinking*)

  I pledge your grace. And if you knew what pains

  I have bestowed to breed this present peace,   300

  You would drink freely ; but my love to ye

  Shall show itself more openly hereafter.

ARCHBISHOP OF YORK

  I do not doubt you.

WESTMORLAND   I am glad of it.

  (*Drinking*) Health to my lord and gentle cousin Mowbray.

MOWBRAY

  You wish me health in very happy season,   305

  For I am on the sudden something ill.

ARCHBISHOP OF YORK

  Against ill chances men are ever merry,

  But heaviness foreruns the good event.

WESTMORLAND

  Therefore be merry, coz, since sudden sorrow

  Serves to say thus : some good thing comes tomorrow.   310

ARCHBISHOP OF YORK

  Believe me, I am passing light in spirit.

294-5 grace. | ⌈HASTINGS⌉] F; ~. *Prince* Q   297.1 *Exit* ⌈*Coleville*⌉] OXFORD; *Exit.* F; *not in* Q
297.2 *Drinks are poured*] This edition; *not in* QF   298.1 *He drinks*] OXFORD; *not in* QF

to discharge the royal army in turn are issued by Prince John at l. 318.

305 **happy** fitting (*OED a.* 5b)
307-8 **Against . . . event** A quasi-proverbial sentiment (cf. 'A lightening before

death' (Dent L277) and 'When men are merriest death says "checkmate"' (Dent M599).

307 **Against** in the face of
311 **passing** extremely

MOWBRAY

So much the worse, if your own rule be true.

Shout within

PRINCE JOHN

The word of peace is rendered. Hark how they shout.

MOWBRAY

This had been cheerful after victory.

ARCHBISHOP OF YORK

A peace is of the nature of a conquest,   315

For then both parties nobly are subdued,

And neither party loser.

PRINCE JOHN (*to Westmorland*) Go, my lord,

And let our army be dischargèd too.

Exit Westmorland

(*To the Archbishop*) And, good my lord, so please you, let
   our trains

March by us, that we may peruse the men   320

We should have coped withal.

ARCHBISHOP OF YORK   Go, good Lord Hastings,

And ere they be dismissed, let them march by.

Exit Hastings

PRINCE JOHN

I trust, lords, we shall lie tonight together.

Enter the Earl of Westmorland ⌈with captains⌉

Now, cousin, wherefore stands our army still?

WESTMORLAND

The leaders, having charge from you to stand,   325

Will not go off until they hear you speak.

PRINCE JOHN

They know their duties.

Enter Hastings

HASTINGS ⌈*to Prince John*⌉

My lord, our army is dispersed already.

Like youthful steers unyoked they take their courses

312.1 *Shout within*] CAPELL; *shout.* Q; *not in* F   318.1 *Exit Westmorland*] F (*Exit., after l.*
320); *not in* Q   322.1 *Exit Hastings*] ROWE 1714; *Exit.* F; *not in* Q   323.1 *Enter ... captains*]
OXFORD; *enter Westmerland.* Q (*after l.* 322); *Enter Westmerland.* F   328 My lord] Q; *not in*
F   already] Q; *not in* F   329 take their courses] Q; *tooke their course* F

321 **coped withal** engaged, fought with
   (*OED, cope, v.² 2 Obs.*)

East, west, north, south; or, like a school broke up,   330
Each hurries toward his home and sporting place.

WESTMORLAND

Good tidings, my lord Hastings, for the which
I do arrest thee, traitor, of high treason;
And you, Lord Archbishop, and you, Lord Mowbray,
Of capital treason I attach you both.   335

> ⌈*The captains attach the Archbishop, Hastings, and
> Mowbray* ⌉

MOWBRAY

Is this proceeding just and honourable?

WESTMORLAND Is your assembly so?

ARCHBISHOP OF YORK Will you thus break your faith?

PRINCE JOHN I pawned thee none.

I promised you redress of these same grievances   340
Whereof you did complain; which, by mine honour,
I will perform with a most Christian care.
But for you rebels, look to taste the due
Meet for rebellion.
Most shallowly did you these arms commence,   345
Fondly brought here, and foolishly sent hence.
Strike up our drums, pursue the scattered stray.
God, and not we, hath safely fought today.
Some guard these traitors to the block of death,
Treason's true bed and yielder up of breath.   *Exeunt*   350

---

331 toward] Q; towards F   335.1–2 *The ... Mowbray*] This edition; *not in* QF   344 rebellion.] Q; Rebellion, and such Acts as yours. F   348 God] Q; Heauen F   hath] Q; haue F
349 these traitors] F; this traitour Q   350 *Exeunt*] F; *not in* Q

---

335 **attach** arrest

344 **Meet for rebellion** The F-only segment
  which follows is rather bland and looks
  suspiciously like a line-filler for Q's hemistich. By arresting the verse at that point,
  as if it were an emphatic caesura, the use
  of the hemistich confers considerable emphasis on the key phrase 'rebellion'. It is
  therefore (*pace* Humphreys, Davison, *et
  al.*) omitted in this edition.

346 **Fondly** foolishly (another pleonastic
  sentence)

347 **stray** stragglers

350 *Exeunt* F (but not Q) explicitly clears the

stage at this point, although neither Q
nor F starts a new scene for the entry of
Falstaff and Coleville. But whereas the
main battle may be over when the rebels'
leaders are tricked and taken prisoners,
skirmishes on the field continue. Thus
much is suggested by Prince John's command to 'pursue the scattered stray', and
his order to stop the chase with 'follow no
further now' (4.2.24). The battle scene is
probably conceived as one long scene,
and Falstaff and Coleville enter immediately after the '*Exeunt*' at l. 350.

4.2   *Alarum. Excursions. Enter Falstaff and Coleville*

FALSTAFF What's your name, sir? Of what condition are
      you, and of what place?

COLEVILLE I am a knight, sir, and my name is Coleville of
      the Dale.

FALSTAFF Well then, Coleville is your name, a knight is   5
      your degree, and your place the Dale. Coleville shall be
      still your name, a traitor your degree, and the dungeon
      your place—a place deep enough, so shall you be still
      Coleville of the Dale.

COLEVILLE Are not you Sir John Falstaff?   10

FALSTAFF As good a man as he, sir, whoe'er I am. Do ye
      yield, sir, or shall I sweat for you? If I do sweat, they are
      the drops of thy lovers, and they weep for thy death;
      therefore rouse up fear and trembling, and do obser-
      vance to my mercy.   15

COLEVILLE I think you are Sir John Falstaff, and in that
      thought yield me.

FALSTAFF I have a whole school of tongues in this belly of
      mine, and not a tongue of them all speaks any other
      word but my name. An I had but a belly of any indiffer-   20
      ency, I were simply the most active fellow in Europe. My
      womb, my womb, my womb undoes me. Here comes our
      general.

4.2.0.1 *Alarum . . . Coleville*] OXFORD (*subs.*); *Alarum Enter Falstaffe excursions* Q; *Enter Falstaffe
and Colleuile*. F   2 place] Q; place, I pray F   6–7 be still] Q; still be F

4.2.0.1 *Alarum. Excursions* 'Alarum' is a
      call to arms (*OED*, *alarm*, *sb*. 4a), usually,
      as here, in conjunction with 'excursion'
      (an issuing forth against an enemy; a
      sally, *OED sb*. 3).

1 **condition** rank

3–4 **Coleville of the Dale** Holinshed (Bul-
      lough, p. 274) mentions a 'sir John Col-
      levill of the Dale' among those who were
      beheaded at Durham, after the King
      moved there from York whose citizens
      he had punished 'by greevous fines'.

7 **dungeon** because both dungeons and
      dales are deep places

13 **drops . . . lovers** Falstaff's sweat-drops
      will be the tears of Coleville's friends.

18–19 **I . . . mine** Falstaff's vast girth speaks
      his name in all languages, i.e. the whole
      world knows him by his unique appear-
      ance. Like Rumour, which is painted 'full
      of tongues', so Falstaff is full of deceit, and
      here in particular he trades on the false
      reputation of killing Hotspur at Shrews-
      bury.

20–1 **indifferency** moderate size

22 **womb** belly (*OED* 1a)

Enter Prince John, the Earl of Westmorland, Sir John
Blunt, and other lords and soldiers

PRINCE JOHN

The heat is past; follow no further now.

Call in the powers, good cousin Westmorland. 25

Exit Westmorland

Now, Falstaff, where have you been all this while?

When everything is ended, then you come.

These tardy tricks of yours will, on my life,

One time or other break some gallows' back.

FALSTAFF I would be sorry, my lord, but it should be thus. I 30
never knew yet but rebuke and check was the reward of
valour. Do you think me a swallow, an arrow, or a
bullet? Have I in my poor and old motion the expedition
of thought? I have speeded hither with the very extrem-
est inch of possibility; I have foundered nine-score and 35
odd posts; and here, travel-tainted as I am, have in my
pure and immaculate valour taken Sir John Coleville of
the Dale, a most furious knight and valorous enemy. But
what of that? He saw me, and yielded, that I may justly
say, with the hook-nosed fellow of Rome, three words, 'I 40
came, saw, and overcame.'

23.1–2 *Enter . . . soldiers*] OXFORD; *Enter Iohn Westmerland, and the rest. Retraite* Q; *Enter Prince Iohn, and Westmerland.* F 24 further] Q, F (*farther*) 25.1 *Exit Westmorland*] ROWE; *not in* QF 40 three words] HUMPHREYS; there cosin (*c.w.* their) Q; *not in* F; Rome there, *Caesar* THEOBALD; Rome, their Caesar SISSON

28 **tardy tricks** delaying ploys
30 **but . . . be** if it were not
33 **expedition** speed
35 **foundered** lamed
35–6 **nine-score and odd posts** more than 180 post-horses
40 **hook-nosed . . . Rome** i.e. Julius Caesar **three words** Q has 'there cosin' on G4^v and the catchword 'their' on G4^r, while F omits the two words altogether. Shakespeare's manuscript must have been hard to read here, and the copyist of the prompt-book clearly failed to make sense of it. Q's compositor's guess cannot quite decide between 'their' and 'there', and its overall reading invites forced interpretations. Even if appeal is made to Falstaff's

irreverence and his relish for effrontery, which alone could justify a form of address like 'There, cousin' to Prince John, 'three words' (Humphreys, p. 134) not only makes good sense, but is strongly supported by one of Shakespeare's favourite and most closely followed sources, Plutarch's 'Life of Julius Caesar'. According to a marginal note in North's translation 'Caesar wryteth three wordes to certifie his victory [over King Pharnaces]' and, in the text, Caesar 'bicause he would aduertise one of his frendes of the sodainness of this victorie, he onely wrote three words . . . *Veni, vidi, vici*: to wit, I came, I saw, I ouercame' (Plutarch, *Lives*, 1579, p. 787).

PRINCE JOHN It was more of his courtesy than your deserving.

FALSTAFF I know not. Here he is, and here I yield him ; and I beseech your grace, let it be booked with the rest of this 45 day's deeds ; or, by the Lord, I will have it in a particular ballad else, with mine own picture on the top on't, Coleville kissing my foot ; to the which course if I be enforced, if you do not all show like gilt twopences to me, and I in the clear sky of fame o'ershine you as much as the full 50 moon doth the cinders of the element, which show like pins' heads to her, believe not the word of the noble. Therefore let me have right, and let desert mount.

PRINCE JOHN Thine's too heavy to mount.

FALSTAFF Let it shine then. 55

PRINCE JOHN Thine's too thick to shine.

FALSTAFF Let it do something, my good lord, that may do me good, and call it what you will.

PRINCE JOHN

Is thy name Coleville ?

COLEVILLE   It is, my lord.

PRINCE JOHN

A famous rebel art thou, Coleville. 60

FALSTAFF And a famous true subject took him.

COLEVILLE

I am, my lord, but as my betters are

That led me hither. Had they been ruled by me,

You should have won them dearer than you have.

---

46 by the Lord] Q; I sweare F   47 else] Q; *not in* F   on't] Q; of it F   59 Is . . . lord] STEEVENS; *as prose* QF

46–7 **a particular ballad** a ballad all about me (cf. *1 Henry IV* 2.2.44–6)

47–8 **with . . . foot** Ballads were illustrated with wood-cuts.

49 **like gilt . . . to me** like counterfeits compared to me. The smaller pieces of silver coins were sometimes gilded to pass them off for coins of higher value, e.g. the twopence piece for the half-crown.

51 **the cinders . . . element** the stars of heaven; cf. the similarly odd and paradoxical comparison of Antony's faults to 'the spots of heaven' (*Antony* 1.4.12)

54 **Thine . . . mount** Probably a hemistich (see rebellion, 4.1.344), like 'Thine . . .

shine', and his other six part-lines in the play which include the very last words before the Epilogue, 'Come, will you hence?' He resolutely refuses to speak prose, even when dealing with Falstaff.

heavy Either (a) spoken ironically: Falstaff's 'desert' is so vast (and he is very fat) that it cannot rise; or (b) 'heavy' here means heinous: cf. 'O heavy deed!' (*Hamlet* 4.1.11).

56 **thick** i.e. in both bulk and opacity

59 **Coleville** The name is trisyllabic (cf. Davison, p. 254).

FALSTAFF I know not how they sold themselves, but thou   65
   like a kind fellow gavest thyself away gratis, and I thank
   thee for thee.

    Enter the Earl of Westmorland

PRINCE JOHN Now, have you left pursuit?

WESTMORLAND
   Retreat is made, and execution stayed.

PRINCE JOHN
   Send Coleville with his confederates   70
   To York, to present execution.
   Blunt, lead him hence, and see you guard him sure.

                Exit Blunt, with Coleville ⌈guarded⌉

   And now dispatch we toward the court, my lords.
   I hear the King my father is sore sick.
   Our news shall go before us to his majesty,   75
   (*To Westmorland*) Which, cousin, you shall bear to
      comfort him;
   And we with sober speed will follow you.

FALSTAFF
   My lord, I beseech you give me leave to go
   Through Gloucestershire, and when you come to court
   Stand my good lord, pray, in your good report.   80

PRINCE JOHN
   Fare you well, Falstaff. I in my condition
   Shall better speak of you than you deserve.

                   Exeunt all but Falstaff

FALSTAFF I would you had but the wit; 'twere better than
   your dukedom. Good faith, this same young sober-
   blooded boy doth not love me, nor a man cannot make   85

---

66 gratis] Q; *not in* F   68 Now] Q; *not in* F   72.1 *Exit … guarded*] F (*Exit with Colleuile.*); *not in* Q   78–80 My … report] *as verse* DYCE; *as prose* QF   80 pray] F; *not in* Q   81–2 Fare … deserve] F; *as prose* Q   82.1 *Exeunt … Falstaff*] CAPELL (*subs.*); *Exit.* F; *not in* Q   83 but] F; *not in* Q

72.1 *Exit Blunt* His only active share in the play, in which he does not speak at all (cf. 3.1.31.1 where QB provides him with an entry but no lines).

80 **Stand** act as
81 **in my condition** i.e. as commander-in-chief

him laugh. But that's no marvel; he drinks no wine.
There's never none of these demure boys come to any
proof; for thin drink doth so overcool their blood, and
making many fish meals, that they fall into a kind of male
green-sickness; and then when they marry they get   90
wenches. They are generally fools and cowards—
which some of us should be too, but for inflammation.
A good sherry-sack hath a twofold operation in it. It
ascends me into the brain, dries me there all the foolish
and dull and crudy vapours which environ it, makes it   95
apprehensive, quick, forgetive, full of nimble, fiery, and
delectable shapes, which, delivered o'er to the voice, the
tongue, which is the birth, becomes excellent wit. The
second property of your excellent sherry is the warming
of the blood, which before, cold and settled, left the liver   100
white and pale, which is the badge of pusillanimity and
cowardice. But the sherry warms it, and makes it course
from the inwards to the parts' extremes. It illumineth the
face, which, as a beacon, gives warning to all the rest of
this little kingdom, man, to arm; and then the vital   105
commoners and inland petty spirits muster me all to
their captain, the heart; who, great and puffed up with
this retinue, doth any deed of courage; and this valour
comes of sherry. So that skill in the weapon is nothing

87 none] Q; any F   103 illumineth] Q; illuminateth F   107-8 with this] Q; with his F

86-8 **wine ... proof** Cf. the proverbial expression that 'Good wine (drink) makes good blood' (Dent W461).

87-8 **come ... proof** turn out well; 'proof' = fulfilment (*OED sb.* 7), but 'proof' may also refer to drink (cf. 2.4.115), although the first recorded usage in *OED* dates from 1705.

90 **green-sickness** A form of anaemia called chlorosis, which affects young women.

90-1 **get wenches** Falstaff suggests that an abstemious diet of 'thin drink' and 'fish meals' diminishes virility, and results in daughters rather than sons. The Porter in *Macbeth* 2.3.29 instead believes that drink induces impotence. The proverb 'Who goes drunk to bed begets but a girl' (Dent B195) flatly contradicts Falstaff.

92 **inflammation** excitement through drink

93 **sherry-sack** sweet white wine from Xeres in Spain

95 **crudy** curdy, thick

96 **apprehensive** quick to perceive; alert **forgetive** inventive (cf. 'forge')

100 **liver** the seat of passion: cf. 1.2.170

103-7 **the face ... heart** The analogy of the human body with the body politic and its organization was common in the period (cf. *Coriolanus* 1.1.94-153, Menenius' fable of the belly). Falstaff's 'vital commoners' are the 'natural', 'animal', and 'vital' spirits which were thought to 'permeate the blood and chief organs of the body' (*OED, spirit, sb.* 16a).

without sack, for that sets it a-work ; and learning a mere   110
hoard of gold kept by a devil, till sack commences it and
sets it in act and use. Hereof comes it that Prince Harry is
valiant ; for the cold blood he did naturally inherit of his
father he hath, like lean, sterile, and bare land, manured,
husbanded, and tilled, with excellent endeavour of   115
drinking good and good store of fertile sherry, that he is
become very hot and valiant. If I had a thousand sons,
the first human principle I would teach them should be to
forswear thin potations, and to addict themselves to
sack.   120

    Enter Bardolph

How now, Bardolph ?

BARDOLPH

   The army is dischargèd all and gone.

FALSTAFF Let them go. I'll through Gloucestershire, and
   there will I visit Master Robert Shallow, Esquire. I have
   him already tempering between my finger and my   125
   thumb, and shortly will I seal with him. Come away.

                                Exeunt

4.3   *Enter King Henry ⌐in a bed⌐, the Earl of Warwick,*
       Thomas Duke of Clarence, Humphrey Duke of
       Gloucester, ⌐and others⌐

KING HENRY

   Now, lords, if God doth give successful end
   To this debate that bleedeth at our doors,

118 human] Q (humane); *not in* F   120.1 *Enter Bardolph*] Q (*after l.* 122), F   126.1 *Exeunt*]
F; *not in* Q

4.3.0.1–3 *Enter . . . others*] F (*Enter King, Warwicke, Clarence, Gloucester.*); *Enter the King,*
Warwike, Kent, Thomas duke of Clarence, Humphrey of Gloucester. Q   0.1 *in a bed*] OXFORD
(*subs.*); *carried in a chair* SISSON; *not in* QF   1 God] Q; Heauen F

111 **hoard . . . devil** Treasures were supersti-
   tiously thought to be guarded by evil
   spirits.
111–12 **commences . . . act** Puns on the
   conferring of degrees at Cambridge
   ('Commencement') and Oxford ('Act'),
   which allowed the scholars to exploit
   their learning at last. According to Falstaff, sack is the great university of life.
115 **husbanded** cultivated
118 **human** secular

125 **tempering** softening, melting (like wax)
126 **seal with him** come to an agreement
   with him; but also 'use him as my seal
   to my purpose', after warming him like
   wax
4.3 The setting is the Jerusalem Chamber in
   Westminster Abbey (not, as Shakespeare
   implies, in the royal palace: see Lee ii.
   163).
2 **debate** struggle

We will our youth lead on to higher fields,
And draw no swords but what are sanctified.
Our navy is addressed, our power collected,   5
Our substitutes in absence well invested,
And everything lies level to our wish;
Only we want a little personal strength,
And pause us till these rebels now afoot
Come underneath the yoke of government.   10
WARWICK
Both which we doubt not but your majesty
Shall soon enjoy.
KING HENRY   Humphrey, my son of Gloucester,
Where is the Prince your brother?
GLOUCESTER
I think he's gone to hunt, my lord, at Windsor.
KING HENRY
And how accompanied?
GLOUCESTER   I do not know, my lord.   15
KING HENRY
Is not his brother Thomas of Clarence with him?
GLOUCESTER
No, my good lord, he is in presence here.
CLARENCE What would my lord and father?
KING HENRY
Nothing but well to thee, Thomas of Clarence.
How chance thou art not with the Prince thy brother?   20
He loves thee, and thou dost neglect him, Thomas.
Thou hast a better place in his affection
Than all thy brothers. Cherish it, my boy,
And noble offices thou mayst effect
Of mediation, after I am dead,   25
Between his greatness and thy other brethren.
Therefore omit him not, blunt not his love,

12–13 Humphrey ... brother?] *as verse* POPE; *as prose* QF

3 **higher fields** i.e. a crusade
5 **addressed** ready
6 **substitutes in absence** deputies
invested empowered
7 **level** readily accessible (*OED a.* 3a)

17 **in presence** present
19–50 **Nothing ... Thomas** See Introduction, p. 21.
27 **omit** neglect

Nor lose the good advantage of his grace
By seeming cold or careless of his will;
For he is gracious, if he be observed,   30
He hath a tear for pity, and a hand
Open as day for meting charity.
Yet notwithstanding, being incensed, he is flint,
As humorous as winter, and as sudden
As flaws congealèd in the spring of day.   35
His temper therefore must be well observed.
Chide him for faults, and do it reverently,
When you perceive his blood inclined to mirth;
But being moody, give him time and scope
Till that his passions, like a whale on ground,   40
Confound themselves with working. Learn this, Thomas,
And thou shalt prove a shelter to thy friends,
A hoop of gold to bind thy brothers in,
That the united vessel of their blood,
Mingled with venom of suggestion—   45
As force perforce the age will pour it in—
Shall never leak, though it do work as strong
As aconitum or rash gunpowder.

CLARENCE

I shall observe him with all care and love.

KING HENRY

Why art thou not at Windsor with him, Thomas?   50

CLARENCE

He is not there today; he dines in London.

KING HENRY

And how accompanied? Canst thou tell that?

CLARENCE

With Poins and other his continual followers.

---

32 meting] Q; melting F   33 he is] Q; hee's F   39 time] Q; Line F   52 Canst...that] F; *not in* Q

30 **observed** paid proper respect
32 **meting** dealing out (*OED*, *mete*, *v.*¹ 6)
34 **humorous** capricious
35 **flaws congealèd** icy squalls (but *OED*, *flaw*, *sb.*¹ 1 glosses 'a flake (of snow)')
    spring of day daybreak
41 **working** exertion

45 **suggestion** (four syllables) promptings to evil
48 **aconitum** Aconite or wolf's-bane, a highly toxic plant and fabled to have been invented by Hecate.
    rash instant, 'operating quickly and strongly' (*OED a.* 2b)

KING HENRY

Most subject is the fattest soil to weeds,
And he, the noble image of my youth,   55
Is overspread with them; therefore my grief
Stretches itself beyond the hour of death.
The blood weeps from my heart when I do shape
In forms imaginary th'unguided days
And rotten times that you shall look upon   60
When I am sleeping with my ancestors;
For when his headstrong riot hath no curb,
When rage and hot blood are his counsellors,
When means and lavish manners meet together,
O, with what wings shall his affections fly   65
Towards fronting peril and opposed decay?

WARWICK

My gracious lord, you look beyond him quite.
The Prince but studies his companions
Like a strange tongue, wherein, to gain the language,
'Tis needful that the most immodest word   70
Be looked upon and learnt, which once attained,
Your highness knows, comes to no further use
But to be known and hated; so, like gross terms,
The Prince will in the perfectness of time
Cast off his followers, and their memory   75
Shall as a pattern or a measure live
By which his grace must mete the lives of other,
Turning past evils to advantages.

---

72 further] Q, F (farther)   77 other] Q; others F

---

54 **the fattest ... weeds** Proverbial: cf.
'Weeds come forth on the fattest soil if it
is untilled' (Dent W241).
58 **The blood ... heart** To weep here means
'To issue in drops; to trickle or fall as
tears' (*OED v.* 4b); the line alludes to the
common belief that every sigh draws a
drop of blood from the heart.

64 **lavish** unrestrained, mild
65 **affections** inclination
66 **fronting** confronting
opposed hostile
67 **look beyond** misconstrue (*OED, beyond,
prep.* 3)
77 **mete** measure, estimate
other others

KING HENRY

'Tis seldom when the bee doth leave her comb

In the dead carrion. Who's here? Westmorland?   80

   Enter the Earl of Westmorland

WESTMORLAND

Health to my sovereign, and new happiness

Added to that that I am to deliver!

Prince John your son doth kiss your grace's hand.

Mowbray, the Bishop Scrope, Hastings and all

Are brought to the correction of your law.   85

There is not now a rebel's sword unsheathed,

But peace puts forth her olive everywhere.

The manner how this action hath been borne

Here at more leisure may your highness read,

With every course in his particular.   90

KING HENRY

O Westmorland, thou art a summer bird

Which ever in the haunch of winter sings

The lifting up of day.

   Enter Harcourt

               Look, here's more news.

HARCOURT

From enemies heaven keep your majesty;

And when they stand against you, may they fall   95

As those that I am come to tell you of!

The Earl Northumberland and the Lord Bardolph,

With a great power of English and of Scots,

Are by the Sheriff of Yorkshire overthrown.

80.1 *Enter . . . Westmorland*] Q (*Enter Westmerland*), F (*after* 'carrion')   93 *Enter Harcourt*] QF (*after l.* 93 *in* Q)   94 heaven] F; heauens Q

79–80 **'Tis . . . carrion** He is not likely ('seldom when' = seldom that) to renounce his pleasures, however corrupt they may be. The image of the honeycomb and dead carrion probably recalls Judges 14: 8, when Samson 'went aside to se the carkeis of the lyon: and beholde, there was a swarme of bees, and hony in the body of the lyon'.

90 **course** line of (personal) action (*OED sb.* 22a)

91 **summer bird** Possibly the lark which starts singing in February (according to Stanley Wells): cf. 'rising of the lark to the lodging of the lamb' (*Henry V* 3.7.31–2); other birds have been suggested, notably the blackbird, the thrush, and the cuckoo (Shaaber, p. 350).

92 **haunch of winter** latter end of winter; cf. 'the posteriors of this day' (*LLL* 5.1.84) and 'the buttock of the night' (*Coriolanus* 2.1.51)

97–9 **The Earl . . . overthrown** At the Battle of Bramham Moor in 1408.

The manner and true order of the fight   100
This packet, please it you, contains at large.

KING HENRY

And wherefore should these good news make me sick?
Will fortune never come with both hands full,
But set her fair words still in foulest terms?
She either gives a stomach and no food—   105
Such are the poor in health—or else a feast,
And takes away the stomach—such are the rich
That have abundance and enjoy it not.
I should rejoice now at this happy news,
And now my sight fails, and my brain is giddy.   110
O me! Come near me now; I am much ill.

He swoons

GLOUCESTER

Comfort, your majesty!

CLARENCE   O my royal father!

WESTMORLAND

My sovereign lord, cheer up yourself, look up.

---

103 full,] F; ~. Q   104 set...terms] This edition; wet...termes Q; write...Letters F
111.1 *He swoons*] OXFORD; *not in* QF

---

101 **at large** in full
102 **these** The use of the plural here was
possible at the time (see 1.1.27).
104 **set...terms** F's 'write' for 'wet' and
'Letters' for 'termes' yield a more
straightforward meaning, and one consonant with the general idea here of Fortune offering her goods contrarily. But
while 'wet' and 'write' could conceivably
be confused when copying or setting
from a manuscript, it is hard to see how
'terms' and 'Letters' could be produced
by the same original. It may be that the
prompt-book copyist read 'write', but
then could not make sense of the line
'write her fair words still in foulest
terms', because 'words' means 'terms'
(according to *OED, term, sb.* 13b, is 'an
expression', 'Any word or group of words
expressing a notion or conception, or denoting an object of thought'). He therefore may consciously have substituted
'letters' for 'terms'. If 'terms' is indeed

what stood in the manuscript, as seems
likely, then the problem lies with 'wet'.
The copyist did not (in this scenario) read
'terms' in the legal sense suggested by
Hilda Hulme's ingenious reading of
the line (*Explorations in Shakespeare's
Language* (1962), p. 295) so that her
reading of 'wet' = wit (in the sense of
'bequeath') also becomes doubtful. A
monosyllable is required, and 'set'
(*OED, set, Comb.* 2, 'set out' g = 'to put
down on paper in express or detailed
form') is a reading which recognizes
that the problem lies above all with
'wet'/'write' rather than 'termes'/'Letters', and accords well with the use of
'words' here meaning promises (*OED,
word, sb.* 8).
105–8 **She...not** Cf. the proverbial expression 'The rich man walks to get a
stomach to his meat, the poor man to
get meat for his stomach' (Dent M366).
107 **stomach** appetite

WARWICK

  Be patient, princes; you do know these fits

  Are with his highness very ordinary. 115

  Stand from him, give him air; he'll straight be well.

CLARENCE

  No, no, he cannot long hold out these pangs.

  Th'incessant care and labour of his mind

  Hath wrought the mure that should confine it in

  So thin that life looks through and will break out. 120

GLOUCESTER

  The people fear me, for they do observe

  Unfathered heirs and loathly births of nature.

  The seasons change their manners, as the year

  Had found some months asleep and leaped them over.

CLARENCE

  The river hath thrice flowed, no ebb between, 125

  And the old folk, times' doting chronicles,

  Say it did so a little time before

  That our great-grandsire Edward sicked and died.

WARWICK

  Speak lower, princes, for the King recovers.

GLOUCESTER

  This apoplexy will certain be his end. 130

KING HENRY

  I pray you take me up, and bear me hence

---

117 out_∧... pangs.] Q; out:... pangs, F   120 and...out] F; *not in* Q

118–20 **Th'incessant . . . out** See Introduction, pp. 22–3. Shakespeare clearly recalls Daniel here, and the F-only line 'and...out' would appear to correspond to Daniel's puzzling 'and his frailty find'. Shakespeare's meaning is clear: the King's pains have made the wall ('mure') of his spirit (i.e. his body) so thin and fragile (i.e. transparent) that life can see through it and will escape from it.

121 **fear** alarm

122 **Unfathered heirs** offspring who are not naturally begotten, i.e. children resulting through a freak virgin birth, or born as the result of sex between a witch and an evil spirit; or it may mean deformed children as in 'loathly births' (l. 122).

123 **as** as if

125–8 **The river . . . died** According to Holinshed (Bullough, p. 276), on 12 October 1412 there 'were three flouds in the Thames, the one following upon the other, and no ebbing betweene'. Shakespeare's connection of this to the death of Edward III does not derive from any of his major sources.

131–370 **I pray . . . die** On Shakespeare's use here of *Famous Victories*, see Introduction, pp. 25–6.

Into some other chamber; softly, pray.

⌈*The King's bed is taken up*⌉

Let there be no noise made, my gentle friends,

Unless some dull and favourable hand

Will whisper music to my weary spirit.   135

WARWICK

Call for the music in the other room.

⌈*Exit one. Music within*⌉

⌈*The King's bed is moved and put down*⌉

KING HENRY (*removing the crown*)

Set me the crown upon my pillow here.

⌈*Clarence*⌉ *sets the crown on the pillow*

CLARENCE

His eye is hollow, and he changes much.

WARWICK

Less noise, less noise.

Enter Prince Henry

PRINCE HENRY   Who saw the Duke of Clarence?

CLARENCE

I am here, brother, full of heaviness.   140

PRINCE HENRY

How now, rain within doors, and none abroad?

How doth the King?

GLOUCESTER Exceeding ill.

PRINCE HENRY

Heard he the good news yet? Tell it him.

GLOUCESTER

He altered much upon the hearing it.   145

---

132 softly, pray] F; *not in* Q   132.1 *The . . . up*] This edition; *They take the King up and lay him on a bed.* HUMPHREYS (*conj.* Capell *subs.*); *The King is carried over the stage in his bed* OXFORD; *not in* QF   136.1 *Exit . . . within*] OXFORD (*subs.*); *not in* QF   136.2 *The . . . down*] This edition; *not in* QF   137 *removing . . . crown*] This edition; *not in* QF   137.1 *Clarence . . . pillow*] OXFORD (*subs.*); *not in* QF   139 *Enter Prince Henry*] Q (*Enter Harry*), F (*Enter Prince Henry.*)   145 altered] Qb, F; uttred Qa

---

132 Q and F clearly envisage the action to be continuous. There are no stage directions in QF to signal exits, and no new scene is signalled, but the King is clearly intended to be in a notionally different location when he speaks at l. 137.

134 **dull** soothing
   favourable kindly, gracious (*OED a.* 2b)
140 **heaviness** sadness
141 **rain** tears
145 **altered** changed (for the worse)

PRINCE HENRY

If he be sick with joy, he'll recover without physic.

WARWICK

Not so much noise, my lords. Sweet Prince, speak low.
The King your father is disposed to sleep.

CLARENCE

Let us withdraw into the other room.

WARWICK

Will't please your grace to go along with us?   150

PRINCE HENRY

No, I will sit and watch here by the King.

> *Exeunt all but the King and Prince Henry.* ⌈*Music*
>   *ceases*⌉

Why doth the crown lie there upon his pillow,
Being so troublesome a bedfellow?
O polished perturbation, golden care,
That keep'st the ports of slumber open wide   155
To many a watchful night—sleep with it now!
Yet not so sound, and half so deeply sweet,
As he whose brow with homely biggin bound
Snores out the watch of night. O majesty,
When thou dost pinch thy bearer, thou dost sit   160
Like a rich armour worn in heat of day,
That scald'st with safety. By his gates of breath
There lies a downy feather which stirs not.
Did he suspire, that light and weightless down
Perforce must move. My gracious lord, my father!   165
This sleep is sound indeed. This is a sleep
That from this golden rigol hath divorced
So many English kings. Thy due from me
Is tears and heavy sorrows of the blood,
Which nature, love, and filial tenderness   170

146 If...physic] *as here* Q; *as verse* F (If...Ioy, | ...Physicke.)   147–8 Not...sleep] *as here*
F; *as prose* Q   151.1 *Exeunt...ceases*] This edition; *not in* QF   156 night—sleep...now!]
This edition; ~,~...~! Q; ~:~...~, F   162 scald'st] QF; scalds THEOBALD   163 downy] Q
(dowlny), F (dowlney)   164 down] QF (dowlne)   165 move.] F; ~ ͜ Q

155 **ports** gates   167 **rigol** circle
158 **homely biggin** plain (i.e. coarse) night-
cap

Shall, O dear father, pay thee plenteously.
My due from thee is this imperial crown,
Which, as immediate from thy place and blood,
Derives itself to me.
> *He puts the crown on his head*
> > > Lo where it sits,
Which God shall guard; and put the world's whole
   strength   175
Into one giant arm, it shall not force
This lineal honour from me. This from thee
Will I to mine leave, as 'tis left to me.   *Exit*
> *The King awakes*

KING HENRY

Warwick, Gloucester, Clarence!
> *Enter the Earl of Warwick, and the Dukes of*
> *Gloucester and Clarence*

CLARENCE   Doth the King call?

WARWICK

What would your majesty? How fares your grace?   180

KING HENRY

Why did you leave me here alone, my lords?

CLARENCE

We left the Prince my brother here, my liege,
Who undertook to sit and watch by you.

KING HENRY

The Prince of Wales? Where is he? Let me see him.
He is not here.   185

WARWICK

This door is open; he is gone this way.

GLOUCESTER

He came not through the chamber where we stayed.

KING HENRY

Where is the crown? Who took it from my pillow?

WARWICK

When we withdrew, my liege, we left it here.

174 *He ... head*] OXFORD (*conj.* Johnson *subs., after l.* 174); *not in* QF   where] Q; heere F
175 God] Q; Heauen F   178.1 *The King awakes*] OXFORD; *not in* QF   179 *Enter ... Clarence*]
QF (*Enter Warwicke, Gloucester, Clarence., after l.* 178)   180 How ... grace] F; *not in* Q
182–4 We ... him] F; *as prose* Q   185 He ... here] *as here* CAPELL; *as prose* Q; *not in* F

KING HENRY

The Prince hath ta'en it hence. Go seek him out.   190
Is he so hasty that he doth suppose
My sleep my death?
Find him, my lord of Warwick; chide him hither.

Exit Warwick

This part of his conjoins with my disease,
And helps to end me. See, sons, what things you are,   195
How quickly nature falls into revolt
When gold becomes her object!
For this the foolish over-careful fathers
Have broke their sleep with thoughts, their brains
          with care,
Their bones with industry;   200
For this they have engrossèd and piled up
The cankered heaps of strange-achievèd gold;
For this they have been thoughtful to invest
Their sons with arts and martial exercises;
When, like the bee tolling from every flower   205
Our thighs packed with wax, our mouths with honey,
We bring it to the hive; and, like the bees,

191–2 Is...death?] *as here* F; *one line* Q   193–5 Find...are] Q; Finde...Warwick) |
Chide...conioynes | With...me. | See...are: F   193.1 *Exit Warwick*] CAPELL; *not in*
QF   199–200 Have...industry] *as here* This edition; Have...thoughts | Their...industry
QF   199 sleep] Q; sleepes F   205 tolling] Q; culling F   206–9 Our...father.] Q; The
vertuous Sweetes...wax, | Our...Hiue; | And...pains. | This...engrossements, | To...
Father. F   206 thighs] F; thigh Q

194 **part** action
201 **engrossèd** amassed
    piled Q's 'pilled' (i.e. plundered, robbed as
    in 'The commons hath he pilled with
    grievous taxes': *Richard II* 2.1.247) is
    possible (and retained by Davison), but
    arguably inappropriate in the context of
    describing solicitous fathers fending for
    the welfare of profligate and thankless
    children.
204 **arts...exercises** The two branches of a
    gentleman's education.
205–6 **When...honey** Folio introduces a
    hemistich 'The virtuous sweets' as the
    direct object of the activity. It is hard to
    see how the Q compositor and proof cor-
    rector could have missed the half-line if it

ever stood in foul papers. The F hemistich
is both bland and unnecessary. It may
well be a consequence of a misreading of
'culling' for Q's 'tolling'. Whereas 'toll'
was used both transitively and intransi-
tively, *OED* only records transitive uses of
'cull', so that 'The virtuous sweets' may
be a filler for a missing direct object (at l.
4.2.40 the same hand may have left out
'three words' when it could not decipher
the phrase).
205 **tolling** taking as a toll, collecting (used
    transitively and intransitively). F's 'cul-
    ling' = selecting is possible, but it is prob-
    ably a misreading of the manuscript (see
    next note).

Are murdered for our pains. This bitter taste
Yields his engrossments to the ending father.
> *Enter the Earl of Warwick*

Now where is he that will not stay so long   210
Till his friend sickness have determined me?

WARWICK

My lord, I found the Prince in the next room,
Washing with kindly tears his gentle cheeks,
With such a deep demeanour, in great sorrow,
drank That tyranny, which never quaffed but blood,   215
Would, by beholding him, have washed his knife
With gentle eye-drops. He is coming hither.

KING HENRY

But wherefore did he take away the crown?
> *Enter Prince Henry*

Lo where he comes. Come hither to me, Harry.
(*To the others*) Depart the chamber; leave us here alone.   220
> *Exeunt all but the King and Prince Henry*

PRINCE HENRY

I never thought to hear you speak again.

KING HENRY

Thy wish was father, Harry, to that thought.
I stay too long by thee, I weary thee.
Dost thou so hunger for mine empty chair
That thou wilt needs invest thee with my honours   225

209.1 *Enter . . . Warwick*] Q (*Enter Warwicke., after l.* 211), F   211 have] RIDLEY; hands
Q; hath F   218.1 *Enter . . . Henry*] Q (*Enter Harry, after l.* 217), F   220.1 *Exeunt . . . Henry*]
OXFORD; *exeunt*. Q; *Exit.* F   222 thought.] F (thought:); ~∧ Q   224 mine] Q; my F
225 my] Q; mine F

208 **murdered** It is the drones and not the
  workers whom the bees kill off after
  swarming. The mistake may be a deliberate 'slip' by the King whose devious-
  ness is in no way lessened by his illness.
  See also *Henry V* 1.2.187–204, where
  the 'lazy yawning drone' is delivered to
  executioners.
208–9 **This . . . ending father** his accumula-
  tions ('engrossments') yield this bitter
  taste to the dying (= 'ending': *OED ppl.
  a.* 2) father
209 **Yields** Use of singular for plural (the

  subject is 'engrossments'); the singular
  accord may have been caused by 'taste'.
  The sentence syntactically replicates the
  inversion of the norm: fathers' rewards
  should be a sweet taste, i.e. gratitude and
  dutiful behaviour from their offspring.
211 **determined** put an end to
213 **kindly** natural, filial
215 **tyranny** cruelty
  quaffed drank
222 **Thy . . . thought** Proverbial: cf. 'We
  soon believe what we desire' (Dent
  B269).

Before thy hour be ripe? O foolish youth,
Thou seek'st the greatness that will overwhelm thee!
Stay but a little, for my cloud of dignity
Is held from falling with so weak a wind
That it will quickly drop. My day is dim.   230
Thou hast stol'n that which after some few hours
Were thine without offence, and at my death
Thou hast sealed up my expectation.
Thy life did manifest thou lovedst me not,
And thou wilt have me die assured of it.   235
Thou hid'st a thousand daggers in thy thoughts,
Whom thou hast whetted on thy stony heart,
To stab at half an hour of my life.
What, canst thou not forbear me half an hour?
Then get thee gone and dig my grave thyself,   240
And bid the merry bells ring to thine ear
That thou art crownèd, not that I am dead.
Let all the tears that should bedew my hearse
Be drops of balm to sanctify thy head.
Only compound me with forgotten dust.   245
Give that which gave thee life unto the worms.
Pluck down my officers, break my decrees;
For now a time is come to mock at form—
Harry the Fifth is crowned! Up, vanity!
Down, royal state! All you sage counsellors, hence!   250
And to the English court assemble now
From every region, apes of idleness!
Now, neighbour confines, purge you of your scum!
Have you a ruffian that will swear, drink, dance,
Revel the night, rob, murder, and commit   255

237 Whom] Q; Which F   241 thine] Q; thy F   249 Harry] Q; Henry F   253 scum!] F
(Scum:); ~ ͺ Q   254 will] Q; swill F

228–30 **for my cloud . . . drop** Clouds were   236 **daggers** See Introduction, p. 26 n. 1
   thought to be held up by the wind; the   237 **Whom** which
   King's breath is so weak that his high   245 **compound** mix
   estate ('cloud of dignity', with a sugges-   248 **form** law and order
   tion perhaps of its flimsiness) is about to   254 **dance** i.e. revel
   collapse.
233 **sealed . . . expectation** confirmed my
   fears

The oldest sins the newest kind of ways?
Be happy; he will trouble you no more.
England shall double gild his treble guilt,
England shall give him office, honour, might;
For the fifth Harry from curbed licence plucks   260
The muzzle of restraint, and the wild dog
Shall flesh his tooth on every innocent.
O my poor kingdom, sick with civil blows!
When that my care could not withhold thy riots,
What wilt thou do when riot is thy care?   265
O, thou wilt be a wilderness again,
Peopled with wolves, thy old inhabitants.

PRINCE HENRY (*kneels*)

O pardon me, my liege! But for my tears,
The moist impediments unto my speech,
I had forestalled this dear and deep rebuke   270
Ere you with grief had spoke and I had heard
The course of it so far. There is your crown;
　　⌈*He gives the King the crown*⌉
And He that wears the crown immortally
Long guard it yours! If I affect it more
Than as your honour and as your renown,   275
Let me no more from this obedience rise,
Which my most inward true and duteous spirit
Teacheth this prostrate and exterior bending.
God witness with me, when I here came in
And found no course of breath within your majesty,   280
How cold it struck my heart. If I do feign,
O, let me in my present wildness die,
And never live to show th'incredulous world
The noble change that I have purposèd.
Coming to look on you, thinking you dead,   285

---

262 on] Q; in F   268 *kneels*] ROWE (*after* 'liege!'); *not in* QF   269 moist] Q; most F
272.1 *He ... crown*] This edition; *not in* QF   277 inward ... and] Q; true and inward F
278–9 bending ... me,] F; ~, ... ~. Q   279 God] Q; Heauen F

---

262 **flesh** plunge into the flesh (*OED v.* 3a)
264–5 **When ... care** When my benevolent
　　rule could not curb your riots, what will
　　you do when riot (in the person of Hal)
　　afflicts you?

268–306 **O ... to it** See Introduction, pp.
　　48–9.
270 **dear** grievous
276 **obedience** obeisance, i.e. kneeling (*OED*
　　3)

And dead almost, my liege, to think you were,
I spake unto this crown as having sense,
And thus upbraided it : 'The care on thee depending
Hath fed upon the body of my father;
Therefore thou best of gold art worse than gold.   290
Other, less fine in carat, is more precious,
Preserving life in medicine potable;
But thou, most fine, most honoured, most renowned,
Hast eat thy bearer up.' Thus, my most royal liege,
Accusing it, I put it on my head,   295
To try with it, as with an enemy
That had before my face murdered my father,
The quarrel of a true inheritor.
But if it did infect my blood with joy
Or swell my thoughts to any strain of pride,   300
If any rebel or vain spirit of mine
Did with the least affection of a welcome
Give entertainment to the might of it,
Let God for ever keep it from my head,
And make me as the poorest vassal is,   305
That doth with awe and terror kneel to it.
KING HENRY O my son,
God put it in thy mind to take it hence,
That thou mightst win the more thy father's love,
Pleading so wisely in excuse of it!   310
Come hither, Harry; sit thou by my bed,
And hear, I think, the very latest counsel

---

287 this] Q; the F   290 worse than] Q; worst of F   291 fine in carat, is] F (~ ~ Charract,
~); ~, ~ karrat∧ Q   294 Hast…liege,] Q; vp. | Thus…Liege) F   thy] Q; the F   most
royal] Q; Royall F   304 God] Q; heauen F   307 O my son] F; *not in* Q   308 God]
Q; Heauen F   put it] F; put Q   309 win] Q; ioyne F

291 **carat** value (*OED* 4)
292 **medicine potable** A liquid drug called
    'aurum potabile' which was thought to
    contain gold and to have great curative
    powers.
294 **eat** a contemporary past form (Abbott
    §343)
296 **try** ascertain the truth or right of (*OED*
    v. 5c)   ·
298 **quarrel** (just) hostility (*OED sb.*³ 2)
300 **strain** high-pitched feeling
302 **affection** inclination (*OED sb.* 5)

307 **O my son** F-only hemistich: see simi-
    larly F-only 'My gracious liege' (l. 350).
    The absence from Q of both has been read
    as prompt-book or actors' interpolations
    (Davison, p. 265), but some form of ad-
    dress is needed in each case (as at l. 268
    where both Q and F use an address), and
    both are retained here.
309 **win** F's 'joyne' may be a misreading of
    manuscript 'winne' (Humphreys, p.
    lxxviii).
312 **latest** last

That ever I shall breathe.
　　Prince Henry rises
　　　　　　　　God knows, my son,
By what bypaths and indirect crook'd ways
I met this crown; and I myself know well   315
How troublesome it sat upon my head.
To thee it shall descend with better quiet,
Better opinion, better confirmation,
For all the soil of the achievement goes
With me into the earth. It seemed in me   320
But as an honour snatched with boist'rous hand;
And I had many living to upbraid
My gain of it by their assistances,
Which daily grew to quarrel and to bloodshed,
Wounding supposèd peace. All these bold fears   325
Thou seest with peril I have answerèd;
For all my reign hath been but as a scene
Acting that argument. And now my death
Changes the mood, for what in me was purchased
Falls upon thee in a more fairer sort;   330
So thou the garland wear'st successively.
Yet though thou stand'st more sure than I could do,
Thou art not firm enough, since griefs are green,
And all thy friends—which thou must make thy
　　　friends—

---

313 *Prince ... rises*] This edition; *not in* QF　God] Q; Heauen F　325 Wounding ... fears]
Q; Wounding .'. Peace. | All ... Feares, F　334 all thy] QF; all my RANN (*conj.* Tyrwhitt)

319 **soil ... achievement** taint of my ac-
　　quisition
321 **boist'rous** violently fierce (*OED a.* 9a
　　Obs.)
325 **fears** objects of fear
328 **argument** theme, subject (*OED 6*)
329 **purchased** In the legal sense of 'ac-
　　quired otherwise than by inheritance or
　　descent' (*OED, purchase, v.* 5a).
331 **garland** crown
　　successively by right of succession
334 **thy ... thy** Both Q and F have the first
　　'thy', and although it is tempting to
　　emend to 'my' as some editions do, this
　　is neither necessary nor warranted, be-
　　cause the King's 'friends' (i.e. allies) and
　　former foes would also be the Prince's. It

seems more likely that the King is telling
his son that he must not take alliances for
granted, but actively create them. During the preceding twenty lines the King
has been equivocal about his own part,
active or passive, in achieving the crown:
he claims to have 'met' it (just as in 3.1
he professed to have been 'compelled' to
kiss greatness), but he also knows that he
orchestrated the encounter through 'bypaths and indirect crook'd ways'. The
point of the double 'thy' seems to be a
lesson in realpolitik. The Prince, his
father tells him, must take nothing for
granted once he is king, least of all the
loyalty of his friends.

Have but their stings and teeth newly ta'en out;   335
By whose fell working I was first advanced,
And by whose power I well might lodge a fear
To be again displaced; which to avoid,
I cut them off, and had a purpose now
To lead out many to the Holy Land,   340
Lest rest and lying still might make them look
Too near unto my state. Therefore, my Harry,
Be it thy course to busy giddy minds
With foreign quarrels, that action hence borne out
May waste the memory of the former days.   345
More would I, but my lungs are wasted so
That strength of speech is utterly denied me.
How I came by the crown, O God forgive,
And grant it may with thee in true peace live!
PRINCE HENRY My gracious liege,   350
You won it, wore it, kept it, gave it me;
Then plain and right must my possession be,
Which I with more than with a common pain
'Gainst all the world will rightfully maintain.
      Enter Prince John of Lancaster, the Earl of Warwick,
      ⌈*and others*⌉
KING HENRY
Look, look, here comes my John of Lancaster.   355
PRINCE JOHN
Health, peace, and happiness to my royal father!
KING HENRY
Thou bring'st me happiness and peace, son John,
But health, alack, with youthful wings is flown
From this bare withered trunk. Upon thy sight
My worldly business makes a period.   360
Where is my lord of Warwick?

---

342 Too...Harry] Q; Too...State. | Therefore...*Harrie*) F   348 God] Q; heauen F
350 My...liege] F; *not in* Q   354.1–2 *Enter...others*] F (*Enter Lord Iohn of Lancaster, and
Warwicke.*), CAPELL (*subs.*); *enter Lancaster.* Q

337 **lodge** harbour   345 **waste** wear out, obliterate
341–2 **look...state** watch, scrutinize (with   350 **My...liege** See above, l. 307.
   a view to rebellion) my affairs too closely   360 **makes a period** comes to an end
344 **hence borne out** endured abroad

PRINCE HENRY   My lord of Warwick!
        ⌈*Warwick comes forward*⌉
KING HENRY
    Doth any name particular belong
    Unto the lodging where I first did swoon?
WARWICK
    'Tis called Jerusalem, my noble lord.
KING HENRY
    Laud be to God! Even there my life must end.   365
    It hath been prophesied to me many years
    I should not die but in Jerusalem,
    Which vainly I supposed the Holy Land.
    But bear me to that chamber; there I'll lie;
    In that Jerusalem shall Harry die.   370
                        Exeunt, carrying the King in his bed

5.1   *Enter Shallow, Falstaff, Bardolph, and the Page*
SHALLOW (*to Falstaff*) By cock and pie, sir, you shall not
    away tonight. What, Davy, I say!
FALSTAFF You must excuse me, Master Robert Shallow.
SHALLOW I will not excuse you; you shall not be excused;
    excuses shall not be admitted; there is no excuse shall   5
    serve; you shall not be excused. Why, Davy!
        Enter Davy
DAVY Here, sir.

361.1 *Warwick...forward*] OXFORD (*subs.*); *not in* Q   363 swoon] Q; swoon'd F
365 God] Q; heauen F   370.1 *Exeunt...King*] This edition; *Exeunt, bearing the King in his bed* OXFORD; *Exeunt.* F; *not in* Q
    5.1.0.1 *Enter...Page*] CAPELL (*subs.*); *Enter Shallow, Falstaffe, and Bardolfe* Q (*opposite*
4.3.369-70); *Enter Shallow, Silence, Falstaffe, Bardolfe, Page, and Dauie.* F   1 pie, sir] Q; Pye
F   6.1 *Enter Davy*] THEOBALD; *not in* QF

364-70 'Tis called...die See Introduction,
p. 18 n.
5.1.0.1 F's stage direction is a block entry
    (see 3.2.0.1) and introduces Davy as well
    as Silence who does not feature in the
    scene at all. But Davy is specifically called
    for twice by Shallow (ll. 2, 6) and should
    properly enter on 'Here, sir' (l. 7).
1 By...pie A mild oath; 'cock' (*OED sb.*[8])
    is a perversion of the word 'God' (cf.
    'cock's body'), and 'pie' is the Roman
    'cock's body'), and 'pie' is the Roman

Catholic ordinal. The choice of this particular oath may be partly due to the cross-
scenic triple rhyme of 'lie–die–pie', and
'pie' of course denotes a dish of food,
while 'cock' already had its bawdy meaning, as Williams, 1994 (pp. 258–61)
shows (although *OED* first records this
in 1618): cf. 'Pistol's cock is up, | And
flashing fire will follow' (*Henry V* 2.1.50–
1). The oath signals the shift into a scene
of comedy.

SHALLOW Davy, Davy, Davy, Davy; let me see, Davy; let
me see, Davy; let me see—yea, marry, William Cook, bid
him come hither.—Sir John, you shall not be excused.   10

DAVY Marry, sir, thus: those precepts cannot be served.
And again, sir: shall we sow the headland with wheat?

SHALLOW With red wheat, Davy. But for William Cook—
are there no young pigeons?

DAVY Yes, sir. Here is now the smith's note for shoeing and   15
plough-irons.

SHALLOW Let it be cast and paid. Sir John, you shall not be
excused.

DAVY Now, sir, a new link to the bucket must needs be
had; and, sir, do you mean to stop any of William's   20
wages, about the sack he lost at Hinckley Fair?

SHALLOW A shall answer it. Some pigeons, Davy, a couple
of short-legged hens, a joint of mutton, and any pretty
little tiny kickshaws, tell William Cook.

DAVY Doth the man of war stay all night, sir?   25

SHALLOW Yea, Davy, I will use him well; a friend i'th' court
is better than a penny in purse. Use his men well, Davy,
for they are arrant knaves, and will backbite.

DAVY No worse than they are back-bitten, sir, for they have
marvellous foul linen.   30

SHALLOW Well conceited, Davy. About thy business, Davy.

---

8 Davy, Davy, Davy, Davy] Q; *Dauy, Dauy, Dauy* F   8–9 Davy; let . . . William Cook] Q; *William Cooke* F   12 headland] Q (hade land), F (head-land)   19 Now, sir] Q; Sir F   21 lost] Q; lost the other day F   Hinkley] F; Hunkly Q   22 A] Q; He F   24 tiny] Q; tine F   26 Yea] Q; Yes F   29 back-bitten] Q; bitten F   30 marvellous] F, Q (maruailes)

9 **William Cook** i.e. William the cook; he is named after his profession (cf. Robin Ostler, *1 Henry IV* 2.1.10–11)

11 **precepts** writs, warrants (*OED*, *precept*, *sb.* 4)

12–13 **headland . . . red wheat** The headland is the strip of land at the end of the furrow of an arable field where the plough turns. It is therefore planted later than the main field, with spring wheat ('red wheat') rather than winter wheat (or 'white wheat').

15 **note** bill

17 **cast** reckoned (*OED v.* 37)

19 **link . . . bucket** (probably) a rope or chain, or a part of either, for a pail (or perhaps a yoke: see 3.2.253)

21 **Hinckley Fair** Every 26 August a famous cattle fair was held at Hinckley, a market town on the border of Warwickshire and Leicestershire, some thirty miles north-east of Stratford. Sugden (p. 250) notes that 'As Henry IV died on March 20th, Davy must have had a long memory!'

23 **short-legged hens** They are better table fare than long-legged birds.

24 **little tiny** Cf. 'He that has and a little tiny wit' (*Lear* 3.2.74).
kickshaws fancy dish

26–7 **a . . . purse** Proverbial: cf. 'Better is a friend in court than (A friend in court is worth) a penny in purse' (Dent F687).

29 **back-bitten** by lice

31 **Well conceited** very witty

DAVY I beseech you, sir, to countenance William Visor of
 Won'cot against Clement Perks o'th' Hill.

SHALLOW There is many complaints, Davy, against that
 Visor. That Visor is an arrant knave, on my knowledge.   35

DAVY I grant your worship that he is a knave, sir; but yet
 God forbid, sir, but a knave should have some countenance at his friend's request. An honest man, sir, is able to
 speak for himself, when a knave is not. I have served
 your worship truly, sir, this eight years. An I cannot   40
 once or twice in a quarter bear out a knave against an
 honest man, I have little credit with your worship. The
 knave is mine honest friend, sir; therefore I beseech you
 let him be countenanced.

SHALLOW Go to; I say he shall have no wrong. Look about,   45
 Davy.   *[Exit Davy]*
 Where are you, Sir John? Come, come, come, off with
 your boots. Give me your hand, Master Bardolph.

BARDOLPH I am glad to see your worship.

SHALLOW I thank thee with all my heart, kind Master Bar-   50
 dolph; *[to the Page]* and welcome, my tall fellow. Come,
 Sir John.

FALSTAFF I'll follow you, good Master Robert Shallow.

                                             Exit Shallow

---

33 o'th'] Q; of the F   34 is] Q; are F   37 God] Q; heauen F   40 this] Q; these F   An]
Q; and if F   42 little] Q; but a very little F   43 you] Q; your Worship F   45 to; I say‚] F
(too, | I say); ~, ~ ~, Q   46 Exit Davy] CAPELL; *not in* QF   47 Come, come, come, off]
Q; Come, off F   50 all] F; *not in* Q   53.1 Exit Shallow] CAPELL; *not in* QF

---

32 **countenance** favour (*OED v.* 5a)

32–3 **William Visor ... o'th' Hill** The two
litigants almost certainly live in Wood-
mancote ('Won'cot'), Dursley, and the
adjoining Stinchcombe Hill ('o'th' Hill')
in Gloucestershire. The name Visor (or
Vizard) was common in the region in
the early seventeenth century, but
Perkes ('Perkis' or 'Purchase') is seldom
found here. The places were locally called
'Woncot' and 'The Hill' (Huntley, Palmer), although Smith only records
'Wormcote' as a contraction of Wood-
mancote. That Shakespeare was familiar
with this particular area is suggested
further by the reference to Berkeley Castle 'by yon tuft of trees' (*Richard II*
2.3.53) in clear view on a copse four

miles from Stinchcombe Hill. Shakespeare is rarely this specific in his references, although one of Falstaff's recruits
(3.2.133) may correspond to a real person. 'Wincot', i.e. Wilmcote near Stratford (as in 'Marian Hacket, the fat ale-
wife of Wincot'—the Induction to *Shrew*:
Hackets lived in that parish in the
1590s), has also been proposed as the
location behind Won'cot.

38 **honest** Used here as a term of apprecia-
tion rather than to describe Visor as a
man of probity.

41 **bear out** support, back up (*OED, bear, v.*[1]
3a)

45 **Look about** be wary

51 **tall** (probably) an ironic form of address
to the small page

Bardolph, look to our horses.

> *Exit Bardolph ⌈with the Page ⌉*

If I were sawed into quantities, I should make four dozen   55
of such bearded hermits' staves as Master Shallow. It is a
wonderful thing to see the semblable coherence of his
men's spirits and his. They, by observing him, do bear
themselves like foolish justices; he, by conversing with
them, is turned into a justice-like servingman. Their   60
spirits are so married in conjunction, with the participation of society, that they flock together in consent like so
many wild geese. If I had a suit to Master Shallow, I
would humour his men with the imputation of being
near their master; if to his men, I would curry with   65
Master Shallow that no man could better command his
servants. It is certain that either wise bearing or ignorant
carriage is caught as men take diseases, one of another;
therefore let men take heed of their company. I will
devise matter enough out of this Shallow to keep Prince   70
Harry in continual laughter the wearing out of six fash-
ions—which is four terms, or two actions—and a shall
laugh without intervallums. O, it is much that a lie with
a slight oath, and a jest with a sad brow, will do with a
fellow that never had the ache in his shoulders! O, you   75

54.1 *Exit . . . Page*] CAPELL (*subs.*); *not in* QF   58 him] Q; of him F   72 a] Q; he F   73 with-out] Q; with F

55 **quantities** fragments
57 **semblable coherence** close correspondence
59 **conversing** consorting (*OED v.* 2)
61 **married in conjunction** intimately joined
61–2 **participation of society** associating
   with one another
62 **flock . . . consent** Cf. the proverbial expression 'Birds of a feather will flock (fly)
   together' (Dent B393).
63 **had a suit** needed to beg a favour
65 **curry** flatter, win favour (*OED, curry, v.*[1]
   4b)
68 **carriage** demeanour (*OED* 14a)
69 **let . . . company** Proverbial: cf. 'Draw to
   such company as you would be like'
   (Dent C565.1).

71–2 **the wearing . . . actions** Falstaff is
   poking fun at the rapid changes in fashion (every two months) and the slowness
   of lawsuits ('actions'), two of which last
   for a whole year (or four terms: the legal
   year consists of Michaelmas, Hilary,
   Easter, and Trinity terms).
73 **intervallums** intervals (specifically between the various legal terms and actions, hence the use of the Latin phrase)
74 **sad** serious
74–5 **a fellow . . . shoulders** free from the
   aches which accompany old age, i.e. the
   Prince is young enough yet to enjoy
   Falstaff's brand of tomfoolery wholeheartedly

shall see him laugh till his face be like a wet cloak ill laid
up.

SHALLOW (*within*) Sir John!

FALSTAFF I come, Master Shallow; I come, Master Shal-
low.   *Exit*   80

5.2   *Enter the Earl of Warwick ⌈at one door⌉, and the Lord
Chief Justice ⌈at another door⌉*

WARWICK

How now, my Lord Chief Justice, whither away?

LORD CHIEF JUSTICE How doth the King?

WARWICK

Exceeding well: his cares are now all ended.

LORD CHIEF JUSTICE

I hope not dead.

WARWICK   He's walked the way of nature,
And to our purposes he lives no more.   5

LORD CHIEF JUSTICE

I would his majesty had called me with him.
The service that I truly did his life
Hath left me open to all injuries.

WARWICK

Indeed I think the young King loves you not.

LORD CHIEF JUSTICE

I know he doth not, and do arm myself   10
To welcome the condition of the time,
Which cannot look more hideously upon me
Than I have drawn it in my fantasy.

---

80 Exit] F (*Exeunt*); *not in* Q

  5.2.0.1–2 *Enter . . . another door*] F (*Enter the Earle of Warwicke, and the Lord | Chiefe
Iustice.*); *Enter Warwike, duke Humphrey, L. chiefe Iustice, Thomas | Clarence, Prince, Iohn
Westmerland.* Qa; *. . . Prince Iohn, Westmerland.* Qb   3 Exceeding . . . ended] Q; Exceeding . . .
Cares | Are . . . ended F

76–7 **like . . . up** creased (from laughing)
like a wet cloak that was badly hung up
to dry
5.2.0.1–2 Q's opening stage direction includes three characters (Prince John,
and the Dukes of Clarence and Gloucester) who enter again at Q 5.2.13, as well
as the supernumerary Westmorland.
This may suggest that Shakespeare did

not at first intend to start the scene with
the Lord Chief Justice but rather to gather
all the mourners for Henry IV before the
entry of the new king. The omission of
Westmorland from Act 5 of the play altogether seems odd and may be an over-
sight. He should perhaps be imagined as
part of a train of 'others' who walk in the
King's procession.

Enter Prince John of Lancaster, and the Dukes of
Clarence and Gloucester

WARWICK

Here come the heavy issue of dead Harry.

O that the living Harry had the temper   15

Of he the worst of these three gentlemen!

How many nobles then should hold their places

That must strike sail to spirits of vile sort!

LORD CHIEF JUSTICE

O God, I fear all will be overturned.

PRINCE JOHN

Good morrow, cousin Warwick, good morrow.   20

GLOUCESTER *and* CLARENCE Good morrow, cousin.

PRINCE JOHN

We meet like men that had forgot to speak.

WARWICK

We do remember, but our argument

Is all too heavy to admit much talk.

PRINCE JOHN

Well, peace be with him that hath made us heavy!   25

LORD CHIEF JUSTICE

Peace be with us, lest we be heavier!

GLOUCESTER

O good my lord, you have lost a friend indeed;

And I dare swear you borrow not that face

Of seeming sorrow—it is sure your own.

PRINCE JOHN (*to Lord Chief Justice*)

Though no man be assured what grace to find,   30

You stand in coldest expectation.

I am the sorrier; would 'twere otherwise.

CLARENCE (*to Lord Chief Justice*)

Well, you must now speak Sir John Falstaff fair,

Which swims against your stream of quality.

13.1–2 *Enter ... Gloucester*] Q (*Enter Iohn, Thomas, and Humphrey.*); *Enter Iohn of Lancaster,*
Gloucester, | *and Clarence.* F   16 he] Q; him F   19 O God] Q; alas F   21 GLOUCESTER *and*
CLARENCE] Q (*Prin. ambo*), F (*Glou. Cla.*)

14 **heavy** sorrowful
18 **strike sail** lower their sails, i.e. submit
34 **swims...stream** Proverbial: cf. 'To
swim against the stream (with the crab,

trout)' (Dent S930.1).
34 **your stream of quality** the current of your
natural inclination and office

LORD CHIEF JUSTICE

> Sweet princes, what I did I did in honour,   35
> Led by th'impartial conduct of my soul;
> And never shall you see that I will beg
> A raggèd and forestalled remission.
> If truth and upright innocency fail me,
> I'll to the King my master that is dead,   40
> And tell him who hath sent me after him.
>   *Enter King Henry the Fifth*

WARWICK Here comes the Prince.

LORD CHIEF JUSTICE

> Good morrow, and God save your majesty!

KING HENRY

> This new and gorgeous garment, majesty,
> Sits not so easy on me as you think.
> Brothers, you mix your sadness with some fear.   45
> This is the English, not the Turkish court;
> Not Amurath an Amurath succeeds,
> But Harry Harry. Yet be sad, good brothers,
> For, by my faith, it very well becomes you.   50
> Sorrow so royally in you appears
> That I will deeply put the fashion on,
> And wear it in my heart. Why then, be sad;
> But entertain no more of it, good brothers,

---

36 th'impartial] Q; th'Imperiall F   38–9 remission. ...me,] F; ~,...~. Q   39 truth] Q; Troth F   41.1 *Enter...Fifth*] F (*Enter Prince Henrie., after l.* 42); *Enter the Prince | and Blunt* Q (*opposite ll.* 41–2)   43 God] Q; heauen F   46 mix] F; mixt Q   50 by my faith] Q; (to speake truth) F

---

38 **raggèd** beggarly
  forestalled remission (probably) a pardon certain to be refused in advance (and therefore not worth asking for)
41.1 *Enter . . . Fifth* Q here introduces 'Blunt': see 3.1.31.1 n.
48 **Amurath** A topical reference to the accession to the Turkish Sultanate in January 1596 of Muhammad III who, like his father Amurath III, also had his brothers strangled. Shakespeare's (unhistorical, and not strictly accurate) claim that one fratricidal Amurath succeeded another Amurath implies that at the Turkish court it does not matter who inherits the throne, because their rulers are all

equally wicked. In England, on the other hand, there is a reassuring continuity in the transition from one Harry to another Harry, which does not, however, negate the real differences between Bolingbroke and Henry V. But in '"Not Amurath an Amurath Succeeds": Playing Doubles in Shakespeare's Henriad', *ELR* 21 (1991), 161–89, Richard Hillman argues that the allusion to Turkish tyranny serves 'as a powerful subversive emblem of the shadow-side of English monarchy' (p. 167), a part of a wider strategy which questions the concept of the Lancastrian warrior-king.

Than a joint burden laid upon us all. 55
For me, by heaven, I bid you be assured
I'll be your father and your brother too.
Let me but bear your love, I'll bear your cares.
Yet weep that Harry's dead, and so will I;
But Harry lives that shall convert those tears 60
By number into hours of happiness.

PRINCE JOHN, GLOUCESTER *and* CLARENCE
We hope no otherwise from your majesty.

KING HENRY
You all look strangely on me, (*to Lord Chief Justice*)
    and you most.
You are, I think, assured I love you not.

LORD CHIEF JUSTICE
I am assured, if I be measured rightly, 65
Your majesty hath no just cause to hate me.

KING HENRY
No? How might a prince of my great hopes forget
So great indignities you laid upon me?
What—rate, rebuke, and roughly send to prison
Th'immediate heir of England? Was this easy? 70
May this be washed in Lethe and forgotten?

LORD CHIEF JUSTICE
I then did use the person of your father.
The image of his power lay then in me;
And in th'administration of his law,
Whiles I was busy for the commonwealth, 75
Your highness pleasèd to forget my place,
The majesty and power of law and justice,
The image of the King whom I presented,
And struck me in my very seat of judgement;
Whereon, as an offender to your father, 80
I gave bold way to my authority
And did commit you. If the deed were ill,

59 Yet] Q; But F   62 PRINCE...CLARENCE] Q (*Bro.*), F (*Iohn, &c.*)   otherwise] Q; other F

69 **rate** chide
71 **Lethe** The river of the underworld the
    waters of which induce oblivion in the
    souls who drink from it.

72 **use the person of** represent
73 **image** symbol
78 **presented** impersonated

Be you contented, wearing now the garland,
To have a son set your decrees at naught?
To pluck down justice from your awe-full bench,   85
To trip the course of law, and blunt the sword
That guards the peace and safety of your person?
Nay, more, to spurn at your most royal image,
And mock your workings in a second body?
Question your royal thoughts, make the case yours,   90
Be now the father, and propose a son;
Hear your own dignity so much profaned,
See your most dreadful laws so loosely slighted,
Behold yourself so by a son disdained;
And then imagine me taking your part,   95
And in your power soft silencing your son.
After this cold considerance sentence me;
And, as you are a king, speak in your state
What I have done that misbecame my place,
My person, or my liege's sovereignty.   100

KING HENRY
You are right Justice, and you weigh this well.
Therefore still bear the balance and the sword;
And I do wish your honours may increase
Till you do live to see a son of mine
Offend you and obey you as I did.   105
So shall I live to speak my father's words;
'Happy am I that have a man so bold
That dares do justice on my proper son,
And not less happy having such a son

95 your] Q; you F   109 not] Q; no F

83 **garland** Cf. 4.3.331.
85 **awe-full** Cf. 4.1.174.
89 **your . . . body** the exercise of your duties
   by a representative
91 **propose** imagine
96 **soft** gently
97 **considerance** sober reflection
98 **in your state** according to your royal
   office
101 **right Justice** justice personified, i.e. an
   ideal figure of justice itself. The absence of
   a comma between 'right' and 'Justice' in
   QF points to this reading rather than a

form of address to the Lord Chief Justice
(as does the preceding dialogue with its
emphasis on the symbolic identity of
office-bearing).
101 **weigh** consider
102 **still . . . balance sword** The confirmation of the Lord Chief Justice by Henry V
   is not historical: see Introduction, pp.
   21–2. The balance and the sword are
   emblems of justice, the scales symbolizing impartiality and the sword the power
   to enforce the law and punish.
108 **proper** own

That would deliver up his greatness so   110
Into the hands of justice.' You did commit me,
For which I do commit into your hand
Th'unstainèd sword that you have used to bear,
With this remembrance : that you use the same
With the like bold, just, and impartial spirit   115
As you have done 'gainst me. There is my hand.
You shall be as a father to my youth ;
My voice shall sound as you do prompt mine ear,
And I will stoop and humble my intents
To your well-practised wise directions.   120
And Princes all, believe me, I beseech you,
My father is gone wild into his grave,
For in his tomb lie my affections ;
And with his spirits sadly I survive
To mock the expectation of the world,   125
To frustrate prophecies, and to raze out
Rotten opinion, who hath writ me down
After my seeming. The tide of blood in me
Hath proudly flowed in vanity till now.
Now doth it turn, and ebb back to the sea,   130
Where it shall mingle with the state of floods,
And flow henceforth in formal majesty.
Now call we our high court of Parliament,
And let us choose such limbs of noble counsel
That the great body of our state may go   135
In equal rank with the best-governed nation ;
That war, or peace, or both at once, may be
As things acquainted and familiar to us ;
(*To Lord Chief Justice*)
In which you, father, shall have foremost hand.

111 justice.' You . . . me,] F (~. You . . . me:); ~ . . . ~: Q   You] Qb, F; your Qa

114 **remembrance** reminder
122–3 **My father . . . affections** Henry V pro-
    claims that he has buried his riotous be-
    haviour with the body of his father.
    There may be an echo here of the Pauline
    notion of shedding the old Adam and
    rising again with a new Christian ar-
    mour of virtues (Ephesians 6: 16).
124 **spirits** sentiments, feelings
    sadly gravely

125 **mock** disprove
128–32 **The tide . . . majesty** Cf. *Othello*
    3.3.456–63.
129 **proudly** with vigour or force (*OED adv.*
    2)
131 **state of floods** majesty of oceans
    (Onions)
134 **limbs** members (anticipating the 'body
    of our state' in l. 135)

(*To all*) Our coronation done, we will accite,   140
As I before remembered, all our state ;
And, God consigning to my good intents,
No prince nor peer shall have just cause to say
'God shorten Harry's happy life one day.'   *Exeunt*

5.3   *Enter Falstaff, Shallow, Silence, Davy, Bardolph, and
       the Page*

SHALLOW (*to Falstaff*) Nay, you shall see my orchard,
    where, in an arbour, we will eat a last year's pippin of
    mine own grafting, with a dish of caraways, and so
    forth—come, cousin Silence—and then to bed.

FALSTAFF Fore God, you have here a goodly dwelling, and a   5
    rich.

SHALLOW Barren, barren, barren ; beggars all, beggars all,
    Sir John. Marry, good air. Spread, Davy, spread, Davy.
        ⌐*Davy spreads the table*⌐
    Well said, Davy.

FALSTAFF This Davy serves you for good uses ; he is your   10
    serving-man and your husband.

SHALLOW A good varlet, a good varlet, a very good varlet,
    Sir John—by the mass, I have drunk too much sack at
    supper—a good varlet. Now sit down, now sit down. (*To
    Silence*) Come, cousin.   15

SILENCE Ah, sirrah, quoth-a, we shall
    (*sings*) Do nothing but eat, and make good cheer,
              And praise God for the merry year,
              When flesh is cheap and females dear,
              And lusty lads roam here and there   20

142 God] Q; heauen F   144 God] Q; Heauen F   *Exeunt*] F, Q (*exit.*)
    5.3.0.1–2 *Enter . . . Page*] Q (*Enter sir Iohn, Shallow, Scilens, Dauy, Bardolfe, page.*); *Enter
Falstaffe, Shallow, Silence, Bardolfe,* | *Page, and Pistoll.* F   1 my] Q; mine F   3 mine] Q; my
F   5 Fore God] Q; *not in* F   a goodly] F; goodly Q   5–6 a rich] F; rich Q   8.1 *Davy . . .
table*] OXFORD (*subs.*); *not in* QF   13 by the mass] Q; *not in* F   17 (*sings*)] ROWE (*subs.*); *not in*
QF   17–22 Do nothing . . . merrily] *as verse* ROWE; *as prose* QF   18 God] Q; heauen F

140 **accite** summon
141 **remembered** mentioned (*OED v.*[1] 3a)
    state government (*OED sb.* 26a)
142 **consigning** setting his seal to (*OED v.* 5)
5.3.3 **caraways** sweetmeats containing car-
    away seeds (Onions)
  8 **Spread** lay the table (*OED v.* 8b)
  9 **Well said** well done

11 **husband** steward
17–22 **Do nothing . . . merrily** All Silence's
    songs are set as prose by QF, except 'Be
    merry . . . merry' (ll. 32–6) which F has
    as verse. Although only one of them can
    be identified ('Do . . . Samingo', ll. 72–4),
    it is probable that the others were also
    popular and traditional tunes and words.

    So merrily,

    And ever among so merrily.

FALSTAFF There's a merry heart, good Master Silence! I'll give you a health for that anon.

SHALLOW Give Master Bardolph some wine, Davy.   25

DAVY (*to Falstaff*) Sweet sir, sit—(*to Bardolph*) I'll be with you anon—(*to Falstaff*) most sweet sir, sit. Master page, good master page, sit. Proface! What you want in meat, we'll have in drink; but you must bear; the heart's all.

Exit

SHALLOW Be merry, Master Bardolph, and my little soldier   30 there, be merry.

SILENCE (*sings*)

    Be merry, be merry, my wife has all,

    For women are shrews, both short and tall.

    'Tis merry in hall when beards wags all,

    And welcome merry shrovetide.   35

Be merry, be merry.

FALSTAFF I did not think Master Silence had been a man of this mettle.

SILENCE Who, I? I have been merry twice and once ere now.   40

    Enter Davy ⌈*with a dish of apples*⌉

DAVY There's a dish of leather-coats for you.

SHALLOW Davy!

DAVY Your worship? I'll be with you straight. (*To Falstaff*) A cup of wine, sir?

---

25 Give] Q; Good F   29 must] Q; *not in* F   29.1 *Exit*] THEOBALD; *not in* QF   32 (*sings*)] ROWE (*subs.*); *not in* QF   32–6 Be merry...merry] *as here* OXFORD; ~ ~ ... wagge all; | And...merry. F; *as prose* Q   34 wags] Q; wagge F   38 mettle] Q (mettall), F (Mettle) 40.1 *Enter...apples*] OXFORD; *Enter Dauy.* Q; *not in* F   41 There's] Q; There is F

---

22 **ever among** all the while

28 **Proface** 'May it do you good', a traditional formula of welcome at dinner in the period (from obs. French 'bon prou vous fasse!').

28–9 **What...drink** Cf. proverbial 'What they want in meat let them take in drink' (Dent M845).

28 **want** lack

29 **bear** put up with

34 **wags** Use of the singular for the plural (Abbott §333: see above, 1.2.71–2). The expression of beards wagging 'in hall' is proverbial (Dent H55: 'It is merry in hall when beards wag all').

39 **twice and once** The inversion and very low frequency (for a man of Silence's age) is for comic effect.

41 **leather-coats** russet apples (which are rough-skinned)

SILENCE ⌈*sings*⌉

      A cup of wine that's brisk and fine,   45
      And drink unto thee, leman mine,
      And a merry heart lives long-a.

FALSTAFF Well said, Master Silence.

SILENCE And we shall be merry; now comes in the sweet
    o'th' night.   50

FALSTAFF Health and long life to you, Master Silence!

SILENCE Fill the cup and let it come. I'll pledge you a mile to
    th' bottom.

SHALLOW Honest Bardolph, welcome! If thou want'st any-
    thing and wilt not call, beshrew thy heart! (*To the Page*)   55
    Welcome, my little tiny thief, and welcome indeed, too!
    I'll drink to Master Bardolph, and to all the cavalieros
    about London.
      He drinks

DAVY I hope to see London once ere I die.

BARDOLPH An I might see you there, Davy!   60

SHALLOW By the mass, you'll crack a quart together, ha,
    will you not, Master Bardolph?

BARDOLPH Yea, sir, in a pottle-pot.

SHALLOW By God's liggens, I thank thee. The knave will
    stick by thee, I can assure thee that; a will not out, a; 'tis   65
    true-bred.

BARDOLPH And I'll stick by him, sir.

---

45 ⌈*sings*⌉] ROWE (*subs.*); *not in* QF   45–7 A cup...long-a] *as verse* ROWE; *as prose* QF
49 And] Q; If F   50 o'th' night] Q; of the night F   52–3 Fill...th' bottom] QF; Fill...
come, | I'll...th' bottom CAPELL   53 th' bottom] Q; the bottome F   56 tiny] Q; tyne F
58.1 *He drinks*] OXFORD; *not in* QF   60 An] Q; If F   61 By the mass] Q; *not in* F   63 Yea]
Q; Yes F   64 By God's liggens] Q; *not in* F   65 that;] F (~.); ~$_\wedge$ Q   65 a...out, a; 'tis] Q
(a...out, a tis); He...out, he is F

46 **leman** sweetheart
47 **a merry . . . long-a** Proverbial (Dent
   H320a: 'A merry heart lives long').
49–50 **the sweet . . . night** Cf. 2.4.362.
52 **let it come** pass it round (a common
   drinking cry)
52–3 **a mile . . . bottom** i.e. the whole cup
   even if it is a mile deep. The expression
   was a common drinking term, as in 'To
   set all a going if it were a mile to the
   bottom' (Dent A207), and in Jonson,
   Every Man In His Humour 5.3.153 (H &
   S, iii. 280).

56 **little tiny** Also used at 5.1.24.
57 **cavalieros** A playful and affectionate
   term for gallants.
59 **once** one day
61 **crack** 'empty, drink' (*OED v.* 10)
63 **pottle-pot** pot of two quarts (i.e. twice the
   amount proposed by Shallow)
64 **By God's liggens** An oath of unknown
   origin; its absence from F is almost certainly due to the 1606 Act (3 Jac. I, c. 21)
   outlawing profanity on the stage (see Introduction, p. 98).
65 **out** drop out

SHALLOW Why, there spoke a king! Lack nothing, be
  merry!

  One knocks at a door within

Look who's at door there, ho! Who knocks?   70

                                              ⌈*Exit Davy*⌉

      ⌈*Shallow drinks again*⌉

FALSTAFF Why, now you have done me right!

SILENCE (*sings*)   Do me right,
                And dub me knight—
                Samingo.

  Is't not so?   75

FALSTAFF 'Tis so.

SILENCE Is't so? Why then, say an old man can do somewhat.

      ⌈*Enter Davy*⌉

DAVY An't please your worship, there's one Pistol come
  from the court with news.   80

FALSTAFF From the court? Let him come in.

      Enter Pistol

  How now, Pistol?

PISTOL Sir John, God save you.

FALSTAFF What wind blew you hither, Pistol?

PISTOL

  Not the ill wind which blows no man to good.   85

69.1 *One . . . within*] Q (*One knockes at doore., opposite l. 67*); *not in* F   70 Look∧] Q; ~, F
70.1 *Exit Davy*] CAPELL; *not in* QF   70.2 *Shallow drinks again*] This edition; *not in* QF
72 (*sings*)] ROWE (*subs.*); *not in* QF   72-4 Do . . . Samingo] *as verse* MALONE; *as prose* QF
78.1 *Enter Davy*] CAPELL; *not in* QF   79 An't] Q; If it F   81.1 *Enter Pistol*] Q (*opposite l.*
80), F   83 God save you] Q; 'saue you, sir F   85 no man] Q; none F   85-6 good. | Sweet
knight,] Q; ~, ~ ~: F

71 **done me right** matched me drink for
  drink; 'do me right' was a drinking challenge: cf. '*Do me right, and dub me knight,*
  | *Balurdo*' in *Antonio and Mellida* 5.2.26–
  7, ed. G. K. Hunter (1965).

72-4 **Do . . . Samingo** Silence quotes an
  idiosyncratic and English version of the
  refrain of a popular French drinking song
  Monsieur Mingo, set to music by Orlando
  di Lasso and first published in 1570 (cf.
  Nashe, *Summer's Last Will and Testament*
  968–71: 'Mounsieur Mingo for quaffing
  doth surpasse, | In Cuppe, in Canne, or
  glasse. | God Bacchus, doe mee right, |

And dubbe mee knight Domingo', *The
  Works of Thomas Nashe*, ed. R. B. McKer-
  row, vol. 3 (1905), p. 264). Silence's
  'Samingo' may be an assimilated version
  of 'Sir Mingo' (Mingo has just been
  knighted through his drinking prowess).
  The fact that 'mingo' is Latin for 'I make
  water, void urine' (ppl. 'mictum', hence
  'micturate') indicates something about
  the unedifying and humorous nature of
  the song about 'Sir Pisser'.

85 **Not . . . good** Cf. proverbial 'It is an ill
  (evil) wind that blows no man good'
  (Dent W421).

Sweet knight, thou art now one of the greatest men in
this realm.

SILENCE By'r Lady, I think a be, but Goodman Puff of
Bar'son.

PISTOL Puff?   90

Puff i'thy teeth, most recreant coward base!
Sir John, I am thy Pistol and thy friend,
And helter-skelter have I rode to thee,
And tidings do I bring, and lucky joys,
And golden times, and happy news of price.   95

FALSTAFF I pray thee now, deliver them like a man of this
world.

PISTOL

A foutre for the world and worldlings base!
I speak of Africa and golden joys.

FALSTAFF

O base Assyrian knight, what is thy news?   100
Let King Cophetua know the truth thereof.

SILENCE (*sings*)

'And Robin Hood, Scarlet, and John.'

---

87 this] Q; the F   89 By'r Lady] Q; Indeed F   a] Q; he F   90–5 Puff... price] POPE; *as
prose* QF   91 i'thy] Q (ith thy); in thy F   92–3 friend, | And] Q; Friend F   96 pray thee]
Q; prethee F   98–101 A foutre ... thereof] *as verse* F; *as prose* Q   101 Cophetua] Q (Coue-
tua); *Couitha* F   102 (*sings*)] JOHNSON (*subs.*); *not in* QF

86 **greatest** most powerful (because of the
new king), but Silence mistakes it to
mean 'largest', as his unwittingly (?)
comic comparison with one Puff makes
clear.
88 **but** except for
Goodman A title for yeomen and farmers
who are below the rank of gentlemen.
89 **Bar'son** Probably Barton north-east of
Stratford, or Barcheston-on-the-Stour
(locally pronounced Barson) to the
south; or perhaps Barton-on-the-Heath
to which Shakespeare may already have
referred in *Shrew* (see above, 5.1.32–3).
95 **of price** 'of value' (*OED, price, sb.* 7)
96–7 **like ... this world** i.e. in plain language (rather than a cryptic jingle)
98 **A foutre . . . world** the equivalent of
'screw the world'
99 **Africa** Associated with wealth and splen-

dour by Marlowe in the *Tamburlaine*
plays, which elsewhere may have influenced Pistol's rhetoric (cf. notes to
2.4.153–5, 161–3, 167 , 172).
100 **Assyrian** (Perhaps) a playful biblical
designation. In the drama of the period
the phrase seems to be associated with
luxury, as in 'Th'*Assyrian* pompe, the
Persian pride' (Jonson, *The Masque of
Queenes* 766, H & S, vii. 316), or 'Assyrian silkes' and 'Assyrian carpets' (T.
Nabbes, *Microcosmus* 3. 216; 5.34).
101 **Cophetua** The story of King Cophetua
from Africa, who disliked all women but
married a beautiful beggar girl, comes
from the popular ballad *A Beggar and
King*. Shakespeare refers to it repeatedly.
102 **'And ... John.'** A scrap from a stanza in
the ballad of *Robin Hood and the Pindar of
Wakefield*.

PISTOL

   Shall dunghill curs confront the Helicons?

   And shall good news be baffled?

   Then, Pistol, lay thy head in Furies' lap.   105

SHALLOW Honest gentleman, I know not your breeding.

PISTOL Why then, lament therefor.

SHALLOW Give me pardon, sir. If, sir, you come with news
   from the court, I take it there's but two ways: either to
   utter them, or conceal them. I am, sir, under the King in   110
   some authority.

PISTOL

   Under which king, bezonian? Speak, or die.

SHALLOW

   Under King Harry.

PISTOL   Harry the Fourth, or Fifth?

SHALLOW

   Harry the Fourth.

PISTOL   A foutre for thine office!

   Sir John, thy tender lambkin now is king.   115

   Harry the Fifth's the man. I speak the truth.

   When Pistol lies, (*making the fig*) do this, and fig me, like

   The bragging Spaniard.

FALSTAFF   What, is the old King dead?

PISTOL

   As nail in door. The things I speak are just.

FALSTAFF Away, Bardolph, saddle my horse! Master Ro-   120
   bert Shallow, choose what office thou wilt in the land,

103–5 Shall...lap] *as verse* F; *as prose* Q   106 Honest...breeding] Q; Honest Gentleman, |
I...breeding. F   108 sir. If] Q; Sir. | If F   109 there's] Q; there is F   110 or] Q; or to F
112 king, bezonian?] Q; King? | *Bezonian* F   115–18 Sir John...dead?] F; *as prose* Q
117 (*making the fig*)] OXFORD; *not in* QF   119 As...just.] *as here* Q; As...doore. |
The...iust. F   120–2 Away...dignities] *as prose* Q; Away...Horse, | Master...wilt |
In...thee | With Dignities. F

---

103 **Helicons** i.e. the Muses (who lived on
   Mount Helicon), and therefore meaning
   true poets like Pistol
104 **baffled** treated with contumely (cf.
   Twelfth Night 2.5.157)
107 **therefor** for that
112 **bezonian** 'needy beggar, knave' (*OED* b)
117–18 **do this...Spaniard** i.e. he chal-

lenges him to put his thumb between
his index and middle fingers in the gesture of contempt known as the fig which
originated in Spain (hence the 'bragging
Spaniard')
119 **As...door** Proverbial: 'As dead (deaf,
   dumb) as a door nail' (Dent D567).
   just true

'tis thine. Pistol, I will double-charge thee with dignities.

BARDOLPH O joyful day!

I would not take a knighthood for my fortune.

PISTOL What, I do bring good news?   125

FALSTAFF (*to Davy*) Carry Master Silence to bed.

⌐*Exit Davy with Silence*⌐

Master Shallow—my lord Shallow—be what thou wilt, I
am fortune's steward—get on thy boots; we'll ride all
night.—O sweet Pistol!—Away, Bardolph!

⌐*Exit Bardolph*⌐

Come, Pistol, utter more to me, and withal devise some-   130
thing to do thyself good. Boot, boot, Master Shallow! I
know the young King is sick for me. Let us take any
man's horses—the laws of England are at my commandment. Blessed are they that have been my friends, and
woe to my Lord Chief Justice!   135

PISTOL

Let vultures vile seize on his lungs also!

'Where is the life that late I led?' say they.

Why, here it is. Welcome these pleasant days.

Exeunt

123–4 O...fortune.] *as here* F; *as prose* Q   124 knighthood] F; Knight Q   126.1 *Exit...*
Silence] OXFORD; *not in* QF   129.1 *Exit Bardolph*] CAPELL; *not in* QF   134 Blessed] Q; Happie
F   that] Q; which F   135 to] Q; unto F   138 these] Q; those F   138.1 *Exeunt*] Q (*exit.*), F

122 **double-charge** overload (with a play on
'charging'—loading—a pistol)

131 **Boot, boot** put on your boots (Onions)

136 **Let...also** Alludes (probably) to the
story of Prometheus who was chained
to a rock by Zeus as a punishment for
stealing the gods' fire. Every day an
eagle came and ate his liver, which
grew back at night, until he was released
from his torment by Heracles. Another
possible candidate is the story of Tityus,
a son of Gaia, who in the underworld had
two vultures tearing away at his liver
(the seat of passion) as a punishment for
assaulting Leto (or Latona) who was a
Titaness and the mother of Apollo and
Artemis (Diana). Both tales are related
in *Aeneid* 6.595–600 and *Metamorphoses*
4.457–8.

5.4 *Enter Beadles, dragging in Mistress Quickly and Doll Tearsheet*

MISTRESS QUICKLY No, thou arrant knave! I would to God that I might die, that I might have thee hanged. Thou hast drawn my shoulder out of joint.

FIRST BEADLE The constables have delivered her over to me, and she shall have whipping-cheer, I warrant her. There hath been a man or two killed about her.   5

DOLL TEARSHEET Nut-hook, nut-hook, you lie! Come on, I'll tell thee what, thou damned tripe-visaged rascal, an the child I go with do miscarry, thou wert better thou hadst struck thy mother, thou paper-faced villain.   10

MISTRESS QUICKLY O the Lord, that Sir John were come! I would make this a bloody day to somebody. But I pray God the fruit of her womb miscarry!

5.4.0.1–2 *Enter ... Tearsheet*] F (*Enter Hostesse Quickly, Dol Teare-sheete, and Beadles.*); *Enter Sincklo and three or foure officers.* Q   1–2 to God that I] Q; I F   4 FIRST BEADLE] F (*Off⟨icer⟩.*, etc.); *Sincklo* Q   5 whipping-cheer] Q; Whipping cheere enough F   6 killed] Q; (lately) kill'd F   8 an] Q; if F   9 I] Q; I now F   wert] Q; had'st F   11 the Lord] Q; *not in* F   I] Q; hee F   12–13 pray God] Q; would F   13 miscarry] Q; might miscarry F

5.4.0.1–2 Q's stage direction clearly suggests that Shakespeare had the actor John Sincklo in mind for the part of the very thin 'First Beadle'. Sincklo is mentioned by name elsewhere by Shakespeare (e.g. F *3 Henry VI* 3.1) and other dramatists (e.g. in the Induction to Marston's *The Malcontent*). From these contexts it appears that he was frequently typecast in the roles of thin men, and he may have played Shadow in 3.2. His parts may have been mostly minor ones, and he is not listed among the 'Principall Actors' in the 1623 Folio. His absence from the F stage direction can (perhaps) be attributed to the fact that the prompt-book closest to F would be the post-1606 one (see Introduction, p. 98), by which time the actor may no longer have been available to play the part; or the first prompt-book (for the 1596–7 performances) may not have reproduced the name because the actor could not be expected to be invariably at hand to play the part even if it were written specifically for him. As well as 'tidy-

ing up' Q, F also introduces Doll and Mistress Quickly who were erroneously omitted from Q's stage direction.

0.1 *Beadles* Officers of a parish who had the power to punish petty offences (cf. *Lear* 4.5.156–9).

5 **whipping-cheer** flogging; (lit.) 'a "banquet" of lashes with the whip' (Onions)

6 **about her** Either 'in her company', or 'because of her'.

7 **Nut-hook** beadle, constable, (lit.) a hooked stick to pull down the branches of trees

8 **tripe-visaged** 'with a face like tripe, (and therefore probably) sallow, pitted' (Onions)

8–9 **the child ... miscarry** Pregnancy would save Doll from the beadles' rough handling and from the gallows (at least till the birth of the baby).

12 **make ... somebody** Cf. proverbial 'To be (make) a black (bloody) day to somebody' (Dent D88).

13 **the fruit ... miscarry** She means the opposite.

FIRST BEADLE If it do, you shall have a dozen of cushions
again; you have but eleven now. Come, I charge you   15
both go with me, for the man is dead that you and Pistol
beat amongst you.

DOLL TEARSHEET I'll tell you what, you thin man in a censer, I will have you as soundly swinged for this, you
bluebottle rogue, you filthy famished correctioner! If   20
you be not swinged I'll forswear half-kirtles.

FIRST BEADLE Come, come, you she-knight errant, come!

MISTRESS QUICKLY O God, that right should thus overcome
might! Well, of sufferance comes ease.

DOLL TEARSHEET Come, you rogue, come, bring me to a   25
justice.

MISTRESS QUICKLY Ay, come, you starved bloodhound.

DOLL TEARSHEET Goodman death, goodman bones!

MISTRESS QUICKLY Thou atomy, thou!

DOLL TEARSHEET Come, you thin thing; come, you rascal.   30

FIRST BEADLE Very well.   *Exeunt*

---

17 amongst] Q; among F   18 you what, you] Q; thee what, thou F   20 bluebottle]
Q; blew-|Bottel'd F   23 God] Q; *not in* F   overcome] Q; o'recome F   25–6 Come...jus-
tice] *as here* Q; Come...come: | Bring...Iustice F   27 Ay] Q (I); Yes F   29 atomy]
Q; Anatomy F   30 Come...rascal] *as here* Q; Come...Thing: | Come...Rascall. F
31 *Exeunt*] F; *not in* Q

---

14 **cushions** implying that Doll is feigning
pregnancy by stuffing cushions under
her gown

18–19 **man in a censer** Censers had low-
relief figures embossed on them. Humphreys (p. 178) points out that Shakespeare frequently compares thin men to
low-relief figures, on e.g. coins, flasks,
brooches.

19 **swinged** thrashed

20 **bluebottle** Elizabethan beadles wore blue
coats.
correctioner An officer from the House of
Correction at Bridewell who inflicts pun-
ishments.

21 **forswear half-kirtles** stop wearing skirts;
a kirtle consisted of a separate bodice and
skirt, hence half-kirtle = skirt

22 **she-knight errant** i.e. prostitute (who
'errs' by night)

23–4 **that...might** The hostess comically
inverts the proverb 'Might overcomes
right' (Dent M922).

24 **of sufferance...ease** Proverbial (Dent
S955).

29 **atomy** i.e. anatomy (as in F) meaning
skeleton. The slip is the correct Elizabethan form for atom, which is also appropriate to the pale thin appearance of
the beadle.

30 **rascal** a lean deer: cf. 2.4.39, where Doll
also uses the word.

5.5   *Enter* ⌈*two*⌉ *grooms, strewers of rushes*

FIRST GROOM More rushes, more rushes.

SECOND GROOM The trumpets have sounded twice.

⌈FIRST⌉ GROOM 'Twill be two o'clock ere they come from
the coronation. Dispatch, dispatch.   *Exeunt*

> *Trumpets sound, and King Henry the Fifth and his train*
> *pass over the stage. After them enter Falstaff, Shallow,*
> *Pistol, Bardolph, and the Page*

FALSTAFF Stand here by me, Master Shallow. I will make   5
the King do you grace. I will leer upon him as a comes by,
and do but mark the countenance that he will give me.

PISTOL God bless thy lungs, good knight.

FALSTAFF Come here, Pistol; stand behind me. (*To Shallow*)
O, if I had had time to have made new liveries, I would   10
have bestowed the thousand pound I borrowed of you!
But 'tis no matter; this poor show doth better; this doth
infer the zeal I had to see him.

⌈PISTOL⌉ It doth so.

5.5.0.1 [two] ... rushes] Q (*strewers of rushes.*); *two Groomes.* F   3 ⌈FIRST⌉ GROOM] F;
3 Q 'Twill] Q; It will F   o'clock] Q; of the Clocke F   4 Dispatch, dispatch] Q; *not in*
F   *Exeunt*] F (*Exit Groo.*); *not in* Q   4.1–3 *Trumpets ... Page*] Q (*subs.*); *Enter Falstaffe, Shallow,*
Pistoll, Bardolfe, and Page. F   5 Master Shallow] Q; M. *Robert Shallow* F   6 a] Q; he F
8 God bless] Q; Blesse F   12 'tis] Q; it is F   14 PISTOL] Q; *Shal.* F

5.5.3–4.3 ⌈FIRST⌉ GROOM . . . *the Page* The
King's ceremonial procession on the way
to the coronation at l. 4 is unique to Q
(both Q and F mark a procession *from* the
coronation at l. 39). It may be that Shakespeare wanted to display the elaborate
pageantry of the coronation twice rather
than once (see Introduction, p. 95; also
Davison, p. 281), even though the First
Groom states that the royal party is coming 'from' the Abbey. It is possible that
Shakespeare imagined the procession
which enters on cue (after 'Dispatch') at
l. 4 to pass across the back of the stage
while the strewers at the front are in
readiness for the return of the procession
over the rushes. By cutting the first ceremonial stage entrance and by removing
the (now redundant) invitation to hurry
('Dispatch, dispatch'), F's text rationa-
lizes the problems posed by Q's stage
directions and dialogue (and may reflect the practicalities of casting: Jowett,

p. 285), but in so doing it may falsify the
author's intention and timing of the action.

6 **grace** honour
leer upon cast a sly glance at (to attract
the passing King's attention)

7 **countenance** (a) look (*OED sb.* 4); (b)
patronage, i.e. approval (*OED sb.* 8)

11 **bestowed** laid out (*OED v.* 5b)

13 **infer** imply (*OED v.* 4)

14 **PISTOL . . . so** Q gives this line, as well as
the next two 'doth' lines, to Pistol,
whereas F gives the first to Shallow
while agreeing with Q on the speech-prefixes of ll. 16 and 18. Although F's attri-
bution seems to acknowledge that
Falstaff's lines are addressed to Shallow
and invite a response of some sort, the
structure of the dialogue in Q suggests
rather that Shallow requires a barrage
of prompting from both Falstaff and Pistol
before agreeing 'It is best, certain'. Q
rather than F appears to recognize the

FALSTAFF It shows my earnestness of affection—   15
PISTOL It doth so.

FALSTAFF My devotion—

PISTOL It doth, it doth, it doth.

FALSTAFF As it were, to ride day and night, and not to
   deliberate, not to remember, not to have patience to   20
   shift me—

SHALLOW It is best, certain.

⌈FALSTAFF⌉ But to stand stained with travel, and sweating
   with desire to see him, thinking of nothing else, putting
   all affairs else in oblivion, as if there were nothing else to   25
   be done but to see him.

PISTOL 'Tis *semper idem*, for *absque hoc nihil est*; 'tis all in
   every part.

SHALLOW 'Tis so indeed.

PISTOL
   My knight, I will inflame thy noble liver,   30
   And make thee rage.
   Thy Doll, and Helen of thy noble thoughts,
   Is in base durance and contagious prison,
   Haled thither
   By most mechanical and dirty hand.   35

---

15 of] Q; in F   19–21 As...me—] *as here* Q; As...night, | And...remember, |
Not...me. F   22 best, certain] Q (~‸ ~); most certaine F   22–3 certain. | FALSTAFF But]
F; certain: but Q   25 affairs else] Q; affayres F   27 *absque*] F2; *obsque* QF1   all] F; *not in*
Q   30–1 My knight...rage] *as verse* JOHNSON; *as prose* QF   32–7 Thy Doll...truth] *as verse*
POPE; *as prose* QF

---

fact that Falstaff has no intention of repaying Shallow under any circumstances, and the rapid-fire dialogue of
Falstaff and Pistol (who is positioned behind Falstaff) has the appearance of a
preconcerted exchange between them.
Even though Falstaff claims here not to
have spent Shallow's money yet, he
either already has (or pretends to), because he professes to be unable to refund
it after the rejection (l. 75).

21 **shift me** change my clothes
27 *semper idem* always the same
   absque ... est apart from this there is
   nothing

27–8 **'tis ... every part** Perhaps intended as
   a loose rendering of the second Latin tag;
   cf. also the proverbial expression 'All in
   all and all in every part' (Dent A133).
30 **liver** See above, 4.2.100.
32 **Helen** i.e. Helen of Troy whose name was
   frequently used jocularly for wives and
   mistresses
33 **durance** confinement, imprisonment
34 **Haled** i.e. hauled, drawn with violence
   (*OED, hale, v.*[1] 1b)
35 **mechanical** belonging to a manual (and
   therefore) base labourer

Rouse up Revenge from ebon den with fell Alecto's
    snake,
For Doll is in. Pistol speaks naught but truth.

FALSTAFF I will deliver her.

    ⌈*Shouts within.*⌉ *Trumpets sound*

PISTOL

There roared the sea, and trumpet-clangour sounds.

    Enter King Henry the Fifth, Prince John of Lancaster,
    the Dukes of Clarence and Gloucester, the Lord Chief
    Justice, ⌈*and others*⌉

FALSTAFF

God save thy grace, King Hal, my royal Hal!   40

PISTOL

The heavens thee guard and keep, most royal imp of
    fame!

FALSTAFF God save thee, my sweet boy.

KING HENRY

My Lord Chief Justice, speak to that vain man.

LORD CHIEF JUSTICE (*to Falstaff*)

Have you your wits? Know you what 'tis you speak?

FALSTAFF

My king, my Jove, I speak to thee, my heart!   45

KING HENRY

I know thee not, old man. Fall to thy prayers.
How ill white hairs becomes a fool and jester!
I have long dreamt of such a kind of man,
So surfeit-swelled, so old, and so profane;
But being awaked, I do despise my dream.   50
Make less thy body hence, and more thy grace.

---

37 truth] Q; troth F   38.1 *Shouts within*] STEEVENS–REED 1793; *not in* QF   *Trumpets sound*] F
(*after l.* 40); *not in* Q   39.1–3 *Enter . . . others*] F (*The Trumpets sound. Enter King Henrie the* |
Fift, Brothers, Lord Chiefe | *Iustice.*); *Enter the King and his traine.* Q   40 God] Q; *not in* F
42 God] Q; *not in* F   47 becomes] Q; become F   50 awaked] Q; awake F

36 **ebon** black
   fell cruel
   Alecto's snake Alecto, one of the Furies,
   is described by Virgil in *Aeneid* 7.346 as
   crowned with snakes.
37 **in** in prison (*OED adv.* 6a)

41 **imp** scion (esp. of a noble house) (*OED sb.*
   3)
43 **vain** foolish
47 **becomes** Cf. 5.2.50; on the use of the
   singular to accord with the plural, see
   1.2.71–2 n.

Leave gormandizing; know the grave doth gape
For thee thrice wider than for other men.
Reply not to me with a fool-born jest.
Presume not that I am the thing I was,   55
For God doth know, so shall the world perceive,
That I have turned away my former self;
So will I those that kept me company.
When thou dost hear I am as I have been,
Approach me, and thou shalt be as thou wast,   60
The tutor and the feeder of my riots.
Till then I banish thee, on pain of death,
As I have done the rest of my misleaders,
Not to come near our person by ten mile.
For competence of life I will allow you,   65
That lack of means enforce you not to evils;
And as we hear you do reform yourselves,
We will, according to your strengths and qualities,
Give you advancement. (*To Lord Chief Justice*) Be it your
    charge, my lord,
To see performed the tenor of my word.   70
Set on.   *Exeunt King Henry and his train*

FALSTAFF Master Shallow, I owe you a thousand pound.

SHALLOW Yea, marry, Sir John, which I beseech you to let
    me have home with me.

FALSTAFF That can hardly be, Master Shallow. Do not you   75
    grieve at this. I shall be sent for in private to him. Look
    you, he must seem thus to the world. Fear not your
    advancements. I will be the man yet that shall make
    you great.

SHALLOW I cannot perceive how, unless you give me your   80
    doublet and stuff me out with straw. I beseech you, good
    Sir John, let me have five hundred of my thousand.

---

56 God] Q; heauen F   66 evils] Q; euill F   68 strengths] Q; strength F   70–1 To...on]
as here POPE; *one line* QF   70 my] Q; our F   71 *Exeunt...train*] CAPELL (*subs.*); *Exit King.*
F; *not in* Q   73 Yea] Q; I F   78 advancements] Q; aduance-|ment F   80 perceive] Q; well
perceiue F   give] Q; should giue F

---

65 **competence of life** supply adequate for   77 **Fear** doubt
    living

FALSTAFF Sir, I will be as good as my word. This that you
　heard was but a colour.

SHALLOW A colour that I fear you will die in, Sir John.　85

FALSTAFF Fear no colours. Go with me to dinner. Come,
　Lieutenant Pistol; come, Bardolph. I shall be sent for
　soon at night.

　　　Enter the Lord Justice and Prince John, with officers

LORD CHIEF JUSTICE (*to officers*)

　Go carry Sir John Falstaff to the Fleet.

　Take all his company along with him.　90

FALSTAFF My lord, my lord—

LORD CHIEF JUSTICE

　I cannot now speak. I will hear you soon.

　Take them away.

PISTOL *Si fortuna me tormenta, spero me contenta.*

　　　Exeunt all but Prince John and Lord Chief Justice

PRINCE JOHN

　I like this fair proceeding of the King's.　95

　He hath intent his wonted followers

　Shall all be very well provided for,

　But all are banished till their conversations

　Appear more wise and modest to the world.

LORD CHIEF JUSTICE And so they are.　100

---

85 that I fear] Q; I feare, that F　86–8 Fear...night] POPE; Feare...dinner: | Come...Bardolfe, | I...night. QF　88.1 *Enter...officers*] CAPELL (*subs.*); *Enter Iustice | and prince Iohn* Q (*opposite ll. 87–9*); *not in* F　92–3 I...away] *as verse* F; *as prose* Q　94 *tormenta, spero me contenta*] Q; *tormento, spera me contento* F　94.1 *Exeunt...Chief Justice*] F (*Exit. Manet Lancaster and Chiefe Iustice.*); *exeunt.* Q (*after l. 93*)

---

83 **as . . . my word** proverbial (Dent W773.1)

84 **colour** pretence

85 **A colour . . . die** in a 'pretence' that will, I fear, be your undoing (with puns on 'die' and 'dye' and, perhaps, on 'colour' and 'collar', i.e. the hangman's noose)

86 **Fear no colours** fear no foe. The expression is proverbial (Dent C520), 'colours' meaning 'military ensigns'.

87 **Lieutenant** Falstaff appears to have been quick off the mark in bestowing this rank on Pistol to whom he promised 'dignities' at 5.3.122.

88 **soon at night** betimes (proverbial: S639.1)

89 **the Fleet** A famous prison north of Fleet Street and to the east side of the Fleet Ditch, near the site of contemporary Shoe Lane. The prison seems to act here as a place of remand accommodation for Falstaff and his companions (including, apparently, Shallow), before a formal hearing in the Lord Chief Justice's court. Although the dispatching to the Fleet of Falstaff and his crew is a punishment, it is only temporary, and the treatment that they can expect at the hands of the Lord Chief Justice's performing the 'tenor' (l. 70) of the King's 'word' seems lenient.

94 *Si . . . contenta* See above, 2.4.179 n.

98 **conversations** behaviour (*OED* 6)

PRINCE JOHN

The King hath called his parliament, my lord.
LORD CHIEF JUSTICE He hath.
PRINCE JOHN

I will lay odds that, ere this year expire,
We bear our civil swords and native fire
As far as France. I heard a bird so sing,   105
Whose music, to my thinking, pleased the King.
Come, will you hence?   *Exeunt*

Epilogue   *Enter Epilogue*

EPILOGUE First my fear, then my curtsy, last my speech.

My fear is your displeasure; my curtsy, my duty; and
my speech to beg your pardons. If you look for a good
speech now, you undo me, for what I have to say is of
mine own making; and what indeed I should say will, I   5
doubt, prove mine own marring. But to the purpose, and
so to the venture. Be it known to you, as it is very well, I
was lately here in the end of a displeasing play, to pray
your patience for it, and to promise you a better. I meant
indeed to pay you with this; which, if like an ill venture it   10
come unluckily home, I break, and you, my gentle cred-
itors, lose. Here I promised you I would be, and here I
commit my body to your mercies. Bate me some, and I
will pay you some, and, as most debtors do, promise you
infinitely. And so I kneel down before you—but, indeed,   15
to pray for the Queen.

---

105 heard] Q; heare F   107 Exeunt] F; *not in* Q
  Epilogue 0.1 *Enter Epilogue*] OXFORD; *not in* QF   9 meant] Q; did meane F   15–16 And
...Queen] Q; *after ll.* 32, F   15 I kneel] Q; kneele F

105 **I...sing** Proverbial (Dent B374).
Epilogue
1 **EPILOGUE** See Introduction, pp. 14–16.
curtsy bow (a sign of respect)
5–6 **making...marring** Cf. proverbial 'To
  make or (and) mar' (Dent M48).
  6 **doubt** fear
  7 **venture** attempt (at delivering the Epilo-
    gue)
  8 **displeasing play** This play has not been
    identified, and in the absence of concrete
    evidence speculation about it is probably
    fruitless.

11 **break** go bankrupt: cf. 'Antonio's cred-
  itors...swear he cannot choose but
  break' (*Merchant* 3.1.105–7).
13 **Bate** remit
16 **pray...Queen** Although a concluding
  prayer for the Queen was customary
  and almost certainly marked the end of
  the only paragraph in the first draft (see
  Introduction, pp. 14–15) of the play, I
  have resisted the temptation to shift it to
  the end of the speech (where Folio and
  Oxford put it). Q alone preserves what
  may well be an intended and cheeky

If my tongue cannot entreat you to acquit me, will you
command me to use my legs ? And yet that were but light
payment, to dance out of your debt. But a good con-
science will make any possible satisfaction, and so   20
would I. All the gentlewomen here have forgiven me ; if
the gentlemen will not, then the gentlemen do not agree
with the gentlewomen, which was never seen in such an
assembly.

One word more, I beseech you. If you be not too much   25
cloyed with fat meat, our humble author will continue
the story with Sir John in it, and make you merry with
fair Katherine of France ; where, for anything I know,
Falstaff shall die of a sweat, unless already a be killed
with your hard opinions. For Oldcastle died martyr, and   30
this is not the man. My tongue is weary ; when my legs
are too, I will bid you good night.   *Exit*

21 would] Q; will F   23 seen] Q; seene before F   29 a be] Q; he be F   30 martyr] Q; a
Martyr F   32 *Exit*] OXFORD; *not in* QF

night/knight pun in the play's last word.
The axe may have come down on the
play's first (k)night, but Shakespeare
wants us to leave the play with Falstaff/
Oldcastle in mind.

18–19 **legs . . . dance** See Introduction, p.
14 n.

21–2 **gentlewomen . . . gentlemen** See similarly *As You Like It*, Epilogue 11–21.
26–7 **continue . . . in it** See Introduction, pp.
15–16.
29 **sweat** venereal disease. On Falstaff and
'sweating', see Introduction, pp. 37–8.

INDEX

This is a guide to selected names, words, phrases, and topics in the Introduction and Commentary. Biblical allusions and proverbial sayings are grouped together. Plays and selected other works cited in the Commentary for cross-reference are also listed. Words which supplement the *Oxford English Dictionary* are asterisked.

A Mad World, My Masters, 3.1.17
abide a field, 2.3.36
ability, 1.3.45
*able, 1.1.43
about her, 5.4.6
abroad, 1.2.92
accite, 5.2.140; *accites, 2.2.56
accommodated, 3.2.64
Ackland, Joss (as Falstaff), pp. 73–4
aconitum, 4.3.48
acts, *n*. Induction, 5
addressed, 4.3.5
advice, 1.2.94
advised, 1.1.172
Aeneid, Induction, 1; 1.1.72; 5.3.136; 5.5.36
affairs, 3.2.176
affection, 4.3.302; affections, 4.3.65
affections of delight, 2.3.29
Africa, 5.3.99
against, 4.1.307
Agamemnon, 2.4.217
agate, 1.2.16
aggravate, 2.4.160
ague, 1.2.95
air and promise, 1.3.28
Alchemist, 2.1.159
Alecto's snake, 5.5.36
Alexander, Peter, 2.4.1–20
all put forth, 1.1.186
All is True, 2.1.92
allow, 1.3.5
altered, 4.3.145
Althea's dream, 2.2.82
Amurath, 5.2.48
Ancient, 2.4.68
Antonio and Mellida, 2.4.246–7; 5.3.71
Antony and Cleopatra, pp. 44, 95; 1.2.163; 2.4.188; 4.2.51
ape, *n*. 2.4.214
Apophthegmes of Erasmus, 2.4.48

apoplexy, 1.2.105
apple-johns, 2.4.1–2
apprehensive, 4.2.96
Arch Street Theatre, Philadelphia, p. 66
Archbishop of York, 1.1.189
argument, 4.3.328
arrant, 2.1.38
as great aim, 3.2.256
As You Like It, 2.4.1–20, 97; Epilogue, 21–2
aspen leaf, 2.4.107
assemblance, 3.2.249
Assyrian, 5.3.100
at large, 4.3.101
atomy, 5.4.29
atonement, 4.1.219
attach, 4.1.335
attached, 2.2.3
avoirdupois, 2.4.252
away with, 3.2.194
awe-full, 4.1.174; 5.2.85

back-bitten, 5.1.29
backsword man, 3.2.61–2
baffled, 5.3.104
Barbary hen, 2.4.97
Barber, C. L., p. 44
Barbican, pp. 67, 73
Bar'son, 5.3.89
Bartholomew boar-pig, 2.4.228–9
Bartholomew Fair, 3.2.303–4
Barton, Anne, p. 45
Barton, John, p. 67
Basingstoke, 2.1.165
bastardly, 2.1.48
bate, Epilogue, 13
battle, *n*. 4.1.152; 3.2.151
Battle of Alcazar, 2.4.153–5, 177
BBC, pp. 67–8, 73, 76, 86
bear out, 5.1.41
bear, *v*., 2.2.16; 2.4.59; 5.3.29

bearherd, 1.2.165
Beaumont and Fletcher, 2.1.159;
    2.4.243
beavers, 4.1.118
*bed-hangers, 2.1.143
being, 2.1.181
Bell, John, pp. 63, 66
Benson, Constance, p. 67
Benson, Frank, pp. 66–7
Berger, Thomas L., pp. 78, 96; 3.2.53
Bergeron, David M., p. 4
Bergman, Ingmar, p. 70
beseek, 2.4.160
beshrew, 2.3.45
best-tempered, 1.1.115
bestow himself, 2.2.161
bestowed, 5.5.11
Betterton, Thomas, pp. 59, 60–2
Bevington, David, pp. 13, 21, 26, 34,
    40, 55, 59, 98; 1.1.161–3
bezonian, 5.3.112
biblical, pp. 6, 30, 42, 72; 1.2.33,
    44–51, 123, 161, 183–4;
    1.3.41–62, 89–90, 99; 2.1.141;
    2.2.23, 111, 123, 135, 142;
    2.4.60–1, 332; 3.2.34–5, 248–9,
    300–1; 4.3.79–80; 5.2.122–3;
    5.3.100
bids, 2.4.332
*big, Induction, 13
Billington, Michael, p. 75
Birmingham Repertory Theatre, p. 67
black ouzel, 3.2.7
Blayney, Peter W. M., p. 91
bleed, 4.1.57
bloodied, 1.1.38
blubbered, 2.4.385
bluebottle, 5.4.20
blunt, Induction, 18
Boar's Head, pp. 1, 54, 80; 2.1.68;
    2.2.138–9
Bogdanov, Michael, pp. 67, 75
boist'rous, 4.3.321
bona-robas, 3.2.21
Book of Martyrs, p. 5
book-oath, 2.1.101
boot, boot, 5.3.131
Booth, Stephen, pp. 32, 34
borne, 2.1.33
borrower's, 2.2.108
bottle, 1.2.206
bottle-ale, 2.4.127
Bowers, Fredson, p. 97

box of th'ear, 1.2.188
Bradbrook, M. C., pp. 52, 55
Bradley, A. C., pp. 44, 46
Bramham Moor, 1.1.0.1
brand, 2.2.82
brawn, 1.1.19
break, *v.* Epilogue, 11
breathed, 4.1.112
Brecht, Bert, pp. 69–70
breeds no bate, 2.4.247
brooches, pearls, and ouches, 2.4.48
bruited, 1.1.114
bung, 2.4.125
burns, 2.4.334
Burrell, John, p. 67
Burton, Richard, pp. 28, 69
busses, 2.4.266
But, 1.1.193
by God's liggens, 5.3.64

Caesar, 1.1.21; 2.2.116; 2.4.152–8,
    164–5; 4.2.40
Cain, 1.1.157
Caird, John, pp. 68, 76
Calder, David (as Falstaff), p. 77
caliver, 3.2.259
calm, 2.4.36
Calydonian boar, 2.2.82
canaries, 2.4.26
candlemine, 2.4.298
capable, 1.1.172–3
Capell, Edward, 1.1.34; 2.4.158
caper with me, 1.2.186
Captain, 2.4.134
carat, 4.3.291
caraways, 5.3.3
carriage, 5.1.68
Cartwright, William, p. 59
case, 2.1.30
cast th'event, 1.1.166
cast, *ppl.* 5.1.17
cause, *n.* 1.3.1,26
cavalieros, 5.3.57
Caxton, William, p. 27
censorship pp. 9, 13, 18, 31, 33, 82–4
certain, 1.1.12
certificate, 2.2.114
Chambers, E. K., p. 29, 1.1.34
chanced, 1.1.87
channel, 2.1.46
Chapman, George, 2.4.109–10
characters, *n.* 1.2.174–5
charge, 1.2.60–1

checked, 1.2.190
Chestnut Street Theatre, Philadelphia, p. 66
Chimes at Midnight pp. 42, 67, 69–71, 75, 77
chipped bread, 2.4.236
chopped, 3.2.264
chops, *n.* 2.4.215
Cibber, Colley, p. 61
Cibber, Theophilus, pp. 61–2
Civil Wars, pp. 18, 21–3, 25, 81; *see also* Daniel
Clare, Janet, pp. 33, 86
Clement's Inn, 3.2.12
close, *v.* 2.1.19
Cobham (Oldcastle), p. 34
Cobham (Lord), Sir William Brooke, pp. 9–15, 29, 31–3, 38, 43, 84
Cobham (Lord), Sir Henry Brooke, pp. 31, 35
cock and pie, 5.1.1
coif, 1.1.6, 147
cold, 3.2.121
colour, *n.* 1.2.240, 5.5.84
come unto it, 3.2.243
commodity, 1.2.243
commotion, 2.4.358
companions, 2.4.92
competence of life, 5.5.65
complices, 1.1.163
compound, *v.* 4.3.245
conceit, 2.4.239
condition, 4.2.1
confirmities, 2.4.58
conger, 2.4.53
considerance, 5.2.97
consigning, 5.2.142
consist, 4.1.185
continent, 3.1.46
continuantly, 2.1.26
conversations, 5.5.98
conversing, 5.1.59
coped withal, 4.1.321
Cophetua, 5.3.101
Coriolanus, 1.1.170–1; 2.2.10; 4.2.103–7; 4.3.92
coronation day, 3.2.176–7
Corporal Bardolph, 2.4.149
Corporate, 3.2.212
*corpse, 1.1.192
correctioner, 5.4.20
costermongers' times, 1.2.164–5
Cotswold, 3.2.19

counsel every man, 1.1.212
countenance, *n.* 4.1.239; 5.5.7
countenance, *v.* 5.1.32
course, 4.3.90
court gate, 3.2.28
cousin, 3.1.65
Coveney, Michael, p. 73
Covent Garden, pp. 61–6, 69
cover, *v.* 2.4.10
Cowl, R. P., 2.1.1
crack, *n.* 3.2.28
crack, *v.* 5.3.61
crafty-sick, Induction, 37
Crane, Ralph, p. 97
creature, 2.2.10
Crewe, Jonathan, p. 4
cribs, 3.1.9
crosses, *n.* 1.2.220
Crowl, Samuel, p. 70
crown and coronation pp. 1, 3–6, 21–6, 41, 45, 48–50, 52, 61, 65, 95; 5.5.3–4.3
crudy, 4.2.95
current, *adj.* 2.1.119
curry, 5.1.65
curtain, 1.1.72
curtsy, Epilogue, 1
cushions, 5.4.14
cuts, pp. 58, 60, 62, 64, 68, 72, 74, 76–7, 88, 91
cyclicality, pp. 66, 69, 72
Cymbeline, 2.1.142; 3.1.69–76

dace, 3.2.315
dance, *v.* 4.3.254
dangerous eyes, 4.1.265
Daniel, Samuel, pp. 16, 18, 22, 81; Induction, 37; 1.1.16–17, 109–11, 127–8; 4.3.118–20
daring of the spur, 4.1.117
Davies, Anthony, p. 71
Davies, R. R., p. 20
Davison, Peter, pp. 14, 30, 95; Induction, 35; 1.1.0.1, 1.1.30, 34, 161–3; 1.2.34–5, 95, 172; 2.4.47, 68, 132–3, 332; 3.1.27, 52–5; 3.2.01; 3.2.273; 4.1.344; 4.3.201, 307; 5.5.3–4.3
dead elm, 2.4.328
dear, 4.3.270
death's head, 2.4.232–3
debate, *n.* 4.3.2
debuty, 2.4.84

decreasing leg, 1.2.176
defensible, 2.3.38
Dekker, Thomas, 2.1.0.2
Delius, N., 2.1.26
Dering, Sir Edward, pp. 58, 86
derives from, 1.1.206
determined, 4.3.211
diff'rence, 4.1.179
discoverers, 4.1.3
disgrace, 1.1.88–9
displeasing play, Epilogue, 8
dog, 1.2.141–2
*dole, 1.1.169
Dolphin Chamber, 2.1.86
Dommelton, 1.2.28
done me right, 5.3.71
Donno, Elizabeth Story, p. 33
double-charge, 5.3.122
doubt, *n.* 4.1.197
doubt, *v.* Epilogue, 6
draw, *v.* 2.1.146
draw our numbers, 1.3.109
drawers, 2.2.164
drollery, 2.1.141
drooping, Induction, 3
Drury Lane, pp. 61–3, 65
dry hand, 1.2.175
dull, 4.3.134
dungeon, 4.2.7
durance, 5.5.33

Eagleton, Terry, p. 44
ears cut off, 2.4.253–4
Eastcheap, pp. 1, 6, 44, 57, 71–3, 81,
    88; 2.1.68; 2.2.138–9
ebon black, 5.5.36
Eddington, Paul, pp. 76–7
Eddison, Robert, pp. 67, 73
elder, 2.4.256
Eliot, John, p. 17; 2.4.152–8
Elsom, John, p. 73
Elyot, Sir Thomas, pp. 16, 21, 27
endeared, 2.3.11
enforcement, 1.1.120
engagèd to, 1.1.180
English Shakespeare Company, pp. 67,
    75
engrafted, 2.2.59
engrossèd, 4.3.201
enlarge, 1.1.204
ensinewed, 4.1.170
entered him, 2.1.10–11

entered the action, 2.1.1–2
entreasurèd, 3.1.84
Ephesians, 2.2.142
Epilogue, pp. 14–16, 37–8, 62, 84,
    93; 2.4.1–20
Erebus, 2.4.155
esquire, 3.2.55
Europa, 2.2.165–6
Evans, G. Blakemore, p. 58
ever among, 5.3.22
Every Man in His Humour, 5.3.52–3
exion, 2.1.29
expedition, 4.2.33

Fabyan, Robert, p. 27
*face-royal, 1.2.22
fain, 2.1.138
faitours, 2.4.157
Falstaff's Wedding, pp. 45, 63
familiarity, 2.1.98
Famous Victories, pp. 4, 16, 21–7, 29,
    73–4; 2.4.11; 4.3.131–370
Fastolf, Sir John, pp. 28, 30, 36, 39,
    43–4
fat rascals, 2.4.41
Fates, 2.2.82
fathers and sons, pp. 4–6, 13, 21, 42,
    46, 48–50, 52
favourable, 4.3.134
fear, *n.* 4.3.121
fear, *v.* 5.5.77
fears, *n.* 4.3.325
Feast of the Garter, pp. 10, 11
feeding, 1.1.10
Fehrenbach, Robert J., p. 33
fell, 5.5.36
Ferguson, W. Craig, p. 78
fetch, 2.2.110
fetch off, 3.2.288
Field, Nathan, p. 34
fiery Trigon, 2.4.263
figure, *n.* 1.3.43
figure, *v.* 4.1.45
fillip, *v.* 1.2.222
Firth, Jonathan, p. 77
fist, *v.* 2.1.21
fit to go, 3.2.160
*flaws congealèd, 4.3.35
fled, 1.1.123
fledge, 1.2.19
Fleet, 5.5.89
Fleming, Abraham, pp. 16, 18, 34
flesh, *v.* 4.3.262

fleshed with conquest, 1.1.149
Florio, John, 2.4.68; 3.2.21
fobbed off, 2.1.33
foining, 2.4.229
fond, 1.3.91
fondly, 4.1.346
foolish-compounded, 1.2.7
for thy heart, 2.4.221
forespent, 1.1.37
forestalled remission, 5.2.38
forgetive, 4.2.96
forlorn, 3.2.298
form, *n.* 4.3.248
forswear half-kirtles, 5.4.21
fortunes, 1.1.23
foul papers, pp. 14, 78–80, 84–90
found the fire, 1.1.74
foundered, 4.2.35
Foxe, John, pp. 5, 33–4, 37
freely, 1.1.27
friends, 3.2.101
fronting, 4.3.66
*fustilarian, 2.1.58

Gad's Hill, 2.4.305
Galen, 1.2.114
gall, *v.* 1.2.143
Galloway nags, 2.4.188
galls, *n.* 1.2.171
gan, 1.1.129
garland, 4.3.331; 5.2.83
Garrick, David, pp. 63–4
Gascoigne, Sir William, pp. 21–2;
    2.1.68
Gaultres, 4.1.2
general, 4.1.167
genius, 3.2.299
gentle, 1.1.189
German hunting, 2.1.142
get wenches, 4.2.90–1
giant, 1.2.1
*gibbets . . . bucket, 3.2.253
Gibbons's Tennis Court, p. 59
Gielgud, John, p. 70
Giles, David, p. 67
gird at, 1.2.6
glass, 2.3.21
glasses, 2.1.140
Gloucestershire, pp. 3, 12, 29, 42,
    55–7, 81; 3.2.19; 5.1.32–3
glutton, 1.2.33
good respect, 2.2.95

good service, 1.2.59
Goodman, 5.3.88
goodyear, 2.4.175
Gossip, *n.* 2.1.93
grace, 1.2.27; 2.1.68; 5.5.6
grate on, 4.1.90
gravy, 1.2.158
greatest, 5.3.86
green, 2.1.96
green-sickness, 4.2.90
Greenblatt, Stephen, pp. 49–50, 55
Greg, W. W., pp. 78, 82, 89–92, 96,
    98; 2.4.1–20, 153–5
grey, 2.3.19
groats, 1.2.229
grows to, 1.2.86
guarded, 4.1.34
Gurr, Andrew, pp. 16, 24; 2.4.68, 243

Hackett, James Henry (as Falstaff),
    p. 66
had a suit, 5.1.63
haled, 5.5.34
half-faced, 3.2.254
Hall, Edward, pp. 16, 19, 21, 24, 27,
    73
Hall, Peter, pp. 67, 69
hallowing, 1.2.183
halt, *v.* 1.2.240
Hamlet, 1.1.169; 1.3.28; 2.3.21;
    4.2.54
Hands, Terry, pp. 5, 60, 67, 71–3,
hangs, 4.1.211
Hankford, Sir William, p. 22
Hanmer, Thomas 3.2.310–11
Hapgood, Robert, p. 70
happy, 4.1.305
Hardy, Robert, p. 69
Hardyng, John, 2.1.24
Harrison, William, pp. 16, 32
Hart, Alfred, p. 86
hasty, 2.1.125
haunch of winter, 4.3.92
Haymarket pp. 61, 63
hearken a'th' end, 2.4.278
heavenly ground, 2.1.137
heaviness, 4.3.140
heavy, 5.2.14
heavy descension, 2.2.165
heavy in, 1.1.121
Hector of Troy, 2.4.216
Hecuba, 2.2.82
heirs of life, 4.1.198

Helen of Troy, 5.5.32
Helicons, 5.3.103
hem, 2.4.29
hemistich, p. 53; 4.2.54; 4.3.205–6, 307
hempseed, 2.1.57
hence borne out, 4.3.344
1 Henry V 1.1.170–1; 1.2.33, 44–5, 62, 155, 184, 190, 206; 2.1.86; 2.2.21–2, 96; 2.3.24; 2.4.1–2, 142–3, 184–5; 3.2.30, 169–70, 289–90, 310–11; 4.2.46–7; 5.1.9
Henry V, 1.2.234; 2.4.152–8, 244–5; 4.3.91, 208
Heroides, 2.2.82
high plot, low plot, pp. 17, 23, 26, 40, 44, 53–5, 80
higher fields, 4.3.3
hilding, 1.1.57
Hillman, Richard, 5.2.48
Hinckley Fair, 5.1.21
Hinman, Charlton, p. 91
Hiren, 2.4.158
history, 4.1.201
history as fiction, pp. 17–20, 21–2, 39, 47
Hobson, Harold, p. 73
Hodgdon, Barbara, pp. 6, 58, 72,
*hold, Induction, 35
hold sortance, 4.1.11
Holinshed, Raphael, pp. 16–22, 24, 26–7, 32–4, 39, 44, 51,70, 73; Induction, 37; 1.1.0.1; 1.1.16–17, 34, 109–11, 127–8, 131, 189; 1.2.62, 101; 1.3.82; 2.1.24; 4.1.0.1–3; 4.1.224; 4.2.3–4; 4.3.125–8
holland, 2.2.21–2
homely biggin, 4.3.158
Honigmann, Ernst, pp. 9, 32, 35, 38–9
hook on, 2.1.158
*horn of abundance, 1.2.44–5
Hotson, Leslie, p. 10
hotter, 1.2.33
household, Induction, 22
Howard, Alan, pp. 5, 72, 74
hulk, 1.1.19; 2.4.64
Hulme, Hilda, 4.3.104
human, 4.2.118
humorous, 4.3.34
humours, 2.1.145; 2.4.161
humours of blood, 2.3.30

Humphreys, A. R. pp. 4, 9, 12, 21, 23, 29, 37, 41–3, 45, 52, 79, 90–1, 94, 95–7; 1.1.0.1; 1.1.30, 34, 161–3, 170–1; 1.2.29, 34–5; 2.1.1, 26, 89; 2.2.6, 21–2, 142; 2.4.11, 19, 128, 179, 246–7; 3.1.52–5, 69–76; 3.2.248–9; 4.1.344; 4.2.40; 4.3.309; 5.4.18–19
Hunsdon (First Lord), Henry Carey, pp. 9, 31, 33
Hunsdon (Second Lord), George Carey, pp. 10, 11, 31–2, 84
hunt counter, 1.2.87–8
hurly, 3.1.25
husband, 5.3.11
husbanded, 4.2.115
Hydra, 4.1.264

image, 5.2.73
imbrue, 2.4.193
imp, 5.5.41
in, 5.5.37
in commission, 3.2.85–6
in common sense, 4.1.259
in few, 1.1.112
*in good case, 2.1.104
in presence, 4.3.17
in question, 1.2.58
in reason, 2.2.46
in your state, 5.2.98
Inchbald, Mrs, p. 64
incision, 2.4.193
indifferency, 4.2.20–1
indited, 2.1.27
infer, 5.5.13
infinitive, 2.1.24
inflammation, 4.2.92
instance, 3.1.102
intended, 4.1.164
intends, 1.2.8
intervallums, 5.1.73
invested, 4.3.6
investments, 4.1.45
invincible, 3.2.299
inward, 3.1.106
iron, 4.1.234

Jacob, E. F., 1.2.105
James, Richard, pp. 13, 36
*Jealousy, Induction, 16
Jenkins, Harold, p. 4
jewel, 1.2.17–18
Johnson, Samuel, pp. 45–6, 81

Jonson, Ben, 3.2.147–52; 5.3.52–3, 100
jordan, 2.4.34
Jove, 2.2.165–6
Jowett, John, pp. 79–81, 87, 95; 5.5.3–4.3
joy, 2.4.47
Julius Caesar, 1.3.33
jumps upon joint-stools, 2.4.245
just, 3.2.79
just distance, 4.1.224
just proportion, 4.1.23
justly, 4.1.67
juvenal, 1.2.18

Kael, Pauline, p. 71
Kastan, David Scott, pp. 14, 31
Keech, 2.1.92
keeper, 1.1.143
Kemble, Charles, p. 65
Kemble, John Philip, p. 65
Kemp, Will, pp. 14–15, 29; 2.4.1–20
ken, 4.1.149
Kenrick, W., pp. 45, 63
Kerrigan, John, p. 56
kickshaws, 5.1.24
Kidd, John, p. 67
Killigrew, Thomas, p. 59
kindly, 4.3.213
King Cerberus, 2.4.166
King Lear, 1.1.153–60, 170–1; 1.2.163; 2.4.120–1, 156; 5.4.0.1
Kirkman, Francis, p. 59
kirtle, 2.4.272
knave, 1.2.34–5
knew for, 1.2.5
Knott, John R., p. 34
Knowles, Richard, Induction, 0.1
Kott, Jan, p. 69
Kyd, Thomas, 2.4.195

lack-linen, 2.4.120–1
land-service, 1.2.131
lanthorn, 1.2.44–5
largely, 1.3.12
latest, 4.3.312
lavish, *adj.* 4.3.64
leather-coats, 5.3.41
Lee, Sidney, 4.3. headnote
leer upon, 5.5.6
leman, 5.3.46
let it come, 5.3.52
Lethe, 5.2.71

level, *adj.* 4.3.7
level, *v.* 3.2.256
Lever, J. W., 2.4.152–8
lewd, 2.2.58
licensing, pp. 82, 84, 86–7
lief, 1.2.40
Lieutenant, 5.5.87
like, *v.* 3.2.81
like a church, 2.4.227–8
liking, 2.1.89
limbs, 5.2.134
Lincolnshire, pp. 12, 81
lined, *v.* 1.3.27
Linthicum, M. Channing, 2.2.14–16, 3.1.0.1
lion, 1.2.190
Lisle's Tennis Court, p. 59
little, 3.1.42
little tiny, 5.1.24; 5.3.56
liver, 4.2.100; 5.5.30
livers, 1.2.170
Locrine, 2.4.153–5
lodge, *v.* 4.3.337
Lombard Street, 2.1.28
look about, 5.1.45
look beyond, 4.3.67
looked, 1.2.41
loosely studied, 2.2.7
Lord Bardolph, 1.1.34
losing office, 1.1.101
Love's Labour's Lost, 4.3.92
Lubber's, 2.1.28
Lupton, D., 1.2.48
lusty, 3.2.14
Lyly, John, p. 42

Macbeth, 1.1.0.1; 3.1.83; 4.2.90–1
Macready, William Charles, p. 65
madcap Hal, pp. 1, 6, 26–7, 46
magnanimous, 3.2.156
make head, 1.1.168
makes a period, 4.3.360
Malcontent, 5.4.0.1–2
mallet, 2.4.240
malmsey-nose, 2.1.38
Malone, Edmond, 3.2.81
Maloney, Michael, p. 76
malt-worms, 2.4.331
man, 4.1.234
man in a censer, 5.4.18–19
man-queller, 2.1.51
mandrake, 1.2.14; 3.2.300–1
manned with, 1.2.16

many, 1.3.91
mark, 2.3.31
marks, *n.* 1.2.187
Marlowe, Christopher, p. 17
married in conjunction, 5.1.61
Marston, John, 2.4.246–7; 5.4.0.1–2
Martin, R. W. F., p. 34
Martlemas, 2.2.96
Mason, Brewster (as Falstaff), pp. 72–3
Master Dumb, 2.4.86–7
mate, *n.* 2.4.121
mayst, 2.2.121
McKeen, David, pp. 29, 31–3
Measure for Measure, 2.4.142–3;
    3.2.30
meat, 2.4.121
mechanical, 5.5.35
medicine potable, 4.3.292
meet for rebellion, 4.1.344
Melchiori, Giorgio, pp. 4,79, 88;
    1.1.0.1; 1.1.30, 34, 161–3, 202;
    2.1.26; 2.4.179
Memorial (later Royal Shakespeare)
    Theatre, Stratford-upon-Avon, pp.
    28, 66–7, 71–3, 75
men of choice, 1.3.11
Merchant of Venice, Epilogue, 11
Meres, Francis, pp. 9, 10
Merry Wives, pp. 7, 10–13, 32, 36, 43,
    62, 70, 72; 1.2.234; 2.1.30; 4.1.236
mess, 2.1.94
metal, 1.1.116
Metamorphoses, 2.2.82, 165–6;
    4.1.264–5; 5.3.136
mete, 4.3.77
meting, 4.3.32
metre, pp. 37–8, 89
Middleton, Thomas, 2.1.0.2; 3.1.17
Midsummer Night's Dream A, 2.4.196;
    3.1.46
Mile-End Green, 3.2.268
Mirror for Magistrates, 2.3.21
misordered, 4.1.259
mock, 5.2.125
moist, 1.2.175
Monmouth, Induction, 29
monstrous, 4.1.260
more and less, 1.1.209
Moreau, Jeanne, p. 70
Morgann, Maurice, p. 46
much, 2.4.129
Much Ado, 2.4.1–20
muddy, 2.4.39

Muir, Kenneth, p. 17
murder, *v.* 2.4.130
Murphy, Gerard, pp. 73–5

Nashe, Thomas, p. 32; 5.3.72–4
national destiny, pp. 48, 64–5, 68–9,
    77
nave of a wheel, 2.4.253
neaf, 2.4.184
necessary form, 3.1.86
new, 2.3.47
New (Albery) Theatre, p. 67
New Inn, 3.2.147–52
new-dated, 4.1.8
nice, 1.1.145; 4.1.189
night-gown, 3.1.0.1
Nine Worthies, 2.4.218
nine-score and odd posts, 4.2.35–6
Noble, Adrian, pp. 67, 75–6
noise, 2.4.11
nomenclature, pp. 7, 15, 27–31, 34,
    39
note, *n.* 5.1.15
notice, *n.* 1.3.85
Nunn, Trevor, pp. 67, 73–5
nut-hook, 5.4.7

obedience, 4.3.276
observed, 4.3.30
occasion, 4.1.72
occupy, 2.4.145
o'erset, 1.1.185
offer, *v.* 4.1.217
offices, 1.3.47
old church, 2.2.142
old utis, 2.4.19
Old Vic, pp. 2, 51, 67, 69, 75
Oldcastle, pp. 7, 9, 13–14, 25, 28,
    31–40
Oliver, H. J., pp. 10–12
Olivier, Laurence, pp. 66–8, 71
omit, *v.* 4.3.27
one, 1.1.157
opener and intelligencer, 4.1.246
opposed, 4.3.66
opposite, *n.* 1.3.55; 4.1.16
orchard, 1.1.4
original, 1.2.112
Ortho-epia Gallica, p.17; 2.4.152–8,
    164–5
ostentation, 2.2.47
Othello, 1.2.175; 2.2.10; 2.4.145;
    5.2.128–32

out, 5.3.65
out-breathed, 1.1.108
*overrode, 1.1.30
overscutched housewives, 3.2.302
owed, 1.2.4
Owen, Jane, p. 34
Oxford, 1.1.161–3; 1.2.34–5;
  2.4.188; 3.2.9, 310–11

pacify, 2.4.79
pagan, *n.* 2.2.146
pallets, 3.1.10
pantler, 2.4.236
parcel-gilt, 2.1.86
parcels, *n.* 4.1.262
Paris, 2.2.82
Park Theatre, New York, p. 66
part, *n.* 4.3.194
part-created cost, 1.3.60
partial, 3.1.26
participation of society, 5.1.61–2
party, 1.2.4
passing, 4.1.311
passion, 1.1.161
pastoral, pp. 55–7, 68
Patterson, Annabel, p. 18
pay, *v.* 2.1.155
peasant, Induction, 33
peascod-time, 2.4.378
Peele, George, p.17; 2.4.153–5, 158
Pendleton, Thomas A., p. 37
Pennington, Michael, pp. 67, 75
Pepys, Samuel, p. 59
perfumes, 2.4.27
Phelps, Samuel, p. 66
Philaster, 2.4.243
philosopher's two stones, 3.2.314
phrases, 3.2.68
physic, 1.1.137
picking, 4.1.196
Pie Corner, 2.1.26–7
piled, 4.3.201
pinches, *n.* 1.2.225
pipe, Induction, 15
Pistol, 2.4.68
pistol-proof, 2.4.113
Pizzle, 2.4.159
Plutarch, p. 17; 4.2.40
point, 1.1.53
point of war, 4.1.52
points, *n.* 2.4.129
Pollard, A. W., pp. 79, 90
Pomfret, 1.1.205

Poole, Kristen, p. 39
Pope, Alexander, pp. 14, 38, 81;
  1.1.161–3
Porter, 1.1.0.1
ports, 4.3.155
post, 2.4.372
post-horse, Induction, 4
Potter, Stephen, p. 68
pottle-pot, 5.3.63
power, 1.1.133
precepts, 5.1.11
pregnancy, 1.2.165
presented, 5.2.78
presently, 2.1.173; 2.4.366
prick him, 3.2.108; pricked,
  3.2.150; pricked down, 2.4.329
proface, 5.3.28
profanity, pp. 90, 93, 98
project of a power, 1.3.29
prompt-book, pp. 14–15, 95,
  97–9
*proof, 4.2.87–8
proper, 2.2.147; 5.2.108
propose, 5.2.91
prose, pp. 54, 61, 66, 68, 80–2
Prosser, Eleanor, pp. 85, 92–3, 95,
  97–8; 1.2.34–5, 44–5
proudly, 5.2.129
proverbs, Induction, 18; 1.1.95–8;
  1.2.50, 80, 149–50, 191–2,
  212–14, 222–4, 230–1; 1.3.8, 28,
  99; 2.1.42, 72; 2.2.44, 63–4, 71–2,
  138–9, 158; 2.4.30–1, 60–1, 107,
  156, 172, 219–20, 244–5, 278;
  3.1.31; 3.2.169–70, 225–9,
  314–16; 4.1.70, 159, 220–1,
  307–8; 4.2.86–8, 90–1; 4.3.54, 58,
  105–8, 222; 5.1.26–7, 62, 69;
  5.2.28–9, 34; 5.3.34, 47, 52–3, 85;
  5.4.12, 23–4; 5.5.27–8, 83, 86–8,
  105; Epilogue, 5–6
puissance, 1.3.9
purchased, 4.3.329
put him to, 3.2.160–1

quaffed, 4.3.215
quality, 4.1.11
quantities, 5.1.55
quarrel, *n.* 4.3.298
Quayle, Anthony, pp. 28, 67–9
quean, 2.1.46
Quin, James, pp. 61, 63
quit, *adj.* 3.2.229

quit, *v.* 2.4.338
quittance, 1.1.108
quiver, *adj.* 3.2.270
quoit 2.4.189

Rackin, Phyllis, p. 7
rage, *n.* 4.1.34
*ragged, 3.2.138
raggèd, 5.2.38
ragged'st, 1.1.151
rain, *n.* 4.3.141
rampallian, 2.1.58
rank, *adj.* 3.1.38; 4.1.64
rascal, 5.4.30
rash, 4.3.48
rate, *v.* 1.3.44; 5.2.69; rated,
    3.1.67
ratsbane, 1.2.40
rearward of the fashion, 3.2.301
recordation, 2.3.61
red lattice, 2.2.75
Redgrave, Michael, pp. 28, 67–9
remembered, 5.2.141
remembrance, 5.2.114
respect, 1.1.184
retrospection, pp. 2, 4, 18, 43, 49–50,
    80, 82, 84
reverent, 1.2.97
revision, pp. 79–81, 89
revolution, 3.1.45
Rey, Fernando, p. 70
rheumatic, 2.4.57
Richard II, 1.1.205; 1.2.105; 1.3.4,
    103–5; 2.1.89; 3.1.52–5, 67–78;
    4.1.71, 80–3, 109, 123; 4.3.201;
    5.1.32–3
Richard III, 1.1.116; 1.2.181–2
Richardson, Ralph, pp. 68, 70
right Justice, 5.2.101
rigol, 4.3.167
road, 2.2.158
Romans, 2.2.116
Romeo, 2.1.14–19; 2.4.1–20, 145,
    182
rood, 3.2.3
roundly, 3.2.16
rousèd, 4.1.116
rowel-head, 1.1.46
Royal Shakespeare Company, pp. 67,
    69, 73
rude scene, 1.1.159
ruff, 2.4.130
Rumour, pp. 73–74, Induction, 0.1

Rutherford, Margaret, p. 70
sad, 5.1.74
sadly, 5.2.124
saltness of time, 1.2.96
Samingo, 5.3.72–4
Samson Stockfish, 3.2.30
sanctities, 4.1.247
Saturn and Venus, 2.4.261
scab, 3.2.265
scaly, 1.1.146
Schafer, Elizabeth, 2.1.89
Scoggin's, 3.2.28
Scrope, 1.1.189
sea-boy, 3.1.27
sea-coal, 2.1.87
seal with him, 4.2.126
Seale, Douglas, pp. 2, 67, 69
*searching, 2.4.27
sect, 2.4.37
security, 1.2.43
semblable coherence, 5.1.57
semper idem, 5.5.27
sensible, 1.2.189
sequel, pp. 1–3, 4, 6, 9, 43, 59–60,
    63, 89
serve, 3.2.131
service, *n.* 3.2.242
set me off, 1.2.13; set off, *ppl.* 4.1.143
Shaaber, Matthias, pp. 29–30, 43, 58,
    65, 81–2, 90, 96; Induction, 35,
    17; 1.1.0.1; 1.1.34, 196–7; 1.2.95;
    2.1.28, 142; 2.2.71–2, 135;
    2.4.109–10, 332; 3.2.299–304;
    4.3.91
Shadow, 3.2.119
Sharpe, Robert Boies, p. 29
she-knight errant, 5.4.22
sherry-sack, 4.2.93
shift me, 5.5.21
short cloak, 1.2.29
short-legged hens, 5.1.23
*shot, *n.* 3.2.264
shove-groat shilling, 189–90
Shrew, 5.1.32–3; 5.3.89
Shrimpton, Nicholas, p. 74
sickness, pp. 1, 20, 40, 47–8
Sidney, Sir Philip, 2.1.89
sights, 4.1.119
signories, 4.1.109
Silence, 3.2.85
silk stockings, 2.2.14–16
Simmes, Valentine, pp. 78–9, 83
Sincklo, John, pp. 29, 90; 5.4.0.1–2

sinful continents, 2.4.283
singing-man of Windsor, 2.1.89
single, *adj.* 1.2.178
Sir Dagonet, 3.2.269–70
1 *Sir John Oldcastle*, p. 35
Sir Thomas More, p.79
Sisters Three, 2.4.196
sleep, 3.1.5
slops, 1.2.29
small beer, 2.2.6
smell a fox, 1.2.151
Smithfield, 1.2.48
smoothy-pates, 1.2.36
sneap, 2.1.120
soft, 5.2.96
Sonnets: 20 (3.2.109–11); 144
    (2.4.48–9); 132 (2.3.19)
sound the bottom, 4.1.277
sources, pp. 16–27
south, 2.4.358
Spanish Tragedy, 2.4.153–5, 195
speaker, 4.1.244
spent, 3.2.115
Spevack, Marvin, p. 55
spirit, 1.1.92
spirits, 5.2.124
spit white, 1.2.206
Sprague, Arthur C., p. 67
spread, 5.3.8
spring of day, 4.3.35
Stamford, p. 12; 3.2.36,
stand, *v.* 3.2.212; 4.1.163; 4.2.80
stand the push, 2.2.35
*stand to, 2.1.62
stand to't, 2.1.5
stand upon, 1.2.36
state, *n.* 3.1.13; 5.2.141
state of floods, 5.2.131
Stephens, Robert (as Falstaff), p. 76
stews, 1.2.51.2.
stick, 1.2.22
stiff-borne, 1.1.177
still, *adv.* Induction, 4
still-discordant, Induction, 19
still-stand, 2.3.64
stomach, 4.3.107
*stop, Induction, 17
stopping, 1.1.78
Stow, John, pp. 16, 21, 26, 73;
    1.1.109–11; 1.2.29; 1.3.82;
    2.1.68
strain, *n.* 4.3.300
strange, 1.1.94

stratagem, 1.1.8
stray, *n.* 4.1.347
strike sail, 5.2.18
structure, pp. 30, 40, 50, 54–5, 80–1
suborned, 4.1.90
substitute, *n.* 4.1.254
substituted, 1.3.84
substitutes in absence, 4.3.6
successively, 4.3.331
suffered, 2.3.57
sufficient, 3.2.91
Sugden, Edward, 2.1.28; 2.2.138–9;
    5.1.21
sullen, 1.1.102
summer bird, 4.3.91
Summer's Last Will and Testament,
    5.3.72–4
supplies, *n.* 1.3.12
supposed sincere, 1.1.202
surety, 1.1.191
Swaab, Peter, p. 71
swagger, *v.* 2.4.97
swaggering, 2.4.70
sway on, 4.1.24
sweat, Epilogue, 29
sweating, pp. 37, 38
swinge-bucklers, 3.2.19–20
swinged, 5.4.19
sworn brother, 3.2.306

ta'en up, 4.1.252
tables, 4.1.199
take, *v.* 1.2.162
take not on me, 4.1.60
*taking-up, 1.2.38–9
tall, 5.1.51
tallow, 1.2.154
Tamburlaine, 5.3.99; *Tamburlaine I*,
    2.4.153–5, 167, 172; *Tamburlaine II*,
    2.4.161–3
tame cheater, 2.4.95
tardy tricks, 4.2.28
Tarlton, Richard, pp. 16, 26
tarry, 3.2.184
taste, *n.* 2.3.52
Taylor, Gary, pp. 9, 14, 35–7, 80–1,
    87, 91, 95, 97–8
temper, *n.* 2.1.79
tempering, 4.2.125
Tempest, 3.2.30
tester, 3.2.265
tetralogy, pp. 1, 4, 15, 26, 47–8,
    67–9, 71, 77–8

Tewkesbury mustard, 2.4.239
thews, 3.2.248
*thick, 2.3.24; 3.2.298; 4.2.56
Thomas Wart, 3.2.133
Thomas of Walsingham, p. 27
Thorndike, Sybil, p. 68
three-man beetle, 1.2.222
tidy, 2.4.228
tilly-fally, 2.4.82
Tillyard, E. M. W., pp. 69, 75
Tilney, Edmund, p. 33
Tilt-yard, 3.2.307
tiring on, Induction, 37
tirrits, 2.4.202
tisick, 2.4.84
title-leaf, 1.1.60
Tito Livio, p. 27
Titus, 2.3.19
tolling, 4.3.205
tonight, 2.1.164
touch ground, 4.1.17
town-bull, 2.2.150
trade of, 1.1.174
translate, 4.1.47
treble hautboy, 3.2.311
Tree, Herbert Beerbohm, p. 66
trilogy pp. 67, 71–2
trimmed, 1.3.94
tripe-visaged, 5.4.8
Troilus and Cressida, 1.2.168–9;
  2.2.82; 2.4.217
Troy, 2.2.82
truncheon, 2.4.138
try, 4.3.296
Turkish Mahamet, 2.4.158
Turnbull Street, 3.2.292
Twelfth Night, 4.1.70; 5.3.104
twenty nobles, 2.1.149–50
twice and once, 5.3.39
Two Gentlemen of Verona, The,
  2.4.340–3
Tynan, Kenneth, pp. 68–9
tyranny, 4.3.215

Udall, Nicholas, 2.4.48
Umfrevile, Sir John, p. 90; 1.1.34,
  161–3
under life, 1.1.141
unequal, 4.1.100
unfathered heirs, 4.3.122
unpay, 2.1.117
unseasoned, 3.1.104
upon the file, 1.3.10

upswarmèd, 4.1.256
Ursula, pp. 45, 63; 1.2.234
usurpation, pp. 17, 46–9, 83, 85

vail his stomach, 1.1.129
vain, 5.5.43
Valentinian, 2.1.159
Valpy, Richard, p.64
vantage, 2.1.77
varlets, 2.1.45
venture, 1.1.59; Epilogue, 7
Venus and Adonis, 2.2.129
verse, pp. 53–4
Vice's dagger, 3.2.304
Vickers, Brian, p. 6
videlicet, 2.2.15
view, *n.* 2.1.22
vile, 1.2.17; 3.1.15
Virgil, Induction, 1 1.1.72; 5.5.36
visitation, 3.1.21

wags, *n.* 1.2.172
Walker, Alice, pp. 86, 96–8
want, *v.* 5.3.28
wanton, 1.1.148
Warbeck, Perkin, 2.1.89
warder, 4.1.123
Wardle, Irving, pp. 72–4
wassail candle, 1.2.154
waste, *v.* 4.3.345
wasted, 4.1.213
watch-case, 3.1.17
water, 1.2.2
waterwork, 2.1.142
wax, *n.* 1.2.155
Webster, John, 2.1.0.2
weigh, 5.2.101
well conceited, 5.1.31
well said, 5.3.9
Welles, Orson, pp. 42, 67, 69–71,
  75
Wells, Stanley, pp. 32, 57; 4.3.91
wen, 2.2.100
West, Gilian, 2.1.24
what the goodyear, 2.4.58–9
Wheeson, 2.1.88
whipping-cheer, 5.4.5
*whoreson, *adj.* 1.2.14,105;
  2.4.206
wicked, 2.4.317
William Cook, 5.1.9
Williams, George Walton, pp. 14, 28,
  58, 78–9, 82, 84, 98; 3.2.53

Williams, Clifford, p. 67
Wilson, John Dorer, 2.4.1–20
win, *v.* 4.3.309
winking, 1.3.33
witnessed usurpation, 1.1.63
Wolner, William, 2.1.89
womb, 4.2.22
Woodvine, John, p. 75

word to sword, 4.1.236
working, 4.3.41
workings, 4.1.248
Woudhuysen, H. R., p. 45
writ man, 1.2.25
wrought out life, 1.1.182

your stream of quality, 5.2.34

A SELECTION OF   **OXFORD WORLD'S CLASSICS**

An Anthology of Elizabethan Prose Fiction

An Anthology of Seventeenth-Century Fiction

APHRA BEHN   **Oroonoko and Other Writings**

JOHN BUNYAN   **Grace Abounding**
The Pilgrim's Progress

SIR PHILIP SIDNEY   **The Old Arcadia**

IZAAK WALTON   **The Compleat Angler**

A SELECTION OF **OXFORD WORLD'S CLASSICS**

The Anglo-Saxon World

Lancelot of the Lake

The Paston Letters

The Romance of Reynard the Fox

The Romance of Tristan

GEOFFREY CHAUCER   The Canterbury Tales
Troilus and Criseyde

JOCELIN OF BRAKELOND   Chronicle of the Abbey of Bury
St Edmunds

GUILLAUME DE LORRIS
and JEAN DE MEUN   The Romance of the Rose

WILLIAM LANGLAND   Piers Plowman

Oriental Tales

WILLIAM BECKFORD   Vathek

JAMES BOSWELL   Boswell's Life of Johnson

FRANCES BURNEY   Camilla
Cecilia
Evelina
The Wanderer

LORD CHESTERFIELD   Lord Chesterfield's Letters

JOHN CLELAND   Memoirs of a Woman of Pleasure

DANIEL DEFOE   Captain Singleton
A Journal of the Plague Year
Memoirs of a Cavalier
Moll Flanders
Robinson Crusoe
Roxana

HENRY FIELDING   Joseph Andrews and Shamela
A Journey from This World to the Next and
The Journal of a Voyage to Lisbon
Tom Jones
The Adventures of David Simple

WILLIAM GODWIN   Caleb Williams
St Leon

OLIVER GOLDSMITH   The Vicar of Wakefield

MARY HAYS   Memoirs of Emma Courtney

ELIZABETH HAYWOOD   The History of Miss Betsy Thoughtless

ELIZABETH INCHBALD   A Simple Story

SAMUEL JOHNSON   The History of Rasselas

CHARLOTTE LENNOX   The Female Quixote

MATTHEW LEWIS   The Monk

A SELECTION OF **OXFORD WORLD'S CLASSICS**

ANN RADCLIFFE
**The Castles of Athlin and Dunbayne
The Italian
The Mysteries of Udolpho
The Romance of the Forest
A Sicilian Romance**

FRANCES SHERIDAN
Memoirs of Miss Sidney Bidulph

TOBIAS SMOLLETT
**The Adventures of Roderick Random
The Expedition of Humphry Clinker
Travels through France and Italy**

LAURENCE STERNE
**The Life and Opinions of Tristram
     Shandy, Gentleman
A Sentimental Journey**

JONATHAN SWIFT
**Gulliver's Travels
A Tale of a Tub and Other Works**

HORACE WALPOLE
The Castle of Otranto

GILBERT WHITE
The Natural History of Selborne

MARY WOLLSTONECRAFT
Mary and The Wrongs of Woman

JANE AUSTEN	**Catharine and Other Writings**
	Emma
	Mansfield Park
	Northanger Abbey, Lady Susan, The Watsons, and Sanditon
	Persuasion
	Pride and Prejudice
	Sense and Sensibility
ANNE BRONTË	**Agnes Grey**
	The Tenant of Wildfell Hall
CHARLOTTE BRONTË	**Jane Eyre**
	The Professor
	Shirley
	Villette
EMILY BRONTË	**Wuthering Heights**
WILKIE COLLINS	**The Moonstone**
	No Name
	The Woman in White
CHARLES DARWIN	**The Origin of Species**
CHARLES DICKENS	**The Adventures of Oliver Twist**
	Bleak House
	David Copperfield
	Great Expectations
	Hard Times
	Little Dorrit
	Martin Chuzzlewit
	Nicholas Nickleby
	The Old Curiosity Shop
	Our Mutual Friend
	The Pickwick Papers
	A Tale of Two Cities

GEORGE ELIOT	Adam Bede
	Daniel Deronda
	Middlemarch
	The Mill on the Floss
	Silas Marner
ELIZABETH GASKELL	Cranford
	The Life of Charlotte Brontë
	Mary Barton
	North and South
	Wives and Daughters
THOMAS HARDY	Far from the Madding Crowd
	Jude the Obscure
	The Mayor of Casterbridge
	A Pair of Blue Eyes
	The Return of the Native
	Tess of the d'Urbervilles
	The Woodlanders
WALTER SCOTT	Ivanhoe
	Rob Roy
	Waverley
MARY SHELLEY	Frankenstein
	The Last Man
ROBERT LOUIS STEVENSON	Kidnapped and Catriona
	The Strange Case of Dr Jekyll and Mr Hyde and Weir of Hermiston
	Treasure Island
BRAM STOKER	Dracula
WILLIAM MAKEPEACE THACKERAY	Barry Lyndon
	Vanity Fair
OSCAR WILDE	Complete Shorter Fiction
	The Picture of Dorian Gray

A SELECTION OF   **OXFORD WORLD'S CLASSICS**

LOUISA MAY ALCOTT	**Little Women**
SHERWOOD ANDERSON	**Winesburg, Ohio**
CHARLES BROCKDEN BROWN	**Wieland; or The Transformation** and **Memoirs of Carwin, The Biloquist**
WILLA CATHER	**Alexander's Bridge**
JAMES FENIMORE COOPER	**The Deerslayer** **The Last of the Mohicans** **The Pathfinder** **The Pioneers** **The Prairie**
STEPHEN CRANE	**The Red Badge of Courage**
J. HECTOR ST. JEAN DE CRÈVECŒUR	**Letters from an American Farmer**
THEODORE DREISER	**Jennie Gerhardt** **Sister Carrie**
F. SCOTT FITZGERALD	**The Great Gatsby** **The Beautiful and Damned**
BENJAMIN FRANKLIN	**Autobiography and Other Writings**
MARGARET FULLER	**Woman in the Nineteenth Century and Other Writings**
CHARLOTTE PERKINS GILMAN	**The Yellow Wall-Paper and Other Stories**
ZANE GREY	**Riders of the Purple Sage**
BRET HARTE	**Selected Stories and Sketches**
NATHANIEL HAWTHORNE	**The Blithedale Romance** **The House of the Seven Gables** **The Scarlet Letter** **Young Goodman Brown and Other Tales**
WILLIAM DEAN HOWELLS	**The Rise of Silas Lapham**

American Literature

British and Irish Literature

Children's Literature

Classics and Ancient Literature

Colonial Literature

Eastern Literature

European Literature

History

Medieval Literature

Oxford English Drama

Poetry

Philosophy

Politics

Religion

The Oxford Shakespeare

A complete list of Oxford Paperbacks, including Oxford World's Classics, OPUS, Past Masters, Oxford Authors, Oxford Shakespeare, Oxford Drama, and Oxford Paperback Reference, is available in the UK from the Academic Division Publicity Department, Oxford University Press, Great Clarendon Street, Oxford OX2 6DP.

In the USA, complete lists are available from the Paperbacks Marketing Manager, Oxford University Press, 198 Madison Avenue, New York, NY 10016.

Oxford Paperbacks are available from all good bookshops. In case of difficulty, customers in the UK can order direct from Oxford University Press Bookshop, Freepost, 116 High Street, Oxford OX1 4BR, enclosing full payment. Please add 10 per cent of published price for postage and packing.